New Philanthropy Benchmarking

New Philanthropy Benchmarking

Wisdom for the Passionate

WORKING BOOK

Prospectus Format

Kristina Anna Kazarian

United
University Press

United University Press is a division of United University (www.unitedu.com). United University seeks to provide world class course content for social sector executives via the Internet.

This publication is designed to provide accurate and authoritative information in regard to the subject matter covered. It is sold with the understanding that publisher is not engaged in rendering legal, accounting, or other professional services. If legal advice or other expert assistance is required, the services of a competent professional person should be sought.

Library of Congress Cataloguing in Publication Data:

Kazarian, Kristina Anna

New Philanthropy Benchmarking: Wisdom for the Passionate / Kristina Anna Kazarian.
       p. cm. — (United University Press)
Includes Index.
ISBN 0-9716446-0-8 (alk. paper)
1. Nonprofit organizations. 2. Benchmarking (Management). 3. Organizational effectiveness. 4. Performance. 5. Philanthropists. 6. Charities. 7. Fund raising. 8. Endowments. I. Kazarian, Kristina Anna. II. Title.

HD62.6 .K39 2002
658'.048--dc21

2001008059
CIP

Printed in the United States of America

10 9 8 7 6 5 4 3 2 1

DEDICATION

"Resplendent and unfading is Wisdom, and she is readily perceived by those who love her, and found by those who seek her."
(NAB, Wisdom 6:12)

"Blessed is she who seeks wisdom, tirelessly cultivating her talents, sowing the rewards to those most deserving."
(St. Hripsime)

"Much will be required of the person entrusted with much, and still more will be demanded of the person entrusted with more."
(NAB, Luke 12:48)

"...He should give away his wealth during his lifetime, using the same acumen that he showed in making it ... the amount which can be wisely given by the individual for individuals is necessarily limited by his lack of knowledge of the circumstances connected with each."
(Andrew Carnegie, The Gospel of Wealth)

"Thus was created a single man, to teach us that every person who loses a single soul, it shall be written about him as if he has lost the entire world, and every person who sustains a single soul, it shall be written about him as if he has sustained the entire world."
(Mishnah, Sanhedrin, IV:5)

"The evil is in the world always comes out of ignorance, and good intentions may do as much harm as malevolence, if they lack understanding."
(Albert Camus, The Plague)

Metz Yeghern

Dedicated to the eternal memory of the millions of victims and their families of The Armenian Genocide. 1.7 million Armenians died and hundreds of thousands suffered.

1894–1923

OVERVIEW SUMMARY

Mission: The unabashedly ambitious mission of *New Philanthropy Benchmarking* is to inspire intense competition among passionate capitalist/philanthropists and provide essential wisdoms whereby they can initiate radically positive transformative change within the social sector.

Competitive Assumption: *New Philanthropy Benchmarking* is predicated upon the assumption that passionate capitalist/philanthropists will instinctively strive for comparable success in the social sector as achieved in the commercial sector. While motivations vary, instincts compelling superior performance or driving a determination to eschew being "dumb money" are considered pervasive and transferable.

NPB Definition: Succinctly put, *New Philanthropy Benchmarking* ("NPB") builds upon a synergist collaboration of commercial sector benchmarking, progressive intersectoral strategies, and contemporary financial markets analytical tools. NPB is evaluated within the context of macro issues, such as stakeholder considerations and comparative conclusionary financial metrics. On a micro level, insights are offered on process as well as organizational execution suggestions.

Power of NPB: The power and compelling attractiveness of NPB is its ability to assist passionate Capitalists/Philanthropists ("CPs") to multiply the impact – create value – of their resource investment relative to other similar social sector initiatives and minimize risk exposure. Relative value creation is not solely based on the value of resources invested in the commercial sector and neither should such be the case in the social sector. For example, NPB seeks to provide CPs with the tools to leverage a $1 million social sector investment to generate a much greater impact, possibly achieving that of comparable $10 million or even $100 million social sector investment. Simultaneously, NPB provides the framework for CP to minimize the risk exposure of NGO or foundation misfortunate developments, wasted funds, or unintended consequences.

Seven NPB Wisdom Points: NPB's key messages are summarized in seven (7) Wisdom Points. These seven points or aphorisms provide a memorable distillation of the entire contents of the Working Book. The seven wisdom points are uniquely customized for passionate CPs. They summarize extensive analytical content including social sector transformation opportunities; world-class CP profile insights; concrete NPB examples; effective conceptual, tactical, and managerial materials; and momentum building specifics. The sources of these wisdom points include the author's value creations, analysis and interpretations of select world-class CPs (Edgar and Charles Bronfman, Bill Gates, Michael Milken, Thomas Monaghan, George Soros, Steven Spielberg, and Michael Steinhardt), assessments of innovative foundations and leading social enterprise investors, and an extensive critical review of leading academic and professional writings.

Social Sector Transformation Opportunities: The Working Book provides a highly practical assessment of major trends effecting the social sector and insights into virtually boundless opportunities for maximum initiative value creation. Intersectoral topics that CPs will discover offer significant NPB measurable value creation include: social enterprise (social entrepreneurship, commercialization, operational philanthropy, and contract services), strategic philanthropy & restructuring (capacity building, collaboration, management efficiency programs, restructuring, and foundation value-creation practices), and social capital markets (innovative financings, social venture capital, blended ROIs, and M&A transactions).

Concepts, Tactics, and Management: To provide for wide application, NPB addresses a diverse range of situations and considers conceptual as well as tactical and managerial issues. Specific and general examples are offered for proactive and passive CP preferences, established and start-up situations, and project or organization-wide assessments. Examples are provided to advance the NPB vision to a concrete understanding with specific quantifications highlighting the extraordinary impact and potential. On a conceptual basis, stakeholder comparative similarities and traditional exaggerations are evaluated in the context of NPB value creation. Three critically important tactics – Deliverable Opportunities, Performance Gaps, and Multiplier/Discount Effects – are advanced in the context of their commercial sector comparables. Managerial issues are addressed throughout with particular note of a CP-focused rapid learning diagram titled "Quality and Value Added Benchmarking Process Pyramid." An extensive review of Internet resources is included on a variety of related topics, including execution services and best practices.

Building Momentum and Avoiding Obstacles: An extensive refinement of momentum building and obstacle avoidance practices is dialogued. Several promising momentum-building topics are social sector capital markets opportunities, traditional and cutting-edge executive educational alternatives, incentive compensation observations, and talent assessment questionnaires. Obstacle avoidance topics positively discussed include: cultural issues, minimization of risk issues, misconceptions, and voices of caution. A statistical comparison of "live-founder/dead-founder" foundations is particularly revealing. The Working Book concludes by proffering compelling common sense perspectives on the realities and myths of fiduciary obligations and potentially contra-fiduciary activities within the social sector.

Success Stories and Illustrations: The Working Book provides practical success stories in four categories: six Best Practice situations illustrating the power and application of NPB, approximately two-dozen Intersectoral practice examples (social enterprise, strategic philanthropy & restructuring, and social capital markets) illustrating NPB assessable value-creation potential, two NPB case studies offering didactic examples of NPB for both single project and multi-project NGOs, and nine compelling examples of publicly traded companies with elements of social sector missions from a list of approximately 200 companies, which offer the potential to serve as NPB best practices in general or for certain specific aspects of operations. Consistent throughout, each facilitates identifying NPB Performance Gaps and Deliverable Opportunities with current best practice social sector only organizations or with best practice commercial organizations (some with social mission elements) thereby advancing value creation (expanding the Multiplier Effect or mitigating the Discount Effect), especially advancing an Intersectoral evolution.

CONTENTS

(continued next page)

INTRODUCTION

New philanthropy is energizing the hearts of capitalists with historically unprecedented power. Passionate capitalists/philanthropists ("CPs") are increasingly seeking to manage and evaluate their philanthropic investments with the most effective strategies and tactics so successfully utilized in the commercial sector. The
social sector's profound transformation offers virtually boundless opportunities.
However, these developments are generating no scarcity of challenges and are
rocking the tectonic plates of the social sector. And, should the economy and
social sector resources be negatively effected by a cyclical rotation, the importance of new philanthropy will only increase.

The ambitious mission of *New Philanthropy Benchmarking* is to inspire intense
competition among passionate capitalist/philanthropists and provide essential
wisdoms whereby they can initiate radically positive transformative change within the social sector.

Succinctly put, New Philanthropy Benchmarking ("NPB") builds upon a synergist
collaboration of commercial sector benchmarking, progressive intersectoral strategies, and contemporary financial markets analytical tools. NPB is evaluated within the context of macro issues such as stakeholder considerations and comparative
conclusionary financial metrics. On a micro level, insights are offered on process
sequence as well as organizational execution suggestions.

New Philanthropy Benchmarking is predicated upon the assumption that passionate capitalists/philanthropists will instinctively strive for comparable success in
the commercial sector as well as the social sector. While motivations vary,
instincts compelling superior performance or driving a determination to eschew
being "dumb money" are considered pervasive and transferable.

Such CPs are no longer satisfied with the so-called nonprofit "results" of old economy philanthropy. They do not tolerate the impulse giving, emotionally-based tactics of those social sector participants who, while often of laudable intentions,
miss major opportunities, waste resources, and all to often suffer from the law of
unintended consequences. Intuitively, they know to aggressively talk external

comparative numbers. Indeed, even obsolete terms such as the non-profit sector and non-profit organizations are being replaced with progressive terms like social sector and Non-Governmental Organizations ("NGOs").

Targeted CPs understand the effort and value of transforming a commercial sector investment of resources into a multiple of its initial value. The competitive comparisons of such investments are extensively and intensively discussed. Such a discourse should and can be the case with social sector investments. Investment of resources should and can be viewed on a comparative basis. Benchmarking can be as powerful in the social sector as in the commercial sector. In short, as was said decades ago in the sixties, if you're not part of the solution, you're part of the problem.

The power and compelling attractiveness of NPB is its ability to assist passionate Capitalists/ Philanthropists to multiply the impact – create value – of their resource investment relative to other similar social sector initiatives and minimize risk exposure. Relative value creation is not solely based on the value of resources invested in the commercial sector and this should not be the case in the social sector either. For example, NPB seeks to provide CPs with the tools to leverage a $1 million dollar social sector investment to generate a much greater impact, possibly achieving that of comparable $10 million or even $100 million social sector investment. Simultaneously, NPB provides the framework for CPs to minimize the risk exposure of NGO or foundation misfortunate developments, wasted funds, or unintended consequences.

NP Benchmarking challenges CP and those interested in the social sector to focus on comparative value of the investment (social sector value creation) rather than a simple tout of how much was spent. Instead of seeing the endless stories and annual ranking of dollars spent by CPs, NPB urges that rankings seek to compare the projected or demonstrated dollar value of the investment. If a smart, high value-added CP teams up with a best-in-class NGO and accomplished with $1 million dollars what another CP spent $10 million or $100 million, then the former should receive the well-earned kudos.

Hopefully, the NPB target audience of passionate CPs are sufficiently immune to the press focus on the so-called "four horsemen" of philanthropy: charity balls, big gifts, soft features about worthy programs, and sensational scandal.[1] These CPs can appreciate the potentially destructive focus on recklessly reducing the hard work of philanthropy to the lowest common denominator stories of just "GIVING IT AWAY." They possess sufficient intuitive wisdom so as not to succumb to the mantra that "the value of agency is immeasurable, for how can anyone quantify a child's happiness or a homeless man's self-esteem."[2] They willingly embrace the goal of emancipating NGOs and social entrepreneurs from their roles as "supplicants," an admittedly "subversive act."[3]

To maximize the application of NPB to CPs, both NGOs and foundations are discussed as appropriate interests. NGOs receive the primary concentration of attention, as these will most likely be the main focus of CP talents. The secondary application to foundations is largely based on a two-fold belief: 1) an NPB evaluation of major foundations is necessary to propel the social sector to achieve greater return on resources, and 2) that certain CPs will chose to channel their talents through managing such organizations.

NPB's key messages are summarized in seven (7) Wisdom Points uniquely customized for passionate CPs. They summarize extensive analytical content including social sector transformation opportunities; world-class CP profile insights; concrete NPB examples; effective conceptual, tactical, and managerial materials; and momentum building specifics. The sources of these wisdom points include my own value creations; analysis and interpretations of select world-class CPs (Edgar and Charles Bronfman, Bill Gates, Michael Milken, Thomas Monaghan, George Soros, Steven Spielberg, and Michael Steinhardt); assessments of innovative foundations and leading social enterprise investors, and an extensive critical review of leading academic and professional writings. These seven points provide a memorable distillation of the entire contents of the Working Book.

As mentioned above, the highly summarized key messages of this Working Book are disclosed at the beginning of each section. The following message box contains the seven wisdom points associated with each section. My research indicates that this format should provide a visual imprint for those CPs wishing to retain the key wisdoms of NPB over an extended period of time. In fact, the paper's readers suggested that this table be of the size for billfold cut out and posted on the Internet for easy access and reference.

Benchmarking Wisdom Points

1. The social sector's profound transformation offers virtually bound
    less opportunities.
2. CPs aggressively talk external comparative numbers.
3. Benchmarking can be as powerful in the social sector as in the
    commercial sector.
4. Application of the commercial sector benchmarking concepts apply
    to social sector benchmarking.
5. Yes, competitive social sector measurement tactics do exist.
6. If you can't measure in the social sector, you can't manage.
7. Generate momentum; expect obstacles.

Section One provides a highly practical assessment of major trends effecting the social sector and insights into opportunities for maximum initiative value creation. The social sector's profound transformation offers virtually boundless opportunities. In Section Two, a quite distinctive target CP profile is developed. Here, CPs are urged to aggressively talk external comparative numbers. The power of benchmarking is reviewed in Section Three. Benchmarking can be as powerful in the social sector as in the commercial sector. Section Four introduces the benchmarking concepts. Application of the commercial sector benchmarking concepts clearly apply to social sector benchmarking. Benchmarking tactics are covered in Section Five. Yes, competitive social sector measurement tactics do exist. Section Six provides a relatively detailed description of benchmarking execution concluding that if you can't measure in the social sector, you can't manage in the social sector. Momentum and obstacles to NPB are covered in Section Seven with these words of wisdom: generate momentum; expect obstacles.

New Philanthropy Benchmarking significantly advances traditional commercial and NGO benchmarking models. A common complaint by NGOs is that not every NGO can be evaluated via a single conclusion "number" like businesses. This critical observation is not without merit. There must be comparisons, analyses, and measurements of the many processes both internal and external to a social sector organization. That is a looming NPB mission to address and remedy. If CPs can't measure in the social sector, CPs can't manage in the social sector.

To provide for wide application, NPB addresses a diverse range of situations and considers conceptual as well as tactical and managerial issues. Specific and general examples are offered for proactive and passive CP preferences, established and start-up situations, and project or organization-wide assessments. Examples are provided to advance the NPB vision to a concrete understanding with specific quantifications highlighting the extraordinary impact and potential. On a conceptual basis, stakeholder comparative similarities and traditional exaggerations are evaluated in the context of NPB value creation. Application of the commercial sector benchmarking concepts apply to social sector benchmarking.

As noted, NPB offers a collaborative approach composed of works from various sectors offering synergistic advancement. And, yes, competitive social sector measurement tactics do exist. Three critically important tactics — Deliverable Opportunities, Performance Gaps, and Multiplier/Discount Effects — are advanced in the context of their commercial sector comparables.

Time-tested commercial sector benchmarking practices provide the material upon which application is transferred to the social sector. Tactics such as Performance Margin and Deliverable Opportunities facilitate the transition. Combining these tools with Best Practice metrics enables the construction of Performance Gap composed of the Deliverable Opportunities. The Performance Gap can be presented in dollars or units for either a specific function or for an organization in the aggregate. In essence, the Performance Gap is analogous to a quantification of a "Value Gap" for a publicly traded company with the Deliverable Opportunities comparable to the "Nuggets of Value" of a commercial enterprise.

Importantly, the culminary tactic provides the necessary comparative quantification and concluding step in the NPB process. A Multiplier or Discount Effect ("M/DE") is calculated as a macro-level assessment of utilization of precious resources, especially monetary.

The Multiplier or Discount Effect provides the means whereby involved social sector participants, especially CPs, can compare the relative return on the investment. For example, the NGO investment yields a multiple of X times better than a prevailing best practice. Did $100,000 invested in a designated NGO achieve the same power as $1 million invested in other NGO, a 10 times Multiplier Effect? Or, did the investment yield only a fraction of an identifiable best practice, possibly a 90% Discount Effect? The best practice is to talk external comparative numbers.

For those CPs who are motivated by competition (and what CP isn't?) there should be the positive motivation of knowing that a social sector investment outperformed a quality benchmark by a multiple of times or that a CP's dollars were so wisely invested in the social sector so as to have the power equaling or exceeding social sector investments made by other CPs. On the other hand, there is the motivating power of concern upon learning that resources were invested so unwisely in a social sector project that dollars invested yielded only a fraction of other apparently more sagacious CPs.

Envision a ranking based not naïvely on the absolute magnitude of dollar of charity, but on the relative quantified dollar impact for specified social sector initiatives.

As is most likely apparent to those CPs active in the social sector, NPB can have direct application to the assessment of human services, including life-determining programs. In a sector where inefficiency prolongs human suffering, unaccountable NGOs can no longer be tolerated.

Opportunities to utilize NPB in connection with the rapidly emerging and progressive intersectoral practices are discussed through out the Working Book. The dual goal of providing such material in the context of NP Benchmarking is to first familiarize the CPs on the most progressive practices and, secondly, to stimulate the application of these practices to maximize Performance Gaps, increase a Multiplier Effect, and/or reduce, eliminate, or reverse a Discount Effect.

Intersectoral practices that CPs will discover offer significant NPB measurable value creation: social enterprise (social entrepreneurship, commercialization, operational philanthropy, and contract services), strategic philanthropy & restructuring (capacity building, collaboration, management efficiency programs, restructuring, and foundation value-creation practices), and social capital markets (innovative financings, social venture capital, blended ROIs, and M&A transactions).

The Working Book presses important opportunities for capital market or social capital market value, including addressing the challenges associated with high cost of funding on restrictive/oppressive terms. Related to this issue is a discussion of the opportunities available through the progressive development of the concept increasingly known as Blended Return on Investment (Blended ROI), which is a combination of a Social Return on Investment (SROI) and a typical

Financial Return on Investment (FROI). In this context, issues of transparency of information are discussed.

Managerial issues are addressed throughout with particular note of a CP-focused rapid learning diagram titled "Quality and Value Added Benchmarking Process Pyramid." Hypothetical examples of the NPB process and metrics are illustrated through both a single purpose case study, Single Function Community Service, and a more complex, multi-service case study called the Comprehensive National Service Organization.

The Working Book addresses the application of NPB to foundations in a narrative fashion. This approach is largely based on the practical observation that a foundation's performance is a large function of the NGOs in which it invests. Therefore, it is obviously essential to build foundation NPB benchmarking by first constructing the NPB elements of its portfolio. Furthermore, foundation NPB arguably merits a unique customized effort more appropriate for a subsequent Working Book. However, such customization is within a reasonable reach.

An extensive refinement of building momentum and avoiding obstacles is dialogued. It becomes incumbent upon CPs to generate momentum, while simultaneously expecting obstacles. Several promising momentum-building topics are social sector capital markets opportunities, traditional and cutting-edge executive educational alternatives, incentive compensation observations, and talent assessment questionnaires. Obstacle avoidance topics positively discussed include cultural issues, minimization of risk issues, misconceptions, and voices of caution. A statistical comparison of "live-founder/dead-founder" foundations is particularly revealing. The Working Book concludes by proffering compelling common sense perspectives on the realities and myths of fiduciary obligations and potentially contra-fiduciary activities within the social sector.

A series of appendices provides supplemental information for those CPs who seek to pursue either individually or direct staff to pursue with NPB or other topics contained in this Working Book.

Appendices A through E contain CP related materials. Appendix A: "Capitalist/Philanthropist Profiles" provides profiles of select world-class CPs addressing such topics as: reasons for giving, foundation goals, successful social sector initiatives, collaboration projects, value-added philanthropic perspectives, foundation financial statistics, analytical insights, and selected personal and related interesting information. Appendix B: "Innovating Foundations" and Appendix C: "Social Enterprise Investors" provide highly summarized Best Practices insights into possibly innovative foundations and pioneering social enterprise investors seeking to create a level of value beyond the norm. Appendix D: "Intersectoral Questions" lists 40 questions that CPs should consider using as a self-diagnostic of their intersectoral familiarity and areas for strengthening or as a resource to assess prospective team members or collaboration partners. For those CPs interested in investigating sectarian guidance, Appendix E: "Sectarian Support for NP Benchmarking" contains brief didactical perceptions of *Tzedakah* and Stewardship.

Appendices F through H offer basic NPB materials. Appendix F: "Concept Comparison Glossary" provides the highlights of practical concept comparison glossary. The terms are organized in two groups: commercial sector benchmarking and NPB Benchmarking-Intersectoral Practices. Appendix G: "Camp's Reasons & Results Chart" outlines a useful comparison of those distinguishing traits between those organizations utilizing and those not adequately utilizing benchmarking. Appendix H: "Best of Best in Commercial Sector" offers the elements of a potentially prophetic vision for the social sector by presenting a list of the benchmarking commercial sector companies in a wide range of functional areas, such as customer service, employee empowerment, health care programs, leadership, marketing, research & development, training, and waste minimization.

Appendix I: "20 Benchmarking Assessment Questions" and Appendix J: "Answers and Explanations" provide a more detailed litmus test to evaluate an individual or an organization's culture with regard to benchmarking in general through a 20-question benchmarking assessment questionnaire and supporting practical answers and explanations. The intent of this material is not so much to assess a numerical evaluation but to provide insight into the base upon which a CP may choose to build upon.

Appendices K through O provide a wealth of hands-on management resource materials. Appendix K: "Dual Steps Benchmarking Process" contain an almost workbook-like list of those suggested steps for both the benchmarking study phase and benchmarking execution. Appendix L: "Selected Blended ROI & Present Value Model Issues and Responses" offers several very preliminary documents from external sources for the more advanced CPs interested in pursuing issues associated with social present value. Appendix M: "Benchmarking Internet Sites" and Appendix N: "Internet Resources" contain reviews of selected on-line resources intended to rapidly condense the CP's learning curve and accelerate NPB execution. The reviews seek to separate the substantial Internet hype of applicable resources from the small added quantity of on-target value. Appendix O: "Benchmarking Advisor Sampling Summary" is an evolving condensation of prospective outsourcing professionals. At present this list is undergoing development and is accordingly integrated as a null set. Appendix P: "Further Reading and Information" is a list of reading utilized both directly and indirectly in the Working Book. The more attentive reader is encouraged to examine the endnotes as they contain an unusually expansive insights.

Appendices Q and T relate to building momentum and avoiding obstacle topics. Appendix Q: "Executive Educational Alternatives" provides a select sampling of premier traditional and cutting-edge executive educational alternatives. Five program offerings are reviewed: Harvard University's programs, Stanford University's programs, Yale University's School of Management, Columbia Business School, and United University. Appendix R: "Illustrative Publicly Traded Companies with Intersectoral Missions" contains a representative list of publicly traded companies with distinguishing elements of social sector missions. Appendix S: "Social Sector Misfortunate Situations" contains abbreviated samplings of illustrated misfortunate situations that have been a source of discussion within the social sector. The situations are categorized in three groups: possible nefarious activities (both foundations and NGOs), unintended consequences, and wasted funds. The intent of this material is to offer a social sector comparable to the commercial sector and capital markets risk of investment disclosure. Appendix T: "Intersectoral Illustrative Examples" contains a useful list of examples from the areas of social enterprise, strategic philanthropy & restructuring, and social capital markets. Appendix U: "Main Outline" provides a time-saving guide to the key sections of NPB.

SECTION ONE

SOCIAL SECTOR TRANSFORMATION

Wisdom 1: "The social sector's profound transformation offers virtually boundless opportunities."

Few credible voices would disagree with the conclusion that profound change is occurring within the social sector. A comprehensive analysis of social sector professionals and CPs leads to the further conclusion that these profound transformations offer virtually boundless opportunities.

Without proceeding into extensive statistical detail, it suffices to indicate those trends most influencing the sector: tides of social sector reform, increasing competitive and commercial pressures, major reductions in social sector government funding, record foundation asset growth, intergenerational transfer of wealth and giving, increasing gap in wealth and knowledge, and a booming economy.

Tides of Social Sector Reform:

The tides of social sector changes are numerous and from multiple sources. One of the better works that seeks to organize and describe these tides is by Paul C. Light, titled "Making Nonprofits Work: A Report on the Tides of Nonprofit Management Reform."[4] Light's work describes four categories of current tides of management reform in the social sector. The tides include: scientific management, the central assumption of which is a set of core practices that makes all organizations effective; liberation management, whose central assumption is that organizations should focus on results, not rules, and be entrepreneurial, a concept championed by Al Gore and the United Way; the war on waste, whose central assumption is that staff, processes, and subsectors can be organized to create maximum efficiency; and the watchful eye, which focuses on transparency and making financial and performance information visible in order to allow competition to weed out inefficiency.

NPB's perspective is both diverse and inclusive, embracing selective elements from the various tides; however, some receive greater focus than others. CPs should gain comfort from the fact that highly valued work from the most progressive elders of the social sector is integrated into NPB. Illustrative of this approach are the works of the following elders.

Those such as Ed Skloot, Bill Shore, and Burton Weisbrod focus on commercialization, which may be considered a form of liberation management as it offers freedom of operations. Jed Emerson's attention is on several areas including social entrepreneurship, social capital markets, and Blended Return on Investment (BROI), which contains elements of all four tides. Harvard's Letts, Ryan, and Grossman on Venture Philanthropy as well as Robert Camp, Gregory Watson and their work on social sector benchmarking over both liberation and scientific management. Michael Porter's focus on foundation practices is comprehensive and inclusive in nature. Gregory Dees of Stanford contributes oversight wisdom, especially his social enterprise spectrum. David La Piana concentrates on strategic restructuring and collaboration initiatives, and the Morino Institute researches and proclaims a chronic NGO capacity undercapitalization, both of which have elements of all four tides.

CPs should be on the alert for the increasing focus on so-called venture philanthropy. A recent research publication by the Morino Institute found that there is much more rhetoric and hype in the field. As noted in its report, "It appears that more people are using the language of the for-profit sector to make foundation activities seem sexy. Relatively, few are truly questioning and exploring what it means to be differently engaged from conventional philanthropy and to reward organizations that demonstrate the best performance, not simply the most interesting people."[5]

Although there are many differences in approaches, there appears to be a common concern that capacity building is needed to advance accountability and managerial effectiveness, especially with those NGOs that have the potential and desire to go-to-scale.

Increasing Competitive & Commercial Pressures:

The second trend of note is the increasing competitive and commercial pressures. In an extensive study, Weisbrod notes, "nonprofits are competing increasingly with for-profit firms, and in an amazing variety of forms…nonprofits have discovered that there are massive potential financial benefits from such symbiotic relationships with private firms – benefits that are not occasional and random, but are systematic consequences of powerful economic forces."[6]

"Competition is not necessarily gentler or less intense because it occurs among nonprofits, although it can be."[7]

CPs should be aware that intense competition among NGOs is significantly greater both for those competing head-on as well as from within the broadly defined social sector capital markets. "[NGOs] vie with each other for revenues, board members, customers, contracts and grants, donations, gifts and bequests, prestige, political power, and volunteers… Their competition with other [NGOs] for customers may involve the production of high-quality products, contesting of market share, or a concerted effort to hold the best reputation. [NGOs] also compete for alliance with for-profit and government entities."[8]

Competition may, indeed, go hand-in-hand with NGO commercialism. Additionally, "…the forces of competition are likely to push nonprofits toward increased use of for-profit business techniques, as least in relation to the products and services they sell in mix-mode settings."[9]

NGO enterprise occurs increasingly along an expanding spectrum (See Dees Social Enterprise Spectrum[10] or Morino's Continuum of Return Expectations[11]) ranging from purely philanthropic to purely commercial. "According to the Urban Institute's Nonprofit Sector Project, approximately 15% of nonprofits actually engage in commerce, but more than 70 percent now earn some money through fees and service charges."[12]

Books such as Ed Skloot's "The Nonprofit Entrepreneur: Creating Ventures to Earn Income" instruct in this arena.[13] Burton Weisbrod's book aptly titled "To Profit or Not to Profit: The Commercial Transformation of the Nonprofit Sector" provides over a dozen impressive articles on a comprehensive range to directly on-point topics.[14] Bill Shore's books "Cathedral Within and Revolution of the Heart" present value-added suggestion of creating value in NGOs.[15] Roberts

Enterprise Development Fund and Jed Emerson have published a number of works describing their processes and metrics, including their seven umbrella organizations that employ 600 people throughout the year and are projected to generate $20 million in sales in 2000, up from $16 million in 1999.[16]

NGO commercial success stories abound. While university technology and life science spin-offs grab headlines (Columbia University is projected to earn over $140 million from licensing its patents in 2000, MIT has embarked on a $500 million to $1 billion Asian Media Lab pact with India,[17] and Stanford earned $61 million annually from its technology transfer activity in 1999),[18] intersectoral success stories can be found in practically every industry.

The American Association of Retired People (AARP), an advocacy association for people 50 years and older, earns $150 million annually from licensing fees. Res-Care Inc., a publicly traded commercial entity, delivers services and supports to people with disabilities and special needs youth. Res-Care Inc.'s 1999 revenues were over $834 million. Charitableway manages donations for charities online. In February 2000, Charitableway closed its second round of financing at $35 million. The College Board, the well known SAT testing firm, is reportedly in the process of preparing for an Initial Public Offering. Edison Schools is a publicly traded company that has assumed management for some of the most challenging public schools in the nation. Phoenix University is a rapidly expanding publicly traded company directly competing with government funded schools. Pioneer Industries, an NGO out of the Northwest, has a $50 million business, winning outsourcing contacts from the likes of Boeing Inc. Two aggressive commercial sector companies, Lockheed Martin IMS and Maximus, are both competing for and winning welfare-to-work contacts. Bancroft Inc., a $67 million/year in revenue residential treatment program in New Jersey for severely developmentally disabled children and adults,[19] is also succeeding in the same area.

There are three additional examples worthy of note. As for Cornell Medical School's recent $750 million agreement to create a branch campus in Qatar, additional information such as terms of the management contract and size of grant to the school have yet to be disclosed. This project is unique in that the branch will give full Ivy League medical degrees.[20] Intel is teaming up with the American Cancer Society, the National Foundation for Cancer Research, the University of Oxford, and United Devices to develop a system permitting home and work PC users to donate excess processing power on their desktops towards solving scientific and medical computing problems.[21] J.K Rowling, author of *Harry Potter*, agreed to donate a month-long effort of writing that expected to generate an excess of $36 million in revenues. Publishers, printers, bookstores, and other companies involved in the production and sale of the books are contributing their services for free or at reduced costs.[22]

As NGOs progress with various commercial strategies and tactics, potential risks are a prudent topic of discussion. CPs should not be surprised to hear a laundry list of unfounded emotional, self-interest based, and even mythic concerns. However, the CPs should keep in mind that the decision not to embrace commercialism could have negative implications. "As a result of not maximizing net revenue, they will also not be able to maximize output of their preferred, mission-related activities, because of the desire to avoid the non preferred activities."[23]

The history of commercial activities with both successes and misfortunes dates far back in history. A recent *New York Times* story, "Modern Marketing Blooms In Medieval Vatican Library" relates commercial efforts dating from well before the Reformation to the latest efforts with e-commerce and licensing. Despite the discontinued project, efforts continue as valuable sources of funding for social mission-focused initiatives. During the Year 2000 events, the Vatican sold 30 licenses for souvenirs and religious items, including an agreement with an on-line retailer to sell reproductions from the Vatican library. Other efforts, such as those to digitize the library's archive of 150,000 rare manuscripts, have yet to become a reality.[24]

Nonetheless, reasonable concerns and analysis is merited. Topics of a comprehensive risk exposure analysis include the so-called "crowding-out" effect where donors, volunteers, and other socially minded stakeholders will depart as commercial activities increase (which affect cost of operations); distributional equity issues where one disadvantaged group is provided with less focus; other disutility issues such as loss of mission, damage to brand name and associated NGO "community trust" images; or even exposure of preferential taxation benefits.

For a more expansive discussion of publicly traded companies with comparable social mission elements refer to Section Seven under Capital Markets NP Benchmarking.

Much of this approach – commercialism – is based on the belief that the social sector must go beyond the simple notion that it is better to teach a person to fish than to give them a fish, but to teach them to build and grow a successful fish conglomerate.

A germane topic for value creation that is somewhat beyond the immediate scope of this Working Book is the potential for creating value in the social sector through collaboration with a wide range of partners. In advanced stages of more strategic application, NPB's focus on quantitative financial metrics and the progressive intersectoral practices should consider the best practices associated with collaborative opportunities. Traditionally, collaborative opportunities have been limited to NGOs. More recently, the value creation potential has expanded to include commercial relationships.[25] Foundations have also begun to capture the collaborative opportunities with a 1998 survey, indicating that two-thirds of all grant makers had collaborated with NGOs, government, or other foundations in the last five years.[26]

As will be discussed later, the CPs profiled in this Working Book have aggressively utilized collaborative opportunities to create value, e.g. Gates and Bronfman.

One of the most respected social sector restructuring professionals offers this astute observation: "Likely nonprofit candidates for strategic restructuring are analogous to businesses with under-valued stock: the necessary elements for success are present, but the organization needs outside help to move it forward. When a business's restructuring is successful, its stock value rises dramatically. When a NGO's restructuring is successful, its ability to fulfill its social mission rises dramatically."[27]

For a further discussion of assessment questions in connection with collaboration see the respective endnote.[28] Also, for the purposes of this Working Book, collaborations are defined to include a wide-range of structural alternatives, including joint venture and other "mixed-mode" settings. (See the endnote for one professional's insightful categorization of holding company and joint venture alternatives.)[29] Coevolution, as practiced in the commercial sector, is also believed to be a viable option for social sector organizations. Coevolution is the notion that by working with direct competitors, customers, and suppliers, a company can create new businesses, markets, and industries – opening the possibility that, in certain situations, nonprofits will indeed collaborate with direct competitors."[30]

Issues associated with NGO conversion as an alternative related to collaboration or restructuring are briefly discussed in Section Seven. These issues cover questions regarding when a conversion is socially appropriate, obligations to modify NGO legal structure, and potential roles for CPs.

Such expanded relationships/alternatives are increasingly common. The value created by these relationships is growing well beyond that envisioned by many of its earliest advocates. For practical purposes, value-creating collaboration is classified within the broader topic of Strategic Philanthropy and Restructuring. Without question, such strategies can expand the Performance Gap and therefore the Multiplier Effect.[31]

A leading social sector sage notes that there is one fundamental reason that NGOs have rarely entered the commercial sector. "They only rarely thought they could. It has been a colossal failure of imagination pervasive to the social sector. That's not to say there are not financial, managerial, and regulatory hurdles to overcome; there are in any business venture. But the limitations on nonprofits starting businesses have by and large been self-imposed."[32] From a CP's perspective, it should be quite informative to learn that some research in the field of pecuniary motives may not be that distanced from decisions whether or not to pursue commercial opportunities. "When faced with large new opportunities for commercialism, many nonprofits seem quite willing to shed their altruistic cover and assume the values and behavior of for-profits."[33]

Throughout this Working Book, topics from both the first and second trend are developed. As mentioned in the Introduction, these items referred to as "Intersectoral Practices" offer CPs significant NPB measurable value creation opportunities. For conceptual organization purposes, CPs can view these under the rubric of three broad categories with several sub-categories. These include the following: social enterprise (social entrepreneurship, commercialization, operational philanthropy, and contract services), strategic philanthropy & restructuring (capacity building, collaboration, management efficiency programs, restructuring, and foundation value-creation practices), and social capital markets (innovative financings, social venture capital, BROIs, and M&A transactions).

Major Reduction in Social Sector Government Funding:

The third trend often identified is the major reallocation in social sector spending by the government, although the trend is not without complicating countervailing considerations. According to one industry advisor, under the congressional budget passed in 1996, NGOs could lose a cumulative amount of $90 billion or 18% of their federal support over the 1997 to 2002 fiscal period. In certain sectors, losses are quite dramatic with social services down 25%, a 48% decline in international aid, and a 51% drop in housing and community development.[34] Under a comparable presidential budget, NGOs will forfeit more than $40 billion in federal revenues during 1997 to 2002. According to one source, private philanthropy must compensate with a triple increase to maintain pre-reduction levels.[35]

As referenced above, there is credible debate as to whether the trend in funding is a true reduction or can be more accurately characterized as a reallocation of governmental or other funding sources. Some observe that increases in state and local government funding may have offset to some extent the decline in federal government budget declines. Others observe that the increase in private giving may have even offset the apparent decline in federal funding, but this requires much further review.

Even assuming the trend of characterization and statistical significance is valid, efforts by the current President Bush appear to indicate a greater focus on outsourcing government projects to faith-based groups. Not unlike former Vice President Gore, the current President Bush sees great potential for philanthropic and social sector initiatives.

As Bush noted during the 2000 campaign, "We could be on the verge of one of the great philanthropic periods in America, where enormous wealth has been generated. The next president needs to encourage that wealth to spread. People need to give back."[36] Bush's view of the roles and opportunities are to some extent influenced or represented in a recent publication by Marvin Olasky, "The Tragedy of American Compassion," which offers a rather conservative perspective.

Bush speaks to an over-reliance on government to deal with many difficult social issues, which he says it has "had a corrosive impact on the great strength of this country, which is individuals helping individuals."[37] He discussed a possible solution during a campaign stop in Indianapolis: "In every instance where my administration sees a responsibility to help people, we will look first to faith-based organizations, charities, and community groups that have shown their ability to save and change lives."[38] For further information, see the endnotes for the seven elements of this plan.[39]

A further countervailing occurrence involves the powerful forces advocating greater funding for "civil society" projects that are more consistent with believers in a "third way" philosophy now increasingly favored by leaders of many industrialized nations. NGOs, functioning as a "third way," are strategically positioned between business and government and are capable of holding both accountable to "civil society" missions. Those such as Bill Clinton (US), Tony Blair (UK), Gerhard Schroeder (Germany), Wim Kok (Netherlands), and Goran Persson (Sweden) reportedly favor this approach. They purportedly want NGOs to become engines of economic development.[40] This direction was evident with a recent World Bank announcement that every country-assistance strategy it approved last year involved NGOs and civil society, which is up from 20% in 1990.[41] According to one source, this bears the imprint of the World Bank's President, James Wolfensohn, who has installed more than 70 NGO specialists in the bank's field offices with even more supporting them at its headquarters in Washington.[42]

Record Foundation Asset Growth:

The fourth trend is a positive one with a record growth in foundation asset growth and giving. Foundation giving is up 17% in 1999, following a 22% increase in 1998. Additionally, endowments increased in asset value to $385 billion in 1998, an increase of 16.7%.[43]

Giving by the nation's nearly 47,000 grant-making foundations grew to $22.8 billion from $19.5 billion between 1998 and 1999. While the 1999 percentage increase was less than 1998, it was still the second largest single year increase since 1985. The two-year increase of 42.3% is an all time record. The inflation adjusted is even more impressive, giving exceeding inflation by 15.1% in 1999. [44]

As mentioned, endowment values increased to $385.1 billion, up 16.7%. This increase was in no small part stimulated by the massive contribution of Bill Gates as well as the exceptionally large gifts and bequests from donors to foundations, which increased by almost 43% to $22.6 billion. An increasing number of new foundations also contributed to the strong increase.[45]

Flow is flowing so rapidly and in such large volumes that *The New York Times* proclaimed in a recent headline that "Harvard's $2.1 Billion Tops Colleges' Big Fund-Raising." As the article mentioned, universities usually don't set fund raising goals they can't achieve; when Harvard in 1992 set a $2.1 billion goal by year-end 1999, the goal seemed herculean. This calculated to approximately one million dollars a day for seven years. But, with over two months remaining, the Boston-based university had already exceeded its goal with $2.3 billion raised.[46]

Even with the declines in market values of late 2000 and early 2001, only approximately 10% of the major foundations surveyed by the Chronicle of Philanthropy predict a decline in grant making.[47] Furthermore, assets only declined by a median of 0.3 percent last year (2000).[48] However, that doesn't mean a more intense focus on resource allocation, such as advocated by NPB, isn't wise even in best of times; cyclical rotations can be around the corner and might bring a significant downward inflection. For example, in the 1975 recession, foundation giving dropped 28% and didn't recover for a decade (accounting for inflation).[49] Should such a decline occur, NPB will be only that much more important. In fact, "during lean economic times, charities typically become more reliant on private foundations because of declines in gifts from individuals and corporations."[50]

The trends continue as indicated in a recently released Foundation Center study on "Foundation Growth and Giving Estimates: 2000 Preview (2001 Edition)." According to the annual report, foundations distributed $27.6 billion last year, up more than 18% from 1999 – the fifth straight annual double-digit increase. From 1995 to 1999, foundations assets nearly double to $450 billion. Commenting on this trend and the increase in proactive philanthropists, a *NY Times* article notes that "donors today increasingly practice 'high impact' philanthropy, in which they look to transform an entire field." [51] The study also notes a trend to increase grant size. "In the early 1990's, grants of $10 million were a rarity. And nationwide, most grants are still for $50,000 or less. Nevertheless, a big commitment is now one of more than $100 million." "Traditionally, when foundations didn't have enough money to have a major impact on an issue, they tried to influence social policy," Ms. Engelhardt of the Foundation Center stated. "Now people have been able to think bigger, and they tend to pick things where they can make a difference."[52]

Intergenerational Transfer of Wealth and Giving:
The fifth trend noted in the schematic refers to the massive intergenerational transfer of wealth, which is just beginning and will only accelerate. In late October of 1999, Boston College researchers published a report in which its researchers concluded that between now and 2005 charities would receive bequests of between $41 trillion to $136 trillion (yes, TRILLION!), measured in 1998 dollars, assuming the estate tax remains unchanged.[53]

The study's authors say that their new statistics indicate that our social sector stands ready to benefit from a "platinum era of giving."[54]

These figures dwarf the previous estimates of $10 trillion widely published from an influential 1993 study by economists Robert Avery and Michael Rendell of Cornell University and cited in such well regarded publications as Lester M. Salomon's "Holding the Center: America's Nonprofit Sector a Crossroad."[55] According to reports, Avery, now an economist with the Federal Reserve, said that while he may have some qualms about the techniques used by the Boston College researchers, the study as described to him sounds like reasonable estimates.[56]

The economic model contains an extensive list of assumptions and extrapolations. One CP relevant note is that the model estimates that for estates of $20 million or more, 39% of the money will go to charity, 23% to heirs, 34% to taxes, and 3% for other expenses. Recent IRS data show that the percentage bequeathed to charity may be low, as in recent years a growing number of individuals are engaging in more estate planning so that more of their money will go to charity after their death.[57]

Of course, if recent discussions of estate tax reduction are enacted, bequests to foundations and NGOs could be much smaller than estimated. Nonetheless, the issue is of such significance that the White House held a major forum during 2000 on the topic of new philanthropy and the ever-growing wealth transfer. A recent conference was titled, "White House Forum on Philanthropy – Gifts to the Future."

But, as a December 2000 article noted, there are some sobering concerns. "The increase in charitable largesse during the 1990's almost entirely was due to the booming economy. A Council of Economic Advisors report concluded that there is "little evidence" to suggest there now is "a more generous attitude toward philanthropy."[58]

Increasing Gap in Wealth and Knowledge and a Booming Economy:

The sixth and seventh trends are essentially intertwined: an increasing gap in wealth and education and an unprecedented period of economic prosperity.

The wealth at the top of our society is increasing at absolutely unprecedented rates. "The US economy generates a new millionaire household approximately every 31 seconds. That comes to about 1 million new millionaire families every year."[59] Even though the US population is growing at slightly more than 1%, the number of millionaires is increasing at a 17% annual rate, according to the Lincoln Financial Group. Incredibly, 90% of these newly-rich have not inherited their wealth.[60] One high profile example is that 2,000 of Cisco's 19,000 employees had become millionaires through their stock.[61]

Since 1994, the number of millionaires in the United States has almost doubled to 7.2 million from 3.4 million in 1994 (an average annual increase of 16%), and is projected to reach 15 million by 2004.[62] More strikingly, the number of pentamillionaries ($5 million in investable assets) has grown more than 500% since 1994 to 590,000; this is up from 90,000 in 1994, which is a staggering annual rate of 46%.[63] And according to the Spectrum Group, the number of pentamillionaries could reach 3.9 million by 2004.[64] The total value of the stock portfolios of this group is estimated to have tripled between 1989 and 1997 to $5.75 trillion. Today, 33% of pentamillionaries' wealth comes from employee stock options and 24% from investment returns.[65]

At an even more rarified level is what Merrill Lynch and Gemini Consulting refers to as the super wealthy, those with $30 million or more in liquid financial assets. Worldwide this group is at approximately 55,000, an increase of 18% from 1998.[66] The group's financial assets are estimated to be $7.9 trillion.[67] However, liquidity issues demand that CPs seek to maximize their philanthropic investment. NPB is a powerful tool, and as dollars free up over time, the available resources should only increase. At latest count, only about one-third of the assets of those individuals whose wealth is in the $10 million range is liquid, while those with $50 million or more have ready access to just 15%.[68]

For the proverbial average American, the wealth remains less than abundant. In the United States, the top 1% of the households has more than 95% of the wealth.[69] Most of the nation's 72 million families feel they cannot make ends meet. Three-quarters earn less than $75,000 a year and 45% of all families earn $30,000 to

$75,000.[70] The average family income gain over the last 10 years is quite meager, with an inflation-adjusted increase of only 4.5% or $2,000 (to $47,000, expected in the 1999 Census).[71] Raising hours has done more to pump up family income and, according to recent studies, stress. Point in fact, from 1989 through 1998, the increase in work time was 3.4 weeks – often from increased spousal employment.[72]

The gap in educational performance is also quite troubling. According to a federal Department of Education study released in August 2000, the gap between test scores of black and white students that had narrowed through the 1980's widened from 1990 to 1999, with the average black 17-year-old reading only about as well as the average white 13-year old.[73] Possibly even more disconcerting is that the gap is widest among children of the best-educated parents, with average scores of white students remaining relatively steady and those of black falling back to the lower achievement of the late 1970s.[74] For instance, the gap between black and white 17-year-olds in science scores widened to 52 points in 1999 from 47 points in 1996, and almost back to the 54-point difference that existed in 1969.[75]

SECTION TWO

TARGET AUDIENCE — CPS

Wisdom 2: "CPs aggressively talk external comparative numbers."

The philanthropic sector has not reached its potential. A lack of benchmarking, measurements, and accountability highlight this point. Some anecdotal accounts can refute this comment, but professionals tend to conclude otherwise. In one of its publications, the Morino Institute bluntly addresses the state of nonprofit organizations. "Current methods of funding and supporting nonprofits can be improved. Nonprofit organizations exist in a culture of dysfunction… This dysfunction makes success highly improbable and calls into question the sustainability of organizations unable to adequately capitalize future growth."[76]

The recognition that the social sector desperately needs improvement leads to the question: what is the cause of this downfall? The James Irvine Foundation provides an answer: "Society is at risk of losing essential nonprofit services because of the poor financial performance and imminent economic collapse of so many of the organizations within which these activities occur."[77] With the problem in the philanthropic sector acknowledged, the task is now to address the problem. And, as Carnegie tells us in his *Gospel of Wealth*, "the rich have the power to benefit mankind."[78]

Technology, rapid expansion, and condensed time are not only the ideas changing the commercial sector, but also those changing the social sector. Understanding the changes in the new economy provides a way to look at the microcosmic changes in philanthropy and benchmarking. Old philanthropy is typified by check writing, in which a good deed done required no accountability. New philanthropy requires measurements, accountability, and benchmarking.

25

The world of philanthropy is being taken over by capitalists who want to see change.

These new capitalists/philanthropists ("CPs") found that the way to turn the social sector into an accountable sector is through applying their commercial sector principles. In all likelihood, CPs are extremely familiar with commercial sector benchmarking. Benchmarking is a regular practice imperative to maintain a successful position. Commercial sector work has developed CP talents and economic treasures. CP talents provide the foundation for a potentially major social impact. CP treasures provide the means by which a CP can quickly and successfully execute a major innovative vision. Management skills may not be a CP's primary talent, but they recognize their value.

As one seasoned observer notes in a recently published book, *What Makes Charity Work?*, "who more than a businessman has the authority to say that no enterprise can prosper that doesn't hold individuals accountable, rewarding merit and punishing failure, keeping everybody's attention focused on results, recognizing that employees can't flourish unless customers do, and giving managers the authority and responsibility for making their operations succeed?"[79]

These potential moral obligations to maximize resources become an opportunity to save lives. Tom Reis of W.K. Kellogg Foundation states that "a new generation of innovators and entrepreneurs – committed to using market-based approaches to solve social problems – is unleashing new ways of using resources for the public good."[80]

The recurring recognition of the potential impact of premier catalysts affirms the notion that CPs opportunities have become obligations. Giving can be done either proactively or passively. While learning about the social sector, there are time limitations that make a passive approach more attractive. However, a proactive approach is ultimately preferable, despite its time demand. Expect direct and to-the-point wisdom. Watered down messages are a waste of valuable time.

Select CP Profiles:
Advocacy of NPB within this Working Book primarily focuses on NGOs with a tangential application to professional foundation. And it should not go without mention that CPs also can and should seek to assess their own performance in a

comparative and quantifiable manner. Such an approach is in part addressed in the comparative strategy and tactics of NPB discussed later, especially a comparative financial metric called "Multiplier/Discount Effect." However, a more complete and comprehensive assessment is probably some distance from this point in time.

Nonetheless, this Working Book embarks upon a pioneering journey by providing a rather detailed review of seven world-class CPs.

As practical research, expansive analysis of material from an extensively wide range of global sources, including IRS filings, as well as several interviews, is useful. This aspect of the Working Book was, in fact, one of the most time consuming and yet the lowest metric yielding. To promote accuracy and high value added content, the material on each CP was provided to each for review in advance of inclusion. Responses varied.

Each with varying talents, the CPs are selected from a range of commercial sectors. They are all highly successful in the commercial sector and all, without question, demonstrate a major and sincere commitment to philanthropy which is met with considerable success. Technology is represented by Bill Gates of Microsoft; consumer product industries by the Bronfman brothers (Charles and Edgar) of Seagram Inc.; consumer services by Tom Monaghan, formerly of Dominos Pizza; investment management by George Soros and Michael Steinhardt, professional investors; multi-media by Steven Spielberg; and financial innovation by Michael Milken.

The summary matrix below provides the highlights of the more extensive profiles contained in Appendix A "Capitalist-Philanthropist ("CP") Profiles." There are several recurring themes cited in the Summary Matrix that are worth noting as they potentially offer both NP Benchmarking comparative information and value-added ideas. These few observations will be followed by a few highlights from both the summary matrix and Appendix A.

There are unmistakable recurring themes that pervade the social sector investments of time, talents, treasures, and tenacity of all seven CPs. Each has embarked, in their own unique way, on a highly ambitious and passionate mission to transform certain areas of the social sector. Consistent throughout is a focus on evolving and quantifiable metrics across an extraordinarily diverse range of projects. Competitive elements consistent with the power of NPB are inspiring. There is a seamless transference of commercial concepts to the social sector initiative; stakeholders in both sectors are all-inclusive. Tactics are focused and intense, especially in contrast with historical social sector practices. Each person embraces hands-on effective management in styles consistent with their highly successful commercial talents. And, without question, each is outstanding in generating momentum and dissolving obstacles.

Value creation is evident in virtually all projects, bringing various special commercial talents previously rare or nonexistent. Intersectoral practices involve social enterprise, strategic philanthropy & restructuring, and social capital markets. Value added includes selecting the best project for collaborating with others to improve performance of participants or to advance the state of knowledge and practice. And, they seek to share their wisdom serving as positive benchmarks to other CPs seeking to accomplish positive missions in the social sector.

These premier CPs' actions may speak as loud as their words. They place a very high present value on social sector accomplishments. The average annual distribution of foundation assets is a considerable multiple of the large foundation norm. There is a message that goals today merit great effort in contrast to building social sector asset bases for professional foundation managers. As would be expected of such a world-class group, they concentrate their efforts on a limited numbers of projects. The average size investment is in the multi-millions versus less than $110,000 for foundations with even larger investment asset bases.

The Bronfman brothers, Edgar and Charles, have achieved many successes in the social sector that some would argue are comparable to those achieved in their commercial lives. They have clearly applied commercial marketing talents honed at Seagram's to their social sector efforts. Edgar's work in combining several major Jewish organizations is an impressive example of strategic restructuring. Charles' co-founding of the BirthRight Israel project is both innovative and a quantifiably measurable initiative. The initiative is also a premier example of collaboration with multiple public and private entities. Edgar's leadership with the Holocaust fund recovery using commercial litigation strategy is already legendary. Valuable perspectives that are both consistent with and support NPB's wisdom points include the concept that measurements illustrate true initiatives and you can't just focus on fundraising – it's simply a tool.

In a personal interview with Edgar Bronfman, he exceeded the author's very high expectations. He began the interview by noting that "giving is so much more than just giving money, it's giving of yourself."[81] His passion is evident: "my heart is not with the little meshugaes, but with the Jewish people and humanity."[82] One of his strengths is investing more time and demonstrating leadership by "taking on projects that others don't want and completing them to exceed expectations."[83] Key to his success is an ability to delegate. "Learn to select the right people. People who are smart, bright, entrepreneurial, and aggressive. With a good person, you discuss, agree, and then you leave, and they go on. In the meantime, they do as much as they can and if they have any questions they will contact you. But, they have to be working, and you must trust them to work and that's how you find good managers."[84] He believes that developing managers in the social sector is more challenging given so many historic cultural issues. As for benchmarking, he displays the instincts of a highly successful CP, and says this is just a part of everyday life. He is a strong proponent of creativity and innovation. "Creativity is when you have a group that is greater than the sum of the parts, and whatever doesn't innovate constantly will die."[85] He has carefully sought to apply his commercial skills, particularly management and marketing, to his social sector endeavors. Also, an interview with Richard Marker, the executive of Edgar Bronfman's foundation, offered several insightfully relevant value-creation related observations. "Regarding our collaboration efforts, we become involved with other organizations so that we can have a greater impact with the program."[86] He also commented that "when assessing grant requests, it's prudent to determine how the recipient plans to measure the impact, as this illustrates their true perspectives."[87]

Bill Gates is known to rigorously analyze initiative proposals for comparatively, which is consistent with the most basic element of NPB. He leverages his technology resources to advance his mission as well as to encourage commercial contacts to participate in social sector initiatives, especially skilled technology and management professionals. His foundation likes to say that the common theme of the Gates giving is "reality is equity." "Right now we have unprecedented opportunities to improve people's lives. The goal of the foundation is to bring some of those opportunities in terms of health and education to people who might not have them."[88] His efforts in collaborative initiatives include a major college merit scholarship program with established NGOs, a library technology program with 3000 libraries in 25 states, and medical vaccine research initiatives with commercial pharmaceutical companies. The major Gates Foundation also appears to be seeking opportunities for strategic initiatives to advance modern science, especially medicine, in what could be highly successful commercial ventures. More recently, Gates has publicly confessed that he was "naïve – very naïve" when he began his more focused engagement in philanthropy back in 1994.[89] Now he assumes a possibly more natural role of a self-described "troublemaker" about the promises of technology.[90] Gates appears to have refocused his belief that global capitalism is capable of solving the most immediate catastrophes facing the world's poorest and suffering, especially the 40,000 deaths a day from preventable diseases.[91] More recently, Gates and his foundation members, including his father, have embarked on a crusade to forestall the repeal of the US estate tax.[92]

Michael Milken, considered one of his generations most innovative and effective investment bankers, has spearheaded in careful fashion a number of initiatives worth mention. His largest, more generally visible effort is Knowledge Universe, ("KU") with his role as lead investor of this now major for-profit company. KU is considered a progressive intersectoral company pioneering areas of education and technology. Currently, the company has completed 30 acquisitions and started over 6 companies, with combined annual revenues exceeding one billion dollars. KU in a collaborative effort obtained funding of approximately $250 million from Larry Ellison, CEO of Oracle. He is an early investor in another intersectoral start-up, UNext Inc., a distance learning company. Possibly one of his most committed efforts involves the founding of CaP CURE, an aggressive cancer research organization which has raised $160 million and is in the process of publishing cancer related research to further its missions.[93] His perspectives on the social sector are quite impressive. An editorial in a prominent international business daily displayed his "six keys to meeting challenging philanthropy." His socio-economic model, which expressively analyzes the elements and relationships of social capital creation has received wide dissemination. And, his focus on ROI in the context of philanthropic initiatives is clearly advancing the creation of value.

Tom Monaghan's talents for innovation, organization, and leadership (amply evident in his building of the Domino's empire) appear in a number of his philanthropic efforts within the social sector. His hands-on approach may merit that he even be termed a social entrepreneur. He is the founder of Legatus, a faith-based organization for business executives to energize and magnify their social sector impact. Such individuals, called Executive Ambassadors, currently number at

1,300 in 25 chapters with a goal of reaching 10,000 members. He has founded an unprecedented initiative, a Catholic law school. He attempted a social enterprise venture via a network of nine Catholic radio stations, is financing a network of Catholic schools, and is the founder of an impact-focused newspaper. He offers valuable perspectives very much consistent with the comparative financial metrics of NPB: objective to return on investment to save as many souls per dollar as possible. And, he reportedly utilizes the same zealous uncompromising approach to the social sector as in commercial sector initiatives.

George Soros, considered by many to be one of the greatest investors of our times, has pressed similar commercial sector intensity to his social sector initiatives. He is the founder of the Open Society Institute/Fund, which is at last count in 30 countries and building solid organization infrastructure. General observations are that his efforts facilitated the transition of Russian communism to multiple democratic countries. He founded the Central European University. His numerous innovative initiatives are evaluated for performance with incentive and phase-out funding plans. The Soros Foundation of Hungary is credited with achieving tremendous results with very little money. As for perspective, two thoughts stand out: The Paradox of Charity, and Open Society. The former states that charity tends to turn recipients into objects of charity, and that is not what it is intended to accomplish. Charity goes against human nature because it makes people dependent. Philanthropy alone cannot be relied upon to change the world; the same as for advocating an "Open Society" that encourages free press, political pluralism, and human rights.

The founding of the Shoah Visual History Foundation may well represent Steven Spielberg's most profiled social sector success. The foundation has leveraged his commercial sector talents into world-class intersectoral initiatives. Shoah has produced several documentaries including a 1999 Academy Award winner; produced its first interactive CD, which is being globally distributed; and developed web based digital research archives of Holocaust testimonials with a goal of 50,000 testimonials. He established the Righteous Person Foundation, using mass media to engage broad audiences and encouraging Jewish learning. In an exceptionally sagacious statement, he dedicated his profits from *Schindler's List* (a highly successful major motion picture) to the Righteous Persons Foundation. In a progressive use of collaboration, he has teamed up with the American Association for School Administrators for a National Tolerance Initiative. Utilizing his networking and financial acumen, he founded the Partners in

History and the Future campaign to assist in funding the Shoah Foundation. Furthermore, his foundations continue to work with outside resources in virtually every aspect of their work. As for perspective, he approves of identifying his name with social sector projects only if it further enhances efforts, which is approximately 20% of the situations.

Michael Steinhardt, one of the world's most respected investors and money managers, has passionately committed his talent to social sector missions. Today, Steinhardt manages a portfolio of enthusiasms, one of which is philanthropy. "What Michael wants to do is be an agent of change, by being very provocative and challenging," says Gershon Kekst, a friend who is also active in Jewish philanthropy.[94] Steinhardt co-founded Birthright Israel, an innovative and quantifiably measured initiative which is also a prime example of collaboration with both private and public entities. He obtained co-ownership of the *Forward* newspaper, possibly the largest Jewish (English language) weekly in the United States. Through considerable effort, he is widely considered an internationally acclaimed proponent and sponsor of universal protection, study, and exhibition of historically significant Judaica. With focused effort, he is an aggressive supporter of multiple New York area high schools and Jewish social and cultural centers. His leadership role supporting the Israel Museum includes global network building and financing. Steinhardt is also the lead sponsor of a visionary project at the Brooklyn Botanical Gardens. A most notable perspective is his mentor role in developing future Jewish community leaders. More recently, he has become increasingly engaged with several higher education institutions, from joining Brandeis University's board, becoming chairman of the board of Tel Aviv University, to pledging $10 million to the School of Education at New York University where he is a trustee. In the spring of 2001, the school will be named in his honor.

Chart 1: <u>Capitalist</u>-Philanthropist ("CP") Profile Summary Matrix

Bronfman Brothers (Charles & Edgar)	Bill Gates	Michael Milken	Tom Monaghan
Marketing talents from Seagram as benchmark	Encourage commercial contacts to participate in social sector initiatives, especially skilled technology and management professionals	Knowledge, Inc: lead investor in K1, which has acquired 30 companies and started up 6. Obtained collaborative funding of $250 million from Larry Ellison at Oracle	Founder of Legatus for Executives to energize and magnify impact. (Executive Ambassadors) 1,300 members, 25 chapters (10,000 member goal)
Combining several major Jewish organizations in strategic restructuring	Seeks opportunities for strategic initiatives to advance modern science, especially medicine, in potentially commercial ventures	Early investor in UNext, a distance learning company	Founder of Catholic Law School, an unprecedented initiative
Cofounder of Birthright Israel, innovative and quantifiably measured initiative	Collaborative initiative, especially Merit Scholarship Program	Founded CaP CURE research organization, raised $75 million	Financing network of Catholic Schools
Holocaust funds recovery using commercial litigation strategies	Collaboration with pharmaceutical companies for medical vaccines	Publisher of Cancer Related Works	Founded impact focused newspaper
Collaboration in Birthright Israel with private and public entities	Library Technology Program. First Year: 3000 libraries in 25 states.	Perspective: Six keys to meeting challenging philanthropy	Attempted social enterprise venture via network of 9 Catholic radio stations
Perspective: Measurements illustrate true initiative	Perspective: Leverage technology resources to advance missions	Perspective: Social capital creative technologies	Perspective: Objective is to return on investment to save as many souls per dollar as possible
Perspective: Can't just focus on fundraising. Fundraising is simply a tool.	Perspective: Rigorously analyzes initiative proposals for comparative merit.	Perspective: Focus on ROI philanthropic giving, e.g. creating viable investments	Perspective: Utilizes the same zealous uncompromising approach to social sector as in commercial initiatives

(continued on next page)

Chart 1: <u>Capitalist-Philanthropist ("CP")</u> Profile Summary Matrix
(continued from previous page)

George Soros	Steven Spielberg	Michael Steinhardt
Founder of Open Society Institute/Fund, active in 30 countries and helping to build solid supporting organizations	Founder of Shoah Visual History Foundation • Produced several documentaries including a 1999 Academy Award winner • Produced its first interactive CD, being distributed globally • Developing web based digital research archives of Holocaust testimonials. Goal: 50,000 testimonials	Co-founder of Birthright Israel, an innovative and quantifiably measured initiative. Also, collaboration in Birthright Israel with private and public entities
General observation is that his efforts facilitated the transition from Russian communism to democracy in multiple countries	Established Righteous Person Foundation, using mass media to engage broad audiences and encourage Jewish learning	Co-Owner of Forward newspaper, possibly the largest Jewish (English language) weekly in the United States.
Founder of Central European University	Dedicated his profits from Schindler's List (commercial movie) to Righteous Persons Foundation	Internationally acclaimed proponent and sponsor of universal protection, study, and exhibition of historically significant Judaica.
Numerous innovative initiatives evaluated for performance with incentive and phased-out funding plans	Collaborative initiative with American Association of School Administrators for National Tolerance Initiative	Aggressive supporter of multiple NY area high schools and Jewish social and cultural centers
Soros Foundation of Hungary credited with achieving tremendous results with very little money	Partners in History and The Future campaign assists in funding Shoah Foundation	Leadership role supporting The Israel Museum, including global network building and financing.
Perspective: The paradox of charity	Outsourcing: The Foundation continues to work with outside resources in virtually every aspect of its work.	Lead sponsor of visionary project at Brooklyn Botanical Gardens
Perspective: Advocating "open society" that encourages free press, political pluralism, and human rights	Perspective: Identifies his name with social sector projects only if further enhances efforts, approximately 20% of situations	Perspective: Mentor role in developing future Jewish community leaders.

Reliance on Foundations as Change Agents:

CPs would be ill advised and disappointed should they seek to rely on major foundations to serve as the necessary change agents for advancing the benefits of New Philanthropy Benchmarking. A general survey will only support foundation assessment research, which concludes that foundations are mostly engaged in a practice of small grants, annual allocations, passive involvement, and non-capacity building projects.[95] However, some in the social sector realize that foundations must change. As a sector wag notes, "the old notion of foundations as 'society's risk capital,' experimenting with new models so that they could later be adopted and widely replicated by government, is essentially dead."[96]

Major foundations clearly have an awesome potential structurally and financially. However, the directors have little training in effective management skills or world-class commercial practices. As is common knowledge in the social sector, many foundations appear more determined to support the IRS 5% mandate for distribution that seeks to accelerate the time table under which their missions can be accomplished.[97] Look no further than reports from the investment advisors to the foundations such as one major investment bank and others proclaiming the 5% as the maximum advisable to maintain and grow the asset base of foundations.[98] In essence, it's more important to grow assets and live forever than deplete assets and accomplish a pyrrhic victory of a completed foundation mission.

What may be even more disturbing is a recent trend whereby so-called "donor-advised funds" are exempt from the 5% minimum and funders are allowed to get the immediate tax deduction and have no obligation to make any annual distribution. "Not everyone is so enthralled with donor-advised funds. Some charities bristle at the fact that contributors can keep their money invested in these funds for years before doling out a single dime. With a foundation, philanthropists must distribute at least 5% of the assets each year, but the government doesn't set any such minimums on donor-advised funds."[99]

Don't expect to hear that biblical principles of "tithing," as expressed throughout the Bible, apply to foundations. Why shouldn't foundations tithe, or donate, 10% of assets annually? Granted, the principle requires an extension to assets from annual income, but foundations are social creatures and should be held to the highest standard. However, even at the annual growth of many foundations over the past decade, they are not even tithing 10% of annual asset appreciation, which is comparable to individual compensation. For further discussion of tithing, see Appendix E: Sectarian Support for NP Benchmarking.

Based on statistics presented in Section One, a single percentage point increase in foundation grants would provide almost $4 billion in additional annual funds, approximately a 17% increase above the current level of $22.8 billion. Increasing the level of annual giving to the tithing level would yield an additional $16 billion, an increase close to 70%. Combine this increase with the increased effectiveness resulting from wide application of NPB, and the accomplishment would be truly monumental.

CPs should be aware that as a general rule, established foundations, by-and-large, view the investing of their assets separately from their mission accomplishments. This has been referred to as the left hand (financial return on assets) moving independent from the right hand (mission).[100] As amazing as it may seem to passionate CPs, most of the professional financial advice (investment banking and management) provided to foundations espouses an investment strategy essentially ignorant to using assets to more effectively accomplishing the foundations missions. Some have gone so far as to fail to compare the present value benefits of satisfying a foundation's mission; instead the sole goal being the size of the foundation's asset base. A 1999 study published by the National Network of Grantmakers and authored by Perry Mehrling at Barnard College/Columbia University sternly criticizes studies defining the 5% standard, stressing that such studies "ignore the possibility that the value and consequence of current grantmaking in solving urgent problems may well be higher now than in the future" and concluding "that a huge and mostly invisible element of the philanthropic field is more concerned with investment banking than grantmaking."[101]

Under this doctrine, a foundation that possesses a prudent and carefully researched project with the potential to satisfy a major foundation, but at the cost of a significant reduction in its investment asset base, would knowingly reject such a project. Thus, CPs should be exceedingly cautious of the professional executive director's preference to perpetuate organization building rather than accelerated mission accomplishments.

This issue is closely aligned with the prevailing pattern of professionally managed foundations to provide grants at the minimum IRS mandated level of 5%. The limited use of investments, such as Program Related Investments ("PRIs"), by foundations to accomplish their mission is also symptomatic of foundation preferences, even though such investments qualify toward the 5% IRS requirement at the time of funding, not at the time of maturity as some in social sector have concluded. This topic is discussed in the capital markets subsection of Section Seven.

Highlighting the disconcerting extent of the independent investment asset management perspective are those foundations that actually seek to maximize investment assets at cross currents to their mission, let alone with any consideration to consistency or potential advancement of mission.

Case in point: Are the concerns raised in several foundations facing ethical challenges over sales of land? In one situation, a local critic comments on the land practices of an environmentally-missioned foundation, " This was an example of a foundation that we thought had different values, behaving very much like a greedy developer.[102] Supporters of the foundation query the greater good theme asking Do you make a financial sacrifice for local environmental reasons and then make it less easy to give grants for worthy causes, including environmental causes elsewhere?"[103] A more neutral observer believes that "until you get a generation of trustees for whom values have changed, in the end people will define fiduciary in the most classic legal terms – that you get the most dollars you can."[104]

An additional word of caution is prudent, especially in the context of executive compensation at foundations. A significant movement developing within the social sector questions the potential contra-fiduciary issues associated with the goal of maximizing return on foundation assets in order to increase investment asset basis with little or no consideration to the present value or opportunity costs of the lost mission. A related source of concern is the apparent relationship between asset size and foundation executive compensation. This issue is addressed with statistical material in the Incentive Compensation subsection of Section Seven.

There are signs of positive change, such as Princeton University's utilization of greater endowment resources to replace student loans with scholarships and modifying parameters to allow more students to qualify.[105]

Should other CPs have the talents and desires of certain world-class CPs, such as Edgar Bronfman, to assume senior roles at established social sector organization, the potential for major change could be phenomenal.

Live-Founder/Dead-Founder Foundation Comparison:
An introductory analysis of the select group of world-class CPs and aggregate data on foundations provides particular insights in the differing *modus operandi*. For purposes of this Working Book, the term "live-founder" refers to those world-class CPs profiled within. The term "dead-founder" essentially refers to the total foundation sector, which includes a small group of proactive CP foundations; however, they are not expected to materially alter the total sector numbers. Indeed, the live-founder foundation designation should be reserved for those foundations where the main contributing financial founder is proactively engaged in advancing the mission of the foundation, well beyond utilizing its assets largely for vanity and so-called "chase after the wind" motives.

For the purposes of this introductory review, NPB's CP metrics are compared to the aggregate foundation data contained in a variety of sources, including Michael Porter's 1999 article "Philanthropy's New Agenda: Creating Value."[106] The CP data reflects an analysis of foundation Federal Tax filings (Forms 990 and 990PF) for the latest periods available and for those associated foundations more representative of their social sector efforts.

A comparison of four characteristics quite illustrative of the differing *modus operandi* includes: annual percentage of qualifying distributions, concentration of top five initiatives, average size of top five initiatives, and percentage of assets invested in indexed equities. The stark contrast confirms common sense expectations.

Consistent with expectations, members of the Working Book CP group registered an annual qualifying distribution percentage of approximately 65%, with a range of 100% to 11%. Even with the wide range, the medium is 43%. This is dramatically higher than the foundation group of 5.5%. This is of little surprise given the almost polar differences between the two. CPs appear to have a much higher regard for the present value of social benefits and are willing to invest more heavily to accomplish social missions and goals. The dead-founder notion of asset building for perpetual existence is a foreign concept to the passionate CP. Furthermore, it would appear adverse for these CPs to allow their foundations to be focused on asset growth and the concomitant increase in foundation executive compensation. Notably, CPs usually have much lower distributions during the early years of a foundation as the organization develops its own systems and processes. Indeed, applicable governing regulations may actually accommodate such a situation.

The 5.5% dead-founder foundations distribution includes expenses (in most cases). And, as most CPs know, the IRS essentially mandates a 5% minimum annual distribution. Not surprisingly, some more progressive professionals in the social sector have analogized dead-founder foundation low-percentage distributions to Ebenezer Scrooge's hoarding of cash. These foundations are savoring the jingling of coins while the souls of their missions suffer a life of ever-growing despair.

The average concentration of top five initiatives for the CPs was generally around 80%.[108] These CPs are focused on the passionate pursuit of a very limited number of missions. Smaller diverse contributions also occur with considerable frequency but to a much more limited extent. The total foundation group is much more expansive with the average foundation making grants in 10 unrelated areas, according to the Porter work.[109] And, these areas contain an extensive list of initiatives. "The average foundation, for example, makes grants in ten unrelated fields every year, where the fields are such broadly defined areas as education and health care. Fewer than 9% of foundations make 75% or more of their grants in a single field, and only 5% focus more than 90% of their grants in one field. Such scattered giving is inconsistent with a clear strategic positioning."[110]

Highlighting this disparity, Porter notes that the average grant size for the total foundation group is surprisingly small. For foundations with between $51 million and $250 million the average grants were only approximately $61,000.[111] And, the average size is only approximately $110,000 for those foundations with assets between $251 million and $999 million.[112] This is such a small amount that NPB or other performance analysis is effectively precluded. Also, the potential for considerable impact is limited as well. Some may say that this is for all intents and purposes a no-win, no-risk situation for dead-founder foundations. The big losers may well be the foundations' mission-based constituencies. These findings are not inconsistent with many of the findings found elsewhere in this Working Book. Further elucidating the concentrated focus of the passionate CPs, the analysis indicates that the average size of the top five initiatives is approximately $30 million. The average size grant was $19 million. The low-end of the range for the top five initiatives was almost one million dollars.

Ninety-five percent of total foundation grants are for one year. Although one-year grants are sometimes awarded for several years in a sequence, there appears to be little evidence that foundations exploit the opportunity to work more closely with grantees over extended periods of time to improve performance.[113]

As for the investment asset size of the equation, the passionate CP group allocated nominal percentage of assets to indexed equities. General industry estimates are that foundations as a whole adhere to a more standard or norm-based approaches, allocating between 40% to 60% to indexed equities. This is to be expected given the non-business/investment backgrounds of dead-founder foundation executives and the allocation of this responsibility to outsourced investment professionals, especially those that earn fee based compensation on asset size, trading, and performance relative to the market indices.

This is not to say that dead-founder foundations do not possess the potential for value creation, measurable by NP Benchmarking. However, cultural barriers and staffing constraints are an issue. Among foundations with $50 to $250 million in assets, there are 35 grants per professional and an average of two staff members to handle grants in 11 unrelated fields.[114] With those foundations holding an excess of one billion in assets, each professional manages approximately 7 grants per year and up to 100 times as many grant requests; on average there are only three professionals for each field.[115] "Staff at the largest foundations may well have sufficient time and expertise to evaluate grants, but it is hard to see how even the most dedicated staff could have much time to assist grantees."[116]

It's little wonder that one extensively published observer noted that "if the practical visionaries who established America's great philanthropic foundations could see their legacy today, they might regret their generosity. Once an agent of social good, those powerful institutions have become a political battering ram targeted at American society."[117]

Value Creation Opportunities for Foundations:
Although not a direct focus of this Working Book, value creation techniques specifically targeted for dead-founder foundations may provide insights for the primary target audience of this Working Book, the passionate CPs.

One of the few sources of value creation suggestions – akin to NPB Intersectoral Practices – for the foundation sector provides sufficiently compelling sights worth inclusion. The following is a modified excerpt from Porter's advocacy material.

Chart 2: Comparison of Live vs. Dead Founders

	Live Founders[107] Seven NPB CPs	Dead Founders
Annual Percentage of Qualifying Distribution	An average of 65%. The range was from a high of 100% to a low of 11%. Even with the wide range, the medium is 43%.	The average is 5.5%.
Concentration of 5 largest Initiatives	The CPs are considerably more focused with their foundations with almost 80% of their social sector investment concentrated on 5 initiatives.	Average foundation makes grants in 10 unrelated areas.
Average Dollar Grant and Average annual Grant for the top 5 Initiatives	The average size annual grant was $19 million and $30 million for the top five initiatives. The range varies considerably, however the low-end of the range for the top 5 initiatives was almost one million dollars.	Average size is $60,000 to $110,000 for foundations between $51million and $999 million.
Percentage of Assets Invested in Indexed Equity	The percentage of indexed equity investments is nominal.	It is estimated that the average foundation maintains approximately 40% to 60% of their investment in indexed equity funds.

Sharing a view comparable to NPB, Porter believes that foundations create value when their activities generate social benefits that go beyond the simple purchasing power of the grant or investment dollars. According to this work, foundations can accomplish this through one of four general strategy categories. The first two are reportedly better known in the social sector but rarely practiced on a systematic basis. The other two are purportedly far more powerful in producing impact but much less common. All four are designed to create value, but there appears to be a hierarchy of increasing impact. Each strategy offering successively higher leverage to a foundation for so-called special assets – resources, expertise, independence, and time horizon, especially as the focus of the activity shifts from the individual recipient to the overall social sector. In other words, the pool of resources affected expands from a single grant to the entire field.

The first approach involves selecting the best grantee. It assumes that each dollar earns a higher social return than a dollar given by a less knowledgeable donor. This is viewed on a single grant basis. Similar to investment managers or corporate executives in the commercial sector, foundations can utilize their expertise (assuming its existence) to allocate resources to the more productive uses within the social sector by funding NGOs that are more cost effective or that address higher preference projects.

The second approach involves signaling others to participate in a social sector investment. The logic here is that by attracting other donors, a foundation effectively improves the return on a larger pool of philanthropic resources. Accordingly, it impacts multiple grants and assumed to impact 3 to 5 more dollars than its single dollar alone. The more social sector-sophisticated CP may observe that this designation and the remaining dollar value impacts designations are somewhat arbitrary and based on a less quantitative process relative to NPB. Nonetheless, its value may rest more with the consistent message of relative value creation and source for appreciating the importance of assessing competitive and innovative ideas.

The third approach is projected to have a potential impact of 50 to 100 fold on social sector dollars. This approach involves assisting the grantee or recipients to improve their own capabilities by increasing the NGO's overall effectiveness as an organization and thus improving the return on funds invested in the social sector. The value created extends beyond the impact of one grant. It increases the social impact of the NGO in all that it does and to the extent that NGOs are willing to learn from one another, it can increase the effectiveness of other organizations as well.

And finally, advancing the state of the knowledge and practice within the designated area of the social sector is deemed to have the greatest value creation impact of 1000 fold or more. More specifically, this approach provides the foundation fund research and a systematic progression of projects that produce more effective ways to address social problems. Arguably, such investments result in a new framework that can shape subsequent investments and efforts in the field, thereby magnifying the effectiveness of future investment by CPs, the government, and other NGOs.

The four approaches appear mutually reinforcing and cumulative in benefit. Successful execution is yet a much bigger issue, and a sound strategy becomes essential.[118] To repeat, "a foundation creates value when it achieves an equivalent social benefit with fewer dollars or creates greater social benefit for comparable cost."[119]

As initially unrelated as it may seem, major universities may provide a compelling benchmark in certain aspects of economic value creation. Their performance in creating value may well warrant further analysis. "In 1998 alone, the Association of University Technology Managers reported, 364 start-up companies were formed on the basis of a license to an academic invention, bringing the total since 1980 to 2,578. The group estimates that overall, university technology-transfer activities generated $34 billion that year, supporting 280,000 American jobs."[120]

Innovative Foundations and Social Enterprise Investors:

CPs are well advised to locate best practices and value creation insights from benchmarking innovative foundation or social enterprise investors. Accordingly, this Working Book provides two appendices containing a select list of such organizations. Twenty-four innovative foundations qualified for this list, while well over 200 were assessed. All seven of the NPB premier CPs have live-founder foundations or affiliated foundations qualified for the select list. As examples, the following are NPB premier CP foundations that create value in four increasing value categories:

- Selecting Best Grantee: Steinhardt NYC schools selection.
- Signalling Other Funders: Bronfman and Steinhardt on Birthright Israel; Monaghan 1,300 plus member Legatus organization.
- Improving Performance of Grant Recipient: Soros's programs at Open Society; Spielberg's work on developing Shoah creations.
- Advancing the State of Knowledge and Practice: Milken's Knowledge Inc, and CaP CURE; Gates Drug research projects.

Although all on the list merit mention, several provide a fair representation of the quality of the group.

Nathan Cummings Foundation
www.ncf.org
The Nathan Cummings Foundation is committed to finding innovative solutions to the challenges faced by the nonprofit sector. To this end, the Nathan Cummings Foundation has supported research on the commercialization of nonprofit spaces, accountability by nonprofits, the professionalization of human services, and new paradigms for corporate giving.

William and Flora Hewlett Foundation
www.hewlett.org
The William and Flora Hewlett Foundation understands that the challenges facing philanthropy in the future will require foundations to be much more active in determining goals and measuring effectiveness. Accordingly, they have devoted significant financial and intellectual resources to grappling with these issues.

James Irvine Foundation
www.irvine.org
Multi-year efforts of the James Irvine Foundation to improve nonprofit management and governance include the support of research in nonprofit, mergers, consolidation, joint ventures, acquisitions, and other strategic restructurings. Newly instituted efforts include the establishment of the Innovation Fund (IF) which supports promising ideas and new strategies that add value to social enterprises.

Ewing Marion Kauffman Foundation
www.emkf.org
The Ewing Marion Kauffman Center is devoted to developing entrepreneurs in the for-profit and nonprofit sectors. By researching, identifying, teaching, and dis-

seminating "state of the art" entrepreneurial skills, the center seeks to increase the success of emerging entrepreneurs. Education and encouragement are the prime drivers of this effort.

W. K. Kellogg Foundation
www.wkkf.org
W. K. Kellogg Foundation's Philanthropy and Volunteerism Efforts seek to "increase the ranks of new givers and to nurture emerging forms of philanthropy." Strong, multi-year, concerted investments of intellectual capital in the areas of social entrepreneurship, e-philanthropy, and venture philanthropy have fueled the W. K. Kellogg Foundation's innovative programs in the intersectoral arena. In particular, its Director of Venture Philanthropy, Thomas K. Reis, has advanced several powerful papers in innovative philanthropy. Regarding best practices, the foundation is developing a computerized knowledge management system to retrieve information on program goals and outcomes and is creating an internal task force to advance its standing as a learning organization. Also, the Foundation has made a strong commitment to education for nonprofit managers by creating distance learning opportunities through a collaboration involving Society for Nonprofit Organizations, University of Wisconsin Extension Service, and Murphy Communications, Inc.

John and Mary Markle Foundation
www.markle.org
Recognizing that the opportunities of the present may be pivotal in solving the challenges of tomorrow, the John and Mary Markle foundation plans to disburse its assets twice as fast as the 5% legal requirement. This innovative move is complemented by the foundation's bold move into intersectoral investing, funding both innovative nonprofit and for-profit entities.

David and Lucile Packard Foundation:
www.packfound.org
The Foundation's Organizational Effectiveness and Philanthropy Program (OE/P) strives to "enhance the effectiveness of Foundation grantees, build the field of nonprofit management, promote philanthropy, and strengthen the nonprofit sector overall." Since 1983, the foundation has worked towards strengthening the management capacity of nonprofit organizations. Multi-year efforts have advanced the causes of organizational assessment, planning, board development, staff training, market research, evaluation design and evaluations, merg-

ers and other restructuring efforts, executive transitions and executive search, and technology assessments and plans.

As for social enterprise investors, the list includes organizations that seek to advance the practice of executing successful investments with inspired social entrepreneurs or (as one social sector elder now refers to them) "new century managers." Taken as a whole, the 21 organizations included in the list have significantly diverse operation models. A sampling of several should provide sufficient motivation for passionate CPs to investigate the prospects of value creation through social enterprise investing. Several examples follow:

Ashoka
www.ashoka.org
Ashoka is a global NGO devoted to social venture capital. Ashoka awards modest ($1,000s) stipends to "pattern changing visionaries." These Ashoka Fellows apply their creativity and determination to solving social problems on a macro scale. Since its inception, 1,000s of Ashoka Fellows in over 40 countries have made society improving changes in the areas of education, the environment, health, human rights, economic development and civic participation.

Japonica Intersectoral
www.japonicaintersectoral.com
Japonica Intersectoral's efforts are focused on the intersectoral segment of the social sector where quantifiable value metrics of the commercial sector converges with the socially powered motivations of the nonprofit sector. Its network of thought leaders, policy experts, and financial experts will apply the firm's global infrastructure to value-creating initiatives which encompass capital market services, strategic financial advisory services, direct investment opportunities, and educational resources. By providing unparalleled financial technologies and a reservoir of industry knowledge to a select group of innovative foundations and NGOs, Japonica Intersectoral seeks to create "best-in-class" returns along a social enterprise investment spectrum.

Morino Institute
www.morino.org
A catalyst, facilitator, and incubator for new, particularly technology-driven, society improving initiatives. Areas of focus include community, youth services, and learning, specifically as they relate to venture philanthropy efforts.

Peninsula Community Foundation
Center For Venture Philanthropy
www.pcf.org
www.pcf.org/pcfsite/stratphil/stratphillinks/cvp.html
The Peninsula Community Foundation's Center for Venture Philanthropy is the "birthplace of venture philanthropy." For over 35 years, the CVP emphasizes giving that has a measurable impact on "civic investment" in the San Francisco Bay Area.

Roberts Foundation
www.redf.org
The Roberts Enterprise Development Fund (REDF). REDF builds on six years of effort to improve economic opportunities for the homeless and very low-income individuals. A proactive leader in social enterprise, REDF operates 23 enterprises in the San Francisco Bay area. REDF takes a social return on investment (SROI) approach to its giving. REDF also "preaches what it practices" by sponsoring, publishing and disseminating a wide range of whitepapers on social enterprise, venture philanthropy, SROI and other innovative approaches to giving.

Robinhood Foundation
www.robinhood.org
Robinhood Foundation seeks to end poverty in NYC. Efforts focus on using venture philanthropy techniques to finding, support and grow strong social enterprise organizations and hold them accountability for their results.

Social Venture Partners
www.svpseattle.org
Social Venture Partners applies the venture capital to its giving. They commit time, money and expertise to create partnerships with not-for-profit organizations. Focus is community based. Original entity is located in Seattle, with affiliated entities in Austin and Arizona.

CPs may wish a tool to evaluate both NGOs and managers' general awareness on a range of intersectoral topics as well as the same for potential network and team members. Accordingly, Appendix D: Intersectoral Questions contains a list of 40 wide-ranging questions pertaining to forays into the Intersectoral arena. The questions are open-ended to encourage an interactive discourse. Questions are classified in six topical areas: key philosophies, minimizing cost and creating value, use of assets, measuring efficiencies, use of assets, social sector and commercial sector, and resistance to new philanthropy.

Motivations:

A significant assumption of this Working Book concerns the sincerity of CP mission and desire to accomplish the most impact with the smallest dollar investment.

Mainstream literature is brimming with opinionated works and more methodical studies analyzing motivations to engage in philanthropic endeavors. Commentary and anecdotal works frequently appear, like an article in *The American Benefactor* titled "Why We Give" and "All That Glitters." The former is an interesting compilation of summary observations by a series of rather well known personalities. As the piece notes, there are as many reasons for philanthropy as there are needs on the planet. The article somewhat innocently assumes static and discrete motivations categories of salvation, selfishness, superstition, grief, giving-to-get, the great whatever, helping, altruism, opening out, obligation, and good feeling.[121]

Others seek greater insights and guidance from faith-based sources. Those of the Jewish faith may study *Tzedakah* and the work of Moses Maimonides, while those of the Christian faith seek the guidance most frequently referred to as stewardship.[122] Andrew Carnegie's *The Gospel of Wealth* continues to be a well-read booklet that offers blend of secular and faith-based insights. His practical theory on "scientific philanthropy" has educated many CPs.

"The scientific philanthropist will target his giving to 'help those who will help themselves,' creating institutions through which those working poor with a 'divine spark' can better themselves economically and spiritually…he should give away his wealth during his lifetime, using the same acumen that he showed in making it."[123]

Certain CPs may further question NPB's consistency with major sectarian theology and teachings. Accordingly, several brief observations are provided below with further summary comment in Appendix E: Sectarian Support for NP Benchmarking. In sum, both Jewish *Tzedakah* and Christian Stewardship provide considerable support and motivation/obligation for CPs to intensely practice NPB and its concepts, strategies and tactics, in the broadest sense.

As stated, both the Jewish *Tzedakah* and Christian Stewardship concepts of philanthropy are extraordinarily consistent with the concepts, strategies, and tactics of NPB. The Jewish teachings on *Tzedakah* are considerably detailed in quantitative formula and calculation, which is consistent with both Wisdom Point Two (CPs aggressively talk external comparative numbers) and Wisdom Point Six (If you can't measure in the social sector, you can't manage). In fact, there are very detailed guidelines relating *Tzedakah* to commercial practices. The highest level (level eight) of *Tzedakah* can be achieved by commercial ventures similar to the progressive intersectoral practices discussed in the Working Book and the material contained in Wisdom Point One. (The social sector's profound transformation offers virtually boundless opportunities.)

The Christian teachings on stewardship offer more general guidance for its words on philanthropy. However, the concept of seeking to maximize return on investments are quite complementary to the seven wisdom points of NPB, all of which guide a foundation to judiciously maximize the return on investment of time, talents, treasures, and tenacity. Surprisingly, the parable of the talents provides a logical foundation of NPB. Wisdom points three, four, and five can gain spiritual support from the Gospel of *Matthew 25: 14-30*. In this parable, the master with the talents seeks to create competition among three servant-providers by quantitatively measuring the performance of each servant-provider (calculating a de facto "Performance Gap" and information for a "Multiplier/Discount Effect"), and then redistributing the resources to the highest performing, allowing for the best practice to, in effect, go-to-scale. See Appendix E for additional summary material.

For those CPs early on in their philanthropic engagement, an ever-growing list of professionals are expanding this advisory niche. Topics covered by such advisory firms range from the most mundane to the highly emotional.[124]

SECTION THREE

POWER OF NP BENCHMARKING

Wisdom 3: "Benchmarking can be as powerful in the social sector as in the

commercial sector."

Summary of NP Benchmarking:

The power and compelling attractiveness of NPB is its ability to assist passionate Capitalists/Philanthropists ("CPs") to multiply the impact – creation value – of their resource investment relative to other similar social sector initiatives and minimize risk exposure. Relative value creation is not solely based on the value of resources invested in the commercial sector and neither should such be the case in the social sector. For example, NPB seeks to provide CPs with the tools to leverage a million dollar social sector investment to generate a much greater impact, possibly achieving that of comparable $10 million or even $100 million social sector investment. Simultaneously, NPB provides the framework for CPs to minimize the risk exposure of NGO or foundation misfortunate developments, wasted funds, or unintended consequences.

Succinctly put, NPB builds upon a synergistic collaboration of commercial sector benchmarking, progressive intersectoral strategies, and contemporary financial markets analytical tools. NPB is evaluated within the context of macro issues, such as stakeholder considerations and comparative conclusionary financial metrics. On a micro level, insights are offered on process as well as organizational execution suggestions.

New Philanthropy Benchmarking is predicated upon the assumption that passionate capitalist/philanthropists will instinctively strive for comparable success in the social sector as achieved in the commercial sector. While motivations vary, instincts compelling superior performance or driving a determination to eschew being "dumb money" are considered pervasive and transferable.

NP Benchmarking is a continuous process of improvement, which helps identify where performance lags and focus on the application of the Best Practices. Benchmarking is more than Best Practices; it is a comparative measurement with active goal setting and implementation.

NPB seeks to perform at two levels, one much more assessment driven and the other application driven. From an assessment perspective, NPB provides the framework to allow a comparative measurement of social sector impact. For example, did one CP's $100,000 social sector investment have a comparable impact to similar CP investment of $5 million or a 50-time multiplier effect? Alternatively, did the latter CP's investment under perform the former by a 98% discount effect? As for the application driven perspective, NPB seeks to provide the information that allows focus on the deliverable opportunities that compose the performance gaps between the two CP investments. With this information, NPB provides the potential for higher returns on social investments and the information to facilitate positive transformative change.

To put NPB in perspective, it could be helpful to some CPs to understand its evolution. NPB's roots hail from classic commercial sector benchmarking, first with internal benchmarking and then later external benchmarking. As the evolution of external benchmarking progressed, the relative levels of quality and value were clarified. The highest level (top of the value-added pyramid) requires database studies of third party internal access information sources and performance gap analysis and recommendations on how best to maximize profit. Application to the social sector has and continues to progress slowly. Its applicability to a wide range of practices, including procurement, transportation, technology, human resources, financial controls, or marketing currently receives limited attention.

The development of Intersectoral value-creation practices is moving at a much faster pace, providing positive energy for the recognition of the power of benchmarking and its application. NP Benchmarking's evolutionary power moves with its concept, tactics, and effective management wisdom points. The

Multiplier/Discount Effect offers a CP the potential to measure relative competitive performance in financial terms – terms familiar to those so successfully utilized in the commercial sector, especially in the financial arena. The Performance Gap and the composing Deliverable Opportunities provide the tools with which to seek well-informed action at both a macro and managerial level. Wisdom offerings on momentum builders and obstacle encounters seek to facilitate progress. Sources of NPB wisdom and best practices are all encompassing, including world class CPs, multi-sector professionals and practitioners, and academia.

Organizations can learn from Best Practices that have accomplished similar objectives in a more efficient, successful, or innovative way. Edward Skloot of the Surdna Foundation emphasizes the value of an entrepreneurial mindset. "Experience has shown that when management spends more time on the financial consequences of its activities, it is generally more rigorous and realistic when making programmatic decisions as well. Thus, the introduction of enterprise brings with it a new mindset within the organization – one that is more calculating and skilled in directing the course of the agency."[125]

Similarly, Jason Saul addresses the application of benchmarking to nonprofits. As President of The Center for What Works, a nonprofit Internet site, he focuses on developing benchmarking techniques for nonprofits. "Simply put, benchmarking is a process of continuous improvement whereby an organization learns from others who are accomplishing similar objectives in a more efficient, successful, or innovative way."[126] Both of these concepts show the importance of benchmarking.

To arrest a red herring issue at the outset, benchmarking is not Total Quality Management ("TQM") as some less than sophisticated observers have mistakenly implied. There are clearly common elements; however, TQM is only a very small element of NPB and fails to merit further attention.

For illustrative purposes, there are basically four alternative philanthropic situations to utilize the power of benchmarking: (1) proactive investor/donor with an established organization; (2) passive investor/donor with an established organization; (3) proactive investor/donor with a start-up organization; and (4) passive investor/donor with a start-up organization.

Some of the most respected commercial sector and NGO professionals advocate new philanthropy and CPs under other names, such as virtuous capital, social venture capital, and venture philanthropy. These themes provide the optimum foundation for promoting benchmarking. The differences, similarities, benefits, and shortcomings of each will be further explained in Benchmarking Concepts, Stakeholders Comparative Similarities and Traditional Exaggerations.

Nonetheless, don't expect much agreement on metrics in general or even in specific areas such as venture philanthropy. As a recent Morino Institute notes, "There is still very little agreement about or utilization of metrics for success. Most funds promise to develop these measures in the future."[127] However, metrics are beginning to emerge, such as the funds to strategic management ratio (the ratio of dollars invested directly in a grant recipient to the total value invested in that grant recipient, including strategic management assistance).[128]

General Quantification of the Magnitude of NP Benchmarking Impact:

The general concept of benchmarking creates an interesting phenomenon with the rapidly expanding utilization of this philosophy. The possibility for $100,000 to have the effect of $1,000,000 is definitely achievable. In commercial sector organizations this opportunity demands attention; so why not utilize this philosophy in the social sector where $1,000,000 can be not only ineffective, but also detrimental? Loss of money is understandably painful, but the loss of lives unforgivable. On the other hand, with the effect of $1,000,000 while spending only $100,000 you are creating $900,000. When $900,000 can save lives – does inefficiency essentially become immoral?

An editorial in the January 13, 2000 *Chronicle of Philanthropy* addresses unaccountable nonprofits: "If one believes that stronger comparative information could lead to a more results-oriented approach to philanthropy, it is alarming to contemplate what the opportunity costs of today's predominantly unaccountable philanthropy are. Just think of the social problems that are not being solved or are not being addressed as quickly as they could be, and the human suffering that, unfortunately, is being prolonged."[129] This opinion reinforces the concept that unaccountable nonprofits will no longer be accepted.

Use of Benchmarking for Proactive and Passive Philanthropic Investments:

Passive giving is most useful when either time or knowledge of the social sector is limited. Still, one should research the organizations most effective in giving, the ones which earn the greatest multiple on each dollar invested. Passive giving should not be viewed as the easy alternative. When applied correctly it still requires significant time. Given the talents CPs possess, proactive giving is the better and usually the more effective choice. The potential for a major social impact is greater when CPs commit their time to managing their philanthropic investments – essentially, being proactive.

Gregory Dees acknowledges the value of entrepreneurial mindsets, suggesting proactive investments. "With growing confidence in the power of competition and the profit motive to promote efficiency and innovation, many observers are suggesting that market discipline should exert more influence in the social sector – especially when those observers have fundamental doubts about the performance of social enterprises."[130]

Applicable to a Diverse Range of Situations:

Benchmarking is equally applicable to investments of $100,000 to $100,000,000. Benchmarking is applicable to established entities or start-ups and proactive or passive investments. Benchmarking is effective in a wide range of organizations varying from local food distribution to the distribution of medical supplies to third world countries. When treasures are invested along with time, the effect of $1,000,000 can be equal to that of $100,000,000. With this opportunity even a smaller organization has endless possibilities.

How many CPs would think that Boston University could serve as a NP Benchmark for Congressional earmarking of funds? And that metrics would even exist? Indeed, they viewed the situation as competitive and responded accordingly. The University's success in obtaining competitive grants increased by 647% during the mid 80's to early 90's, receiving a total of $56.5 million in funds in 1984, 1988, and 1992.[131] During 1981 to 1994, Boston University paid Cassidy and Associates, the most renowned academic lobbying firm, $7.9 million.[132]

An Example of Proactive Benchmarking:
Both the examples provided in this section and the next are very early illustrations of benchmarking. The evolution of the Working Book will demonstrate the transition to New Philanthropy Benchmarking.

Michael Porter, a Harvard professor, comments on one of the effects of old philanthropy: "For those who care deeply about social problems and work tirelessly to make a difference, current foundation practices not only diminish effectiveness, they inevitably reduce the satisfaction that donors, staff, and trustees derive from their work."[133]

These pressures emanate from many directions. For example, a CP on the board of a NGO began suggesting changes to promote productivity and effectiveness. The changes began increasing the workloads at the senior management level. When he suggested benchmarking for Best Practices, several members of the board informed him that they disliked his commercial sector attitude and that the changes he was requesting were unreasonable. The CP advised the board that if they did not heed his advice he would establish a similar organization with a similar mission statement in close proximity – essentially creating competition within the organization's benchmarking. With the knowledge that their jobs were at stake, the other board members considered, deliberated, and then approved his proposal to benchmark.

Burton Weisbrod reminds us that "the relative simplicity of gauging a firm's profitability stands in sharp contrast to the multi-dimensional social goals that, whether attained or not, often characterize nonprofits. The complexity is not a weakness of nonprofits but rather a source of considerable difficulty in identifying and measuring their success or failure, and, thus, in making them 'accountable.'"[134]

An Example of Passive Benchmarking:
The example below is not the typical approach to passive philanthropy, characterized by a "just write a check" mentality, or "impulse giving" as it is often referred to in several classic *Tzedakah* teachings. The CP approach provided includes a more demanding standard of passive benchmarking.

A NGO executive approached a CP seeking money to fund a food distribution program. The CP became rather interested in the program, and with a very minimal time investment, found a source to obtain the food at a lower cost. The CP contacted the organization and provided them with the exciting news. To the CP's surprise, the organization rejected his proposal and told him that if he were going to approach his donation in a business manner, they would no longer be soliciting his donation.

This example illustrates that a passive approach can be effective but nominal research needs to be done to insure the people controlling your investment rigorously seek efficiency and effectiveness. Jed Emerson, Executive Director of the Roberts Enterprise Development Fund, acknowledges that "the quiet secret of the philanthropic community has been its inability to evaluate effectively whether its grant-making activities have substantively altered the conditions of individuals, communities, or society at large."[135]

Even consumer-targeted publications are moving in the direction of comparative quantification. In an article found on the SmartMoney web site, 100 of the largest charities are quantitatively ranked according to a review of three years of financial data. Comparisons are within categories. Three metrics form the basis for the ranking: program expenses as a percentage to total expense, funding raising costs as a percentage to total costs, and funds saved percentage. Each of the three receives weighting of 60%, 30%, and 10%, respectively. The final column provides the ranking on a scale of 0 to 100. It is a good start, however, verification of the supporting math is less than clear from the material presented.[136]

Addressing Initial Queries:

If our research provides any indication of the initial queries to be expected when the topic of NP Benchmarking is first raised, it is probably appropriate to alert CPs to several such queries in advance.

The first comment a CP will most likely encounter is that "for many of those active in the social sector, it has been taken as a virtual given that most elements of social value stand beyond measurement and quantification. Anyone who advocates the social sector be held to greater accountability and report on the progress achieved toward the attainment of societal goals are told in no uncertain terms that indeed, 'some things simply can't be measured and social value is one of them.'

Such logic defies our own reality. There are numerous way to 'triangulate' around a given element in order to understand its worth from a variety of perspectives – numeric or otherwise."[137]

Next, expect to hear that there is really no place to begin. In reality this could not be further from the truth. There are a number of alternative starting points. One such point could be for a CP to commission an industry subsector benchmarking study. This approach has been utilized by industry and government entities for some time. The CP will need to utilize creative persuasion and imagination to encourage NGOs in the sector to participate.

A valuable resource for collecting NGO and foundation information is Guidestar at www.guidestar.org. This is a rapidly improving site that contains 990 tax filing information.

One such interesting example occurred when a branch of the Canadian government sought to facilitate such a study, by funding the study and encouraging participation, in conjunction with the Canadian Book Publishers Association. Precedent for this effort has started in the United Kingdom over 20 years before, with a program called the Interfirm Comparison Program. In it, the activities of 20 to 39 companies in an industry sector are analyzed and the data are normalized for comparability. Each participant receives objective information by which to compare and determine performance gaps. The identification and quantification of the gaps allow the organizations to consider prospective enables such as processes, programs, and policies.

"Potential savings were substantial. If the best practices and technology were applied to Canadian book publishing firms, their fulfillment cost base would be reduced from 35% to 50%; returns – a serious source of non-value-added expense in the book distribution industry – could be reduced by 70%."[138]

Should the CP wish to consider the steps further, Appendix K provides an abbreviated list of the eight suggested phases. In particular, note phases 4 to 7, which focus mission critical aspects essential to constructing gaps. Phase 4 focuses on processes involved with information gathering, suggesting that CFOs serve a central role. Phase 5 addresses data analysis, normalization, and input. Normalization receives particular mention, as all numbers should be calculated on a relative scale to extract the greater possible meaning and minimize avoidable distortions. Phase

6 advances the process by developing internal performance objective, especially seeking to standardize data into a bell curve distribution. Phase 7, titled "Firm-level performance evaluation," provides the link to NP Benchmarking by creating a system to measure Performance Gaps.

This list consists of the more customary 10 step internal benchmarking process, utilized within the commercial sector. This list is also displayed in Appendix K. While all 10 steps are indispensable to internal benchmarking execution, steps 1 to 5 merit particular mention. These steps are critical to establish a credible foundation upon which to build a process in a skeptical environment. The steps begin with identifying what to benchmark, identifying what organizations to benchmark, determining data sought and collection methods, determining the current Performance Gap, and projecting future level of performance. The remaining steps focus more on follow-up execution, while the earlier steps provide CPs with the insights upon which to assess resource allocation and prioritization. As indicated, Step 4 concentrates on identifying Performance Gap opportunities. Yet other queries CPs may encounter involve use of the ubiquitous phrase "benchmarking study information" or reference to the commercial sector's progressive levels of benchmarking.

Value-Added Benchmarking:
The quality of benchmarking study can vary as incredibly. Chart 3 provides a unique pyramid perspective of the quality and value-added of benchmarking process. Of course, there will be situations where a lower rung value benchmarking study yields more value than a study at the higher portion of the pyramid, but such situations should be considered unusual.

Based on an extensive survey of the outstanding literature and discussions with benchmarking industry professionals, it is not unreasonable to conclude that approximately half of the studies conducted on benchmarking are restricted to internal-only information. This is the lowest rung of the value-added pyramid, as comparisons are limited to internal historical information and external competitive information is ignored. This may be of greater use if there are multiple entities within one organization with which to compare; however, this is most often not the case. Next on the value-added pyramid are benchmarking studies that do utilize external information, but do so on a qualitative or anecdotal basis. They are smaller in percentage and are a useful advance over internal only, falling far short of useful quantitative metrics.

Chart 3: <u>Quality and Value-Added Benchmarking Process Pyramid</u>

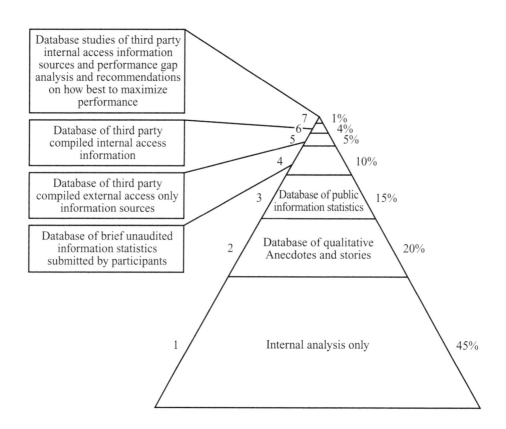

The third level that we identified involves quantitative information, but is based on publicly available information statistics. Examples of such information are public filings with various government agencies or offices as well as publications by a wide range of organizations, including commercial sector organizations such as consulting firms or investment banks. The information may indeed be quite useful relative to the more typical situation, however, still a rather average approach.

The fourth level of the pyramid is a significantly higher level of value-added and is estimated at top 10% of the value-added studies. Here, databases are brief third unaudited information statistics submitted by participants. The benefit of this level is that the information advances to the internal level. The significant shortcoming is that it is submitted by participants on an unverifiable basis, which therefore mandates a high level of caution not typically associated with internal access information.

It is reasonable to assume that a slightly higher value-added database would be information statistics compiled by professionals utilizing external information sources well beyond the typical information generally available to the public. This assumes that the professional compiling the statistics utilizes rigorous practices to assure the quality and comparability of the information.

For rather obvious reasons, a higher value-added level is obtained when the database is third party compiled with access to internal information. However, this is quite rare.

The highest value-added and the approach we urge CPs to seek may be even less than 1% of the studies conducted, which is in part attributable to the difficulty of obtaining commercial subsector cooperation. This is an obstacle that may be less so in the social sector where collaboration may be considered a more acceptable and expected attribute. This highest value-added entails database studies of third party internal access information sources with performance gap analyses and recommendations as to how best to maximize performance.

As for the second point mentioned above regarding the commercial sector's progressive levels of benchmarking, there are varying views on how benchmarking evolved and what is the higher, more elevated, form of benchmarking. Some benchmarking professionals say performance benchmarking is more advanced than process benchmarking and some say strategic benchmarking is more eval-uated than performance. Others say global best practice benchmarking is even more advanced than any other form of benchmarking.

NPB addresses this issue directly by stressing that the type of benchmarking survey is most importantly determined by the quality of the information and – importantly – evaluated by the relative and absolute value-added to the social sector organization. As will be discussed later in the Working Book, NPB seeks to assess for the entire organization or project as well as components, which are logically classified into three component categories of process, policies, and programs. Expect that NPB's focus on the entire organization and its performance gaps as well as its relative comparison to the best practice will engender a significant level of discussion, and at a minimum require an extended commitment of discourse.

Current State of Social Sector Benchmarking:
There is an exceedingly wide range of quality in current social sector benchmarking. It would appear that the primary reasons relate to the corresponding wide range of experience and skills in the social sector audience. As mentioned earlier, there is a general absence of readily accessible social sector benchmarking information. This is in no small part attributable to the limited quality and availability of internal NGO financial controls. Pockets of quality information clearly exist, but obtaining such information will take effort. CPs are advised to focus on commercial sector practices for both direct social sector comparables and for indirect comparables.

In all likelihood, most of the CPs will feel quite comfortable using the top percentile social sector benchmark case studies or examples. Among the top percentile case studies are those gathered in a magnus opus compiled by Robert Camp, appropriately titled "Global Cases in Benchmarking," which contains an impressive selection of social sector case studies (see endnote.)[139] As for benchmarking examples for the aspiring CPs, consult the Further Readings Appendix P for works by Letts, Ryan, and Grossman, and Saul.

Three high quality case studies and four introductory examples are very briefly reviewed below. The first of three sophisticated case studies is a landmark study of mortality rates for cardiac surgery at Northern New England Cardiovascular Disease Study Group (Dartmouth Medical School). The title of the case study is

"Improving the Outcomes of Cardiac Surgery: A Benchmarking Study." The process benchmarked was coronary artery bypass surgery. "After implementation of some of the findings there were 74 fewer deaths (a 24% reduction) than would have been expected based on historical data. The original three-pronged approach of data, improvement tools, and benchmarking site visits showed significant reductions in mortality rates."[140]

A second case study benchmarking enrollment management at Babson College in Boston, Massachusetts. Babson overseers were concerned with early attrition rates and this merited an extensive competitive benchmarking study. Specifically, the benchmarking process was designed to evaluate the attrition from those who inquire about Babson, who apply, who are admitted, and who attend. The improvement of the enrollment process is deemed essential to Babson, especially given its business school degree programs. The study's presumptions included the precepts that Babson must segment its markets and understand its clients expectations/needs. The goals included obtaining significant insights to diagnose and create an action plan for recruiting and program delivery and servicing students to exceed expectations. The study concludes "that it is probably safe to observe that if the benchmarking had not been conducted the consequences would continue to show themselves in declining performance measures, if not more severe consequences."[141]

A third case from Australia entailed benchmarking culture change. The Australian Post is the seventh largest organization in the country with 32,000 employees and five business units. Although this is a governmental situation, its relevance to NGO culture change provides beneficial instruction. This case study addresses improving the process of planning and implementing strategic cultural change via an employee attitudinal survey; and is worthy in seeking to measure qualitative concerns, such as culture and benchmarking its best practices. To supplement its internal benchmarking, the Post compared its outcomes with 20 external partners including automotive firms; multinational subsidiaries in electronic; chemical, petroleum, and technology firms; as well as large Australian organizations in brewing, airlines, and the armed services. The study shows five areas where Performance Gap existed. Also, improvements in process were isolated and integrated into an evolving measurement process.

As for the four introductory examples, two receive brief treatment in Chapter Five of High Performance Non-Profit Organizations, CARE USA and The Boston

Ballet. Two others receive a cursory reference in Chapter 4 of "Improving Quality and Performance in Your Non-Profit Organization," studies of the Museum of Contemporary Art in Chicago (MCA) and STRIVE in New York. CARE USA is an internal benchmarking study where the lesson learned includes concentrating initially on areas of strength, preparing organizations for stress, and using NGO culture as an advantage. The Boston Ballet focused on fund raising, image enhancement, and getting the organization's multiple stakeholders involved. MCA regularly benchmarks its fund raising events. STRIVE is reportedly a model in welfare-to-work initiative.

Appendix H: Best of Best in Commercial Sector offers the element of a potentially prophetic vision for the social sector by presenting a list of the benchmarking commercial sector companies in a wide range of functional areas, such as customer service, employee empowerment, health care programs, leadership, marketing, research & development, training, and waste minimization.

SECTION FOUR

NPB CONCEPTS

Wisdom 4: "Application of the commercial sector benchmarking concepts

apply to social sector benchmarking."

NPB Value Creation in Context:

From a macro perspective, NPB concepts seek to provide the foundation with the strategies and tactics that can be utilized to energize competition with the social sector and create substantial value. The highest value concepts of commercial benchmarking are applied to create additional value; select intersectoral practices seek to further advance their value creation; and concepts originating from the financial capital markets provide further value creation fuel through comparative value creation and performance on investment metrics.

An early step may be for CPs to evaluate team member knowledge with the professional aspects of traditional benchmarking. Through a 20-question benchmarking assessment questionnaire and supporting practical answers and explanations, Appendices I: 20 Benchmarking Assessment Questions and J: Answers/ Explanations provide a more detailed litmus test to evaluate an individual or an organization's culture with regard to benchmarking in general. Questions are grouped in three sections: benchmarking, implementation process, and best practices. The intent of this material is not so much as to produce a numerical evaluation, but to provide insight into the base upon which a CP may choose to build upon.

An example question is:

When assembling a benchmarking team, what are the characteristics you look for?

> a) A large group composed not of organizers or managers, but of intellectuals.
> b) A small team of motivated people who are comfortable with data, well networked, and management focused.
> c) A small group of individuals, each assessing different projects on their specific qualifications.
> d) One person who assesses all the data and then makes the decision.

Although still just one tool for evaluation, these questions are a step beyond simply measuring the level of resistance when the benchmarking topic is raised or judging the extent of non-value added comments or admittedly biased efforts to attack the effort without seeking to first gain additional information. CPs will find that quite often the first reaction of social sector executives or managers is to aggressively seek one flaw in a benchmarking presentation or proposal. Such individuals will tentatively claim to have discovered a major credibility flaw via a potentially rather insignificant number in even a hypothetical example or even an obscure footnote. They may also discuss one very high challenge application of benchmarking (such as global warming or a new trend in the art world) in order to condemn benchmarking to the netherworld of universal inapplicability, worthlessness, or even destructive potential. (Note: Even in both these situations NPB can be applied to assess various processes, programs, or policies. Intersectoral practices can be utilized to create value through branding, licensing, or collaboration ventures.) Remember, many industry professionals strongly believe that 90% of benchmarking success is related to a positive culture and attitude.

Stakeholders Comparative Similarities and Traditional Exaggerations:
Commercial sector organizations and NGO constituencies are considerably similar, yet differences are largely exaggerated. Both commercial sector organizations and NGOs have multiple stakeholders.

One of the main sources of resistance in social sector cultures will be the claim that NGOs and commercial organizations can not be compared. The falsity of this claim will become apparent through the comparison of stakeholders. While the concept that NGOs have stakeholders may seem basic, the resistance will be over-whelming.

Stockholders logically compare to funders/sponsors, in that they both require reports of success. However, the powerful oversight role of stockholders in the commercial sector is currently quite limited. As one social sector observer notes, "Managers (and directors) and their preferences can influence nonprofit organizations' behavior greatly because there is only a weak functional equivalent of private firms' stockholders – the IRS – and there is no threat of corporate takeover as there is in the private-enterprise sector."[142] Commercial customers are NGO clients/patrons: the recipients of your goods and services – a basic yet disregarded comparison.

The next four are best understood through countering the misguided arguments readily asserted to dismiss each comparison. Managers are managers and different mission statements do not change their function: managing. Whether driven by profit or performance, employees in both commercial organizations and NGOs are highly focused on quality to maintain their effectiveness. Suppliers are suppliers; all organizations are expected to find the most cost-effective suppliers who provide the best quality product needed.

NGOs have a community – either the population affected by the distribution of your product or your internal community. NGOs often actively object to this philosophy, saying that communities vary and therefore can not be compared. Most of these social sector traditional exaggerations are unfounded and therefore need to be overcome.

The highly respected Peter F. Drucker has founded a foundation with a website associated with the Peter F. Drucker Foundation that seeks to advance social sector benchmarking. This website is a premier example of the efforts of a person who has realized the need to structure social sector ventures like commercial ventures. His example echoes the concepts presented in Stakeholder Comparative Differences and Tactical Exaggerations. "A key objective at the foundation is to dismantle the walls separating the nonprofit, business and government sectors. It contends that good managers are good management in no matter what sector, and it has pushed leaders of nonprofits to think in the same league as their business counterparts."[143]

The comparisons drawn are similar to Emerson's. Emerson's discussion of the shift in Social Venture Capital from old language to new language reinforces the thoughts presented in Stakeholder Comparative Differences and Tactical Exaggerations.

Chart 4: <u>Stakeholders Comparative Similarities and Traditional Exaggerations</u>

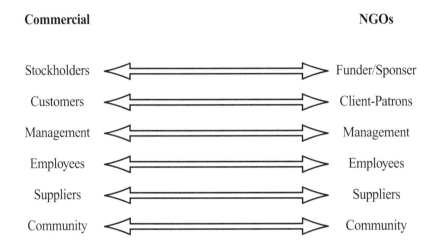

Commercial   **NGOs**

Stockholders ⟵⟶ Funder/Sponser

Customers ⟵⟶ Client-Patrons

Management ⟵⟶ Management

Employees ⟵⟶ Employees

Suppliers ⟵⟶ Suppliers

Community ⟵⟶ Community

Benchmarking Applied to NGO Start-ups and Established Organizations:
NGO start-ups and established organizations each have their own benefits.
Established NGOs differ from start-ups because they are easier to learn from while
getting acquainted with NGOs and their cultures. Established NGOs teach about
all of the resistance in a social sector culture. Valuable knowledge can be gained
when starting up a CP's own organization. A CP can learn while not needing to be
overly involved.

But when you start to invest more time and money in an organization to see it run
more effectively, either one of the two following processes will occur. The social
sector culture will accept your changes or the existing management will resist and
try to negate any changes. Accepting changes is a great process of adapting to positive change, but a process more likely to occur in commercial organizations. The
second process is that of resistance. In the culture you have been learning, the
imbedded culture will take any course of action to avoid implementing your
processes, even force you to leave and take your treasures elsewhere. The established culture will claim to be the most efficient and alterations opposed claiming
a unique mission statement. Employees will argue with changing compensation
structure because of the increase of demand for their jobs. There will be claims

Chart 5: <u>Factors Affecting Benchmarking in NGO Start-ups and Established Organizations</u>

<u>NGO Start-ups</u>

- New Team

- Undeveloped Culture

- To-be Developed Processes

- Relatively Open Compensation Opportunities

- Possible Clean Slate of Past Issues

- Zero-based Budget

- Relatively Greater Resources Allocated to Start-up Functions

<u>Established NGO's</u>

- Existing Management

- Imbedded Culture

- Established Culture

- Accepted Compensation Structure

- Historical Issues

- Certain Fixed Costs as well as Assets and Liabilities

- Relatively Greater Resources Allocated to Administrative Functions

that history issues prevent change. An established NGO is great to learn from if you can make changes within the organizations, but often it is more efficient to allocate your time and treasures to a start-up.

Starting up a NGO allows opportunities to create a team, mold an undeveloped culture, develop processes, create open compensation opportunities for the most qualified people, and have a zero based budget and relatively greater resources to allocated to start-up functions. Both start-ups and established NGOs have their own advantages, but once well versed in NGOs and their cultures, start-ups are a more attractive opportunity.

Review of NPB Best Practice Illustrative Situations:

It's appropriate that the information contained in Chart 6 be viewed primarily as a didactic instrument. Collecting benchmark information is no small task, and collecting the necessary information for a comprehensive NPB analysis requires even greater effort. The six examples require considerable estimates and judgement calls in order to progress to the next stage of dialog. The Best Practices utilized in the chart are assumed to be the most readily available at the time of the decision. This should in no way be confused with the higher value Best Practice information obtainable through more comprehensive processes. (See Chart 3: Quality And Value Added Benchmarking Process Pyramid). As NPB progresses, higher quality information will inevitably develop; however, in the interim, CPs should make the estimates and informed judgements necessary to advance and not be hindered by the view that no quantification is better than early best-effort quantifications. Your social sector mission deserves no less.

TB Treatment in Middle East Program:

With new strains of TB rapidly spreading in the Middle East and beyond, investments to restrict its growth seem reasonably justifiable. Given the increasing common calls of alarm, those with a known humanitarian interest are likely to receive numerous proposals. Appeals arrive from the most and least sophisticated, those genuine-at-heart, and those with less noble interests. One such proposal provides a compelling presentation by comparing its program with that of others in circulation and generally verifiable. The impressive program not only indicates the size of its competitive advantage, its Performance Gap, but also the major components of the differences or Deliverable Opportunities.

Among the Deliverable Opportunities are the superior level of procurement which benefited from leveraging procurement with a major medical center, aggregating quantities from several suppliers, successive competitive stages, and offering positive community press communications. Transportation by both ground and air is piggybacked for gratis by networking with existing routes that have excess space. Transport security and delivery of the medication is coordinated with a medical group, which has a consistent pre-existing travel plan and comparable mission. Although the numbers provided as best practices are more an accurate assessment of at-market rates or possibly a combination of retail and wholesale rates, the analysis indicates an almost $5 million Performance Gap and a 31 Multiplier Effect. The proposal also provides a convincing narrative on strategies and tactics to minimize risks, such as medication "shrinkage" during transportation and during physician delivery, adequate controls to insure the quality of medication, and program constraints to guard against obsolescence from advancing hybrid strains. For those CPs seeking to engage in a social sector mission with comparable characteristics, this program clearly appears to have merit as a potential Best Practice.

As information sharing expands and as the pace of drug developments advances, other initiatives such as the following Gates funded program may provide considerably greater value creation and much larger Multiplier Effect. There are, however, practical limitations related to scalability that would constrain a $5 million investment from obtaining a 31 Multiplier Effect or $155 million in impact.

In October of 2000, The Global Alliance for TB Drug Development, (a public-private partnership dedicated to the discovery of new drugs to treat one of the world's dealiest infectious diseases), was inaugurated at the International Conference on Health Research for Developement (www.conference2000.ch/), in Bangkok, Thailand, by various stakeholders in government, the social sector, and the pharmaceutical industry. Total funding for the alliance is expected to exceed $150 million over the next five years. The Bill and Melinda Gates Foundation (www.gatesfoundation.org) has already announced a grant of $25 million. and the New York City-based ROckefeller Foundation (www.rockfound.org) is expected to commit $15 million.[144]

International Religious Organizational Website:
The emergence of the Internet as a powerful force in all sectors of life and enterprise has created its own momentum. Even the most non-technological social sec-

tor organizations are moving to participate in the movement. Not surprising to any engaged CP, the level of waste or less than optimal investment is significant. The risk of waste or worse becomes greater as the level of sophistication of the organization funding the project drops.

One such situation would probably include a proposal by a major publicly traded web site construction firm to an international religious organization that is located domestically. Assume the proposal specified the development and hosting of basic brochure web site for a budget to exceed $250,000 over a two-year period, a large project for the organization. The content is quite basic but the language, presentations, and promises are impressive to say the least. The visionary benefits of this web site include vastly increased participation, donations, and youth involvement. This all would materialize by simply listing basic information about the church and riding the Internet wave and attracting a young audience.

Fortunately for the organization, members of its community engage the project and offer to complete the project at no expense to the organization. The newly engaged members also provide marketing and technology talent to completely redesign the site, including numerous interactive features, and they also implement a professional marketing plan. The marketing plan includes detailed metrics on agreed upon energized goals. The team extensively benchmarks their efforts against top-tier commercial and social sector Internet offerings, discovering numerous value-added best practices.

During the benchmarking process, several pro bono team members begin negotiations with a start-up software company to serve as a beta site for a suite of software programs still under development. As a major value creation leap, the team obtains options in the start-up and a major funding foundation dependent upon the site's success in attracting members. Generating momentum through the project is essential to its progress, especially given the frequent obstacles. The options offer the potential to accrue in value from $2 to $3 million dollars, versus an initial cost estimate of $250,000. The potential Performance Gap is $3,250,000 and at a minimum $250,000. The Multiplier Effect is essentially infinite.

Soviet Satellite Country Ethnic Group Educational Program:
The political changes confronting former soviet satellite countries present many challenges, none less significant than those of providing education to previously

unfavored minorities. Partly in response to this situation, a highly regarded international organization embarks upon a project to provide educational instruction via satellite to multiple remote locations. The relative absence of current technology infrastructure and the lack of skilled local talent make this challenge greater.

Consistent with a prudent approach, the organization seeks to assess the viability of the project by obtaining a professional proposal to provide a turnkey solution. Upon review of the proposal, several engaged and passionate commercial professionals embark upon a methodical benchmarking process to assess best practices in the area and seek to leverage networking connections. Through various contacts and redefining critical elements of the project, a refined proposal offers the potential to accomplish the key elements of the original at a fraction of the cost. The initial proposal, while admittedly preliminary, estimates the investment cost at approximately $2 million. The revised program offers comparable potential at only 10%. This is a Performance Gap of $1.8 million and a Multiplier of 10 times.

Key differences between the two approaches start with a sophisticated understanding of best practices and aggressively talking numbers. While obtaining exact details in this situation is particularly difficult, forming a smart team of industry knowledgeable individuals is clearly essential. The more wisdom contained in the team the less a methodical process is necessary and the higher the potential for extraordinary value creation. Leveraging excess capacity in communication networks, utilizing the procurement power of larger organizations, and accessing a somewhat proprietary trading market for second generation and odd-lot equipment require special talents. And, in a project of this nature, contract negotiations and strategic planning are time consuming resources.

United States Regional School Email and Software Education:

NPB can be more easily applied in simple situations such as one where a CP receives a specific proposal to fund a rather exclusive private school program to educate pre-K to 8th grade teachers on the use of email, and possibly basic Microsoft Word use. As surprising at this may seem to some, in the mid to late 90's this may not have been so atypical. Furthermore, comparable trait situations are likely to occur again and again.

Simple benchmarking in this case would alert a potential funder to free email and Word instruction at a public library, within 5 minutes of the school. Classes would be at night or on weekends so as not to conflict with the workday. And, the library offers flexibility to arrange classes for large groups. The outsourced proposal on the table required $60,000 in funding, with a core group of teachers traveling by plane for instruction and returning to teach their fellow teachers. Computers would be leased for the classes, and substitute teachers hired while the full time teachers receive training during the day.

Despite the disparity of the two alternatives, the headmaster chooses the $60,000 program and obtains funding from a local Dead-Founder Foundation. It would seem that a fair assessment would conclude that a $60,000 Performance Gap existed, yielding a 100% Discount Effect.

Domestic Resources Facility Building:

Campaigns to raise funds for brick and mortar are clearly among the most easily funded, especially in contrast to those related to capacity building. In this example, an NGO seeks to move from it current leased location and into a soon-to-be-purchased facility. A small subcommittee of the board researches the project and presents the full committee with a complete package to purchase the building and the material supporting the decision. The purchase price is stated at $350,000 and the building is said to be in excellent structural condition, which would make a major renovation much easier. The decision is made to borrow the funds, a campaign to raise the funds begins, and renovations immediately commence.

An involved CP evaluating the funding request finds several less than attractive aspects. First, the purchase contract contains a provision that provides the seller with a second mortgage equal to the increase value of the building several years from the date of purchase. No mention of this almost certain contingent liability is in the early financial statements, which an independent appraiser to the CP estimated at $500,000. Next, the building's roof is determined to be in unsafe condition and requires almost $100,000 of additional repair. Also, there is no initial disclosure of the prior business relationship between the committee members and the seller. Should it also come as a surprise that an independent appraisal of the facility came in at $165,000? So, is the Performance Gap to be $785,000 and the Discount Effect an unfortunate 83%?

Winter Clothing Program For A Soviet Satellite Country:

The smallest situations in dollar terms of the six examples contained in Chart 6 involves a winter clothing program for a former Soviet Satellite country. Although the dollars are small relative to the other situations and possibly fall below the radar screen of a more extensive NPB, several brief observations may provide applicable to relatively small social sector situations. As with the situation profiled, CPs can expect a greater number of competing projects the smaller the funding size and can expect more playing on heartstring appeals with limited sophistication. The illustrative specifics here are as simple as the Best Practice – showing a cost of $53,000 – being the first proposal and the second proposal with a cost of $22,500 (adjusted to normalized for comparable performance specifics). The sponsors of the first proposal provided laudable value-added by arranging to purchase the clothing from a local warehouse club and arranging for volunteers to provide local transportation. The sponsors of the second proposal are even more innovative, by arranging to buy seconds directly from the manufactures and collaborating with another group to obtain more cost effective international transportation and distribution. The comparison shows a Performance Gap of $30,500 and a Multiplier Effect of 2.4 times.

Mission-Oriented Organizations:

Although not reviewed in the chart, CPs interested in innovative models for increasing the capacity of socially-redeeming NGOs, will find the work of Ryan Streeter of use in facilitating a framework for NPB analysis. The three models profiled include job partnerships (community partnerships), business partnerships, and investor partnerships. Within the context of each model, case studies are reviewed.[145]

Best Practice Matrix Cumulative Total:

Had each of these situations occurred as described and each of the six superior situations been funded by one CP and each of the less preferred comparable been funded by another CP, the difference would be compelling to even the largest and least proactive CPs. Even without the potential value of the stock options described in the second situation, the one CP would have accomplished with approximately $750,000 what would have cost the other CP $8.4 million. The results: an approximately $7.6 million Performance Gap and a Multiplier Effect of 11.2 times.

Chart 6: <u>Best Practice Matrix Situation</u>

Situations	Situation Cost	Best Practice Cost	Performance Gap	Multiplier/Discount Effect	New BP
TB Treatment in Middle East Program	$163,366	$5,076,250	$4,912,884	31 multiplier	Yes
International Religious Organizational Website	$3,000,000 (proj.)	$250,000	$3,250,000	inverse multiplier	Yes
Soviet Satellite Country Ethnic Group Educational Program	$200,000	$2,000,000	$1,800,000	10 multiplier	Yes
United States Regional School Email and Software Education	$60,000	-	$60,000	100% discount	No
Domestic Resources Facility Building	$950,000	$165,000	$785,000	83% discount	No
Winter Clothing Program For A Soviet Satellite Country	$22,500	$53,000		2.4 multiplier	Yes

BENCHMARKING TACTICS

Wisdom 5: "Yes, competitive social sector measurement tactics do exist."

Best Practice Situation Matrix:
The best practice matrix contains six premier examples, utilizing the Multiplier Effect or Discount Effect for measurement. Each example is quantified by its Performance Margin, Performance Gap, (dollar or metric model) and its Multiplier or Discount Effect. These situations provide examples of NGOs that either utilize their available resources or act in what unfortunately is the standard NGO fashion: being unproductive.

Tactic Comparison:
The Tactic Comparison illustrates the five key tactics of both commercial sector and NGO benchmarking. This comparison provides CPs with a comparison of familiar commercial sector tactics to the NGO tactics. This will enable them to understand better the approaches that need to be taken and to benchmark. Each of the five tactics of the commercial sector/NGO similarities and contrasts will be explained in the following sections.

Market Multiple vs. Multiplier/Discount Effect:
In the commercial sector, one of the more frequently used tools of measurement is market multiples, especially for public companies and in situations of private

market transactions. As most CPs probably know, historically the most widely recognized multiple was the price/earnings multiple ("P/E Ratio"). More recently the
multiples have expanded to include revenue and cash flow multiples. Even more
recently with the explosion of the new economy, market multiples of a wide range
of measurement have developed, including market value to vision.

Currently CPs are realizing the need for a similar NGO measurement. There are
two philosophies on measurements that come close to accomplishing what the
ROI does.

Chart 7: <u>NPB Tactic Comparison</u>

Public/Commercial Companies		NGOs
Market Multiples	vs	Multiplier/Discount Effect
Value Gap	vs	Performance Gap
Nuggets of Value	vs	Deliverable Opportunity
Best Practices	vs	Best Practices
Profit Margin	vs	Performance Margin

An example of the Multiplier Effect and an example of the Discount Effect can
provide a further understanding to the usefulness of these measurements. An
example of a Multiplier Effect is in a NGO aiming to provide Tuberculosis and
Mediterranean Fever treatment in Middle East Countries with a Multiplier Effect
of 31 times. The CP proactively running this investment decided to figure out
what the retail price to fund efforts would be and what the price to fund the efforts
with his value added would be. The CP located, using his value added, discounts
on the retail price of medication and laboratories, free transportation, and free
physicians. The total retail cost of both the TB and MF was $5,076,250 and the
foundation's costs were $163,366. This difference creates a 31 times multiplier.

In contrast to that, a Discount Effect can be seen through a NGO United States Regional School Email and Software Education Program. A regional private school requested $10,000 to educate faculty and administrators on the types of email. An additional $50,000 was requested to educate faculty and administrators on word processing. A local CP informed the school that public libraries in close proximity to the school offered free educational email and software classes providing informational CD's and user booklets to anyone at no cost. The school did not heed the CP's advice and solicited and received the funding from another source. In contrast to the previous 31 multiplier, the regional private school had a 100% discount effect, investing all of their money wastefully. The Multiplier/Discount Effect is in its initial stages. The Multiplier/Discount Effect is not a panacea. Hopefully, future works will further advance the application and integrity of the Multiplier/Discount Effect.

Value Gap vs. Performance Gap:

The Value Gap is a powerful concept in the commercial sector and is the difference between a company's current value and its potential value approximately two years subsequent to investment. Value gap is based on utilizing existing business lines only. In the social sector, the Value Gap for entire organization can be referred to in NGOs as the Performance Gap.

The Performance Gap is either the aggregate dollar or unit difference between the situation output or deliverable being assessed and the best practice performance metric. The gap is obtained by multiplying the difference (the Performance Margin) to the number of units involved. Performance Gap can be for one specific deliverable or output, a group, or for an entire organization. A Performance Gap is powerfully utilized when applied to an entire organization.

The company's initial costs begin at $30 million. These costs can measure an example of commercial sector Value Gap after benchmarking $24 million. This creates a $6 million Value Gap. The same method is used when assessing NGO Performance Gap. In the Religious Informational website, the Performance Gap is measured by comparing the original price paid and the best practice price. An initial cost proposal of $250,000 cost to a $3 million profit proposal creates a $3.25 million Performance Gap.

Nuggets of Value vs. Deliverable Opportunities:

Nuggets of Value represent specific opportunities to create value by improving current operations or by financial engineering previously ignored by the market and management. Comparing current operations to the practices of selected benchmark companies often provides ideas for these Nuggets. Similar to the commercial sector concept of Nuggets of Value, Deliverable Opportunities are specific situation outputs or deliverables, be they processes, programs, or policies, that offer opportunities for improved performance in an NGO.

A basic example of commercial sector nuggets are the different areas a commercial organization assesses. Some possibilities could vary from the number of products per hour per employee to the average number of hours worked a day per employee. The possibilities for commercial nuggets are endless.

Best Practices vs. Best Practices:

Best practices are the byproducts of the benchmarking process. They are successful innovations or techniques of top performing organizations, which are often classified into processes, programs, or policies. Most effectively applied, Best Practices are represented as quantified metrics. Quantification of a Best Practice is often referred to as a Best Practices metric. The same terminology exists in the commercial sector as the social sector.

Profit Margin vs. Performance Margin:

As virtually every CP is aware, a Profit Margin is a term which is commonly used in commercial organizations and is defined in using various percentage calculations including pre-tax margin, after tax margin, gross margin variable contribution margin, etc. Performance margin is the difference between the situation output or deliverable being measured and the best practice. This can be expressed in dollars or unit terms and preferably in its most basic form. Illustrative examples include cost per meal, percentage of utilized assets, and fees paid per physician visit.

Although not necessarily a percentage calculation, the Performance Margin in the social sector is compared to the Profit Margins in the commercial sector given the similar objective of measuring and comparing a comparable metric.

After a commercial sector organization has determined its possible Nuggets of Value and established their Value Gap the Profit Margin can be determined. The Value Gap is multiplied by the quantity. A brief commercial sector illustration should be sufficient to assure understanding of this basic concept.

A northeastern factory sought to determine the Profit Margin increase the company could obtain by benchmarking their primary competitor's distribution rates. The competitor's output was 10 times greater per hour for equal quality product. That would calculate to 70 additional products every day. With each product having a market value of $200, this creates a daily Profit Margin of $14,000. For the entire year the company had the possibility for an additional $4.8 million Profit Margin.

A comparative example of NGO Performance Margin illustrates the characteristics through two social sector Winter Clothing Programs for Soviet Satellite Countries, both competing for a donation of $2 million. NGO "A" was paying $45 per child to provide hats, coats, gloves, and scarves, purchasing all clothing from a local warehouse. NGO "B" was purchasing seconds (clothing unable to be sold because of one missed stitch) from the manufacturer for $22.50. On this sole feature of the winter clothing program NGO "A" was paying $45,000 to clothe 1,000 children. NGO "B" was paying $45,000 to clothe 2,000 children. NGO "B" Performance Margin was 1,000 extra children clothes at the same cost. This was only one of the three different main features that were compared between the two NGOs.

Other Potential Non-NPB Tactics:

Obviously, there are other non-NPB tools that offer potential for CP consideration. Many are heavily tied to current social sector practices or are purely commercial sector tools pushed to apply to the social sector. However, there are two developing non-NPB tactics that merit mention as tools to provide unique benefits to the progressive and rapid development of a greater social sector mission.

The first such concept, and by far the most important, is a social sector Return on Investment approach increasingly known as a Social Return on Investment ("SROI") or more recently as a Blended Return on Investment ("Blended ROI").

The primary difference between commercial ROI and Blended ROI is that in commercial ROI the returns are calculated solely by determining what is received by the investor, while the Blended ROI is much more inclusive in considering both the commercial/financial return as well as the return to the community. Within the Blended ROI there are two returns referred to as a FROI (financial) and SROI (social).

There should be no question that this is a highly innovative avenue for tremendous value creation. Indeed, the social sector elder of this approach, Jed Emerson, a Harvard Business School Senior Research Fellow and leader of the cutting edge Roberts Enterprise Development Fund (REDF), is forging new ground daily and setting increasingly ambitious goals.

"In contrast to a traditional Investment/Return framework with its implicit 'sinking economic returns' assumption, a Blended Value Proposition of any given investment understands that both functions are integrated and to be fully assessed must be advanced into their highest quadrant...wherein they maximize social and financial value creation and shareholder value."[146] This observation becomes particularly relevant as CPs assess pure NGO investments relative to Intersectoral alternatives. Such Intersectoral opportunities are reviewed in Section Seven under Capital Markets NP Benchmarking and Publicly Traded Companies as Potential NPB Best Practices and Social Sector Investments.

The ambitious nature of the Blended ROI is well illustrated in Emerson's intent on linking this to the development of nothing less than a global Social Sector Capital Market, a capital market that will ingeniously and efficiently allocate funds based on varying degrees of dual objective, both financial and social. His effort is quite expansive, including:

- Theoretical underpinnings of the concept.
- Application of Blended ROI to social enterprise.
- Case studies of actual investment and applications.
- Utilization in the context of venture philanthropy.
- Implication for accounting systems and practices (Social MIS).
- Related concepts of value creation.
- Creation of a social sector stock market.
- Potential for innovative financing instruments.

One of the initial key challenges in applying Blended ROI is the ability to obtain accurate financial information upon which to calculate the social portion of the combined return calculation. REDF had progressed with its efforts on this front via a series of progressive stages. The latest development is an Internet based system called the REDF Ongoing Assessment of Social Impacts (OASIS). It is no small task to assess the impact of social programs or projects, especially those that are involved with complex human service efforts operational over long periods of time, possibly generations. Interested NPB CPs are recommended to review the latest SROI Reports contained on the REDF web site. In addition to reading the basic explanatory information, the Rubicon Bakery and Nu2U and Nu2U2 reports offer real world value-added.[147]

Material provided on the REDF web site provide sufficiently detailed illustrations of those calculations composing the Blended ROI. Emerson's latest work addressing the Blended ROI, "The Nature of Returns: A Social Capital Markets Inquiry into Elements of Investment and The Blended Value Proposition can be found on the Internet at www.hbs.edu/social enterprise/download. The works also provide ample examples of the concept's application. By far, the application encompasses virtually all in the entire social sector, particularly with the human services social sector.

To facilitate CPs' understanding of Blender ROI and its benefits in prospectively complementing NP Benchmarking, the associated chart provides a comparative analysis. First, its merits mention that both strategies possess many similarities. For example, each seeks to energize superior performance of NGOs, especially through Intersectoral practices such as social enterprise, strategic philanthropy and restructuring, and venture philanthropy. Also, both offer potential to advance the development of the social sector capital markets.

Important distinguishing aspects include NPB's focus on relative best practices and performance gaps in contrast to entire social sector comparative assessments and relative investment measurement statistics. NPB focuses more on enablers in contrast to returns. Blended ROI provides application to a wide range of portfolio management and corporate finance techniques in contrast to NPB's application to operational benchmarking and management financial tools. NPB seeks to offer competitive evaluation of resource utilization compared to a greater focus on social impact outcomes and financial returns. Both focus on internal information, while NPB requires external comparative information to advance. While both offer capital markets and managerial application, it is potentially easier to envision NPB's application more to the latter and Blended SROI to the former; however this may soon prove to be a moot point.

There remain opportunities and challenges to advance the Blended ROI concept even further. Efforts to develop or simulate supply-demand equilibrium market return rates by funders and social subsectors or uses-of-funds remains an issue; this includes determining a quantification of the risk and reward preferences of the funders. Technically, there may also be a requirement that the single number return statistic be bifurcated to allow two distinct statistics, one measuring return and the utilized as a discount rate. Dual statistics would allow a presentation of the higher rate for more prized investment and simultaneously a lower statistic for a discount rate to provide for a greater present value of more treasured future benefits.

CPs will also be challenged to consider programs that seek to achieve greater so-called "second-order" effects. These are programs that provide, for examples, education or employment ventures, with the goal that the benefits will inure in the future, in comparison with programs that address current needs such a food, clothing, and shelter. Commenting on this issue, one multi-billionaire CP observed: "The nation's needs far outstrip any fortune, so he hopes to build a more systemic fix. 'We're hoping to build something that gets more children fed through second-order effect.' For instance, an educational venture could attract employers and create jobs."[148] Some social sector researchers even comment upon the need to assess a "third-order" effect, especially in the higher education subsector where universities are engaging in a greater level of commercial research and industrial ventures. "We know little at this point about the commercial efficacy of different forms of university organizations, but we suggest that a third-order effect of enhanced commercial efforts is to change the calculus by which political and economic leaders evaluate universities."[149]

Another less ambitious effort to assess social impact involves that utilized by those seeking to estimate the economic impact on the effected community. These approaches are conceptually akin to those utilized by governmental bodies professing to determine the economic impact of certain programs or projects. Such economic models usually require an extraordinary number of projected assumptions and extrapolations. However, there are little comparative or competitive elements to this approach nor is there enough to provide managerial insights or measure the impact of investments beyond taxpayer or community economic impact variable.

Nonetheless, this approach clearly has valuable application in certain situations.[150]

The second tactic worth note is referred to in the social sector as an Outcome Based Management ("OBM") approach, which is focused on determining relative and effective use of monetary resources. The Multiplier/Discount Effect differs from OBM in that it seeks wisdom and insight to enhance effectiveness and efficiency through internal and external comparative analysis. The limitations of OBM become more apparent as the nebulous and more abstract nature of the mission increases.

Chart 8: NPB & Blended Return on Investment: Selected Comparative

New Philanthropy Benchmarking ("NPB")	Blended Return on Investment ("BROI")
• Best Practice Comparable Assessment	• Entire Social Sector Comparative Assessment
• Relative performance gap statistics	
• Focus on enablers of performance gap	• Relative Investment Measurement Tactics
	• Return on investment, both social and financial
• Applicable benchmarking and management financial tools	• Applicable to both portfolio management and corporate finance methodology
• Competitive evaluation of resource utilization	• Greater focus on social impact outcomes and financial returns
• Requires both internal and external comparative focus	• Primary internal performance analysis
• Dual purpose to enhance internal management and stimulate competitive allocation of social sector funding	• Focus to assess impact and facilitate development of social sector capital market

Present Value Implications:
Present value methodology is considered by many to be a relatively contemporary concept and its application to determining the present social value of social sector investments quite progressive. However, research indicates that one of the legendary CPs, Andrew Carnegie, may have qualitatively expressed a supportive voice with his words on fully investing in the social sector prior to a CP's death.

"Knowledge of the results of legacies bequeathed is not calculated to inspire the brightest hopes of much posthumous good being accomplished by them. The cases are not few in which the real object sought by the testator is not attained, nor are they few in which his real wishes are thwarted. In many cases the bequests are so used to as to become only monuments of this folly. It is well to remember that it requires the exercise of not less ability than that which acquires it, to use wealth so as to be really beneficial to the community."[151]

In the context of both NPB and Blended ROI, the issues associated with the present value of social sector investment are quite real and arguably of vital significance. This is especially on-target as it relates to the annual distribution percentages for the so-called dead-founder foundations. However, the resistance – whether latent or manifest – is understandable, especially for so many social sector participants whose livelihood relies on the notion that the value of achieving a social sector goal today is no more valuable than achieving the same goal at some point in the distant future.

Developing the present value analytical tools will expedite the advancement of NPB by increasing the positive pressure on social sector funders to understand their competitive performance. This is similar to the way NGOs or commercial sector companies measure relative performance or investment managers in the commercial sector measure performance against the indices and other comparable funds.

CPs may be well advised to consider NPB benchmarking best-practices in determining annual distribution targets. Once a foundation has established the necessary capacity, the IRS 5% minimum seems woefully shallow. At a minimum, is it not better to assume the 10% tithing standard?

Although arguably only a tangential and qualitative observation, one social sector professional envisions present value as a tool to assess NGO conversions. "Even more difficult is evaluating the social value of the firm in its nonprofit form. Theoretically it is the present value to society of the services that those assets would deliver over the remainder of their life, if they remain under nonprofit control, less any net subsidies the firm would use in delivering those services."[152]

Foundations should either be morally or ethically compelled to seek answers to many related questions such as the following: What Blended ROIs merit distributions higher than 5%? How should a foundation balance attractive BROIs with level of distributions? What BROI would justify a planned 100% investment of assets in social sector initiatives? Analytically, at what point does the present value of projected future financial assets – discounted by currently obtainable BROIs – decline below the current value of investment assets?

As said earlier in the Working Book, maybe it is not so surprising that certain of the more progressive professionals in the social sector have analogized dead-founder foundation low percentage distributions to Ebenezer Scrooge's hoarding of cash. These foundations savor the jingling of coins while the souls of their missions suffer a life of ever-growing despair. Why are there so few reports of foundation planning for an intended-year 100% social investment strategy?

The Olin Foundation's 10-year plan to full social investment is currently quite extraordinary and a benchmark to be classified as best practice. In 1998, under the direction of William E. Simon (former U.S. Treasury Secretary), the Olin Foundation announced a plan to divest 100% of its fund over a seven to 10 year period.[153]

Although well beyond the scope of NPB, the more advanced CPs – interested in pursuing issues associated with present value – should find the in-process materials in Appendix L (Selected Blended ROI and Present Value Model Issues and Responses) quite enlightening.

SECTION SIX

EFFECTIVE NPB MANAGEMENT

Wisdom 6: "If you can't measure in the social sector, you can't manage."

The first question often confronted by an advocate of benchmarking involves who or what to benchmark. Some NGOs claim that they are so unique that there is no organization with which they could benchmark. This is one of the more frustrating myths encountered in the social sector. When deciding whom to benchmark, first an organization needs to determine what processes or strategies to benchmark. Comparisons are drawn more easily when organizations are similar to one another.

On the other hand, an organization can benchmark others in different fields as long as the other organization provides a best practice example. Don't limit your scope. In order to maintain continuous improvement and continuous betterment, an organization needs to benchmark premier organizations. Remember to look at organizations from which your organization can learn – this is particularly important for those in the social sector. Camp reminds us that "in benchmarking the manager's goal is to identify those companies, regardless of industry, which demonstrate superior performance in functions to be benchmarked so that their practices, processes, and methods can be studied and documented."[154]

Even in a situation involving the influential charity, Oxfam, which seeks to force multinational drug companies to cut prices on their life-saving drugs to poor nations, NPB can provide comparative information and tactics to improve effectiveness.[155] This serves as a reasonable illustration of how clearly everything cannot be measured, but all can be compared.

Assessing Best Practices:

When assessing Best Practices there is one wisdom that you need to remember: if you can't measure it, you can't manage it. This is an important philosophy as best practice metrics provides CPs with a means to measure and benchmark. Metrics also allow CPs to look at different aspects in the best practice: track records, sustainable results, replicable ideas, and cost effectiveness of an idea. All of these different points become important when trying to determine which parts of an organization can be improved most effectively.

Internal vs. External Comparisons:

Internal benchmarking is most frequently used when NGOs claim their unique circumstance does not compare with others, a statement frequently proved untrue. Internal benchmarking can be useful, yet it should not be used as a result of the claim that there are no possible external benchmarking options. There are always external benchmarking options.

Internal benchmarking focuses on historical performance and future goals compared to past variations in changes and historical records. This can be an effective method of benchmarking, yet it also falls short in many ways. Internal benchmarking does not tell how to meet goals or to improve. In fact, there are no comparisons to the competition or others in your same field when benchmarking is limited to internal analysis. A disadvantage is created when internal benchmarking is employed, because it is rare that your performance can accurately indicate the impact of economic change.

External benchmarking is a way to look at other organizations that are doing what you do, only faster, better, and cheaper. This strategy provides techniques, strategies and assessments functional for other organizations. The short fall of external benchmarking contrasts favorably to internal benchmarking: though certainly more complex, the benefits reaped are greater.

Practical Concerns of Execution:

When investing in philanthropic endeavors, CPs are well advised to consider the four "Ts" with regard to their investment. This differs somewhat from an expanded list of five issues that foundations and NGO management should consider.

The first and most important "T" is time; regardless of gift size, your time is necessary to ensure that you are helping rather than hurting. Time is an especially precious gift because of the high value placed on CP time. The second "T" is the talent of each CP – talents that have enabled them to become highly successful. These talents become great assets to philanthropic efforts. The third "T," treasures or financial resources, is often found in positive correlation with the possession of both time and talents. The fourth "T," tenacity of effort, is obviously invaluable and evident when the efforts are self-motivated rather than externally forced.

As highlighted at the top of both Charts 9 and 10, foundation and NGO management is advised to assess and manage five issues associated with each prospective NPB Deliverable Opportunity. The five include (1) time, talents, and tenacity (costs), (2) treasures (financial-monetary costs), (3) significance of impact, (4) probability of accomplishment, and (5) time to accomplish. It should come as no surprise that the success of NPB is essentially reliant on the quality analysis, judgements, and execution skills of foundation or NGO management and other involved team members.

A further word of note on the importance of utilizing the all-in-cost approach is calculating cost of initiatives. The integrity of the analysis merits that attention be given to including both direct and indirect costs associated with a project, program, policy, or organization under review. An activity-based cost accounting approach can be quite helpful but is time consuming and not justifiable in many situations. (Activity-based cost accounting entails an evaluation of time and motion studies of those individuals involved in an effort under study, e.g., how much time on average over a representative time period during the work day do human service officers actually spend on processing paper or attending to non-assigned matters.) CPs may also be well advised to consider the accrual method of cost accounting as this offers the benefits associated with a longer-term perspective. This would include accounting as an expense in the current period of time. And the probability adjusted cost of some future potential expense, such as risk events, uninsured liabilities, or even project related legal or regulatory challenges (law suits).

Single Function Community Service Comparison:
The Single Function Community Service ("SFCS") comparison is admittedly quite simplistic; however, its purpose is as an educational instrument. The SFCS

hypothetical illustrates all the five tactics profiled in Chart 7: Tactic Comparison to this situation in order to facilitate rapid comprehension.

In Chart 9 below, two organizations are compared. SFCS-Boston is referred to as the previous best practice. Comparing the SFCS-Boston with the SFCS-New York, which is the organization conducting NPB, creates a Performance Margin comparing cost per meal. There are two Performance Gaps illustrated. The Performance Gap dollar option compares the cost to feed a set number of meals, saving $70,000. The Performance Gap meal option compares the number of meals that can be served with the money spent by the former Best Practice; an increase in the number of meals served by 140,000. These two options allow a NGOs to assess their productivity from two perspectives. Note that the NGOs need not be of identical size or composition to allow for a valuable relative NPB comparison.

The final calculating line of the chart provides the Multiplier/Discount Effect metrics. Although SFCS-Boston had been considered the best practice, SFCS-NYC is now out performing with a Multiplier of 2.4 times, i.e., each NYC dollar is 2.4 times as powerful as the Boston dollar or NYC only must spend $1 for each $2.40 of Boston's SFCS. Boston metric is now sub-one with a Discount Effect of 58%, i.e., of ever dollar spent, 58% is essentially wasted (or conversely, NYC's 42 cents spent has the same performance as one dollar expended by Boston's SFCS). The calculations are elementary math and are detailed in the chart's footnotes.

Of course, there can be many reasons for the difference. However, a CP is well advised to motivate NGO and foundation management to look for Deliverable Opportunities as well as intractable differences.

Remember, even in the most politically sensitive situations, benchmarking has considerable value-added. One government related example, Seattle's Department of Public Health, determined to benchmark its highly regarded comparable San Francisco entity. Seattle's spokesperson provided an interesting observation. "You have to realize that there isn't one answer to a question, but a series of answers. People in cities are different…We stole everything we could from San Francisco. But we also had the luxury of watching their mistakes."[156]

As reviewed in several sections of this Working Book, CP and management focus should include both the micro and macro factors as well as associated issues and consequences. NPB is predicated on quality analysis focusing on what Bogan refers to as the "enablers" supporting NPB Deliverable Opportunities. Clearly, dealing with culture issues is essential. And – as mentioned above – the judgement decisions and execution actions in the categories at the top of Chart Seven are essential elements in determining the level of NPB success. Instruction on process and worksheets maybe quite helpful, but the performance of team members should be a primary focus of the proactive CP. And, remember, there is no substitute for quality wisdom and judgement. Even the seven NPB wisdom points will only be successful if wisely and effectively applied.

Chart 9: NPB for Single Function Community Service ("SFCS") Comparison — Boston vs. NYC

Issues to Assess and Manage:	• Time, talents and tenacity • Treasures (monetary costs) • Significance of Impact • Probability of accomplishments • Time to accomplish	

	SFCS - Boston (Former Best Practices)	**SFCS - NYC** (Current Best Practices)
Quantity	100,000 meals	200,000 meals
Situation Cost	$1.20	$0.50
Best Practice	$0.50	$0.50
Performance	$0.70	$0.00
Performance Gap (meals)	140,000	0
Performance Gap (dollars)	$70,000	$ 0.00
Multiplier/Discount	58% Discount	2.4 Multiplier

Analysis Conclusion

• SFCS-Boston possess a "Discount Effect" of 58% (($120K-$50K)/$120K) relative to SFCS-NYC, based on costs.

• SFCS-NYC offers a "Multiple Effect" of 2.4 times relative to SFCS-Boston ($240K/$100K), based on performance

Comprehensive National Service Organization:
The Comprehensive National Service Organization NPB – as illustrated in Chart 10 – is an example of the application of benchmarking to a more complex organization. Unlike the SFCS, the Comprehensive National Service Organization ("CNSO") benchmarks nine different aspects of its organization. The CNSO assesses nine deliverables and measures the potential impact of each.

Before offering insights into the chart, two computational observations may be of assistance to those CPs who have yet to work through certain areas of preceding text.

First, the Performance Margin shown in the chart is calculated as the difference between the CNSO metric and the Best Practice metric. The Performance Gap is calculated as the quantity associated with the Deliverable Opportunity under consideration multiplied by the Performance Margin, and is in terms of dollars. The total Performance Gap is the sum of all the Deliverable Opportunities less an Inter-organization adjustment.

Second, the Multiplier/Discount Effect for each Deliverable Opportunity is calculated as either the Performance Margin as a percentage of the CNSO Metric or the Performance Gap as a percentage of the Quantity, whichever is more practical. The Multiplier/Discount Effects for subtotals are calculated as the weighted average of each Deliverable Opportunity Multiplier/Discount Effect. The total calculation can be calculated using either the same weighted average methodology or - as seen in Chart 10 - calculated by dividing the total Performance Gap less the Adjustment for Inter-Organization Eliminations by the total dollars expended for all the Deliverables indicated by the organization. Ideally, the Deliverables would encompass an organization wide NPB. For purposes of Chart 10, the weight is based on the absolute dollars in the Performance Gap. This weighted could also be calculated based on the absolute dollars expended for each by CNSO.

Although no Multiplier Effect is encountered in CNSO, such calculations would apply the same approach described in the previous SFCS example. And, subtotals and total calculations would utilize the approach discussed above.

The Benchmarking Deliverables provide illustrations within each of the three primary categories: process, program, or policy. Within the process category, average employee cost of absenteeism, average facility cost, and opportunity cost of asset utilization are represented. The CNSO metrics are in both dollars and percentage data points, the latter of which is converted into dollar terms to allow calculation of NPB metrics. The program deliverables cover cost of meals, medication, and clothing costs. Policy deliverables are somewhat more abstract, yet quantifiable, and include third-party fund raising costs, clerical wages, and physician visit fees.

As CPs will note, each deliverable has a series of corresponding items including three items of necessary information: quantities, CNSC Metrics, and Best Practice Metrics. These items provide the data to calculate the NPB metrics: Performance Margins, Performance Gaps, and the Multiplier/Discount Effect. Unlike the SFCS Boston to NYC comparison, the CNSC NPB analysis utilizes Best Practice Metrics from various organizations, as comparable as possible, from whatever sector most appropriate, including both social and commercial.

Without delving into each significant detail of Chart 10 (which the intrigued CP may find quite useful), several general observations and conclusions should suffice. Note that not only does each Benchmarking Deliverable have its own NPB metric, but so do the three primary categories as well as a combined total for the entire CNSO. As for the process category, the Performance Gap offers the smaller of the absolute dollar Performance Gaps at $900,000 However, the second largest Discount Effect is at 45%. Sixty percent of the total is attributable to the average cost per employee of absenteeism. The second category, Program, offers both the largest absolute dollar Performance Gap at $7.6 million and the largest Discount Effect at 67%. By far the largest single dollar contributor resides in this category. Cost per person of annual medication provides $5.0 million and also has the largest Discount Effect of 67%. The cost to clothe one person Deliverable at $2.3 million is also one of the CNSO's largest. As for the policy category, the Performance Gap is $3.9 million, but it is worth noting that it has only a 33% Discount Effect. This highlights that the largest dollars need not have a correspondingly high Discount Effect or visa versa. Within policy well over half the Performance Gap is attributable to fees paid per physician visit at $2.5 million.

As Chart 10 indicates, a $1.9 million dollar adjustment has yet to be allocated among the specific deliverables or the three categories. Such an allocation is essential to the integrity of any NPB analysis, and will require considerable sound wisdom and judgement. In all likelihood, the allocation process will become quite politically charged. CPs familiar with activity-based cost accounting (which involves actually measuring the significant resources of time, people, assets, and dollars utilized in connection with a specific deliverable) may find that this prac-

Chart 10: <u>Comprehensive</u> National Service Organization[a]

Five Issues to Assess & Manage:
- Time, talents, and tenacity (costs)
- Treasures (direct financial monetary costs)
- Significance of impact
- Probability of accomplishments
- Time to accomplish

Benchmarking Deliverables or Outputs	Quantity	CNSO Metric	Best Practice Metric	Performance Margin (criteria)	Performance Gap (dollars)	Multiplier/ Discount Effect[b]
Process:						
• Average Cost Per Employee of Absenteeism	1,000 employees	$800.00	$300.00	$500.00	$500,000.00	63% Discount
• Average Cost of Facility Per Square Foot	20,000 sq. ft.	$27.50	$15.00	$12.50	$250,000.00	45% Discount
• Annual Opportunity Cost of Unutilized Assets	$750,000	60%	80%	20%	$150,000.00	20% Discount
Subtotal					$900,000.00	51% Discount
Program:						
• Cost Per Meal	500,000 meals	$1.20	$0.50	$0.70	$350,000.00	58% Discount
• Cost Per Person of Annual Medication	50,000 people	$150.00	$50.00	$100.00	$5,000,000.00	67% Discount
• Cost to Cloth One Person	150,000 people	$30.00	$15.00	$15.00	$2,250,000.00	50% Discount
Subtotal					$7,600,000.00	62% Discount
Policy:						
• 3rd Party Cost For Raised Funds	$3 million	29%	10%	19%	$570,000.00	19% Discount
• Average Annual Wage for Clerical Workers	200 workers	$13.00	$11.00	$2.00	$832,000.00	15% Discount
• Fees paid Per Physician Visit	250,000 visits	$30.00	$20.00	$10.00	$2,500,000.00	33% Discount
Subtotal					$3,902,000.00	27% Discount
Aggregate Subtotal					$12,402,000.00	
Adjustment for Inter-organizational eliminations (15%)					$1,860,300.00	
CNSO Quantity					$10,541,700.00	37% Discount

(a) As this is a hypothetical case study, detailed notes of elaboration serve a more heuristic purpose in contrast with the detailed notes for a situation specific evaluation and analysis. However, it should not go without mention, especially to the more managerial skilled CP's, that careful selection of comparable benchmarks is essential. Furthermore, it's essential that tools such as fishbone or elements analysis be conducted in order that the reasons for the Performance Gap are carefully understood. Camp's Business Process Benchmarking book's Chapter 5 (Analyze the Performance Gap) provide a useful overview of analyzing the elements of a Performance Gap; Watson's Strategic Benchmarking book Chapter 3 (Understanding the Essentials of Process Benchmarking) offers a useful cautionary review of false enablers as well as techniques for assessing the validity of prospective enables, and - to a lesser extent- Bogan and English's book Benchmarking for Best Practices contains useful insights in Chapter 11 (Benchmarking and Change Management). At the same, it may well serve as a warning litmus test if the first reaction of a viewer of this chart to seek analytical disparities before even realizing that it is a hypothetical analysis.

(b) Subtotals are weighted averages and total is separately calculated based on total numbers.

tice is a good starting point. This is in contrast to simple expense allocation based on out-dated and possibly arbitrary cost allocation schemes, e.g., total expenses based on percentages of office space or production space occupied by a group or based on total annual dollars spent by a group.

It's important to again stress the absolute need for CPs to require that the enablers contributing to each Deliverable Opportunity be assessed and understood. Be wary of the ubiquitous "false enablers," for they can cripple an otherwise sound NPB. Furthermore, it's essential that the "five issues to assess and manage" shown at the top of both charts nine and ten form an integral part of NPB. Without careful attention to these five, NPB has little hope of fulfilling its potential. To repeat, these include: time, talents, tenacity (costs), treasures (financial-monetary costs), significance of impact, probability of accomplishments, and time to accomplish.

The final calculating line of the chart provides both the aggregate Performance Gap and the Discount Effect metrics. The total Performance Gap for CNSO relative to the best practice in each of the deliverables measured is $10.5 million, after adjustment for Inter-Organizational eliminations. CNSO's Discount Effect is 37%. In effect, NPB is challenging CNSO and its funders to address a potential wasting of 37 cents on each dollar relative to best practice metrics. This aggregate impact of a 34% Discount Effect results in a less than optimal allocation of $10.5 million; which – as will be highlighted in Chart 11 – is on CNSO total expenditures of $28.4 million.

The footnote to Chart 10 provides supplementary observations and suggestions. Of special note, CPs may well find an early warning litmus test of NGO cultural obstacles if the first reaction of NGO managers in viewing the chart is to seek analytical disparities even while realizing that CNSO is a hypothetical example designed as an educational tool.

Chart 11: NPB CNSO Performance Gap and Discount Effect Schematic provides an effective tool in visualizing the magnitude of the dollars involved in CNSO and the relative size of the Benchmarking Deliverable components of the Performance Gap.

As the CP will note, the total dollars involved is $28.4 million with the best practice expending only $16.8 million resulting in a Performance Gap of $12.5 million pre-inter-organizational eliminations and $10.5 million post. The Performance Gap pie chart illustrates the relative sources of the Gap, especially noting that the

Chart 11: <u>NPB CNSO Performance Gap and Discount Effect Schematic</u>

Total Dollars Invested at CNSO Rate

Facility 2%
Unused Assets 1%
Meals 2%
Absenteeism 3%
Medication 25%
Physicians 25%
Clothing 15%
Fund Raising 10%
Workers 17%

Total: $28.4 Million

Total Dollars Invested at Best Practice Rate

Facility 2%
Unused Assets 1%
Meals 1%
Absenteeism 2%
Medication 14%
Clothing 13%
Physicians 29%
Fund Raising 14%
Workers 24%

Total: $16.8 Million

Total Performance Gap

Meals 3%
Unused Assets 1%
Facility 2%
Absenteeism 4%
Medication 40%
Physicians 20%
Workers 7%
Clothing 18%
Fund Raising 5%

Total: $12.4 Million

Discount Effect: 37%

annual medication cost is 40% of the Gap while comprising only 25% of the total CNSO expenditures. In contrast, annual wages for clerical workers work consumes 17% of the CNSO expenditures, yet composes only 7% of the Performance Gap. As mentioned earlier, the Discount Effect is a sizable 37%.

As repeatedly stressed, these numbers are simply a starting point. It is essential that each Deliverable opportunity is carefully analyzed for root causes. Savvy CPs are well aware of false enablers in the commercial sector and should be similarly wary in the social sector.

Additionally, it should not go without saying that CPs should display the same care in evaluating the five issues to assess and manage prior to initiating significant action. It is important to remember the importance of the "first, do no harm" rule with social sector endeavors.

Identifying Performance Gap Components/Cultivating Assets
CPs seeking to create maximum value from existing resources and appropriate supplements are advised to identify Deliverable Opportunities that compose existing and prospective Performance Gaps from a diverse range of sources. Driving much of the analysis will be the search for an NGO's perceived and real core competencies (competitive advantages) as well as the alternate side of the coin (competitive shortcomings).

The Deliverable Opportunities can be measured relative to social sector organizations or commercial sector organizations. The best practices can be benchmarked against both existing and potential processes, programs, or policies.

Assessing the Performance Gap between two social sector NGOs may be relatively straightforward. However, the comparison of social sector organizations is still no simple task. The Best Practice comparison can begin by locating those NGOs of comparable characteristics, which have effectively created value via outstanding performance. For example, certain NGOs have performed amazingly well in cultivating asset value. These cultivations include revenue harvesting from a membership base; maximizing income from brand identification of NGO logos; commercial collaborations generating income from product or service sales to NGO members, NGO target group members, and nonmembers; sales of instructional materials; or sales from of-interest publications.

CPs with an insatiable desire to maximize the Multiplier Effect are advised to commission an NPB study to measure the Performance Gap between NGOs in terms of relative revenue and income from internally asset cultivation. The Deliverable Opportunities will provide components of the Performance Gap and facilitate an assessment of the various issues to assess and manage. CPs should encourage a discourse of potential risks, including crowding out and negative brand impact. Be wary of easy or absolute conclusions, both positive and negative. Research shows that negative reactions from NGO managers will predominate and be supported by unique and mismanaged misfortunate horror stories. Nevertheless, herein lies the potential to maximize the Multiplier Effect by closing a Performance Gap.

Assessing the factors affecting the Performance Gap with commercial sector organizations will probably provide a greater challenge. As a general practice, it may be advisable to first gain a general understanding of the distinguishing macro factors and then advance to the more operational items. Of course, there will be Performance Gaps that exist but provide little or no significant impact.

Such factors to evaluate could include the following and many more: cultural differences, operating margins, free cash flow metrics, growth rates, acquisition and scalability opportunities, public market funding, social capital market funding, tax rate differences, customer base composition, executive and staff/volunteer team member composition, quality of management, impact of legal and regulatory differences, service or product mix and profit margin deltas, stock option impact, impact and importance of innovation and technology, and competitive factors.

In many situations, a key to maximizing value creation requires effectively applying the quantitative tools of NPB to understand the Performance Gaps and the Deliverable Opportunities relative to best practice. A further word of caution: simply measuring the level of social sector funding for an NGO relative to its commercial sector cousin could actually mask the potential for value creation. How many successful commercial sector companies could have achieved their success without access to the commercial sector capital markets, for both private and public funding?

Use of External Assistance:

The use of external assistance can provide invaluable resources if utilized wisely. External assistance can vary from consultants to incentive compensation. Selective use of consultants can help in benchmarking when assessing your productivity, performing comparative analyses, analyzing business strategies, defining market demand, and designing business strategies, which are just a few examples.

Hiring consultants can reduce costs by out-sourcing rather then hiring an in-house professional. Outsourcing consultants can be a cost-saving use of external assistance. Planning the process of phasing out consultants' requirements is essential so that an organization learns to be self-sustaining. That said, a Morino Institute survey noted that one of the biggest impediments to its success was the shortage of qualified social sector consultants.[157]

CPs must be wary of the fact that research for this Working Book has uncovered initial evidence of what could be a quite disturbing practice regarding social sector consultant compensation. In several situations, highly regarded social sector consultants have convinced social sector organizations, including top tier foundations, to pay extraordinarily high fees, sometimes a multiple of those found for comparable talent within the commercial sector. One example was a $250,000 annual retainer for "on-call" foundation best practices advisory; another achieved daily billings of $5,000. The 990 of one NGO listed comparatively outrageous fees (tens of millions) for external PR and advertising consulting services for its medium size organization. Beware of the profiteers that lurk in the social sector.

Another example of a beneficial form of external assistance would be tying compensation to year-end success. External assistance is frequently used in commercial sector organizations to continually motivate managers through out the year. This concept parallels commercial sector incentive compensation, when if and only if the year end goals are obtained do employees reap benefits. If the goals are not met then full payment is not received. NGOs commonly resist any incentive compensation or external assistance claiming that they can perform their functions better when they are under less stress and working alone.

Jim Collins, author of one of the Drucker Foundation's anthologies, "Leading Beyond the Walls," predicts that "one day we will look back on the present system of a single job with a fixed employee as a somewhat barbaric form of organization, much in the way we view indentured servitude today."[158]

To facilitate more efficient and effective management by the passionate CP, Appendix O: Benchmarking Advisor Sampling Summary contains a sampling of benchmarking advisor firms. Clearly this list is by no means all-inclusive, nor should the listing of any firm be considered a vote of confidence. The intent of the material is to provide a starting point whereby a CP can begin the benchmarking process of evaluating firms. The CP should begin the selection process by asking each candidate to benchmark themselves against those they believe as best for the project. The CP should consider the extent to which certain firms prove reluctant or weak in this task as an early warning signal. Furthermore, the CP should probe the candidate firm's familiarity with all three sectors: commercial, social, and Intersectoral. Compensation should be heavily tied to performance, and the terms of engagement should address minimizing the risk for low value added and project lengthening issues.

Three firms are profiled in the appendix: a boutique, a mid-size firm, and a multinational organization. Each profile contains an introductory summary, strength and weakness highlights, and a seven criteria assessment. The seven criteria include: prior relevant experience in benchmarking, performance benchmarking, the social sector, and internationally; project compensation; time to completion; quality of previous presentations; flexibility; and previous background.

As part of the assessment, each was asked to respond to a hypothetical social sector-subsector project. The text of the assignment is as follows:

Parameters of assignment provided to each prospective benchmarking advisor included the following: evaluation of five organizations of which two will be NGOs and three commercial firms; social sectors of interest will be in the areas of either health care, low income housing, education, or human services; assessment of approximately 30 to 50 different parameters; field research will include one day of research at each organization; the process will adhere to a customary eight phase format and written output presentation will include determining benchmarking metrics and operating practices, quantification of Performance Gap evaluation, best practice identification, and performance improvement observations addressing quantification of costs and benefits of Deliverable Opportunities and Multiplier/Discount Effects.

The introductory summaries should provide a general sense of each firm; however, CPs should only use this information as the beginning of an assessment.

Charles E. Napier Company, Ltd. ("CEN") is a small boutique management consulting firm focused primarily on commercial sector performance benchmarking and improvement. Its managing executive, Harvey Goodwin, possesses an excellent understanding of the highest value-added levels of benchmarking for firm wide performance. CEN's expertise includes a limited number of NGOs. Prior assignments include a diverse group of global initiatives. The firm's work product appears ideally suited for New Philanthropy Benchmarking, as it offers organization and process level Performance Gap metrics, Deliverable Opportunity observations, and execution and assessment information that facilitate the determination and improvement of Multiplier/Discount Effects.

Best Practices, LLC (herein referred to as BP) is a small business research and consulting firm specializing in best practice benchmarking. BP maintains its own proprietary best management practice database, which is constantly updated through its own ongoing research. President and founder Chris Bogan is a recognized expert and author of highly acclaimed books concerning benchmarking and best practice performance improvement. BP's expertise includes a large number of Fortune 1000 companies but a limited number of NGO's. Prior assignments include a wide range of diverse companies studying areas such as customer service, knowledge management, sales and marketing, strategic partnerships, and leadership. Although BP (as of this writing) has limited experience with the investor perspectives of New Philanthropy Benchmarking, the firm does possess sufficiently impressive talents to allow them to be considered as an alternative. However, BP may require a comparatively greater investment of CP time to advance subsector studies, and the firm's traditional incentive compensation structure may sire unproductive counter-currents.

Arthur Andersen LLP is one of the largest consulting and accounting firms in the world with nearly 80,000 employees worldwide. The Metro New York Not-for-Profit Group ("NFP") consists of a group of professionals with expertise in accounting, auditing, tax, and consulting matters. One of the most significant areas of growth in this practice has been in the area of operational reviews (agreed upon procedures format). Arthur Andersen has significant experience reviewing the current operations of NGO clients and analyzing their policies, procedures and internal controls from a best practices perspective. The Metro NY NFP group is able to draw upon the significant resources throughout the firm and frequently work with practices areas within the firm such as the National Higher Education consulting practice. Its performance with NPB is currently under review, especially concerning macro-level NGO performance metrics. Team structure and terms of engagement will probably parallel characteristics of other major multi-national consulting organizations.

Internet Resources:

For purposes of NPB, Internet resources are grouped into two categories: benchmarking and general resources. A wealth of useful material is offered in both commercial sector and social sector benchmarking sites. Appendix M: Benchmarking Internet Sites contains a brief review of three commercial sector and four primarily social sector sites. The commercial sector sites are significantly more advanced. They offer both commercial metrics that can be directly or indirectly applied to social sector organizations and a more limited, but growing, selection of social sector information. The four social sector sites are emerging and offering a mixed-range in quality of content.

Currently, the concept of benefiting from sharing benchmarking information is rapidly expanding in the social sector. In the commercial sector many firms allow on-location visits by their competitors seeking to gain knowledge and increase productivity. This concept should be especially applicable with NGO's given that mission statements frequently tend to be similar. Finding Best Practices tends to be a quite common goal. However, as of this publication, the absence of sharing of hard metrics limits the quantity and quality of metrics within the more social sector focused Internet sites.

A few lines on each of the three commercial sector sites:

APQC (International Benchmarking Clearinghouse)
www.apqc.org.
APQC's approximately 500 members including over 100 social sector organizations in industries including higher education, government, health and human services, and faith based organizations. APQC's members receive access to proprietary best practices data in over 350 categories of value to NGOs.

Benchnet
www.benchnet.com
Benchnet is a large scale, daily updated, subscription based web service devoted to sharing experiences, superior business practices, and increasing the quality industry

quality standards. The 2,500 companies in 50 countries that are members of Benchnet engage in online forums and email surveys, which collect, evaluate, and disseminate quality benchmarking data. Members may initiate on-line email surveys.

Best–in-Class
www.best-in-class.com
Best practices LLC is a research and consulting firm that specializes in best practices benchmarking. Emphasis is on qualitative, as opposed to quantitative, data and analysis. Site offers a very limited social sector database.

Several words on four social sector sites:

The Center for What Works
www.whatworks.org
This website is currently under construction, but the description of its search functions takes a step towards creating a benchmarking society much like the established commercial sector. Assessment is withheld until further developments.

The Peter F. Drucker Foundation for Nonprofit Management
www.pfdf.org
The Peter F. Drucker Foundation's mission is to "lead social sector organizations toward excellence in performance." To this end, the foundation collects, evaluates, and disseminates "Innovations of the Week."

The Inter-Agency Benchmarking and Best Practice Council and The National Partnership for Reinventing Government
www.va.gov/fedbest
www.npr.gov/initiati/benchmk
These sites grew out of Al Gore's national partnership for reinventing government. The sites have excellent benchmarking background material but they are no longer very active.

The London Benchmarking Group (The Corporate Citizenship Company)
www.corporate-citizenship.co.uk/benchmrk.html
The London Benchmarking Group, a consulting firm, specializes in corporate community relation benchmarking. It seeks to "better define measures of efficiency and effectiveness of all types of community involvement activity by using benchmarking techniques."

As for the general Internet sites, five are recommended as offering potential worthy of CP consideration in connection with NPB. They have been selected to illustrate the vast range of relevant offerings on the Internet. Appendix N: Internet General Resources contains a brief summary, of which just a few words are provided below. As noted earlier, it is appropriate to note that these sites are in development and quality, comprehensive financial metrics are quite rare.

Alliance for Community Technology
www.communitytechnology.org
Alliance for Community Technology contains an extensive online database of technology tools for NGOs.

E-philanthropy Database
www.communitytechnology.org/databases/ephil
Organization effectiveness resources for NGOs. Currently the best-in-class database.

GuideStar
www.guidestar.org
A valuable resource for collecting NGO and foundation information is Guidestar. This is a rapidly improving site that contains 990 tax filing information. As of November 2000, Guidestar says that every week approximately 6,000 visitors read a 990, a small fraction of the 2.5 million Web page hits that it records weekly.[159] Apparently, most of those who utilize the service are grant officers at foundations, charity regulators, watchdogs, and journalists.[160]

The Roberts Enterprise Foundation
www.redf.org
REDF's website is based on venture philanthropy. This site offers free publications from REDF on philosophy and practice of social entrepreneurship, venture philanthropy, and the ever-changing social sector. Additional papers are available by other individuals exploring the many challenges of social sector enterprise and investing in social change organizations.

UK Charity Commission
www.charitycommission.uk.org
The United Kingdom took an exemplary step by establishing a commission that has the power of a court to review and regulate NGOs. This commission differs

from the IRS in that if offers guidance and best practice examples for NGOs and that it has objectives aimed at restructuring NGOs to become more accountable.

Further Reading:

Appendix P: Further Reading and Information contains a rather expansive listing of materials utilized both directly and indirectly in the Working Book. It is envisioned that at some point following publication of this work, the list will be periodically updated via the Internet and organized via a database search engine to facilitate interactive inquiry.

Also, CPs may wish to research George Bush's proposed program for benchmarking information. According to campaign material, George Bush will establish a Compassion Capital Fund that will access federal and private money to pay for research to determine the best practices among charities, support training so charities can use those practices, and provide start-up capital to qualified charities that want to emulate or expand model programs.[161] This appears to be an extension of the former Vice President Gore's initiative for Reinventing Government, which is profiled within NPB's Internet Resources section and appendix.

Bush is also strongly pushing the involvement of faith-based organizations as contractors to the government in serving those in need. Though this plan has increasing support, it has also earned its share of critics, including conservatives. The surprisingly critical comments from expected advocates are in part based on concern that the government will effectively gain control over the faith-based organizations via increasing reliance on its funds. Some suggest that tax-deductions are a more effective method to accomplish the same without raising constitutional and control issues.[162]

Section Seven

Momentum and Obstacles to NPB

Wisdom 7: "Generate momentum, expect obstacles."

Suggestions To Improve Probability of Success:

Improving the probability of success in the social sector requires a clear focus on critical factors and a concentrated effort to maintain simplicity. CPs are well advised to keep in mind these five key points.

First, concentrate on continuous improvement, which is a focus on improving processes. Second, focus on continuous betterment, and the outcome of the activity will improve. Third, keep it simple. All too often NGOs become distracted by the possibilities rather than staying close to the goals of its mission statement. Doing a few things very well is better then doing much with mediocrity.

Fourth, everyone has his or her own area of expertise; utilize your own. Remember that "benchmarking attacks only 10 percent of the problem; the other 90 percent involves changing your culture, processes, and whole philosophy so you can encourage your employees to learn and share ideas."[163] A New York Times article discussed how benchmarking can help significantly more than it can hurt. Cultural issues will be addressed later and are most likely the greatest cause of resistance.

The fifth and possibly most valuable of the five points: initially assume your situation performance statistics are average and that the benchmarking group is essentially a normal distribution. The statistical measurement of bell curves applies to practically every situation. About 97 percent of NGOs will claim that they are the best, that virtually everyone is comparatively great, and that there is really no way to measure the difference between NGOs. This claim is untrue, and there will be resistance when you challenge the status quo. Your goal is to challenge the staff to prove, with hard metrics, that your bell curve assumption – with them being average – is inaccurate.

Jed Emerson comments on responsible grant making: "a foundation's grants are viewed as part of a program area and grants are awarded on an individual basis with little respect for the aggregate value to those investments. For the foundation, there is minimal risk exposure in making a grant, as the process of grant-making is what fulfills the mission of the organization."[164] Emerson suggests that foundations need to be presented with consequences when they deal with grants inefficiently.

Intuitive Benchmarking:

Not unlike the commercial sector, CPs should expect to hear of the common existence of the skills known as intuitive benchmarking. As the name suggests, this is a self-proclaimed skill in the social sector that is claimed to be a prominent and well understood as the term "non-profit." Indeed, some organizations and consulting firms seeking to sell the prominence of benchmarking will design their definitions to prompt the participants to designate almost any causal comparison of information as benchmarking. Some studies have gone so far as to conclude that 80%+ of the NGO participants practice some form of benchmarking – even without knowing it. Encouraging classification of intuitive benchmarking as true by social sector managers should be strongly discouraged. Perpetuating solely on intuitive analysis is irresponsible at best.

One of the more respected commercial sector benchmarking professionals strongly cautions against similar weak practices. "Relying on intuition, opinion, or assumption only leads to 'guesstimates' that cannot ensure validity or reliability. At the risk of overstatement, these two factors are essential to an effective process. A benchmarking process must follow a 'management-by-fact, data driven approach to business process analysis rather than a 'management-by-gut' intuition approach."[165]

Yes, a select number of CPs and super-skilled NGO managers may have a unique gift to simulate a methodical benchmarking process via intuitive judgement, but this is exceedingly rare and should be deemed as such. George Soros, Michael

Steinhardt, and Michael Milken may have intuitive skills for finance; Bill Gates for technology; and Edgar Bronfman, Spielberg, and Monaghan for understanding the American public; but building long-lasting organizational capacity and strength requires process. A passionate CP is advised to treat the claims of intuitive benchmarking by NGO managers as much more of a sign of weakness of process and a considerable cause of concern.

The educational process of maximizing the potential of benchmarking requires a considerable investment, especially in education and culture development.

Reference Issues To Be Resolved:

Emerging ideas promote a number-based return on equity to assess NGOs. However, the existence of number manipulation is not a surprise. The government fully funds the SEC to prevent public companies from number manipulation to sell a story. There is little reason to think that NGOs differ.

An instance of social sector number manipulation occurred with a museum measured on attendance. The museum had busloads of local school children shipped in for visits to boast attendance numbers. Only when the revenue per attended number was assessed was the tactic revealed. The revenue was initially hidden by not including the school program into the ratio of percentage of paid attendees to total attendees by including a footnote stating that school programs were excluded. However, school attendees were included in total attendee numbers.

An example of number manipulation reminds us that numeric measurements will not be the Holy Grail, as there are many different reference issues to resolve when assessing Best Practices. These reference issues to be resolved reinforce the concept that there is no replacement for sound judgement. Numbers are not the sole answer.

Momentum:

John Whitehead comments that "running a not-for-profit is definitely more difficult than running a for-profit company."[166] The statement provides another reason for the importance of motivation in benchmarking implementation. The momentum will need to be provided by someone who can maintain the process and be undeterred by resistance. This maintenance will need to be provided on a daily basis and the managers should have the skills to communicate and provide a strict structure.

Resistance should be expected not only by lower employee levels, but also by senior manager levels. Managers should be aware of the frequently repeated advice that the more changes occur, the greater the stress – that benchmarking creates the imperative for change creating stress and anxiety. Implementing new processes will take time. Paul Light reminds us that "innovating organizations are stressful places, healthy and natural but still stressful."[167]

The importance of demonstrating performance success early and then expanding to more challenging projects is imperative so that you gain the support of your culture. A culture change can effectively prohibit resistance in many NGOs utilizing the goal of increasing positive ideas to improve productivity. A key thought to remember: don't try everything from the start, as it is necessary to keep it simple and accomplish small goals first.

The frequently misplaced social sector managerial hubris brings to mind a telling comic mimicking the sales pitch of a prospective executive to an executive recruiter: "I've had quite a bit of experience running non-profit organizations. I've headed four corporations, and none of them has made a profit."[168]

CPs Claim a Subsector:

CPs should consider fostering significant change by serving as social sector catalysts in organizing and managing subsector benchmarking studies. High quality benchmarking information is essential and without question requires a considerable investment of time and talents. Obtaining a representative selection within a subsection will require powerful leadership to motivate NGO to participate in the process, dedicate the required time, and strive to provide quality information.

Illustrations of successful subsector benchmarking do exist in various forms. Somewhat surprisingly, several insightful case studies hail from Canada. In particular, one well-developed and documented example found the Canadian government serving as a sponsor seeking to improve a designated industry. Although not a social sector industry, the goals of community enhancement and the role of an impartial catalyst can serve as a useful role model for CP generated programs. The case study is an excellent example of the application of performance measurement and benchmarking at both the organization level and sector level. Details of the case study can be found in Chapter 14 of a case study anthology titled "Global Cases in Benchmarking."[169]

It suffices to say that considerable effort was expended in assuring outstanding quality of information. Professionals with considerable sector management and financial experience team up with premier benchmarking professionals to lead the process of internal analysis and global external comparative analysis, thereby fostering successful application by narrowing performance gaps via management application of deliverable opportunities.

Little hope for rapid substantial success can be expected from either external-only benchmarking studies, self-compiled surveys, or consultant-only projects. Although some may claim that the latter category of approaches is an acceptable baby step, such a half-hearted approach should be viewed as nothing more than a weak and timid alternative.

Strongly Incentivized Leadership:
Without question, successful NPB requires motivated leadership and team members. Cultural issues abound and change will be required highly-incentivized social sector competitive compensation.

CPs should expect to hear that statistics from benchmarking – especially NP Benchmarking – are essentially a foreign language. To the contrary, CPs should incentivize NGOs to talk quantitative success story situations, especially on a competitive basis. Encourage NGO executives to focus on benchmarking for processes, programs, and policies. Incentivize them to prepare and present macro NPB assessments of their entire organization. Don't fall for the social sector myth that only in the social sector can superior performance get criticized given the lack of agreed upon metrics.

In the commercial sector, new management teams often arrive on the scene and have less than favorable words for the prior well-thought of management. Likewise, more aggressive investors demand even greater performance than what had previously been considered quite acceptable.

In addition to incentivizing NGOs to present Performance Gap and Multiplier/Discount Effects, challenge them to move to understand the enabler underlying these measurement and adapt, not simply adopt.

Without strong leadership, NGOs will be particularly challenged in their ability to successfully implement benchmarking efforts. Superior management must receive high percentage compensation. No longer willing or able to work for, as David La Piana describes, "discounted labor," skilled nonprofit managers are leaving the social sector for more lucrative positions in the for-profit sector.[170]

Commercial sector to social sector compensation disparity starts early. In a study of recent Cornell undergraduates, researchers observed that earnings for those employed by commercial sector firms were 250% of NGOs, even accounting for gender, GPA, and college curriculum.[171] The disparity only magnifies with an increase in seniority. It is not uncommon for CEOs of commercial firms to earn tens if not hundreds of times more than their social sector counterparts. Faced with this sort of disparity, attracting and retaining quality social sector managers has become increasingly challenging.

One veteran of the social sector notes: "The challenge today is to insure that students from the business, law, and professional schools at Harvard, Stanford, and other great universities don't view working in this sector as a career detour, but rather as a career builder."[172]

Several points of pressure are increasing the need for competitive compensation in the social sector. There should be little question that compensation issues are increasingly driving attraction and retention of employees.

First, there is growing competition for employees within the sector. With a small pool of trained managerial talent, competition for social sector executives is fierce. Increasingly, compensation is even being used as a tool to attract social sector executives. Gordon Gee, for instance, was recently hired away from Ivy League Brown University to head Vanderbilt University where his compensation package was reportedly doubled.

Competition from the commercial sector is also placing pressure on social sector employee attraction and retention. A tight labor market, particularly for skilled managers, has led to an increased interest in managers of social sector enterprises by commercial sector entities. Dr. John Rowe, for instance, was recruited from Mt. Sinai Hospital to run Aetna Insurance's $26 billion total assets even though he had nominal large public company experience. His management experience in the social sector, however, was excellent preparation. In a Wall Street journal article, he notes that "the challenges are not as great as they might seem on the surface. There are many similarities in managing a hospital, which can be formidable."[173] The commercial sector is also increasingly attracting talents from the government sectors. As covered in a front page story in the September 2000 New York Times, senior scientists making $90,000 at a government laboratory can go to private companies and increase their salaries by 50%; and add lucrative stock options.[174] The attrition among scientists increased from a traditionally 4% to recently double digits.[175] The attrition among scientists in the computing division at Los Alamos has more than doubled in the past two years; with the Advanced Computing Laboratory hardest hit losing 41%.[176]

Finally, pressure for employees is being felt via head to head competition. A need for new revenue sources as well as the increasing size of the social sector market has increased commercial sector movement into the social sector and hence the pressure upon employee attraction and retention. For instance, Charitableway is a commercial entity provides many of the same services as the social sector United Way. In many cases, these "intersectoral" organizations are commercial subsidiaries or spin-offs of NGOs managed by executives with commercial backgrounds and compensation expectations. The College Board, for instance, recently hired a former high-ranking executive from Dupont Corporation to run a commercial spin-off.

Not surprisingly, the structure of compensation packages receives – as it should – careful attention. Packages that directly relate pay to performance encourage value creating action by managers, while those that lack this linkage foster at best indifference towards value creation and at worst encourage value destroying behavior. Pay packages developed by Stern Stewart & Co. for the US Postal Service, for instance, linked pay to creation of Economic Value Added (EVA). In this way, the successful completion of the US Postal Service's objectives were aligned with management compensation.[177]

In contrast, the index linked option plans advocated by certain accounting firms do not directly link pay to performance. These plans provide the social enterprise executive with options on an index of stocks, often at a strike price below the market price of the stock. This creates an opportunity for significant financial gain for the social enterprise executive.

The price of the index, and hence the value of the options, however, are not related to the performance of the social enterprise. Consequently, there is not an alignment between the successful completion of the social enterprise's objectives and management's objectives.

Regardless of the package selected, the CP should insure that fair and complete disclosure be made in the proper venue. Inadequate disclosure and the appearance of obfuscation can eviscerate even the most potentially effective package.

A word of caution is necessary, especially in the context of executive compensation at foundations. A significant movement is developing within the social sector questioning the potential contra-fiduciary issues associated with the goal of maximizing return on foundation assets in order to increase investment asset basis with little or no consideration to the present value or opportunity costs of lost mission. A related source of concern is the apparent relationship between asset size and foundation executive compensation. The information contained in the chart 12 below indicates a common sense expected correlation.

Statistically, it appears quite clear that the salary compensation levels – for all intents and purposes – moves in step with the foundation asset dollar value. In fact, the relationship in virtually all cases is a compelling positive correlation. An increase in asset base of 20% from the $25 to $49 million to the $50 to $99 million range shows a corresponding median increase of 25% or a 74% increase in maximum compensation. And breaking the $250 million asset level from the $100 to $249 million level has a corresponding median salary increase of 52% or a maximum salary level of $570,000, a 75% increase.

Chart 12: Summary Foundation CEO Salaries by Asset Group

Asset Group (in millions)	Median	Mean	Max	# of FDNS
• $250 or more	$ 217,000	$ 243,960	$ 570,000	112
• $100 to $249.9	$ 142,500	$ 151,762	$ 325,000	92
• $50 to $99.9	$ 100,000	$ 109,207	$ 270,000	77
• $25 to $49.9	$ 80,000	$ 84,233	$ 155,000	76
• $10 to $24.9	$ 65,000	$ 70,944	$ 171,400	110
• $5 to $9.9	$ 51,250	$ 55,382	$ 126,075	38

Source: Council on Foundations. Preliminary data from 2000 salary survey database, subject to change. As of February 1, 2000.

A simple economic model indicates that over a several year period, the difference between a full payout of foundation asset appreciation and a 5% payout could mean a cumulative impact equal to approximately one-third of the CEO's current salary, which is quite material. Alternatively, if the CEO of a $10 million plus asset foundation increases the assets of his foundation by 20% per year, his median salary (after approximately 5 years) could equal $80,000, an increase of over 23%. Assuming 5% average inflation (per year over 5 years) the figure would equal $102,000, an increase of over 57%!

Executive Educational Alternatives:

As NP Benchmarking requires sound decision making beyond the NPB process itself, solid educational training is a decided positive. Given the current state of social sector management, CPs should anticipate the need to encourage executives in this sector to further their professional education with executive level courses that provide commercial content targeted to the progressive social sector or intersectoral manager. Chart 13: NPB Executive Education Matrix provides a summary of the strengths and weaknesses of the five profiled programs. Appendix Q: Executive Educational Alternatives provides a select sampling of alternatives currently and prospectively available. Two of the established executive education programs reviewed are the Harvard Business School and Stanford Business School social sector executive educational offerings. Yale's recently evolved program is profiled; however, its executive education offering appears to require larger groups and customization. Columbia Business School offers a unique several week program customized for progressive social sector executives. As for a more cutting-edge alternative, the distance learning offerings of United University are reviewed (www.unit-edu.com).

By and large, the educational alternatives evaluated are staffed by highly qualified professionals. Technology receives an increasing level of attention, with Stanford understandably offering an impressive integration. Networking contacts appear strong across the board. Most offer sufficient selection of basic courses, with an increasing emphasis on more progressive Intersectoral Practices at Harvard, Stanford, and 2U (prospectively). Yale has a particularly extensive selection of more traditional social sector courses, with an expanding focus on more contemporary topics. The multiple graduate programs at the major schools are a plus in offerings and staffing. Case content is good but possibly too heavily focused on the social sector, from a policy perspective in contrast to a more Intersectoral purview. Most of the established schools are increasing the number of workshops and special programs. The flexibility of course offering and schedules is rather limited with the exception of the currently under-development 2U. As Yale's offering is quite limited, it offers the opportunity to structure programs for groups.

In all, the programs are impressive, but offer considerable room for advancement in Intersectoral offerings and value creation teachings.

For those CPs interested in assessing further human resource and team building information with it in the social sector, The Harvard Business School offers a "Guide to Careers in the Nonprofit Sector." This guide is a good introductory work touching on employee motivations, social enterprise, career continuum, job search processes, industry subsector definitions (which are summaries in the associated endnote), expectations and cultural differences, and career resources.[178]

A few relevant words of caution from one industry compensation observer: be alert to comparable compensation numbers. In particular, the private education industry compensation numbers often require numerous adjustments in order to compare with other social sector NGOs. Within private educational institutions, it is not uncommon for educators to receive other benefits (which may be treated favorably for tax purposes) such as housing and free or subsidized tuition for relatives. In one example, a high school teacher received a home with an average annual lease value of $20,000 and full tuition for three children of varying ages for a total of $250,000 over 10 years or an average of $25,000. Before the benefits of tax preferences are included, the initial package of compensation of $60,000 is increased to $105,000. Additionally, the teacher received three months off for the summer where he earned $10,000 for two months of tutoring, retaining one month as vacation time. This provided a comparable package of $115,000 or almost 100% normalizing adjustment for other social sectors.

The controversy over performance pay for teachers offers an on-point example in a social subsector pressed for accountability and reform. There appears to be relatively less disagreement that performance-based pay is one of the better tactics to improve teacher performance. This is considered especially relevant in a subsector where 40% of the new teachers leave after the first year.[179] However, the situation is very complex and challenging to implement. During the summer of 2000, the primary reason the National Education Association rejected a conservative proposal to endorse performance-based pay reportedly involved issues of equity.

Chart 13: New Philanthropy Benchmarking, Executive Education Matrix

School	Strengths	Weaknesses
Columbia University	1. Low student-teacher ratio 2. Diverse student body 3. Large number of faculty practitioners 4. In-depth instruction 5. State of the art instructional resources	1. Little emphasis on technology 2. Little stated distance learning or web-based initiatives
Harvard University	1. Instructors researched and wrote many of the case studies used and are highly involved in social sector 2. High quality senior level students with diverse (cultural, educational, and professional) backgrounds 3. Networking opportunities 4. High level of peer-to-peer interaction 5. Name recognition	1. Small selection of programs focused on NGOs and social enterprise 2. Short duration of program 3. High student-teacher ratio
Stanford University	1. Within MBA program, Public Management Initiative including workshops, conferences, work-service projects 2. Internship Fund and Loan Forgiveness Program 3. Professors strong in health care 4. Close proximity to Silicon Valley	1. Few executive education courses for the social sector professional. 2. Lack of depth 3. High student-teacher ratio
United University	1. Extensive intersectoral course offerings -- prospective 2. Value creation course content 3. Social sector transformation mission focus 4. Unique exec. time value sensitivity 5. Structured class interaction and 24/7/365 access 6. Mostly faculty practitioners	1. Requires proactive approach. Non-passionate need not apply. 2. Designed primarily for senior mgt. 3. Emerging initiative
Yale University	1. Unique public/private sector program 2. Many faculty practitioners 3. Vast selection of course offerings 4. Broad network of contacts 5. Strong ties to other graduate schools	1. Relatively weak technology program 2. Not as strong as the top schools in traditional MBA disciplines (e.g., finance, marketing, technology) 3. Relatively weak recruiting effort

"In general, teachers don't believe a fair and objective system has yet been developed that can ensure that evaluations would be truly based on merit, instead of the whims of an administrator."[180] As noted in Wisdom Point Seven, "Generate momentum, expect obstacles." NP benchmarking can provide reliable information especially if elements of competitive pressures can be developed, i.e. Wisdom Point Five ("Yes, competitive social sector measurement tactics do exist.")

NPB CPs should be attentive to other on-line educational developments. For example, MIT announced in April of 2001 that it will commence a 10-year initiative, dubbed OpenCourseWare, to create public web sites (free-access) for almost all of its 2,000 courses and to post materials like lecture notes, problem sets, syllabi, exams, simulations, and even video lectures online. The Chairman of the project, Professor Steven Lerman, noted that "selling content for profit, or trying in some ways to commercialize one of the core intellectual activities of the university seemed less attractive to people at a deep level than finding ways to disseminate it as broadly as possible." The cost is estimated at $100 million.[181]

Addressing Prospective NPB Voices of Caution:
Not surprisingly, there are a certain number of respected social sector professionals who voice strong words of caution over many of the emerging trends associated with NPB. In fact, some claim that the complexities of NGOs require managers with skills and talents unique to and possibly superior to the commercial sector. One such article proclaims as its title, "What Managers Can Learn from Nonprofits."[182]

Others attack the notion of applying commercial practices such as venture philanthropy. One of the more frequently touted sages in this regard has a lead article titled "If Pigs Had Wings." His primary theme is well summed up in his articles opening line: "It's sexy to compare grant making to venture capitalism. It's also dead wrong."[183] Some even go so far as to strongly criticize using quantification to measure result, such a one mid-west NGO association head who says that "I think it's heading in the wrong direction. It's turning human lives and communities into some kind of statistical formula. I don't think that's the way nonprofits serve their missions and help their communities …[such efforts] drive you to do only what you can measure instead of measuring what you should be doing."[184]

There should be little question that both perspectives have considerable validity. The former is correct in noting that NGOs are more complex to manage, especially given the challenges associated with many more qualitative missions and goals as well as the lack of organization capacity. Also, the latter expresses worthy words of caution, especially highlighting the dangers of unqualified foundation offices proactively meddling in the operations of NGOs. Yes, there are dangers in unqualified individuals with assets and power pushing control over day-to-day operations and seeing the all too real law of negative unintended consequences.

Recognizing these words of caution, CPs should approach their efforts with caution, but with many of the same talents – including tenacity – that they utilize to accomplish their successes.

As for the issue of the complexity of managing in the commercial sector, it would be quite naïve to think that there are not multiple constituencies with conflicting agendas in almost every successful commercial operation. Issues of long-term versus short-term, capital allocation, and community/employee issues are constantly in a state of dynamic tension.

Furthermore, the claim that the employees of commercial operations are myopically and solely focused on profit is inconsistent with a reality where most employees' daily focus is on issues associated with customer satisfaction, positive vendor relationships, and strong employee relationships. To act otherwise would be contrary to long-term organization building.

Let it also be said that the vast majority of major innovations in marketing, organizational management, financial engineering, technologies, and compensation programs have been sired from the commercial sector.

As for the concerns of foundations damaging NGOs with proactive involvement, several observations are appropriate. First, successful CPs have a vastly different skill base than many currently passive foundation professionals. Second, it is inconceivable to pretend that the allocation of the lifeblood of foundations' funding does not have a profound impact on the direction of NGOs. This is especially true given the astronomical fund-raising costs and restrictive/oppressive terms under which these fund are raised. Third, the weaknesses of current foundation professionals will change, sooner or later, as those influential overseers realize that uncompetitive compensation packages are forcing many of the most talented, motivated, and creative managers and professionals to dismiss the social sector as a viable career path in favor of the commercial sector.

More directly on point in response to claims of risks associated with applying NPB, CPs should endorse the principal that knowledge is power and power is freedom. Building organizational capacity via a compressive understanding of best practices, performance margins, deliverable opportunities, performance gaps, and multiplier/discounts have a greater probability of serving as catalysts for positive change than the risks associated with unintended consequences. As for those who claim that it is better for unskilled managers to be shielded from such information, as they don't have the skills to properly assess or will mis-assess the information and take actions that will have reign of negative consequences, it is enough to say that such attitudes obviously mandate major culture changes to be inline with the basic tenets of contemporary democratic society.

Misconceptions:

Misconceptions of benchmarking can be seen in the following two quotes. Sievers, author of "If Pigs Had Wings," states that "there is no counterpart in the nonprofit world to the for-profit world's single bottom-line variable, return on investment (ROI). ROI is essential to the logic of venture capital; indeed, it is the entire point of the investment."[185]

This statement is true. There is no single bottom line in the social sector; there are multiple bottom lines. The reason benchmarking is so effective is because it assesses individual processes. But as any senior manager knows, there is rarely just one metric of concern – even the ROI – which can be used to the exclusion of all others. Any successful analysis requires multiple measures and metrics.

In addition, there is the inevitable conflict over studies and numbers, which really is little different than CPs' daily experience in the commercial sector. One on point social sector example involves the controversy over the effectiveness of the national Drug Abuse Resistance Education (DARE) program. A growing number of elected officials are seeking to end funding for the program in their communities. DARE classes are now part of the curriculums in approximately 10,000 school districts in the United States and at schools in 54 other countries.[186]

One mayor commented that "DARE is a complete fraud on the American people, and has actually done a lot of harm by preventing the implementation of more effective programs."[187] Citing the fruits of his research, "to my amazing dismay, all the peer-reviewed research shows that DARE is a complete waste of money and, even worse, fritters away the opportunity of implement a good drug-prevention program in schools."[188] In response, defenders of the program say such statistics are unfair and the results have long-term unquantifiable benefits.

Here is a prime situation where NPB could seek to assess the disparity in views. Comparable programs could be evaluated and components of a Performance Gap calculated as well as a Multiplier/Discount Effect. Such a NPB analysis could be conducted at a minimum with internal DARE statistics and preferably with external statistics of comparable programs.

A second misconception is illustrated by a quotation from Stephen Nelson author of "What Can Managers learn from Nonprofits?" Nelson claims, "they (nonprofits) must be cutting edge in order to survive – and the only way to do that is to fertilize and grow cutting edge people."[189] True, NGOs must be cutting edge, but there are a few fields where they are not cutting edge and can learn from the commercial organizations. In areas such as the Internet, finance, and management, commercial firms often assert the cutting edge. In these areas among others, NGOs could benefit from the skills of commercial sector organizations.

Listing a small sampling of social sector misconceptions relating to benchmarking provides a CP with a basic idea of the unreasonable and massive amount of resistance likely encountered. Claims that benchmarking conflicts with the social sector mission are patently false.

In virtually all situations, social sector missions are to help, and benchmarking can be used to increase productivity and mission goals. Therefore, assisting an NGO to become more productive and increase the probability of helping more people can not be against an NGO mission statement.

Another frequently espoused misconception is that benchmarking uses negative commercial sector principles. The claim that benchmarking is too similar to maximizing profit is slightly true because benchmarking in the commercial sector is used for performance maximization. However, accusations of guilt-by-association appeal falsely to a cultural bias. NGOs also claim that they can't be compared to others; NPB asserts that everything can be compared, especially when discussing bell curves.

NGOs claim that assessments following productivity implementation can be humiliating. While this is a true statement, those who are wasting money and having a harmful effect should be informed of the effect of their processes. The previously mentioned Michael Porter also wrote about the effect of evaluations and accountability on philanthropy. "Until foundations accept their accountability to society and meet their obligation to create value, they exist in a world where they cannot fail. Unfortunately, they also cannot truly succeed."[190]

As for those in the social sector who continue to claim that business has little place, especially in the very life sensitive areas, consider the following observation by a well regarded national executive. John Rowe, the recently named CEO of Aetna U.S. Health Care, and former highly successful president and CEO of Mount Sinai NYU Health, provided a high value observation in response to the question "Is there a danger in mixing business with medicine as a doctor?" His response, "I don't think it's a bad thing. I've been a business-oriented manager for a long time and being that way has permitted us to serve more patients better than we could have if were not business-oriented."[191]

Not surprisingly, NPB CPs will not need to look far to find rampant public controversy over NPB related issues. Within a small several week period, major newspapers were carrying front page stories on such controversies. Such an example includes an ownership debate at National Public Radio (NPR), the Edison Schools' bid to manage several failing Brooklyn schools, and a *NYT* editorial questioning the merits of considering the student as a customer.

The NPR debate centered around an erudite radio talk show "The Connection" owned by the Boston station WBUR-FM and the effective rebellion by its host. The host, Christopher Lydon, reportedly left over a dispute involving proprietorship and revenue splits of his program, which had grown to reach over 400,000 listeners in the Boston area. Mr. Lydon reportedly wanted to own some form of equity or earn increased compensation based on WBUR's expansion of the show to other public radio stations. The station proposed a base salary increase to $230,000. For Lydon's part, he wanted to share in the growth of the broadcasts in "new markets, new media, and new revenue streams." Comments on the radio station's Internet site highlight the fundamental controversies to be expected as NPB and other Intersectoral initiatives grow. Mr. Lyon writes, "I have known all along that we weren't picking Jane Christo's (the radio station manager) cotton. It's our cotton." One station competitor comment, "The mission of public radio has never been to make money. This crazy private venture stuff is changing the whole picture and putting a bad taste in everyone's mouth. They assume, wrongly, that we're all the same." Lydon respond that " she can do what suits her, I think there's also an entrepreneurial spirit in the land, in the culture, and in our program that points another way. This is not a sort of priesthood. It is not a Civil Service job." In response to the WBUR's claim that Lydon was seeking a share of underwriting revenues, he wrote, "he never would touch the listeners donations, which he calls 'the church money.'" Of course, NPB CPs know that dollars are fungible and such a claim is unrealistic. One industry observer astutely noted that he thought the fight was unfortunate, but in an industry where many are in financial peril, the fight may be a good sign for the industry: "Thank God that somebody's making money."[192]

The Edison schools ran into a public buzz saw in bidding to manage several failing Brooklyn, New York public schools. The *New York Times* headline "Confusion, The Fervent Opposition to a Plan to Privatize 5 Schools" hints at the controversy surrounding the circumstances.[193] At one public forum, "the speakers evoked the wounds of past discrimination, the [school] board's neglect of their schools, of the divisive decentralization battles of the 1960's, and of programs imposed by a Republican mayor and central school board that are deeply mistrusted in many of the affected communities. Edison representatives and board officials listened in shock. 'Nobody expected this highly emotional opposition,' said Seymour Fliegal, President of the Center for Educational Innovation-Public Education Association, a policy group. 'They way underestimated what could happen.'" The plan failed, leaving all to consider other alternatives, but with the schools, student, and communities still in desperate need. Much of this debate is affected by the controversy over standardized scores utilized especially by for-profit schools.[194] "Opponents contend that some, if not all, of the improvement in the school's scores on standardized tests stem from a change in a school's population under Edison. It now has fewer impoverished black students and more middle-class and Hispanic students." Edison refutes these claims and also notes that either way more children are doing better.[195]

A *New York Times* editorial by Michele Tolela Myers, president of Sarah Lawrence College, pines for the lost days when those running the colleges determined direction without the pressure of today's market forces. She decries the application of many commercial sector principles to education, especially being judged relative to

other schools. At a recent conference she learned about various new "ways to operate more efficiently and make the most of our assets, we begin learning about outsourcing, for-profit ventures, and the buying and selling of intellectual property."
She warned that such focus has pushed universities to "bid for student talents,"
building the "Star Value" into the student body so as to affect a school's "Brand
Value" – "its prestige, its ranking, its desirability, and ultimately its wealth and its
ability to provide more 'value per dollar to its 'customers.'" She questions the need
to be driven by being the 'best in the world." She asks, "Have we really come to
believe that we can only measure ourselves in relation to others, and that value and
goodness are only measured against something outside the self? Do we really want
to teach our children that life is all about beating the competition? Are we ready to
think that we should only teach what students want or be driven out of business?"[196]
NPB – pragmatically applied – clearly has its view.

Culture Issues:

There will be excessive resistance to new approaches, which often cause the implementation to get stuck. Some of the culture resistance excuses are: insisting on the best,
that only current approaches will work, compensations may be out of sync with organization, or that senior management may be left out of loop. The absence of meaningful discussion and use of comparative performance numbers adds to cultural issues.

One of the greatest issues that would not be tolerated in a commercial sector firm is
the minimal consequence of inaccurate representations, especially numeric. Stephen
Goldsmith was mayor of Indianapolis for eight years and served as advisor to former Texas Gov. George W. Bush. He comments that "government bureaucrats themselves at all levels are resilient and tend to operate, through not explicitly, for their
own interests, and will fight strenuously to protect themselves from losing too much
authority."[197] NGOs claim that social sector organizations do not act in their own
interests but all the evidence and data confirms that even senior management creates
problems when changes are implemented.

"Benchmarking is such a change to the management process of most organizations.
It must be treated as a significant change and handled carefully, or, like many other
systematic transformations, it may suffer rejection, much like a heart transplant that
doesn't take,"[198] according to Gregory Watson.

This commercial sector idea is analogous to NGOs with these three social sector complaints: "1) many nonprofits may find their service cultures at odds with a learning approach like benchmarking, 2) the analysis and innovation that benchmarking can generate are wholly consistent with their ultimate goal of service: doing public good, and 3) nonprofits may believe that comparing benchmarking is too demanding for a staff and the organization involved."[199] These three concepts, explained by Letts, Ryan and Grossman in the previously mentioned book, are all illustrative examples of social sector resistance and need to be kept in mind when dealing with NGO cultures.

CPs should also expect noise from the ranks, especially if NPB wisdom is applied to large and diverse organizations. By way of example, the latest rumblings at the United Way (the September 2000 resignation of its president) appears to be in some part attributable to efforts to impose national standards on the 1,300 local United Ways that included requiring rigorous and public self-examination of their effectiveness every several years.[200] The move reportedly in some way influenced locals to withhold dues and another to consider a name change.

And don't expect too much in the way of transparency. Yes, GuideStar is a plus, but getting more detailed information runs into obstacles from both the lack of capacity as well as a culture of distrust. As Emerson notes in the recent Morino Institute publication, a representative cultural attitude of a rather typical old-school social sector manager, "we can't be too honest with our investors, since we still need to raise additional money in the future."[201]

Minimize Risk of Investment:

"The evil in the world always comes out of ignorance, and good intentions may do as much harm as malevolence, if they lack understanding."[202] However, "It is a moral and logical fallacy to conclude that because aid can do harm, a decision not to give aid would do no harm."[203]

Unfortunate situations and developments should be anticipated and preventive programs developed. Such situations can arise from multiple sources in isolation or some form of combination. Without striving for or advocating defined categories, the Working Book's observations in this area of misfortunate situations are generally classified in three areas: nefarious activities, unintended consequences, and wasted funds.

Although not covered extensively in the press or social sector literature, operating NGOs and foundations experience their share of misfortune covering all three areas. Appendix S: Social Sector Misfortunate Situations contains abbreviated samplings of illustrated misfortunate situations that have been a source of discussion within the social sector. The intent of this material is to offer a social sector comparable to the commercial sector and capital markets' risk of investment disclosure.

It is important for CPs to appreciate that even failure can offer benefits if lessons are shared openly with those interested in social sector initiatives. One article in The July/August 1998 issue of *Philanthropy* appropriately titled "Failure in Philanthropy" distinguishes between a well investigated and shared-information disappointment and a hidden failure. "Like the rest of us, foundations do not like to admit mistakes, and they like even less to publicize their failures."[204] The writer compares a 1982 to 1988 Rockefeller Foundation program and 1996 Oprah Winfrey initiative. The former shares the details as lessons learned; the latter was less than open. In a quite insightful observation, "One thing is certain, however. The costs of failing to document, communicate, and appreciate failed grants will surely prove more costly in the long run than any grantmaker now neglecting this task can possibly foresee."[205] "An open discussion of failed grants may be a first step in bringing some reality and frankness to the increasingly strained and distorted communications between foundations and their grant recipients."[206]

Although this is not the appropriate forum, several situations involving NGOs, contained in the appendix, offer examples of concerns that are quite traumatic: the United Way's New York senior executive in the early 90's, the impending collapse of the New Covenant charter School in New York, the costly lessons of the Los Angeles Community Development Bank, charges of dozens and dozens of NGO officers for fraud in connection with federally funded meal programs for deserving children, serious allegations of shoddy medical practices at Operation Smile (who count among their donors on this Working Book world class CPs such as Bill Gates), or the turmoil at Adelphi University. Others mentioned include Project Pathways, NGO name confusion, American Parkinson Disease Association, and Harvard University's Russian project.

Foundations have experienced several rather high-profile misfortunes as of late, including the fiasco surrounding the Saint Francis Assisi Foundation and the intense litigation of well known author Tom Clancy's Kyle Foundation. The criticisms of America's Promise appear less clear, but less than positive. There are also the self-dealing issues at the Bernice Pauahi Bishop Estate, and the important lessons learned from the New Era Foundation.

As for unintended consequences in the social sector, the occurrence has gained notoriety with the phrase "the law of unintended consequences." Michael Maren's book *The Road to Hell* provides a compelling, fact-driven exposé on the ravaging effects of foreign aid and international charity.[207] Or, a recent situation where a major United States funded organization must curtail funding of its foreign student exchange program given that instead of encouraging students to return home with their knowledge, virtually all participants have chosen to stay in the States and are encouraging their peers to leave for the United States as well, thus exasperating the 'brain-drain.'

Some social sector professionals are candid with their concern. As one individual noted, "we honestly think we are doing good work, but sometimes what we encourage can turn out to be a real disaster for the NGOs and the communities we serve."[208]

CPs also face the risk (as does the social sector) of being labeled "Dr. Evil Donor." The increasing power of billionaire CPs raises a number of interesting issues that are more appropriately addressed in an ethics forum.[209]

The exposure to the risk of unintended consequence violates the foremost rule of philanthropy: do no harm. Others have gone even further with words of caution regarding the subsector of welfare reform: "if you're doing something that doesn't work – that probably even makes things worse – the prudent course is to stop doing it."[210]

A chronicle of the situation in the Nuba Mountains of Sudan offers similar stories of concern but also works for hope that lesson of the past may alter international aid efforts in the future. The opening of the assessment notes the harsh reality, "but for all the mouths fed, the easy rock-star sloganeering of the 1980's Ethiopian famine ("Feed the world!) has been flattened by a more complicated reality –international relief can do more harm than good."[211] The call is now to build capacity, which is very consistent with the wisdoms of NPB and the with the emerging venture philanthropy sector. A significant concern in the Nuba situation is to avoid destroying the population's tough self-reliance.

In this context, Mary B. Anderson, who is currently considered the most influential theorist in the world of humanitarianism, is an intellectual force behind what is referred to as the "do no harm movement." "Her method is not poetry. She advises a strict analysis of the good and bad of any aid effort and to find ways around the bad. Practical ways, for example, to end soldiers' stealing food. Aid agencies, she argues, can work more closely with parts of society that have a greater commitment to peace or, at least, to functioning as envisioned. She does not, however, advocate going so far as to stop giving aid. 'Not to give aid can also cause harm,' she says. 'The decision not to give aid plays into war. We are embroiled whether we like it or not."[212] Offering further words on experience, she notes, "The challenge we see for aid workers — and for the large number of generous and caring individuals who support their work with financial and material contributions — is to figure out how to do the good they mean to do without inadvertently undermining local strengths, promoting dependency, and allowing aid resources to be misused in the pursuit of war."[213]

CPs are often aggressive and risk tolerant individuals who should practice a much higher level of risk aversion and risk minimization strategies in the social sector. Even well- intentioned and innocent efforts for expanding parochial school schol-arship programs can result in beneficiary schools being ejected from public school league or pushing already over-stressed educational infrastructures beyond capaci-ty. CPs should be careful not to rein unbridled financial hubris to the social sector. Although praised by an editorial in a major daily business publication, a million dollar insurance payment offer to inner city schools that convert to private status and revert back if unsuccessful is patently naive – indeed highly inconsiderate – of the potential human life consequences at state. And to think that a one million-dol-lar offer paid to the school system that fails the venture is both an appropriate incen-tive and an adequate compensation for the potential damages is quite unwise.[214]

Other situations summarized include student foreign exchange programs sponsored by United States, a potential example of high-risk challenge philanthropy. Although no examples are provided, the CP should be cognizant of a risk often referred to as the "crowding-out effect." Here, an NGO risks loss of either charitable funding or volunteer support in response to certain actions and events, perceived or real. Several frequently cited examples involve the loss of unrestricted donations as health care organizations move partially or completely into the commercial sector.

More controversial situations where harm or benefit is debated receive concentrated attention in Marvin Olasky's book, *The Tragedy of American Compassion.*

Also, CP generosity can trigger elevated expectations and competing institutional interests. Rensselaer Polytechnic Institute ("RPI") in Troy, N.Y, recently received an anonymous donation of $360 million, perhaps the largest gift ever to a U.S. college. RPI has indicated an interest in using the gift "to catapult RPI into the top tier of technological-research universities."[215] As it begins to invest these monies, it may be well-advised to assess from an NPB perspective the experience of Indiana's DePauw University, the recipient of a $128 million gift in 1995, and the unintended consequences of such an undertaking.[216]

Then, of course, there is the all too real risk of simply wasting funds. This is a particularly difficult topic to address as it is one that is customarily kept out of the public light. However, the real risks are highlighted by the observations of several CP benchmarks. "You know, it would be possible to blow $100 billion, and have no impact at all," says Patricia Stonesifer, who manages the $21 billion Bill and Melinda Gates Foundation."[217]

George Soros offers a relevant observation with his response to a query during a Brown University speech when asked whether good-intentioned philanthropy can create an undesirable and depressing trait of dependency on charity. "Charity goes against human nature. One of the paradoxes is that it makes people dependent. You can't rely on philanthropy to change the world."[218]

Another on-target statement appears in Andrew Carnegie's *The Gospel of Wealth*, where he cites not only the large waste of charity funds but also the risks of unintended consequences.

"Of every thousand dollars spent in so-called charity today, it is probable that nine hundred and fifty dollars is unwisely spent – so spent, indeed, as to produce the very evils which it hopes to mitigate or cure."[219]

An executive at one of the more respected foundations for its efforts on grant evaluation, The Robert Wood Johnson Foundation, candidly commented that "we are probably batting between .300 and .500… If we try 10 things – hard things like dealing with substance abuse or teenage smoking, programs where you are taking a risk – and three or four work, that's a great success rate. Think about it. Most things people do to improve things don't work."[220]

Other examples summarized in this section include: a discomforting perspective on Ted Turner's United Nations gift, the potentially high cost of endowment fund raising in connection with certain projects, the Drug Abuse Resistance Education program's effectiveness, and over-investment in NGO facilities.

There should be little question that NP Benchmarking can assist in providing a framework to greatly advance a social sector mission. At the same time, a NP Benchmarking framework offers the potential to isolate prospective concerns, thus allowing for more effective risk management. Powerful CPs should strongly consider requesting NGOs and possibly their foundation executives to provide a written discussion of risk assessment plans and programs.

Don't be surprised if such a request is met with considerable skepticism, indignation, or is even ridiculed as totally inapplicable. Keep in mind that for virtually every social sector manager or team member you interact with, concepts such as metrics, benchmarking, rigorous impact statistics, or competitive assessments are viewed with hostility. So, why should a CP expect a professional risk assessment statement or discussion to be viewed with anything other than even greater scorn?

The fact that the commercial sector has numerous situations where such risk discussion is effectively utilized is alone a strong reason for consideration in the social sector, but also will serve as sufficient for many less progressive thinkers in the social sector to be dismissive.

As NGOs progress with various commercial strategies and tactics, potential risks are a prudent topic of discussion. CPs should not be surprised to hear a laundry list of unfounded emotional, self-interest based, and even myth-like concerns. Nonetheless, reasonable concerns and analysis are merited. Topics of a comprehensive risk exposure analysis are limited to: the so-called "crowding-out" effect where donors, volunteers, and other socially minded stakeholders will depart as commercial activities increase (which affect cost of operations); distributional equity issues where one disadvantaged group is provided with less focus; other disutility issues such as loss of mission; damage to brand name and associated NGO "community trust" images; or even exposure of preferential taxation benefits.

An ideal opportunity for such disclosure is in connection with such capital markets funding as discussed in the Capital Markets NPB subsection. The discussion could take the form of three sections similar to those mentioned above: 1) policies and processes to protect against nefarious activities, 2) disclosure of potential "unintended consequences" considered by management based on careful research of other external and internal appropriate situations and programs to minimize such risks, and 3) discussion of risks of wasted funds, specific metrics to be utilized in measuring this risk, and disclosure of the approximate dates to which the metrics apply.

As mentioned in Wisdom Point Two, "CPs aggressively talk external comparative numbers," see the Social Sector Misfortunate Situations subsection or Appendix S for a summary review of selected publicly covered examples.

Capital Markets NPB:

Recognition and importance of the social capital markets is increasing, especially as professional attention gathers greater publication.

Within the social sector, an upcoming work by REDF and HBS's Jed Emerson, titled "The Nature of Returns: A Social Capital Markets Inquiry into Elements of Investment and The Blended Value Proposition" propels the understanding and importance of this topic to a new level. Prior works on the topic note, "Historically, discussions of funding in the nonprofit sector have touched primarily on grants, annual funding campaigns, direct mail and endowment funds. Only recently have these discussions evolved toward a realization that the resources supporting the work of the social sector are more than simply a variety of charitable fundraising efforts, but actually form a distinct capital market: The Nonprofit Capital Market."[221] Other works such as those by Caroline Williams and various governmental finance organizations are generating important instructional materials in this topic area.[222]

More recently Emerson has tri-authored a piece "Going Mainstream: NPO's Accessing the Capital Markets - Exploring the Use of Traditional Financing Methods, Processes and Debt Instruments for Expanding the Capital Structure of Non-Profit Community and Economic Development Organizations." Although most of the material is basic, the checklists could be of assistance in training and there are several innovative applications suggested.[223]

The issue of the importance of the capital markets and/or financial technologies may vary, but its vital role merits considerable study, especially with regard to NPB. CP Michael Milken promotes a philosophy he created at age 19 whereby social prosperity conceptually equals an equation where financial technology is allocated equal weight and is multiplied by the sum of human capital, social capital, and real assets.[224]

Although views on the importance of capital will inevitably vary, a successful CP will need little further comment as to its essential role. George Soros provides insightful comments with his observation on "reflexivity"(involving the interplay between perceptions and the flow of financial capital), the financial markets, and business. Gates' Microsoft business model was fundamentally driven by the equity markets and stock options to compensate team members. As for the social sector or Intersectoral situations, the increased level of competition discussed in Trend Two and the demands for operational efficiency and high cost of technology covered in Trend One only serve to reinforce the applicability to those with elements of social mission. Of course, this is not to say that access to capital is the sole criteria for success in any sector. Nor is there any shortage of examples where excess financial resources corresponded to prolific waste and even fraud, especially in situations with under evaluated endowments.

The issue of supply and demand is gaining increasing sector study as illustrated by an October 2000 study for the Ford Foundation appropriately entitled, "NO EXIT: The Challenge of Realizing Return on Community Development Venture Capital Investments."[225] However, such work doesn't even begin to address the necessary issues of developing the tensions of balancing supply and demand. The demand for the funds are essentially insatiable, which makes it impossible for them to establish an equilibrium with a limited supply of funds. This is directly a result of NGO managers willing to accept unlimited funds with no Blended ROI hurdle and other NGOs more than happy to place excess annual funds in a meager 5% distribution endowment.

In this context, costs of raising capital for NGOs is an area especially appropriate for NPB. Wide disparities exist between what is considered acceptable. A recent report by the New York Attorney General's office, www.oag.state.ny.us/charities/charities.html for example, concluded that over 70% of every dollar raised by professional solicitors in New York is kept by fundraising companies. Massachusetts and other states report even a lower percentage of proceeds to charities.

Within the Morino Institute's 2001 Venture Philanthropy publication, the profile on the Entrepreneur's Foundation of Cupertino, California, identifies fund-raising cost as one of its three "biggest impediments to success: "Most [NGOs] are spending over 50% of their time on fundraising, instead of running their organization, due to the dysfunctional capital market for this sector."[226]

One highly academic study notes the possibility that in some industries "the marginal return on fundraising is exceeded by the cost."[227] During the process of researching NPB, a significant number of such situations appeared likely, where even only direct costs exceeded revenues.

The Better Business Bureau, however, believes that fund-raising costs should not exceed 35% of related contributions.[228]

Importantly, none of these figures include indirect cost of fundraising (e.g., senior management time).

Bill Shore, founder and executive director of Share Our Strength, a NGO that has raised more than $82 million to support anti-hunger and antipoverty efforts worldwide comments on the heavy cost of fund raising on NGO executives: "The most committed and thoughtful social-change activists, those upon whom our society depends to solve social problems, are forced to spend most of their time and energy raising money to support their work, rather than devoting their ingenuity, problem-solving skills, and other talents to devising effective strategies and programs."[229]

A potential arena of counter-examples to the high cost of fund may reside in the social subsector of private education, especially the so-called "elite schools." Harvard's $2.3 billion capital campaign previously mentioned is an on-target example. The alumni network supplies a considerable amount of the human capital, in effect acting a pro-bono labor. And when the funds go into an endowment, the term for use of the funds is essentially timeless, even if the funds are held in restricted accounts.

However, it has been argued that in certain circumstances the cost of endowment fund raising is much higher than meets the eye on first inspection. One example cited in this regard concerned the efforts by a major east coast college to raise a $3 million endowment for a specific (from-scratch) faith-based center. The project sponsors indicated that only the IRS minimum of 5% would be established as the distribution hurdle and that fund management expense were estimated at approximately 2%. Even though the fund was clearly projected to earn much more given a planned heavy equity and alternative investment mix, some have urged that the cost really be measured relative to the amount distributed, or 40% (2%/5%).

Furthermore, the same observers have urged that the project overseers and funders view the cost of this fund raising approach as even much higher. This observation is quite critical of the annual use of such a small portion of the fund, i.e., $90,000 ($3 million times 3% net funds spent). They contend that the opportunity cost of not utilizing a much greater percentage of the fund in a 3 to 5 year time frame carries a huge social cost. Given the social mission of the project, that this social opportunity cost can be added into the all-in-cost of funding.

These individuals contend that the timeless commitment of funds breeds waste and inefficient use of the funds, which should also be somehow included in the cost of funds analysis. As proof of this concern, they astutely note that this project has no benchmarks, performance metric, strategic plan, assessment of risks, or impact consideration. The current project coordinators, who are also fund managers, have made it abundantly clear that no such progress will be adopted. Hence, the risk of wasted funds is notably significant.

Could a CP with a comparable passion and a powerful several-year strategic and tactics plan accomplish even greater faith-based goals with only 5% to 10% or less than the $3 million sought to be raised? If so, that would give the CP a 20X to 10X Multiplier Effect (and 95% to 90% Discount Effect for the endowment funders) and a Performance Gap of $2.7 million at the low end.

Chart 14: "Select Intersectoral Capital Market Challenges" provides a conceptual overview of these trends and issues. The center of the diagram highlights the target of transformative change, which is the "Astronomical Fundraising Cost on Restrictive/Oppressive Terms," these costs being both internal and external. The seven identifiable trends illustrated in the diagram have been discussed earlier in the Working Book in Section Two. The supplemental points notes include reference at the top of the chart to three subjective assessments: 1) Absence of Powerful and Consistent Intellectual Capital, 2) Market Forces of Capitalism Must Be Unleashed, and 3) Milken's social prosperity formula.

Chart 14: <u>Select Intersectoral Market Challenges</u>

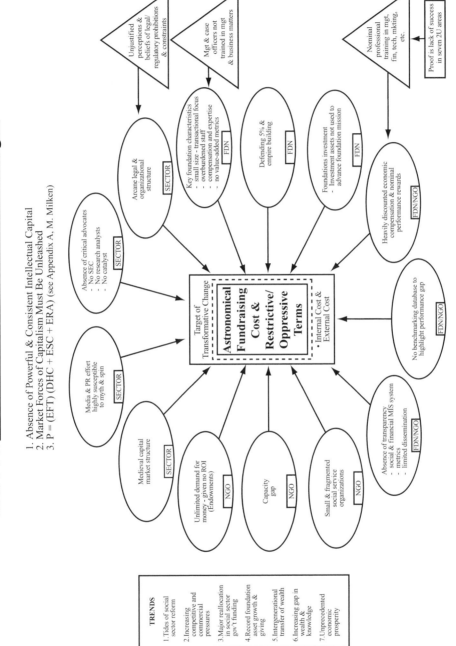

1. Absence of Powerful & Consistent Intellectual Capital
2. Market Forces of Capitalism Must Be Unleashed
3. P = (EFT) (DHC + ESC + ERA) (see Appendix A, M. Milken)

TRENDS

1. Tides of social sector reform
2. Increasing competitive and commercial pressures
3. Major reallocation in social sector gov't funding
4. Record foundation asset growth & giving
5. Intergenerational transfer of wealth
6. Increasing gap in wealth & knowledge
7. Unprecedented economic prosperity

Unjustified perceptions & beliefs of legal/regulatory prohibitions & constraints

Mgt & case officers not trained in mgt & business matters

Nominal professional training in mgt, fin, tech, mkting, etc.

Proof is lack of success in seven 2U areas

Arcane legal & organizational structure — SECTOR

Key foundation characteristics
- small size - transactional focus
- overburdened staff
- compensation and expertise
- no value-added metrics — FDN

Defending 5% & empire building — FDN

Foundations investment
- Investment assets not used to advance foundation mission — FDN

Heavily discounted economic compensation & nominal performance rewards — FDN/NGO

Absence of critical advocates
- No SEC
- No research analysts
- No catalyst — SECTOR

Media & PR effort highly susceptible to myth & spin — SECTOR

Target of Transformative Change

Astronomical Fundraising Cost & Restrictive/ Oppressive Terms
- Internal Cost & External Cost

No benchmarking database to highlight performance gap — FDN/NGO

Medieval capital market structure — SECTOR

Unlimited demand for money - given no ROI (Endowments) — NGO

Capacity gap — NGO

Small & fragmented social service organizations — NGO

Absence of transparency
- social & financial MIS system
- metrics
- limited dissemination — FDN/NGO

Although time and space do not allow a detailed discussion of the multiple influencing factors to be identified, four relate to the social sector in general (medieval capital structures, media & PR effort highly susceptible to myth and spin, absence of critical advocates, and arcane legal and organizational structures often confirmed by unjustified perceptions),[230] three are assigned to NGOs (unlimited demand for funds, capacity gap, small and fragmented social service organizations), three are assigned to foundations (key foundation characteristics, defending the 5% empire building , and foundation investment strategy unrelated to mission), and three to a combination of foundations and NGOs (absence of transparency, limited benchmarking, and heavily discounted compensation and nominal performance reward).

CPs can have a direct and powerful impact in applying NPB to the capital market issues of their target NGOs. The process may not be all that complicated to the extent that best in class NGOs can be isolated. Yes, innovative ideas and risk will be part of the process.

Furthermore, the enablers or deliverable opportunities composing the Performance Gap may not be so simple to determine. However, in addition to NGO's setting new standards in the cost and composition of their capital structure, they may also locate opportunities for commercial ventures as a positive alternative to the more traditional capital market instruments.

In this regard CPs interested in advancing in this area may find the insights offered by Dees in his social enterprise spectrum or Morino's Continuum of Return Expectations to be on point.[231] This material complements the works mentioned earlier in this Working Book of Emerson, Skloot, Shore, and Weisbrod.

CPs seeking a readily available, although somewhat basic, structural vehicle to facilitate both their social sector investments and effective implementation of NP Benchmarking should consider Program Related Investments ("PRI"). PRIs are essentially investments in NGOs or other mission-consistent ventures that qualify toward a foundation's 5% IRS hurdle. Basically, such investments can be in multiple forms as long as three tests are met, none of which are particularly onerous if a worthy purpose exists for the investment (see the PRI definition in the Glossary). There should be no misconceptions; properly designed PRIs can create pressure to perform and heavy judgmental financial metrics for both the receiving organization and the investor, CP or foundation. (For informative sources of foundation perspectives see associated endnote).[232] PRIs do offer considerable flexibility and can be structured along a wide spectrum such as: social purpose deposits, loan to loan funds, loan guarantees, cash flow loans, seed capital loans, bridge loans, real estate loan, asset purchases, and stock purchases.[233] "PRIs can and have been used to fund almost every conceivable type of project."[234]

According to one study, PRI investments total only $718 million, including more than $400 million outstanding since their beginning.[235] However, PRIs continue to be referred to by professionals in the industry as "new tools for philanthropy."[236] One publication also provides findings that the sector should not expect to see a deluge of requests for such structured and quantifiable investments from either NGOs or socially focused entities.[237] Nor should one expect that traditional foundation funders will seek to engage in PRI. Reading between the lines, PRIs (much like NP Benchmarking) require a commitment to commercial sector and progressive inter-sectoral concepts and tactics. Confirming Wisdom Point Seven: "Generate Momentum, expect obstacles," a study found considerable foundation resistance to the commercially disciplined PRI. Among the primary reasons for not making PRIs was the belief that they are "inappropriate vehicles" for foundation funding and 4 out of 5 funders don't expect to make any in the future.[238] From another perspective, don't be surprised if professional advisors offer little quality knowledge on PRIs and parrot hackneyed general characteristics of the existing PRI market rather than discuss the many benefits for a passionate CP to create Performance Gaps and increase the Multiplier Effect of their intersectoral investments.

Some PRI professionals advocate a positive role for investing in and cultivating intermediaries in this field. A leading PRI investor observes that foundations can achieve enormous leverage by investing in organizations that use capital, rather than grants alone, to address important social problems that are usually too large and complex to be solved through direct intervention by grantmakers.[239] PRIs give private foundations an opportunity to make direct social contributions that far exceed the normal reach of grant programs.[240] Other advantages include: leveraging limited staff, accessing niche expertise, more extensive capacity building network, greater distance from enforcement decisions and consequences, and magnified impact of funds. PRIs can also be used in connection with NGO mergers, similar to those reviewed in David La Piana's latest book, *The Nonprofit Mergers Workbook: The Leader's Guide to Considering Negotiating, and Executing a Merger.*[241]

NPB CPs should also be aware of Intersectoral opportunities to acquire dot-coms or their assets to advance a CP's philanthropic mission. In February of 2001, the National Wildlife Foundation ("NWF") acquired/rescued eNature. eNature provides online guidebooks about plants and wildlife. NWF agreed to spend $4 million in cash to bolster the site's presence in cyberspace. [242]

There is considerable reason to be confident that the potential exists for the social sector capital market instruments. A study published by the Social Investment Forum noted that socially responsible investing in the United States exceeded $2 trillion, up 82% from 1997. And, socially responsible indexes continue to outperform the S&P 500. Two socially responsible indexes benchmarked to the S&P 500 achieved 24.5% and 29.6% relative to the S&P 500 at 21.1% for calendar year 1999, a spread of 340 and 850 basis points, respectively.[243] These social investment indexes have outperformed the S&P 500 on a total return basis since their inception on May 1990 and December 1994, respectively.[244] Of course, the definition of socially responsible is quite all-inclusive.

Developing highly-skilled, dedicated, and niche-focused financial intermediaries, especially investment banks and merchant banks, in the social sector is essential to advance the positive transformation of the social sector capital markets. An example of a firm that appears to be seeking a pioneering role in this sector is Japonica Intersectoral. Its web site offers an informative introduction to its ambitious mission. At some point tactics such as spin-offs and tracking stock will be a powerful topic of conversion of the better social sector executives and among the more sophisticated social sector board members.

"Japonica Intersectoral is an investment bank dedicated to creating value in the intersectoral markets. The firm proactively cultivates opportunities in the segment of the social sector where quantifiable value metrics of the commercial sector converge with the socially powered motivations of the social sector. Here, "doing good and doing well" is synergistic. Japonica Intersectoral continually seeks to strategically optimize its financial and intellectual capital for the benefit of its multiple constituencies, including: emerging growth NGOs, established NGOs, foundations, institutional investors, social sector professionals, and social sector executives/board members. The firm's value creating initiatives encompass capital market services, strategic financial advisory services, direct investment opportunities, and educational resources. Japonica Intersectoral's global constituents share a common mission of seeking best-in-class performance along a social enterprise spectrum of bringing transformative value to society."[245] As for the firm's criteria for investing in or providing investment banking services to the social sector, such information is located on its web site.[246] The following table provides a brief summary.

Preliminary Criteria for Selecting Intersectoral Investments

- Strong internal and external team, with a sound program of substantial opportunities for value-added.
- High relative market share and good relative perceived quality of offerings.
- Strong core competencies.
- Substantial, identifiable opportunities to improve services and offerings.
- Attractive opportunities for blended ROI investments, especially via technology.
- Potential opportunities for value harvesting and commercial success stories.
- Receptive avenues for mega transformative organizational changes.

Researchers in the social sector note a number of other relevant considerations, most important of which may be the impact of existing management's unwillingness or aversion to commercially related strategies and tactics. This is a two-edged sword which also may impair the effectiveness of the NGO's social mission. "As a result of not maximizing net revenue, they [NGOs] will not be able to maximize output of their preferred, mission-related activities, because of the desire to avoid the non-preferred activities."[247] Also, keep in mind the importance of legal structures and the relationship of national organizations to local entities.

As for the concern that increasing sources of revenue would have a de facto negative impact on donations, that does not appear to be the case. One frequently cited study notes the following: "Focusing on whether revenue from other sources affects donations to a nonprofit organization, we find evidence that revenue from either government grants or from the organizations' own program sales activity generally does not crowd out private donations. To the contrary: in most industries there are significant positive effects."[248]

Publicly Traded Companies as Potential NPB Best Practices and Social Sector Investments:

Despite the apparent sparsity of intersectoral companies, publicly traded companies with elements of social sector mission do exist. Such companies offer the potential to serve as NPB best practices in general or in certain aspects of their operations. The availability of comprehensive public filings, research reports, and stakeholder relations material offers fertile ground for NPB research. These companies may even serve as essential resources or elements for various intersectoral practice strategies, e.g. merger candidates, joint venture partners, or sundry strategic alliances. Innovative benchmarking intersectoral ideas offer CPs the prospective opportunities to create value and thus positively impact Performance Gap and Multiplier/Discount Effect metrics.

From a consistent competitive perspective, CPs may wish to utilize NPB to evaluate both social sector initiatives and somewhat comparable publicly traded companies as alternative investments. NPB provides the framework for assessing competitive performance in a number of areas, including process, program, and policy. The Blended ROI offers the potential to integrate the prospects of a financial return. It would seem quite practical and prudent for CPs or progressive foundations (those who are willing to utilize their assets consistent with their mission and significantly exceeded the minimum 5% IRS requirement) to consider the benefits associated with successful investments. What could be more consistent with the NPB wisdom points than making an investment that offers competitive social sector mission benefits and provides a significant financial return for future reinvestment? The polar and all-to-common contrast is a non-measured social sector investment (blind charity) with no financial return for donors to reinvest in future social mission projects. This comparison offers interesting opportunities for present value analysis.

Appendix R contains a list of over 200 publicly traded companies with social-sector missions. Broadly, these companies can be classified into eleven major sectors: Arts & Culture, Biotechnology, Community Development, Education, Educational Publishing, Edutainment, Environment, Financial, Health Care, Human Services, Long Term Care, Medical Devices, Professional Services, Technology, and Other. Within each of these categories, publicly traded companies stand out as having outperformed to some extent their social sector equivalents, in both their fiscal health and the quality of their service. In essence, a very real performance gap exists between equivalent NGO and commercial firms. Hence, social-sector organizations can benefit from drawing upon the best practices of public companies in the inter-sectoral area.

Although several success stories in the intersectoral area are easily identified, like Pacificare and HCA, there are a number of smaller companies that provide more rel-evant benchmarks for intersectoral companies. For example, Total Renal Care (TRL) is the second largest provider of kidney dialysis services in the United States. It operates over 500 dialysis centers in the United States and serves over 40,000 patients per year. Financially, the company is also strong. Last year it had EBITDA of $70.1 million on $1.49 billion in sales. With a market capitalization of over $800 million and YTD stock performance of 43%, Total Renal Care is a model intersec-toral company. Likewise, ITT Educational Services (ESI) is another example of a successful intersectoral company. It operates 67 educational institutes and serves over 26,000 students. Last year, it had sales of $330 million and EBITDA of $48.5 million from its educational activities. As an investment, ITT Educational Services has a YTD return of 83.5% and a market capitalization of $674 million. In an era when social service organizations are encountering increasing difficulties in both serving their constituents and maintaining their fiscal health, successful intersectoral companies provide a compelling model for their struggling social sector counter-parts.

Successful intersectoral companies are spread among a number of different indus-tries, such as childcare, correctional health care, and environmental protection. For example, Bright Horizons Family Solutions operates over 300 day-care centers at work places. Last year, it provided care for over 37,000 children, increased compa-ny services to employees, and enabled many parents to return to work. At the same time, the company had revenues of $262.6 million and EBITDA of $15.9 million. Bright Horizons Family Solutions has a market capitalization of $300.9 million and is up 35% YTD. America Service Group, which provides health care solutions to correctional facilities and the military, is another successful intersectoral company. It had sales of $308 million and EBITDA of $17.9 million. American Service Group has a market capitalization of $84.2 million and has increased by 48.3% YTD. Ecology and Environment, Inc. provides environmental consulting to minimize the impact of development on the environment. Last year, it had sales of $66.8 million and EBITDA of $2.16 million. It has a market capitalization of $27.3 million and has increased 32.7% YTD.

Successful intersectoral companies also exist in the Arts & Culture segment. For instance, Baldwin Piano and Organ (BPAO) and Steinway Instruments (LVB) are both successful manufacturers of top-quality instruments. In addition, A.C. Moore Arts & Crafts supplies artists with a wide variety of tools necessary for their success. Even the Gallery of History (HIST) has managed to successfully bridge the gap between the social and commercial sectors. As the success of these companies indicates, the pursuit of a social sector mission does not preclude an organization from achieving fiscal self-sufficiency or raising money through the equity markets. In fact, a strong case exists for organizations that are fiscally self-sufficient and publicly traded to be more successful in reaching their target audiences than traditional social sector organizations.

NGO Conversion:

Having reviewed a rather comprehensive listing of topics as they relate to NPB, one still remains: NGO conversions. An NGO conversion may be considered the ultimate progression for an organization's formal migration from the tax-preferred social sector to the taxable commercial sector. Formal conversion of the entire organization is not necessary; in many situations the conversion occurs for only a portion of an NGO's operations. Conversion is an attempt to address the issue of transition or exit from a social sector investment. Conversions have occurred mostly in the health care sector but in other subsectors as well.

A highly publicized recent example of a pending conversion involves Empire Blue Cross and Blue Shield. Its CEO states that "the insurer's 'continued viability' would be jeopardized and its potential for public health service dissipated unless the company was allowed to restructure as a for-profit company owned by investors." He also indicated that Empire needed access to shareholder capital to compete with for-profit managed-care companies. Empire proposed to establish a $1 billion charitable foundation that could bring health care to 10,000 uninsured children or buy prescription drugs for 50,000 low-income elderly people in New York as part of the conversion plan. Expressing a diametrically opposed view, the president of the Greater New York Hospital Association stated, "The benefits of the foundation pale in comparison to the havoc wreaked on the provider community by an investor-owned entity that does not care about providers but instead cares about stock prices on Wall Street."[249]

NPB provides the tools to assess comparative performance issues, providing the analytical framework to assess an organization's ability to successfully navigate the conversion. CPs are advised to ask a series of challenging questions: Should they believe a significant Performance Gap can be expanded by the conversion? When is a conversion socially appropriate? What are the obligations to modify the legal structure? What is the most effective role for a CP as a proactive social sector entrepreneur/investor?

Generally speaking, a conversion is appropriate when the assets of the NGO will produce greater social value under commercial legal structure. Circumstances, such as market forces and economic conditions, change, and what was once an optimal legal structure may no longer be appropriate. "Presumably conversion occurs when the advantages of for-profit status outweigh the advantages of non-profit status. This may be socially desirable if price finance is now so widely feasible that a public good has been turned into a private good, if access to equity is important to expand facilities, and if donations are no longer a large potential source of revenue."[250]

The initial reaction of some may be emphatically negative, with the proclamation "once an NGO, always an NGO." However, the NGO tax-exempt status should not remain unquestioned throughout the lifetime of the organization. One highly respected industry professional provided the following astute observation: "It is difficult to argue that conversion of a non-profit firm to for-profit can never advance social welfare. Because of the stronger incentives for minimizing costs and responding to consumer demands that come with private ownership of assets, as well as possibly greater flexibility associated with access to equity capital, the same resources could plausibly produce greater value in the for-profit than in the non-profit sector."[251]

This observation leads to the second question: What are the obligations to modify the legal structure? The rapid growth of the social sector has also elevated the discourse of NGO justification of tax-exempt privileges. CPs should remember that with NGO status comes the cost to society of the lost tax revenues to the government for re-distribution determined by our elected officials. Some critics even see "crass motives" behind the goals of some NGOs "taking advantage of public subsidies and public trust to support inefficiency; they posit that some NGOs are nothing more than 'for-profits in disguise' (FPIDs)."[252]

In fact, one industry professional goes so far as to offer this challenging observation. "As a countertheory, then, we might hypothesize that pecuniary rather than altruistic objectives dominate the decisions of many nonprofits. These 'false' nonprofits – which Weisbrod (1998) referred to as 'for-profits in disguise' – may maximize profits that they then distribute in disguised form (as higher wages and perks), or they may maximize revenues that lead to power and prestige for their managers."[253]

Furthermore, the issue of internal corruption within NGOs complicates conversion possibility. "There is more scope for such abuse in the nonprofit sector because nonprofits are not subject to financially motivated takeover bids that limit abuse among for-profits. Favoritism, nepotism, kickbacks, self-dealing, and other abusive power relationships can govern nonprofit allocation, particularly when allocation criteria require subjective judgements on the part of the nonprofit employee."[254]

What's next? The IRS, as mentioned in Section Four, is a rather weak proxy – in many circumstances – for a threat to a corporate take over.

What is the most effective role for a CP as a proactive social sector entrepreneur/investor? Let's assume that sufficient NGO commercialism motives exist, conversion is socially appropriate, varying obligation pressures develop, and a significant NPB value creation opportunity exists. There are possible reasonable concerns that the NGO may be appropriately classified as a "false non-profit" or that its operations include the nefarious elements cited above.

Do civic-minded activists have a role and responsibility to initiate a proactive effort with management, board, and/or regulatory authorities? Could an advocacy effort encompass varying forms of the three points noted above, depending upon the audience? In a capitalistic driven economic system, what are the appropriate and most effective roles for profit-driven entrepreneur catalysts, e.g. a proactive social entrepreneur/investor (CPs)?

What will happen should NGO conversion pressures materialize, from various sources, when social benefits diminish relative to the social cost of tax-exemption privilege? What are the most effective strategies and tactics for facilitating socially beneficial conversions, e.g. externally funded case studies for NGO discussion, externally funded social cost/value analyses, catalyst presentations to NGO management and board, IRS communications, congressional initiatives and public relations tactics?

As a tactical matter, can a change of control be facilitated by an offer to the board with the logical advantages of increasing value and maximizing social benefit to the public if such a suggested proposal is adopted? Injection of funds or subsidiary spin-off could have a positive impact. Importantly, the regulatory and legal guidance cited in the Capital Markets NP Benchmarking subsection of Section Seven indicate the opportunity for the 501(c) NGO to continue to hold stock and use the funds to advance other social missions.

And, to expand a CP's perspective, there may even be opportunities for reverse conversions, i.e., from commercial to social sector. Such is the case with Culturefinder.com, which made such a transition.[255]

CONCLUSION

This Working Book has reviewed a comprehensive expanse of information within its body, appendices, and endnotes. To begin a conclusion there is probably little better way than to reiterate the NPB Working Book mission, the NPB competitive assumption, and the seven NPB Wisdom Points. Next, in appreciation of the high premium on CP time, and somewhat contrary to standard practice, concluding NPB observations are presented in a subsection titled Educational Perspectives. This is then followed by more methodical brief observations on each of the seven wisdom point sections.

Mission:
The unabashedly ambitious mission of *New Philanthropy Benchmarking* is to inspire intense competition among passionate capitalist/philanthropists and to provide essential wisdom points whereby CPs can initiate radically positive transformative change within the social sector.

Competitive Assumption:
New Philanthropy Benchmarking is predicated upon the assumption that passionate capitalist/philanthropists will instinctively strive for comparable success in the social sector as achieved in the commercial sector. While motivations vary, instincts compelling superior performance or driving a determination to eschew being "dumb money" are considered pervasive and transferable.

Educational Perspectives:
From an educational perspective, NPB builds on a synergistic collaboration of a classic benchmarking pyramid, progressive Intersectoral practices, and the key NPB metrics. See visual presentation in Chart 15.

The classic benchmarking pyramid components include hard metrics to insure quality management and financial statistics, third party verifiable metrics to increase the probability of obtaining comparable information on a timely basis, and extensive comparative internal metrics to move to the highest levels of comparable organization information. Constructing a quality benchmarking pyramid provides the foundation upon which to build a process to create value in the social sector.

Creating substantial value can be enhanced through successful execution of progressive Intersectoral practices. The three general categories to consider are social enterprise (social entrepreneurship growth, commercialization initiatives, and operational philanthropy opportunities), strategic philanthropy & strategic restructuring (organizational restructuring, collaboration programs, management efficiency programs, and capacity building investments), and social capital markets developments (innovative financings, Blended ROIs, M&A transactions, and social venture capital practices).

Building upon the classic benchmarking pyramid and creating value through progressive intersectoral practices, NPB analytical tools facilitate competition by identifying the Performance Gaps between or among organizations or processes, policies, or programs. NPB seeks to assist in isolating the Deliverable Opportunities to better understanding the Performance Gap and potentially addressing/advancing an under-performing situation. The culmination of initial NPB analytical progress is the calculation of an organization's specific deliverables. The MDE offers the comparable competitive assessments designed to capitalize and exploit passionate CPs instincts to strive for comparable success in the social sector as achieved in the commercial sector. While motivations vary, instincts compelling superior performance or driving a determination to eschew being "dumb money" are considered pervasive and transferable.

The more passionate and proactive CPs may seek to motivate both NGOs and foundations by advancing the obligations associated with the proper understanding and application of fiduciary responsibility of social sector executives, board members, and trustees.

In pressing to increase the Multiplier Effect or reduce a Discount Effect, the best insights of the seven wisdom points can provide a good faith framework. Nonetheless, motivating recalcitrant individuals in positions of influence may require much more than compelling logic, persuasive studies, and overwhelming proof of success.

Within NGOs, fiduciary responsibility should merit the methodical development of metrics and careful analysis to insure optimal advancement of mission. If necessary, CPs should firmly remind NGO executives and oversight boards that the absence of such information could be considered grounds for contra-fiduciary actions and may actually fall under the rubric of the Federal inurement protection provisions (the 1996 Intermediate Sanctions Act), which contain personal liability provisions. Furthermore, should pursuit of purely financial goals (outside of the primary social mission) be connected with increased compensation of executives or oversight members and at the expense of attractive potential social sector mission present value returns, CPs may wish to consider issues associated with legal or regulatory consequences. (See subsection discussion "Strongly Incentivized Leadership" within Section Seven, which provides clear evidence of the correlation between larger foundation asset size and increasing levels of compensation.) All too often the research indicates an absence of quality metrics assessing an NGO's mission has been tolerated. Hundreds of millions of dollars of NGO funds are expended with little or no attempt to measure efficiency or effectiveness with either internal historical information or comparable entity information.

As for the foundation members of the social sector community, the confusion and consequences of proper fiduciary responsibility may be even greater. The research unquestionably indicates an almost complete absence of quality social sector mission performance metrics. In fact, protests proclaiming the concept of hard metrics as impossible, quixotic, and actually damaging are overwhelming. The defense of the 5% IRS mandated distribution/payout standard seems to motivate the dead-founder foundation sector more universally than any other issue. Not to be outdone, the defensive arguments include essentially *prima fascia* positions that the perpetual growth of foundations investment asset base is sacrosanct, any attempt to measure the present value of accomplishing a social mission sooner is under serving, and investment assets should not be utilized to advance social mission. Eerily, hired legal counsel almost universally defend what may in fact be blatant contra-fiduciary actions by advising that the asset side of the foundation can essentially be managed separately from a foundation's primary social sector mission. Need it be restated that this is an environment without mission metrics, competitive performance measurements, and with executive compensation so closely correlated with asset size?

Questions and doubts still abound. Should it be little wonder that perpetuation and growth of the foundation investment asset base increases outside fees and executive compensation? Should it be little wonder that investment bankers are running to defend the growth of a foundation's investment asset base or that professional compensation studies support greater executive compensation for larger asset base foundations? How often will a CP see outside service providers suggesting greater compensation for more rapid and successful execution of a foundation's mission? Is the quest for growth of a dead-founder foundation's asset base any different than a commercial sector executive's quest to build revenues through whatever means possible, including ill-advised acquisitions? Is this one of the few situations where foundation executives are aggressively adopting commercial sector practices, an action which coincidentally corresponds to compensation growth? Should CPs view this confluence of practices as blatantly contrary to the effective, successful, and early success of a foundation's social sector mission?

Can NPB provide a start for passionate CPs to achieve comparable success in the social sector? Unquestionably.

Benchmarking Wisdom Points

1. The social sector's profound transformation offers virtually bound less opportunities.
2. CPs aggressively talk external comparative numbers.
3. Benchmarking can be as powerful in the social sector as in the commercial sector.
4. Application of the commercial sector benchmarking concepts apply to social sector benchmarking.
5. Yes, competitive social sector measurement tactics do exist.
6. If you can't measure in the social sector, you can't manage.
7. Generate momentum; expect obstacles.

Wisdom Point One: *"The social sector's profound transformation offers virtually boundless opportunities."*

The social sector transformation offers CPs the opportunity to apply their skills as effectively as they have done in the commercial sector. Recall the tides of change discussed in Section One, especially the increasing application of social enterprise and commercialization. The time is ripe, as the pressures demanding performance from all of the CP's talents are growing exponentially greater by the moment.

CPs inevitably must lead the way to major positive change. Change of dramatic proportion demands outstanding talents and judgements, which many of the most successful CPs possess and will wisely share. Talents of professional management are essential, including finance, marketing, technology, venture capital and restructurings, benchmarking, compensation design, and budgeting. Opportunities for collaboration with select world-class foundations should be aggressively engaged; however, there is no shortage of practical constraints. Motivations will vary but desire for positive change should be a common goal.

This Working Book provides a highly practical assessment of major trends effecting the social sector and insights into virtually boundless opportunities for maximum initiative value creation. The following Intersectoral topics offer significant NPB measurable value creation, as the CP will discover: social enterprise (social entrepreneurship, commercialization, and operational philanthropy), strategic philanthropy & restructuring (capacity building, collaboration, management efficiency programs, restructuring, and foundation value-creation practices), and social capital markets (innovative financings, social venture capital, Blended ROIs, and M&A transactions).

Regarding success stories, the material in this section contains descriptions of numerous positive situations in the Intersectoral practice arena (social enterprise, strategic philanthropy & restructuring, and social capital markets). CPs should seek to integrate NPB where practical, benchmarking other situations as offering best practice insights, and capturing value creation opportunities. The examples provide insight as to how NPB can facilitate identifying Performance Gaps and Deliverable Opportunities between current social sector-only organizations and best practice social mission commercial organizations, thereby advancing value creation and forging an Intersectoral evolution.

Wisdom Point Two: *"CPs, aggressively talk external comparative numbers."*

As CPs engage more passionately and more extensively within the social sector, they will find, according to one industry sage, a culture of dysfunction. More efficient and effective philanthropic initiatives demand measurements, accountability, and benchmarking. Deeply entrenched cultural barriers opposing metrics require a more assertive response: aggressively talking external comparative numbers.

CPs should identify best practices, whether they are from other CPs, foundations, or social enterprise investors. The world-class CPs profiled in this NPB Working Book offer a diverse range of success stories, especially intersectoral practices. Quantification of innovative practices is the next stage to challenge even those perceived to be the current best practices. CPs are advised not to rely on foundations, especially dead-founder foundations, as change agents.

There are unmistakable recurring themes that pervade the social sector investments of time, talents, treasures, and tenacity of all seven featured CPs. Each has embarked – in their own unique way – on highly ambitious and passionate missions to transform certain areas of the social sector. Throughout is a constant focus on evolving and quantifiable metrics across an extraordinarily diverse range of projects. Competitive elements consistent with the power of NPB are inspiring. There is a seamless transference of commercial concepts to the social sector initiative; stakeholders in both sectors are all-inclusive. Tactics are focused and intense, especially in contrast with historical social sector practices. Each hands-on effective management style is consistent with their highly successful commercial talents. And, without question, each is outstanding in generating momentum and absolving obstacles.

Value creation is evident in virtually all projects, bringing various special commercial talents previously rare or nonexistent. Intersectoral practices involve social enterprise, strategic philanthropy & restructuring, and social capital markets. Value added ranges from selecting the best project, collaborating with others, improving performance of participants, and advancing the state of knowledge and practice. These CPs seek to share their wisdom, serving as positive benchmarks to other CPs seeking to accomplish positive missions in the social sector.

These premier CPs' actions may speak as loud as their words. They place a very high present value on social sector accomplishments. The average annual asset distribution of CP foundation is a considerable multiple of the large dead-founder foundation norm. There is a message that goals today merit great effort in contrast to building social sector asset bases for professional foundation managers. As would be expected of such a world-class group, they concentrate their efforts on a limited numbers of projects. The average size investment is in the multi-millions, versus less than $110,000 for dead-founder foundation with even larger investment asset bases.

Expanding on this topic, the Working Book offers a comparison of four key characteristics illustrating the differing *modus operandi* between so-called Live-Founder (aka CP Foundations) and Dead-Founder foundations: annual percentage of qualifying distributions of CPs averaged 27% compared to the aggregate foundation groups 5.5%; 90% of CP funds were concentrated in five initiatives compared to 10 unrelated areas for the foundation group; the average annual dollar amount to top five initiatives was $6.5 million for the CPs and only between $60,000 to $110,000 for foundations with assets between $51 million and $999 million; and CPs invested nominal amounts in indexed equities versus an estimated 40% to 60% for foundations.

While motivations vary considerably, teachings from virtually all realms, both secular and sectarian (e.g. *Tzedakah's* aversion to impulse giving and Stewardship's "parable of the talents") are consistent in advocating a proactive and measurement focus to CP philanthropic efforts. NPB positively complements such teachings.

CPs are suggested to review the appendices for relevant benchmark information on world-class CPs, social sector investors, and innovative foundations. Also, the intersectoral and benchmarking questionnaires could provide a sound starting point for initiating assessment of team members.

Wisdom Point Three: *"Benchmarking can be as powerful in the social sector as in the commercial sector."*

The power and compelling attractiveness of NPB is its ability to assist passionate CPs to multiply the impact (create value) of their resource investment relative to other similar social sector initiatives and minimize risk exposure. Relative value creation is not solely based on the value of resources invested in the commercial sector and neither should such be the case in the social sector. For example, NPB seeks to provide CPs the tools to leverage a million dollar social sector investment to generate a much greater impact, possibly achieving that of comparable $10 million or even $100 million social sector investment. Simultaneously, NPB provides the framework for CPs to minimize the risk exposure of NGO or foundation misfortunate developments, wasted funds, or unintended consequences.

The framework to transfer the power of commercial sector benchmarking to the social sector is especially critical given the absence of resources, knowledge base, and culture barriers. The current state of social sector benchmarking information provides easy opportunities for improvement. Seeking to progress to the higher level of the NPB pyramid can facilitate the process and provide a sound foundation. In particular, note "the value of database studies of third party internal access information sources and Performance Gap analysis and recommendations on how best to maximize performance."

NPB is diverse in its application and its power can be applied to (1) proactive investors/donors with an established organization; (2) passive investors/donors with an established organization; (3) proactive investors/donors with a start-up organization; and (4) passive investors/donors with a start-up.

Wisdom Point Four: *"Application of the commercial sector benchmarking concepts apply to social sector benchmarking."*

From a macro perspective, NPB concepts seek to provide the foundation whereby strategies and tactics can be utilized to energize competition within the social sector and create substantial value. The highest value concepts of commercial benchmarking are applied to create additional value; select intersectoral practices seek to further advance the value creation; and concepts originating from the financial capital markets provide further value creation fuel through comparative value creation and performance on investment metrics.

Commercial sector and social sector constituencies are considerably similar, yet differences are largely exaggerated. Both commercial sector firms and NGOs have multiple stakeholders. One of the main sources of resistance in social sector cultures will be the claim that NGOs and commercial sector firms cannot be compared. The fiction of this claim is apparent through the comparison of stakeholders. While the concept that NGOs have stakeholders may seem basic, the resistance will be overwhelming.

Although information is quite rare in the social sector, illustrative examples offer sufficient constructive vision. Perhaps most easily viewed at a project level, the applicability of the concepts is illustrated in several NPB examples where range of performance runs from significant multiples to relative discount performance.

The NPB Best Practice Situations Matrix provides a practical review on the application potential of NPB. Had each of these situations reviewed in the matrix occurred as described, each of the six superior situations been funded by one CP, and each of the less preferred comparable been funded by another CP, the difference would be compelling to even the largest and least proactive CPs. Even without the potential value of the stock options described in the second situation, the first CP would have accomplished with approximately $750,000 what would have cost the other CP $8.4 million. The results: an approximately $7.6 million Performance Gap and a Multiplier Effect of 11.2 times.

Wisdom Point Five: *"Yes, competitive social sector measurement tactics do exist."*

The presentation of NPB tactics and the comparison to their commercial sector brethren should leave little question that competitive social sector measurement tactics do exist. Six tactics are reviewed, with the three most important to CPs being Deliverable Opportunities, Performance Gaps, and Multiplier/Discount Effects ("M/DE").

The three critical tactics will empower CPs to establish a common language whereupon they can begin to assess and create value. Importantly, the culminary tactic – M/DE – provides the necessary comparative quantification and concluding step in the NPB process. It is the macro-level assessment of utilization of precious resources, especially monetary.

For those CPs who are motivated by competition, (and what CP isn't?), there should be the positive motivation of knowing that a social sector investment out performed a quality benchmark by a multiple of times or that a CP's dollars were so wisely invested in the social sector so as to have the power equaling or exceeding social sector investments made by other CPs. On the other hand, there is the motivating power or concern of learning or having others learn that resources were invested so unwisely in a social sector project that dollars invested yielded only a fraction of the efforts of other apparently more sagacious CPs.

Envision a ranking based not naively on the absolute magnitude of dollar of charity, but on the relative quantified dollar impact for specified social sector initiatives.

Wisdom Point Six: *"If you can't measure in the social sector, you can't manage."*

Two hypothetical examples are provided to further illustrate the sixth wisdom point, "If you can't measure in the social sector, you can't manage in the social sector." Whether CPs are passively or proactively engaged with a single function or multi-function NGO, comparative metrics associated with NPB provide the framework for measurable value creation. On the one hand, NPB can be utilized as a possibly more passive tool to evaluate organizational or project outcome, or as a more proactive tool to evaluate process, programs, or policies. The latter provides information upon which management actions can be implemented to close or expand a Performance Gap.

Either way, a first question often confronting a passionate CP seeking to advance NPB involves who or what to benchmark. Some NGOs claim that they are so unique that there is no organization with which they could benchmark. This is one of the more frustrating myths encountered in the social sector and an early obstacle to obtaining measurement information. When deciding with whom to benchmark, an organization first needs to determine what processes or strategies to benchmark. Comparisons are drawn more easily when organizations are similar to one another.

Alternatively, an organization can obtain benchmark measurement information from others in different fields as long as the other organization provides a best practice example. Don't limit your scope. In order to maintain continuous improvement and continuous betterment, an organization should obtain measurement information from premier organizations. Remember to look at organizations, regardless of sector, from which your organization can learn. This is particularly important for those in the social sector.

There are external resources available to the passionate CPs which may not be readily apparent. CPs should look in both the commercial and social sector for quality resources and talents. The Working Book provides an extensive list of Internet resources on general intersectoral topics, benchmarking, prospective external resources, and potential networking and best practices organizations.

Both the SFCS and CNSO examples provide a useful, hands-on illustration for NPB. As these analyses indicate, NPB should not be completely delegated to individuals with insufficient skills and judgement. The quality and value creation result will in large part be determined by decisions made regarding five issues to be assessed and managed: (1) time, talents, and tenacity (costs), (2) treasures (direct financial monetary costs), (3) significance of impact, (4) probability of accomplishment, and (5) time to accomplish.

Wisdom Point Seven: *"Generate momentum; expect obstacles."*

An extensive refinement of momentum building and obstacle avoidance practices is dialogued. Several promising momentum-building topics are social sector capital markets opportunities, traditional and cutting-edge executive educational alternatives, incentive compensation observations, and talent assessment questionnaires. Obstacle avoidance topics positively discussed include cultural issues, minimization of risk issues, misconceptions, and voices of caution. This Working Book concludes by offering compelling common sense perspectives on the realities and myths of fiduciary obligations and potentially contra-fiduciary activities within the social sector.

With regard to generating momentum, CPs may find a particularly high return on their time and resources by focusing on three areas: incentive compensation, executive educational alternative, and social sector capital markets. As for prospective obstacles, CPs are well served to carefully focus on social sector misconceptions and minimization of investment risk issues.

Incentive compensation can work both for and against social sector success. A well-designed value creation program can be a powerful motivator if properly tied to social mission. However, a passive executive compensation program can lead to management more along the lines of a dead-founders foundations.

A word of caution is necessary, especially in the context of executive compensation at foundations. A significant movement is developing within the social sector questioning the potential contra-fiduciary issues associated with the goal of maximizing return on foundation assets in order to increase investment asset basis with little or no consideration to the present value or opportunity costs of lost mission. A related source of concern is the apparent relationship between asset size and foundation executive compensation. The information contained in the Working Book, not surprisingly, indicates an apparently strong correlation.

As for educational alternatives, social sector executives unfortunately have received insufficient training on Intersectoral topics. There are several more established programs that offer a useful curriculum, although the field still needs to develop much further. There are emerging alternatives that appear quite promising, and CPs are advised to monitor their progress, especially those offering highly 24/7/365 global access and networking.

Social sector capital market opportunities are especially promising for positive sector transformation, and NPB can help advance its progress. The issue of the importance of the capital markets and/or financial technologies may vary, but its vital role merits considerable study, especially with regard to NPB. Some firmly espouse a view that social prosperity conceptually equals an equation where financial technology is allocated equal weighting and multiplied by the sum of human capital, social capital, and real assets.

"Historically, discussions of funding in the nonprofit sector have touched primarily on grants, annual funding campaigns, direct mail and endowment funds. Only recently have these discussions evolved toward a realization that the resources supporting the work of the nonprofit sector are more than simply a variety of charitable fundraising efforts, but actually form a distinct capital market – The Nonprofit Capital Market."[256]

In this context, costs of raising capital for NGOs is an area especially appropriate for NPB. Wide disparities exist between what is considered acceptable. Estimates of cost of fundraising range as high as 70% and even one oversight group advocates 35% as an acceptable target not be exceeded.

Large bodies of knowledge firmly indicate that performance and capital are inextricably intertwined, and that the benefits of capital include information technology, organizational effectiveness, and enhanced competitiveness.

Chart 14: Select Intersectoral Capital Market Challenges provides a conceptual overview of these trends and issues. The center of the diagram is focused on the target of transformative change, which is the "Astronomical Fundraising Cost on Restrictive/Oppressive Terms." Among the issues highlighted are the absence of powerful and consistent intellectual capital and the importance of unleashing the market forces of capitalism.

CPs can have a direct and powerful impact in applying NPB to the capital market issues of their target NGOs. The process may not be all that complicated to the extent that best-in-class NGOs can be isolated. Innovative ideas and carefully managed risk will be part of the process.

The enablers or deliverable opportunities composing the Performance Gap may not be so simple to determine. However, in addition to NGOs setting new standards in the cost and composition of their capital structure, they may also locate opportunities where commercial ventures are a positive alternative to the more traditional capital market instruments.

This section provides a sampling of successful publicly traded companies with social sector mission elements for a database of over 200 publicly traded companies with such mission elements. Broadly, these companies can be classified into eleven major sectors: Arts & Culture, Biotechnology, Community Development, Education, Educational Publishing, Edutainment, Environment, Financial, Hospitals, Health Care Services, Health Support Services, Human Services, Long Term Care, Medical Devices, Professional Services, and Technology. Within each of these categories, publicly traded companies stand out as having outperformed to some extent their social sector equivalents, in both their fiscal health and the quality of their service. In essence, a very real Performance Gap exists between equivalent NGOs and commercial firms.

Social-sector organizations can benefit from drawing upon the best practices of public companies in the Intersectoral area. NPB facilitates identifying Performance Gaps and Deliverable Opportunities between current social sector-only organizations and best practice social mission commercial organizations, thereby advancing value creation and forging an Intersectoral evolution.

There is considerable reason to be confident that the potential exists for the social sector capital market instruments. Developing highly skilled, dedicated, and niche-focused financial intermediaries, especially investment banks and merchant banks, in the social sector is essential to advancing the positive transformation of the social sector capital markets.

CPs are directed to collaborate with experienced talent to understand and assess risk factors similar in framework to those in the commercial sector. Minimization and management of risk factors is arguably much more important in social sector initiatives. Much tenacious pioneering in this area will in all likelihood be necessary as not only will cultural issues present challenges, but consideration of exposure to unintended consequences, the realities and myths of fiduciary obligations, and potentially contra-fiduciary actives within the social sector are formative at best.

[Supplemental note: An extensive NPB revolution will undoubtedly create uproar. As Sievers and Nelson suggest, complaints are often largely based on superficial cultural barriers. Passionate CPs can be catalysts of major transformation within the social sector. NPB addresses both processes and comparative assessment, which is clearly a caveat solution. NPB does not claim to be a panacea, although NPB is a positive opportunity to bring measurements, comparisons, and greater value creation to the social sector. Further ideas and collaboration create the possibility for a more advanced discourse as the NPB Working Book is only one step towards "New" Philanthropy.]

Chart 15: <u>Educational Components of New Philanthropy Benchmarking</u>

Classic Benchmarking Pyramid + *Progressive Intersectoral Practices* + *NPB Analytical Tactics*

Hard Metrics → Social Enterprise → Multiplier/Discount Effect

3rd Party Verifiable Metrics → Strategic Philanthropy & Restructuring → Performance Gap

Extensive Comparable Internal Metrics → Social Capital Markets → Deliverable Opportunities

Closing Words of Thanks

Many individuals and organizations provided useful insights and assistance in the formulation and construction of this Working Book. My advisor at Lincoln School, Joan Countryman, provided strong encouragement and support from the inception of the project. Mr. Jed Emerson provided practical insights during the preparation of the paper, valuable support to allow my devotion to its preparation, and whose works merit his designation as one of the most influential individuals in the social sector. Mr. Edgar Bronfman, Sr. and Mr. Richard Marker of the Seagram Foundation provided exceptionally valuable insights and inspiration during the early stages of the Working Book's preparation.

Messrs. Michael Levin, Jason Wall, and Ricardo Soto, affiliates of the Japonica Foundation, provided numerous social sector insights and emendations. Other individuals to whom I owe a considerable statement of gratitude for varied assistance include Mark F. Ogan, Tito Cohen, and Jason Saul.

I'm especially indebted to many members of my family who committed time and effort well beyond reasonable expectations, including my siblings (Paul, Ani, Sema, and Charlie), my parents (Harriet and Paul), and my grandparents.

However, it's important to note that I accept full responsibility for all the materials and views expressed in this Working Book, especially those that are most likely to generate controversial dialogue.

APPENDIX A

CAPITALIST/PHILANTHROPIST ("CP") PROFILES

Within Appendix A, Capitalist/Philanthropist ("CP") Profiles, seven CPs are profiled: the Bronfman Brothers (Edgar Sr. & Charles – counted as one), William H. Gates, Michael Milken, Thomas Monaghan, George Soros, Steven Spielberg, and Michael Steinhardt.

Each profile's section contains Sections A to O:

Section A	Overview
Section B	Foundations
Section C	Foundation Goals
Section D	Assets of Foundations
Section E	Successful Ventures
Section F	Attempted Ventures
Section G	Biography
Section H	Personal Assets
Section I	Why Give
Section J	Religious Influence
Section K	Books Written
Section L	Books Read with Substantial Impact
Section M	Quotations
Section N	Interesting Facts
Section O	Internet Resources

Bronfman Brothers - Edgar Sr. and Charles

A. Overview:

Brothers Edgar and Charles Bronfman have achieved many successful initiatives in the social sector. Some would justifiably note that these successes are comparable to those achieved in the commercial sector. Both have clearly applied commercially relevant marketing talents honed at Seagram's to their social sector efforts. Edgar's work in combining several major Jewish organizations is an impressive example of strategic restructuring. Charles, co-founder of the Birthright Israel project, is innovative and possesses a quantifiably measurable initiative. The initiative is also a premier example of collaboration with multiple public and private entities. Edgar's leadership efforts utilizing commercial litigation to recover funds for Holocaust survivors is already legendary and a blueprint for other victims of similar crimes. Valuable perspectives that are both consistent with and support NPB wisdom include measurements that illustrate true initiatives and the concept of focusing above and beyond fundraising, reiterating that "it's simply a tool."

Summary of author's notes of interviews with Edgar Bronfman and foundation executive Richard Marker:

A personal interview with Edgar Bronfman exceeded this author's very high expectations. He began the interview by noting that "giving is so much more than just giving money, it's giving of yourself." His passion is evident: "My heart is not with the little meshugaas, but with the Jewish people and humanity." One of his strengths is investing more time and demonstrating leadership by "taking on projects that others don't want and completing them to exceed expectations." A key to his success is an ability to delegate. He says, "Learn to select the right people. People who are smart, bright, entrepreneurial, and aggressive. With a good person, you discuss, agree, and then you leave, and they go on. In the meantime, they do as much as they can, and if they have any questions they will contact you. But, they have to be working, and you must trust them to work and that's how you find good managers." He believes that developing managers in the social sector is more challenging given so many historic cultural issues. As for benchmarking, he displays the instincts of a highly successful CP, and says this is just a part of everyday life. He is a strong proponent of creativity and innovation. "Creativity is when you have a group that is greater than the sum of the parts, and whatever doesn't innovate constantly will die," he explains. He has carefully sought to apply his commercial skills, particularly in management and marketing, to his social sector endeavors.

Richard Marker, Executive Vice President and a trustee of Edgar Bronfman's largest foundation, offered several insightful, relevant value-creation related observations. "Regarding our collaboration efforts, we become involved with other organizations so that we can have a greater impact with the program." He also noted that "when assessing grant requests, it's prudent to determine how the recipient plans to measure the impact, as this illustrates their true perspectives."

Both interviews occurred in New York City; Edgar Bronfman's on October 12, 1999, and Richard Marker's on September 25, 1999.

This Working Book quantifies four metrics that benchmark the efficiency and effectiveness of foundations. Edgar Bronfman's initiatives rank quite favorably in comparison to both CP foundations profiled (Live-Founder Foundations) and foundations in the aggregate (classified for simplicity as Dead-Founder Foundations).[257] Although the former is a subset of the latter, a recalculation of the aggregate metrics without the Live-Founder Foundation would only strengthen the comparative conclusions.

> • *Annual Percentage of Qualifying Distribution:* Calculates the percentage of distributions paid out of each foundation's net asset value. Foundations as a group distribute approximately 5.5%. Bronfman's foundations paid out 43% in 1998, well above the average. The weighted average for the Live-Founders profiled as best-in-class CP was an average of 65%. The higher average percentage is in part logically based on Edgar's philanthropic strategy of dedicating his primary efforts to NGOs and utilizing his foundations for more diverse initiatives. Several other CPs utilize their foundations as effective operating initiatives, which results in a significantly higher annual percentage distribution. In certain instances, CPs achieve an annual percentage in excess of 100%, and then replenish the foundation with new resources.

> • *Concentration of 5 Largest Initiatives:* Measures the percentage of annual dollars expended to five largest initiatives. These initiatives may be a specific NGO initiative or closely aligned projects, such as several spe-

cific ethnic group schools within one geographic region or medical treatment projects in various countries but affiliated through a common initiative. The greater level of concentration is assumed to indicate a higher level of specific expertise and offer a greater probability of contributing value-added or risk minimization. Dead-Founder foundations (foundations in the aggregate) make grants in 10 unregulated areas according to a recent study. Bronfman foundations concentrated 53% of their distributions to their top 5 initiatives. The Live-Founders group averaged a greater concentration at 79%, which is in part attributable to the 90%+ focus of several CP foundations.

• *Average Dollar Grant and Average Annual Grant for the Top 5 Initiatives:* Average annual dollar distributions is for all grants in excess of $10,000 and the average annual grant for the top five initiatives is based on the methodology indicated in the Concentration of 5 Largest Initiatives endnote. Larger amounts are assumed to indicate a higher value-added and passionate commitment to social sector initiatives. This is somewhat analogous to the commercial sector investment strategies of limited number of concentrated investment versus an index approach of making a sufficiently large number of small investments so no one investment can have a material impact on the investing entity's aggregate performance. The Dead-Founder foundations (with assets between $51 million and $999 million) average $60,000 to $110,000 in individual grants, which effectively prohibits detailed performance analysis. The Samuel Bronfman Foundation made grants averaging $934,000 to each of top five initiatives metric. The average was more in-line with foregoing based in part on Edgar's concentration on leading major NGOs. The Living-Founders studied averaged $29 million to their top five initiatives and $19 million for average dollar grants.

• *Percentage of Assets Invested in Indexed Equities:* Compares the average percentage of foundation assets invested in indexed equity funds in contrast to more aggressive alternative investments. Dead-Founders are approximately 40% to 60% invested in indexed equity funds. The Samuel Bronfman Foundation is invested principally in Seagram's stock (recently acquired by Vivendi). For the Living-Founder foundations as a group, indexed equity investments are essentially nominal.

B. Foundations:

> **Edgar:**
> 1. President, The World Jewish Congress
> 2. President, The World Jewish Restitution Organization
> 3. Chairman, Foundation for Jewish Campus Life
> 4. Chairman, The Samuel Bronfman Foundation
>
> **Charles:**
> 1. Chairman, United Jewish Communities
> 2. Founder, Andrea and Charles Bronfman Philanthropies
> 3. Co-founder (with Michael Steinhardt), Birthright Israel
> 4. With other Canadian billionaires like Galen Weston and Harrison McCain, launched www.histori.ca, site dedicated to Canada's culture and history

C. Foundation Goals:

The **World Jewish Congress** (WJC) is an international federation of Jewish communities and organizations. As an umbrella group it represents Jews from the entire political spectrum and from all Jewish religious denominations. Serving as a diplomatic arm of the Jewish people to world governments and international organizations, it tries to preserve the principle of unity in diversity and always seeks consensus. Since 1987, the WJC has sponsored the Israel Council on Foreign Relations, which is directed by the organization's Israel office. The WJC strives to coordinate the common interest of its members, defending Jewish rights and status without interfering in domestic affairs. The plenary assembly, convening every five years, is the supreme authority of the Congress; the governing board meets between the assemblies, and its executive committee conducts the affairs of the organization. Source: www.virtualjerusalem.com/orgs/orgs/wjc/what.htm

The WJC is organized to foster the unity of the Jewish people, to strive for the fulfillment of its aspirations, and to ensure the continuity and development of its religious spiritual, cultural, and social heritage, and to that end it seeks:

> 1. To intensify the bonds of world Jewry with Israel as the central creative force in Jewish life and to strengthen the ties of solidarity among Jewish communities everywhere.

2. To secure the rights, status, and interests of Jews and Jewish communities and to defend them wherever they are denied, violated, or imperiled.
3. To encourage and assist the creative development of Jewish social, religious, and cultural life throughout the world.
4. To coordinate the efforts of Jewish communities and organizations with respect to the political, economic, social, religious, and cultural problems of the Jewish people.
5. To represent and act on behalf of its participating communities and organizations before governmental, intergovernmental, and other international authorities with respect to matters which concern the Jewish people as a whole.

The WJC strives to cooperate with all peoples on the basis of universal ideals of peace, freedom and justice. Source: WJC Charter.

World Jewish Restitution Organization is an umbrella organization seeking restitution of Jewish property for Holocaust survivors from European governments, Swiss banks, and other European institutions.
Source: www.virtual.co.il/orgs/orgs/wjc/what.htm

United Jewish Communities resulted from the merger of the Council of Jewish Federations, the United Israel Appeal, and the United Jewish Appeal. Its stated mission is to:

• Utilize our financial and human resources to improve the quality of Jewish life worldwide – honoring the covenant that "All Jews are Responsible One for the Other," and that only through unified action can we solve our community's most pressing problems;
• Nurture vital experiences of Jewish life and learning in North America to create a compelling culture of shared meaning, shared responsibility, and shared values, such as Klal Yisrael, or "one people in all its diversity," combined with a shared commitment to its future;
• Join in partnership with fellow Jews in Israel to build unity and mutual respect and solidify Israel's central role in our Jewish identity and future;
• Inspire Jews to fulfill the mitzvah of Tzedakah, securing the financial and human resources necessary to achieve our mission of caring for those in

need, rescuing Jews in danger, and ensuring the continuity of our people;

• Provide the strategic resources, assistance, and direction to help local federations fulfill their individual, regional, and collective responsibilities of Tikkun Olam, community building and Jewish renaissance; and

• Involve more of our fellow Jews in the work of our community and provide opportunities for a new generation of leaders to continue our sacred work of caring for one another.

Source: www.uja.com/ourmission/mission.htm

Birthright Israel offers to present lifelong Jewish values to young Jewish adults worldwide through a first educational peer-group trip to Israel. Made possible through a $210 million partnership from a group of prominent philanthropists, local Jewish Federations, the people of Israel through their government, Keren Hayesod and The Jewish Agency for Israel.

Source: www.israelexperience.org/birthright_gift_about.htm

Foundation for Jewish Campus Life ("Hillel"): Hillel's mission is to maximize the number of Jews doing Jewish activities with other Jews. Hillel actively seeks to engage uninvolved Jewish students on their own terms: to provide them with opportunities to do Jewish activities and traditions that are meaningful and appealing to them. Students are empowered to take responsibility for their Jewish identity, whether they wish to participate in community service projects, express themselves artistically, participate in social events, engage in informal Jewish learning or attend religious services. Any student may participate in Hillel – no membership is required. Hillel is committed to a pluralistic vision of Judaism that embraces all movements.

The Hillel Board of Directors, chaired by Chuck Newman of Ann Arbor, Michigan, sets Hillel policy. Members of the board include volunteer and student leaders from North America and abroad. The Hillel International Board of Governors provides counsel and advice to the Board of Directors. The chairman of the Board of Governors is Edgar M. Bronfman of New York, NY, and co-chairs are Michael Steinhardt of New York, NY, and Charles Schusterman of Tulsa, OK. Richard M. Joel is the President and International Director of Hillel.

Source: www.hillel.org/hillel/newhille.nsf

Andrea and Charles Bronfman Philanthropies: Support efforts to provide educational programs to Israeli children and to run educational programs about environmental conservation. Makes grants to projects that improve relations between

Israeli and Palestinian people and that strengthen connections between Jews in Israel and Jews in the rest of the world. CRB Foundation supports efforts that strengthen unity of Jewish people around the world or that promote Canadian culture and heritage.
Source: The Chronicle of Philanthropy, 11/18/99 www.philanthropy.com/free/articles/v12/i03/03000802.htm

D. Assets of Foundations:

World Jewish Congress American Section, Inc.
501 Madison Avenue - 17th Floor
New York, NY 10022
Fiscal Year: 1998 Assets: $9,204,625 Income: $9,458,227
EIN: 13-1790756 Ruling Year: 1953

The Foundation for Jewish Campus Life
1640 Rhode Island Avenue, NW
Washington, DC 20036
Fiscal Year: 1998Assets: $12,775,465 Income: $12,027,362
EIN: 52-1844823 Ruling Year: 1993

Samuel Bronfman Foundation, Inc.
375 Park Avenuet
6th Floor
New York, NY 10152
Fiscal Year: 1998 Assets: $20,907,756
EIN: 13-6084708 Ruling Year: 1952

Andrea and Charles Bronfman Philanthropies, Inc.
375 Park Ave. - 6th Floor
New York, NY 10152-0002
Financial Info Assets: $ 0
EIN: 13-3984936 Ruling Year: 1998

United Jewish Communities
111 Eighth Ave. Suite 11E
New York, NY 10011-5201
www.jewishcommunities.org
Fiscal Year: 1997
Assets: $31,910,166
Income: $323,114,918

E. Successful Ventures:

1991 The Jerusalem Report
1997 Swiss Bank Restitution
1999 Birthright Israel

F. Attempted Ventures: TBD

G. Biographies:

Born: Edgar 1929
         Charles 1931

Faith: Jewish

Early years:

Recently: Edgar Sr. inherited U.S. assets after father Sam died in 1971; in 1994 passed reins to son Edgar Jr. who transformed Seagram's into an entertainment giant.

H. Personal Assets:

Bronfman Family (mainly through brothers Edgar and Charles and Edgar's son Edgar, Jr.) own 24% of The Seagram Company Ltd. (4 segments - music, filmed entertainment, recreation and other, and spirits and wine). Company started by Samuel Bronfman, father of Edgar and Charles, as Spirits Company in 1924. Seagram's merged into Vivendi, creating a fully integrated global media and Communications Company for the wired and wireless world. Value of all stock deal - US$34 Billion.

Edgar: $4.1 billion, *Forbes*, October 9, 2000.
Charles: $3.3 billion, *Forbes*, July 2, 2000

I. Why Give:

Edgar: Create unity between Jewish people and their heritage, gain restitution for Holocaust survivors and the Jewish Community

Charles: On Birthright Israel: "I'm trying to make Jews. You can live a perfectly decent life not being Jewish, but I think you're losing a lot – losing the kind of feeling you have when you know throughout the world there are people who somehow or other have the same kind of DNA that you have." Hockstader, Lee, "Selling Jewishness to Jews": A $210 million program that aims to connect young Jews with their heritage is sending 6,000 to Israel. *Washington Post*, January 17, 2000

J. Religious Influence:

Edgar: Avoided religion as rebellion against father until father died. Edgar was then recruited as chairman of World Jewish Congress.

K. Books Written:

Bronfman, Edgar M. *The Making of a Jew.*
Bronfman, Edgar M. *Good Spirits: The Making of a Businessman.*

L. Books Read with Substantial Impact: TBD

M. Quotations:

Edgar:
• Giving is a Jewish person's obligation.
• *Tzedakah* establishes priorities.
• Giving of oneself is more valuable than one's treasures.
• Utilize tactical benefits to influence others.
• Create value through collaborating.

• The key to management is delegation.

• Measurements illustrate true initiatives

"If only the Swiss bankers had offered him a chair, and if only they had not offered him $30 million to shut up and go away."

Charles:

On merger of UJA and CJF into UJC, decision to handle disputes internally, and frustrations during tenure as chairman of the UJC:

"It's going to take a number of years for this group to sort itself out and figure out who it is and what it is."

"When a person like me gets into an organization like this, it's going to be frustrating, and I was frustrated. I'm no longer frustrated because I understand the bounds of what I can get done. It's not like business."

Gootman, Elissa, "UJC Prepares to Squelch Public Airing of Disputes, Curb Overseas Allocation," *The Forward*, 5/12/00.

Bronfman hopes consolidation will make his new group more effective. "In business, we've had this going on for over a decade," he said. "Downsizing and taking a look at ourselves and being more productive." Beth Gardiner, Jewish charities find fund-raising harder. *The Atlanta Journal - The Atlanta Constitution* 11/27/99.

On giving and fund-raising:

When one is responsible for raising funds, "all you care about is raising more than the last guy" who ran a fund-raising effort. "You can't just focus on [fund-raising] competition. Fund raising is not a Jewish goal. It's just a tool" to build Jewish communities, he said. "Bronfman Creating Center in Bid to Wed Federations, Foundations," *The Forward*, 5/3/99.

On group of 20 wealthiest and most influential US Jewish businessmen (The Study Group):

"The Study Group's members want to take a more entrepreneurial and strategic approach to giving, learning from one another, contributing to one another's causes, launching projects together." [e.g. Birthright Israel]

N. Interesting Facts:

Edgar: Awarded Medal of Freedom. Member United States Holocaust Memorial Council.

Charles: Oversaw merger of United Jewish Appeal and Council of Jewish Federations into United Jewish Communities

O. Internet Resources:

World Jewish Congress: www.virtualjerusalem.com/orgs/orgs/wjc

The World Jewish Restitution Organization:
www.geocities.com/Paris/Rue/4017/wjro.htm

Foundation for Jewish Campus Life: www.hillel.org

The Samuel Bronfman Foundation (Bronfman Youth Fellowships):
www.bronfman.org/index.html

United Jewish Communities: www.uja.com

Andrea and Charles Bronfman Philanthropies:
philanthropy.com/free/articles/v12/i03/03000802.htm

Birthright Israel: www.israelexperience.org

William H. Gates

A. Overview:

It is widely known that Bill Gates rigorously seeks comparisons in his analysis of new business proposals. That practice is consistent with the most basic element of NP Benchmarking. In his philanthropic endeavors, he leverages his technology resources to advance his foundation's mission. Gates encourages commercial contacts to participate in social sector initiatives, especially skilled technology and management professionals.

Gates Foundation notes that the common theme of its benefactors' giving is "reality is equity." "Right now we have unprecedented opportunities to improve people's lives. The goal of the foundation is to bring some of those opportunities in terms of health and education to people who might not have them."[258]

Efforts in collaborative initiatives include a major college merit scholarship program with established NGOs, a library technology program with 3000 libraries in 25 states, and medical vaccines research initiatives with commercial pharmaceutical companies. The major Gates Foundation effort also appears to be seeking opportunities for strategic initiatives to advance modern science, especially medicine, in what could be highly successful commercial ventures.

More recently, Gates has publicly confessed that he was "naïve - very naïve" when he began his more focused engagement in philanthropy in 1994.[259] Now he assumes possibly the more natural role of a self-described "troublemaker" about the promises of technology.[260] Gates appears to have refocused his belief that global capitalism is capable of solving the most immediate catastrophes facing the world's poorest and suffering, especially the 40,000 deaths a day from preventable diseases.[261]

This Working Book quantifies four metrics that benchmark the efficiency and effectiveness of foundations. William Gates' initiatives rank quite favorably in comparison to both CP foundations profiled (Live-Founder Foundations) and foundations in the aggregate (classified for simplicity as Dead-Founder Foundations).[262] Although the former is a subset of the latter, a recalculation of the aggregate metrics without the Live-Founder Foundation would only strengthen the comparative conclusions.

• *Annual Percentage of Qualifying Distribution:* Calculates the percentage of distributions paid out of each foundation's net asset value. Foundations as a group distribute approximately 5.5%. Gates' foundations paid out 11%. The weighted average for the Live-Founders profiled as best-in-class CP was an average of 65%. Gates percentage is understandable given the growth of his fund and absolute dollar size, which now stands in excess of 50 times larger than the nearest NPB CP. Gates Foundation distribution is still twice as high as the typical foundation at 5.5%. Several other CPs utilize their foundations as effectively operating initiatives, which results in a significantly higher annual percentage distribution. In certain instances, CPs achieve an annual percentage in excess of 100%, and then replenish the foundation with new resources. Such an approach is highly impractical and – indeed unwise – especially given the massive relatively liquid asset base of the Gates Foundation.

• *Concentration of 5 Largest Initiatives:* Measures the percentage of annual dollars expended to five largest initiatives. These initiatives may be a specific NGO initiative or closely aligned projects, such as several specific ethic group schools within one geographic region or medical treatment projects in various countries but affiliated through a common initiative. The greater level of concentration is assumed to indicate a higher level of specific expertise and offer a greater probability of contributing value-added or risk minimization. Dead-Founder foundations (foundations in the aggregate) make grants in 10 unregulated areas according to a recent study. Gates' foundations concentrated 60% of their distributions to their top 5 initiatives metric. The Live-Founders group averaged a greater concentration at 79%, which is in part attributable to the 90% plus focus of several CP foundations.

• *Average Dollar Grant and Average Annual Grant for The Top 5 Initiatives:* Average annual dollar distributions is for all grant in excess of $10,000 and the average annual grants for the top five initiatives is based on the methodology indicated in the Concentration of 5 Largest Initiatives endnote. Larger amounts are assumed to indicate a higher value-added and passionate commitment to social sector initiatives. This is somewhat analogous to the commercial sector investment strategies of limited number of concentrated investment versus an index approach of making a sufficiently large number of small investments so no one investment can have a material impact on the investing entity's aggregate performance. The Dead-Founder foundations (with assets between $51 million and $999 million) average $60,000 to $110,000 in individual grants, which effectively prohibits detailed performance analysis. The Bill and Melinda Gates Foundation made grants averaging $66 million to each of top five initiatives and $3.5 million on average. The dollars to the top five initiatives is obviously a significant multiple of the average NPB CP. However, the size of Gates' fund is so much larger that it is – in some respects - a study in contrast compared to the other CPs. Worthy of note, the average NPB CP grant is larger than Gates even with its massively larger asset base, some 22 times larger than the closest CP. The Living-Founders studied averaged $29 million to their top five initiatives and $19 million for average dollar grants. Overall, Gates' high impact philanthropy approach is very consistent with the messages of NPB.

• *Percentage of Assets Invested in Indexed Equities:* Compares the average percentage of foundation assets invested in indexed equity funds in contrast to more aggressive alternative investments. Dead-Founders are approximately 40% to 60% invested in indexed equity funds. Indexed equity investments are essentially nominal because such successful business people and investor are rarely interested in average and more focused on the impact of their funds and distributing them as quickly as possible.

B. Foundations:

Bill & Melinda Gates Foundation
(In 1999, the William H. Gates Foundation and the Gates Library Foundation were consolidated into the Bill & Melinda Gates Foundation.)

C. Foundations Goals:
Places a major focus on helping to improve people's lives through health and learning. "We will continue to look for strategic opportunities to extend the benefits of modern science and technology to people around the world, especially where poverty serves as an obstacle to participating in these benefits. As in the past, we will invest in partnerships with indi-

viduals and organizations that bring experience, expertise and commitment to their own efforts to help people through better health and learning. Source: www.gatesfoundation.org/about/default.htm

The Bill & Melinda Gates Foundation is dedicated to improving people's lives by sharing advances in health and learning with the global community. Led by Bill Gates' father, William H. Gates, Sr., and Patty Stonesifer, the Seattle-based Foundation has an asset base of approximately $21 billion. Preventing deadly diseases among poor children by expanding access to vaccines, and developing vaccines against malaria, HIV/AIDS and tuberculosis are central priorities. Other major efforts include extending unprecedented opportunities for learning by bringing computers with Internet access to every eligible public library in the U.S. and Canada and providing scholarships to academically talented minority students in the U.S with severe financial need through the Gates Millennium Scholars Program (www.gmsp.org).

D. Gates Foundation Information

Bill & Melinda Gates Foundation
1551 Eastlake Avenue East
Seattle, WA 98102
Fiscal Year: 1999
Assets: $15,515,454,543
EIN:91-1663695
Ruling Year: TBD

E. Successful Ventures:

Microsoft
Cascade Investments

F. Attempted Ventures: TBD

G. Biography:

Born: 1955, Seattle, WA

Faith: Congregationalist by birth.

Early years: At 13 Gates wrote his first computer program. Soon after
wards, he and his friend and Microsoft co-founder Paul Allen
wrote scheduling program for the school. Still in high school,
Gates and Allen founded a company called Traf-O-Data, which
analyzed city traffic data. Founded Microsoft in 1975 as a partnership in 1975 and incorporated in 1981.

Recently: Stepped aside as CEO of Microsoft, naming college classmate
Steve Ballmer as the new CEO. Federal Judge ruled against
Microsoft in an antitrust trial (now under appeal) and wants the
company split in two. Its Internet plan to rollout Microsoft.Net, a
$4.4 billion subscription based Web service, has not impressed
investors. Using his own Cascade Investments to buy stakes in
both old economy companies – shipbuilder Newport News
Shipbuilding, real estate firm Castle & Cooke and in one that has
yet to materialize; ICO-Teledesic Global, the satellite-based
"Internet in the sky" venture founded by Craig McCaw.

H. Personal Assets:

$63 Billion, *Forbes*, 10.9.00.

I. Why Give:

"By word and example, his parents taught young Bill the virtues of giving generously. . . . [Gates] inherited his parents' social liberalism and
empathetic view of poor people. In a nation turning away from affirma-
tive action, he has firmly restated his support of it and backed up his
words with the billion-dollar Millennium Scholars Program for minority
students." Williams, Roger M., *Foundation News & Commentary*,
May/June 2000. [Father was prominent lawyer, active in United Way and
other charities. Mother, deceased, was a "charity activist."]

"We have a social imperative to work together to address basic inequity" that leaves [third world] children without vaccines for years. "The objective that we all have to shares is to help every child in the world enjoy the health and the length of life that a child born in Seattle can expect today." Williams, *Id.*, quoting Gates.

Vartan Gregorian - "More important than why he's doing this is what he's doing. The proof will be in the pudding." Strouse, Jean, "How to Give Away $21.8 Billion" *New York Times* Magazine, 4.16.00

Gates' father provided insight into their family's view on repeal of the US estate tax in responding to a New York Time interviewer's questions. In response to the question, 'If the estate tax is repealed, charities will most likely suffer. Does that mean a lot of Americans are giving to charity not out of generosity?' Gates replied, "That's true. I think there are mixed motives, both charitable and selfish. The motive is to do something good and to do something to save yourself money. A double motive." He later comments that "without the tax motivation, there will be a serious diminishing of charitable giving."[263]

J. Religious Influence: TBD

K. Books Written:

> *Business @ the Speed of Thought: Succeeding in the Digital Economy*
> *Business @ the Speed of Thought: Using a Digital Nervous System*
> *The Road Ahead*
> *Los Negocios En La Era Digital* (Jose Antonio Bravo, Translator)

L. Books Read with Substantial Impact:

> Carnegie, Andrew. *Gospel of Wealth*.

M. Quotations:

> Gates, quoting Winston Churchill, "We make a living by what we get, we make a life by what we give." Annual Reports for the William H. Gates Foundation and the Gates Library Foundation, 12.98.

Well aware that effective philanthropy requires as much time and creativity as building a business does, Gates considers himself "very early on the learning curve of this stuff," he says. "there are just an infinite number of things to be figured out." Strouse, *NYT*.

Gates has publicly confessed that he was "naïve - very naïve" when he began his more focused engagement in philanthropy back in six years ago in 1994.[264]

"We have found that giving away money in a strategic and meaningful way is as challenging, and interesting, as working in technology." Bill & Melinda Gates Foundation, 1999 Annual Report.

Regarding Vartan Gregorian: when Gates first met him, he thought, "Why is this guy spending time getting to know me? First, he was at Brown. So I wondered, does he want a bunch of money for Brown? And then he'd come and see me and we'd talk about what were good causes, or what was going on with foundations." It turned out that Gregorian just wanted to encourage Gates to think about giving money away, not ask for any. Strouse, *New York Times*.

"The only way great vaccines will be created is by working with the pharmaceutical industry and encouraging them to take more risks, knowing that governments and philanthropists will work with them to make sure there is a market." Bank, David, "Gates Earmarks $750 Million to Spur Work on Vaccines," *WSJ*, 8/27/99.

"Vaccines should be given a high priority because they carry with them the promise of staving off billions of dollars in health-care costs." Verhovek, Sam Howe, "Elder Bill Gates Takes on the Role of Philanthropist," *NYT*, 9.11.99.

"Man who dies thus rich dies disgraced" AC WC "Knowledge is power. Information is liberating. Education is the premise of progress, in every society, in every family."

N. Interesting Facts:

- Twin focal points for grant making: global health and learning. In some pronouncements, access to technology is a third. Williams, *Id.*

- Biggest foundation: $21.8B, surpassed Britain's Wellcome Trust; Fastest-ever ramp-up: 11-fold growth since end of '98; Biggest gifts ever by living donor in fields of education and health. Williams, Roger M., *Foundation News & Commentary,* May/June 2000.

- In my years at Ford [Foundation], says Perkin [Gordon Perkin director of health program], "we had about one staff person per $1 million in grants. Here we handle $550 million in grants with a staff of five." Williams, *Id.*

- "You know, it would be possible to blow $100 billion" and have no impact at all, says Patricia Stonesifer, who manages the $21 billion Bill and Melinda Gates Foundation. Hardy, Quentin, The Radical Philanthropist, *Forbes Magazine,* 5/1/00.

- 2000 – Disburse $1B, almost all going to learning and health. Corcoran, Elizabeth, The World's Richest Donors, *Forbes Magazine,* 5/1/00.

- Gates Library: first year worked with 7,000 libraries in 25 states based on poverty status.

O. Internet Resources:

Bill & Melinda Gates Foundation: www.gatesfoundation.org

Michael Milken

A. Overview:

Michael Milken, considered one of his generation's most innovative and effective investment bankers, has carefully spearheaded a number of important relevant initiatives. His largest, most visible effort is possibly Knowledge Universe, ("KU") with his role as lead investor of this now major public company. KU is considered a progressive multidimensional company pioneering areas of education and technology. Today, the company has completed 30 acquisitions and started over 6 companies, with combined annual revenues exceeding one billion dollars. KU, in a collaborative effort, obtained funding of approximately $250 million from Larry Ellison, CEO of Oracle. Milken is an early investor in another multidimensional start-up, UNext Inc., a distance learning company. Possibly one of his most committed efforts involves the founding of CaP CURE in the 1993, an aggressive cancer research organization. CaP CURE has raised $160 million (, and is publishing cancer-related research to further its missions.[265] An editorial in a prominent international business daily displayed his "six keys to meeting challenging philanthropy" (see below). Milken's socio-economic model exclusively analyzing the elements and relationships of social capital creation has been widely disseminated. Also, his focus on ROI in the context of philanthropic initiatives is clearly advancing the creation of value.

This Working Book quantifies four metrics that benchmark the efficiency and effectiveness of foundations. Michael Milken's initiatives rank quite favorably in comparison to both CP foundations profiled (Live-Founder Foundations) and foundations in the aggregate (classified for simplicity as Dead-Founder Foundations).[266] Although the former is a subset of the latter, a recalculation of the aggregate metrics without the Live-Founder Foundation would only strengthen the comparative conclusions.

> • *Annual Percentage of Qualifying Distribution:* Calculates the percentage of distributions paid out of each foundation's net asset value. Foundations as a group distribute approximately 5.5%. Milken's foundations paid out 18%. The weighted average for the Live-Founders profiled as best-in-class CP was an average of 65%. The lower average percentage compared with the other CPs is in part logical based on Milken's interest in managing his funds to create business assets and these business assets are not intended to be distributed. These metrics

represent an strategy of Intersectoral investing that is consistent with the focus of NPB. Several other CPs utilize their foundations as effectively operating initiatives, which results in a significantly higher annual percentage distribution. In certain instances, CPs achieve an annual percentage in excess of 100%, and then replenish the foundation with new resources.

- *Concentration of 5 Largest Initiatives:* Measures the percentage of annual dollars expended to five largest initiatives. These initiatives may be a specific NGO initiative or closely aligned projects, such as several specific ethic group schools within one geographic region or medical treatment projects in various countries but affiliated through a common initiative. The greater level of concentration is assumed to indicate a higher level of specific expertise and offer a greater probability of contributing value-added or risk minimization. Dead-Founder foundations (foundations in the aggregate) make grants in 10 unregulated areas according to a recent study. Milken foundations concentrated 83% of their distributions to their top 5 initiatives metric. The Live-Founders group averaged a greater concentration at 79%, which is in part attributable to the 90% plus focus of several CP foundations.

- *Average Dollar Grant and Average Annual Grant for The Top 5 Initiatives:* Average annual dollar distributions is for all grant in excess of $10,000 and the average annual grants for the top five initiatives is based on the methodology indicated in the Concentration of 5 Largest Initiatives endnote. Larger amounts are assumed to indicate a higher value-added and passionate commitment to social sector initiatives. This is somewhat analogous to the commercial sector investment strategies of limited number of concentrated investment versus an index approach of making a sufficiently large number of small investments so no one investment can have a material impact on the investing entity's aggregate performance. The Dead-Founder foundations (with assets between $51 million and $999 million) average $60,000 to $110,000 in individual grants, which effectively prohibits detailed performance analysis. Michael Milken's foundations and initiatives made grants averaging approximately $1.4 million to each of top five initiatives, making it well above the dead founder average, by 12 to 22 times. The Average Dollar Grant reaches almost $700,000. The number maybe relatively smaller than the other NPB CPs, but this is to some extent a function of Milken's relatively smaller foundation asset base. The Living-Founders studied averaged $29 million to their top five initiatives and $19 million for average dollar grants.

• *Percentage of Assets Invested in Indexed Equities:* Compares the average percentage of foundation assets invested in indexed equity funds in contrast to more aggressive alternative investments. Dead-Founders are approximately 40% to 60% invested in indexed equity funds. Indexed equity investments are essentially nominal because such successful business people and investor are rarely interested in average and more focused on the impact of their funds and distributing them as quickly as possible.

B. Foundations and Initiatives:

1. Milken Family Foundation
2. Association for the Cure of Cancer of the Prostate ("CaP CURE")
3. Milken Institute - a think tank that conducts and publishes scholarly research
4. Knowledge Universe

C. Foundations/Initiative Goals:

Discover and advance inventive and effective ways of helping people help themselves.

Education: rewarding outstanding educators and expanding their professional leadership, encouraging talented young people to become educators, stimulating creativity and productivity among educators by using technology, fostering involvement of families and communities in schools, building vibrant communities in disadvantaged areas or involved with special needs children.

Medical: advancing and supporting medical research especially of prostate cancer and epilepsy, recognizing and rewarding outstanding scientists, supporting basic health care programs.

D. Milken foundations Information:

The Milken Family Foundation
1250 Fourth Street, Sixth Floor
Santa Monica, CA 90401
Fiscal Year: 1998
Assets: $285,857,297
EIN: 95-4073646
Ruling Year: TBD

The Milken Institute
1250 Fourth Street, Sixth Floor
Santa Monica, CA 90401
Fiscal Year: 1998
Assets: $35,829,868
EIN: 95-4240775
Ruling Year: TBD

E. Successful Ventures:

In 1993 Milken set up CaP CURE and currently raised $160 million.

Milken invested $250 million in Knowledge Universe in 1996; friend Larry Ellison (Oracle) also donated $250 million in 1996. In 1998 Knowledge Universe acquired 30 companies and started up 6 more. Knowledge Universe has quietly acquired companies in businesses ranging from day care centers to computer training, with combined revenues of $1.2 billion [in 1998].[267]

Knowledge Universe sales jumped from $17 million in 1997 to $80 million in 1999; total sales for Knowledge Universe in 1999 was $1.5 billion

F. Attempted Ventures:

Knowledge Universe spin-off – Nextera, a consulting firm gone public, whose stock is not doing well.

G. Biography:

Born: 1946, Los Angeles, CA

Faith: Jewish

Early years: As a boy he helped his accountant father prepare returns at tax time. Milken married his high school girlfriend after graduating from the University of California: Berkeley and then earned his MBA from Wharton before joining Drexel, Burnham, Lambert in 1970. He led the firm into the 1980s, using high-risk, high-yield bonds to finance corporate takeovers. *The Economist* said his financial innovations "are credited with fueling companies with bright ideas to get the money they need to develop them." This created millions of jobs, leading a *Time Magazine* to write in 1997, "Milken was right in almost every sense."

Recently: He is focused on the education industry, battling prostate cancer (now in remission), and his philanthropic efforts.

H. Personal Assets:

$800 Million, America's 400 Richest People, *Forbes*, 2000 Edition, 10.9.00.

I. Why Give:

"It is better to focus on the future – that is what gives me energy." Morris, Kathleen, "The Reincarnation of Mike Milken," *Business Week*, 5.10.99.

On Milken's self-image as a social scientist:

"I think I've had three missions in life," he explained. "The first mission in my view was the democratization of capital. I believe that mission succeeded by the early 1980s. The next mission we perceived was the democratization of knowledge . . . and then the third one would be the solution to what we would call the health problems. " White, Michael (AP), "Decade After Fall, Former Junk Bond King Presides Over New Empire" 4.27.99.

J. Religious Influence: TBD

K. Books Written:

> *The Taste for Living Cookbook: Mike Milken's Favorite Recipes for Fighting Cancer* (September 1998)

> *The Taste for Living World Cookbook: More of Mike Milken's Favorite Recipes for Fighting Cancer and Heart Disease* (October 1, 1999)

L. Books Read with Substantial Impact: TBD

M. Quotations:

> Six keys to meet challenge of philanthropy:
> 1. Follow your passion;
> 2. Get personally involved;
> 3. Think big;
> 4. Foster teamwork;
> 5. Fight the zero-sum game mentality (don't "spend" money on grants; invest in society to produce greater return); and
> 6. Transfer skills, not just money.

> Milken, Michael, Commentary: Manager's Journal: Advice for Bill Gates - "Follow Your Passion," *WSJ*, 10.4.00.

> "Funding expanded medical research would produce one of the greatest returns on investment in social capital . . . The main benefit would be an incalculable, but magnificent, reduction in human suffering; and the economic benefit of lives saved would be in the tens of trillions of dollars — all for the annual investment that is the equivalent of what Americans spend on beauty products." Milken, Michael, Commentary: Prosperity and Social Capital, *WSJ*, 6.23.99.

> Milken comments on his idyllic life and the shock of the 1965-Watts riot.

> "I'm out of this Happy Days family in the San Fernando Valley, and I couldn't understand why people were burning buildings that they were

living in or might have worked in," he said. Two days later, he drove to Watts, where his father had clients, and talked to a man who had set fire to his own workplace. "He had no savings and now he had no job. I asked him why and he told me that he wasn't a part of the system," Milken said. "He wasn't living the American Dream." When he returned to Berkeley a few days later, Milken switched his major from math to business with a vague idea of trying to change the financial system. Eventually he came to the conclusion that the system could be opened to more people by providing credit based on a company's potential instead of its past history. Junk bonds became the vehicle. "I viewed that as an opportunity. I viewed that as my own little revolution," he said. White, Michael (AP), "Decade After Fall, Former Junk Bond King Presides Over New Empire" 4.27.99.

"It is better to focus on the future - that is what gives me energy." Morris, Kathleen, "The Reincarnation of Mike Milken," *Business Week,* 5.10.99.

N. Interesting Facts:

Philosophy created at age 19, $P = \sum FT\ (\sum HC + \sum SC + \sum RA)$. Prosperity (P) equals the sum of financial technology ($\sum FT$) times the sum of human capital ($\sum HC$), social capital ($\sum SC$) and real assets ($\sum RA$).

Originally focused on "financial technology" and "democratizing capital." Then turned attention to "access to knowledge, and access to social capital," i.e. cancer research, education and public policy.

Venture into cancer research triggered by 1993 diagnosis of incurable prostate cancer and given 12-18 months to live. Radically changed life style and founded CaP CURE.

"In so many ways, he is who you hope your kids become. He is diligent, loyal, a great listener, grounded, persistent, optimistic, generous to a fault," say Joseph Costello. Morris, Kathleen, "The Reincarnation of Mike Milken," *Business Week,* 5.10.99.

Philanthropy, although probably not at same level and focus, began two decades ago. In the 1980s he began tutoring inner-city children.

The Milken Family Foundation was cited in a November 1999 paper by Thomas Backer ("Innovation in Context: New Foundation Approaches to Evaluation, Collaboration, and Best Practices") for its University-Community Outreach Program. The programs offer ways for universities to become more engaged in urban community development. The efforts include university-based entrepreneurship training and technical assistance through MBAs as technical advisors.

Worth Magazine ranked Milken #6 ahead of the Rockefeller brothers and behind Bill Gates.

O. Internet Resources:

Mike Milken: www.mikemilken.com
Milken Family Foundation: www.mff.org
Milken Institute: www.milken-institute.org
Knowledge Universe: www.knowledgeu.com
CaP CURE: www.capcure.org

Thomas Monaghan

A. Overview:

Thomas Monaghan's talents for innovation, organization, and leadership (amply evident in his building of the Domino's empire) are reflected in a number of his social sector philanthropic efforts. His hands-on approach earns him the title of a social entrepreneur. He is the founder of Legatus, a faith-based organization, for business executives to energize and magnify their social sector impact. Members are known as Executive Ambassadors of whom there are currently 1,300 in 25 chapters; the goal is to reach 10,000 members. He has founded an unprecedented initiative, a Catholic law school. Monaghan is financing a network of Catholic schools, is the founder of an impact-focused newspaper, and attempted a social enterprise venture via a network of nine Catholic radio stations. He offers valuable perspectives very much consistent with the comparative financial metrics of NP Benchmarking. His objective is to measure the return on investment by maximizing how many souls are saved per dollar. Monaghan reportedly utilizes the same zealous uncompromising approach to the social sector as he has done in his commercial sector ventures.

This Working Book quantifies four metrics that benchmark the efficiency and effectiveness of foundations. Thomas Monaghan's initiatives rank quite favorably in comparison to both CP foundations profiled (Live-Founder Foundations) and foundations in the aggregate (classified for simplicity as Dead-Founder Foundations).[267] Although the former is a subset of the latter, a recalculation of the aggregate metrics without the Live-Founder Foundation would only strengthen the comparative conclusions.

> • *Annual Percentage of Qualifying Distribution:* Calculates the percentage of distributions paid out of each foundation's net asset value. Foundations as a group distribute approximately 5.5%. Monaghan's foundations paid out 200%, well above the average. Obviously the in-excess of 100% metric is in part a function of a significant foundation during the year and a correspondingly high distribution. The weighted average for the Live-Founders profiled as best-in-class CP was an average of 65%. The higher average percentage was excluded out of the average because his intention is to deplete his assets. This extreme percentage may begin to decline with the establishment of Ave Maria's Law School. Several other CPs utilize their foundations as effectively oper-

ating initiatives, which results in a significantly higher annual percentage distribution. In certain instances, CPs achieve an annual percentage in excess of 100%, and then replenish the foundation with new resources.

- *Concentration of 5 Largest Initiatives:* Measures the percentage of annual dollars expended to five largest initiatives. These initiatives may be a specific NGO initiative or closely aligned projects, such as several specific ethic group schools within one geographic region or medical treatment projects in various countries but affiliated through a common initiative. The greater level of concentration is assumed to indicate a higher level of specific expertise and offer a greater probability of contributing value-added or risk minimization. Dead-Founder foundations (foundations in the aggregate) make grants in 10 unregulated areas according to a recent study. Monaghan foundations concentrated 93% of their distributions to their top 5 initiatives. Monaghan averaged a greater concentration than the 79% average for Live-Founders, both of which are outstanding metrics.

- *Average Dollar Grant and Average Annual Grant for the Top 5 Initiatives:* Average annual dollar distributions is for all grant in excess of $10,000 and the average annual grants for the top five initiatives is based on the methodology indicated in the Concentration of 5 Largest Initiatives endnote. Larger amounts are assumed to indicate a higher value-added and passionate commitment to social sector initiatives. This is somewhat analogous to the commercial sector investment strategies of limited number of concentrated investment versus an index approach of making a sufficiently large number of small investments so no one investment can have a material impact on the investing entity's aggregate performance. The Dead-Founder foundations (with assets between $51 million and $999 million) average $60,000 to $110,000 in individual grants, which effectively prohibits detailed performance analysis. Thomas Monaghan Foundations made grants averaging $3.3 million in its top five initiatives metric and $1.4 million in Average Dollar Grants. The numbers may be smaller then other foundations, but it is a function that it is a smaller foundation. The Living-Founders studied averaged $29 million to their top five initiatives and $19 million for average dollar grants.

- *Percentage of Assets Invested in Indexed Equities:* Compares the average percentage of foundation assets invested in indexed equity funds in contrast to more aggressive alternative investments. Dead-Founders are approximately 40% to 60% invested in indexed equity funds. Indexed equity investments are essentially nominal because such successful business people and investor are rarely interested in the average and more focused on the impact of their funds and distributing them as quickly as possible.

B. Foundations:

1. Ave Maria Foundation
2. Legatus
3. Spiritus Sanctus Academy

C. Foundations Goals:

Ave Maria Foundation:

The Ave Maria Foundation has focused on Catholic education, Catholic media, and community projects in the Greater Ann Arbor area and other Catholic Charities. In 1998, the Ave Maria Institute was established as a two-year Catholic liberal-arts college that is expected to expand to a four-year institution in the future. In April 1999, the foundation announced its plans to spend $50 million to build a world class Catholic law school scheduled to open in the fall of 2000. The Ave Maria School of Law, a not-for-profit educational corporation, will be the latest educational institution added to a new campus of Catholic schools in the Ann Arbor area. The new school will offer students a comprehensive legal curriculum enriched by its grounding in natural law and the enduring teachings of the Catholic faith; a faith which holds among its primary tenets that objective truth exists, that it is universal, and that it is knowable. Timeless truths about the nature of God, humanity, and society form the foundation of justice.

Its motto is *"Fides et Ratio"* (Faith and Reason), reflecting that one can pursue both strong religious convictions and academic excellence.

Legatus:

To study, live and spread the Faith in our business, professional and personal lives. The Legatus Mission:

"Our threefold purpose is:

Study: Ongoing education is at the heart of Legatus. We are matching members, who have a thirst for knowledge, with the most profound and convincing body of religious knowledge in the history of human thought.

Live: Translating the teachings of Christ and the social teaching of the Church into practical applications helps our members become eminently pragmatic about their faith.

Spread: Legatus is the Latin word for "ambassador". Our members don't typically wear their faith on their shirtsleeves. They spread the faith through good example, good deeds and high ethical standards.

Legatus currently provides service to over 950 businesses in 37 chapters across the U.S., and internationally on three continents. Our members enjoy the benefits of:

• Networking
• Education
• Peer Support
• Spiritual Growth
• Spouse Membership
• No Age Limits

D. Monaghan Foundations Information:

Ave Maria Foundation
24 Frank Lloyd Wright Dr.
Ann Arbor, MI 48106-0373
Fiscal Year: [YEAR]
Assets: $ 249.6 million
Income: $ 242.2 million

EIN: 38-2514364
Ruling Year   1983

Legatus
P.O. Box 511
Ann Arbor, MI 48106-0511
Fiscal Year: 1998
Assets: $1,289,440
Income: $1,305,502
EIN: 38-2776542
Ruling Year: 1989

Spiritus Sanctus Academy
2600 Via Sacra
Ann Arbor, MI 48105-9366
Fiscal Year: 1996
Assets: $220,642
Income: $608,440
EIN: 38-2951387
Ruling Year: 1992

E. Successful Ventures:

Domino's Pizza

F. Attempted Ventures:

Catholic Family Radio, network of nine Catholic radio stations that lacked a large enough audience to attract sufficient advertising dollars.

G. Biography:

Born: 1937, Ann Arbor, MI

Faith: Roman Catholic

Early years: Fatherless at 4, raised for several years in a Catholic orphanage, later was a seminarian and then a Marine. He bought

DomiNicks, a storefront pizza shop, with his brother in 1960. The following year he bought out his brother with a VW car, renamed the store Domino's and built it into a worldwide chain with more than 5,300 stores.

Recently: In 1998, he sold the company to Bain Capital for $1 billion, retaining a 7% share plus the company's Ann Arbor headquarters and 300 surrounding acres. Now works full time for God. He donated $248 million to the Ave Maria Foundation; provided $50 million to open a Catholic law school and is presently building an elementary school and a convent.

H. Personal Assets:

$600 Million, America's 400 Richest People, *Forbes*, 2000 Edition, 10.9.00.

I. Why Give:

"My overall goal in giving is to save as many souls for the buck as I can. To me that's why we're here. That's why we were created: to be with God forever in heaven" Marchetti, Domenica, Delivering on His Word, *The Chronicle of Philanthropy,* 10.7.99.

J. Religious Influence:

Father died when 4; two years later mother placed brother and him in Catholic orphanage. Youth "saturated" with ritual. Drifted away as young man. Drifted back beginning in 1973 when saw story that Don Shula, coach of Miami Dolphins, went to Mass daily.

K. Books Written:

Pizza Tiger

L. Books Read with Substantial Impact:

Lewis, C.S. *Mere Christianity.*
McFarlane, Bud. *Pierced by a Sword.*

M. Quotations:

Rebutting criticism for financing a cathedral in Nicaragua rather than helping homelessness or poverty, Monaghan points out that poor children attend schools he has financed, and as for soup kitchens and homeless shelters, "There are a lot of people doing that sort of thing. There's no one doing the spiritual, morality kinds of things. There's more of a need there." Miller, Lisa, "Thomas Monaghan's Scope, Style Stir Rancor in His Local Diocese" *WSJ*, 6.21.00.

"There's nothing wrong with most Catholic schools, except they're not Catholic." *Ibid.*

N. Interesting Facts:

Since the mid-1990s, he has started a Catholic law school, newspaper, online bookstore, and law practice. Bought Catholic radio station and Internet dating service for singles.

Miller, Lisa, "Thomas Monaghan's Scope, Style Stir Rancor in His Local Diocese" *WSJ*, 6.21.00.

Started Catholic schools out of frustration with what he sees as a lack of rigorous religious education at Catholic schools. *Id.*

Plan is to build and support numerous Catholic education institutions and to support other Catholic causes for next 20 yrs. — and then "to die broke."

So committed to anti-abortion movement, uses date he was conceived, rather than birth date, to calculate his age. Marchetti, *Id.*

Anonymously provided high-school and college scholarships to children at Catholic schools, requiring in return that they promise to recite rosary daily for rest of lives. *Id.*

Has deliberately downsized his life, after taking a run at collecting cars and once owning the Detroit Tigers, a $53-million investment at the time. Details of his philosophy are in a 1986 autobiography, *Pizza Tiger*. And he's now got his hobbies down to basics, daily running (while saying a rosary) and reading (a current favorite is *Pierced by a Sword* by Bud McFarlane). Source: Bullard, George, "Monaghan ponders nation's soul" *The Detroit News,* 5.21.99.

Monaghan has taken a "millionaire's vow of poverty;" he stopped flying first class. "I don't deprive myself of comforts," Monaghan says " but I won't indulge in luxuries, because I don't want to commit the sin of pride."

Monaghan has pledged to give to Catholic charities most of the $1 billion he received for selling Domino's.

Put up $50 million to found Ave Maria Law School in Detroit. *Id.*

O. Internet Resources:

Legatus: www.legatus.org

Ave Maria: www.avemariafoundation.org

George Soros

A. Overview

George Soros, considered by many to be one of the greatest investors of our times, has translated his commercial sector intensity to his social sector initiatives. He is the founder of the Open Society Institute/Fund, which is in 30 countries at last count and is building a solid organizational infrastructure. It is generally observed that his efforts facilitated the transition of Russian communism to multiple democratic countries. He founded the Central European University. His numerous innovative initiatives are evaluated for performance with incentive and phase-out funding plans. The Soros Foundation of Hungary is credited with achieving tremendous results by greatly leveraging his investment.

As for perspectives he has provided, there are two themes that stand out: The Paradox of Charity and Open Society. The former posits that charity tends to turn recipients into objects of charity, and that result is not what charity is intended to accomplish. In fact, charity goes against human nature; it makes people dependent. Philanthropy can't be relied upon to change the world. "Open Society" encourages free press, political pluralism, and human rights as a mechanism for empowering people to improve their situation.

The Soros Charitable Foundation is one of several that he utilizes to fund his major initiative that is the Open Society Institute. Soros is considered by many to be the most influential non-elected politician East of the Alps. He maintains 50 offices from Haiti to Mongolia and does not hide the fact that there is a political bias to his foundations. His aim is to replace old left-wing dictatorships, not with free market democracies, but with left-wing democracies.

In 2000, he recanted his 1998 prediction that global capitalism would disintegrate in two years, but he still worries that globalism continues to be a threat to democracy.

This Working Book quantifies four metrics that benchmark the efficiency and effectiveness of foundations. George Soros' initiatives rank quite favorably in comparison to both CP foundations profiled (Live-Founder Foundations) and foundations in the aggregate (classified for simplicity as Dead-Founder Foundations).[268] Although the former is a subset of the latter, a recalculation of the aggregate metrics without the Live-Founder Foundation would only strengthen the comparative conclusions.

• *Annual Percentage of Qualifying Distribution:* Calculates the percentage of distributions paid out of each foundation's net asset value. Foundations as a group distribute approximately 5.5%. Soros' foundations paid out 49% in 1998, well above the average. The weighted average for the Live-Founders profiled as best-in-class CP was an average of 65%. This high 49% still exceeds that majority of NPB CPs. Several other CPs utilize their foundations as effectively operating initiatives, which results in a significantly higher annual percentage distribution. In certain instances, CPs achieve an annual percentage in excess of 100%, and then replenish the foundation with new resources.

• *Concentration of 5 Largest Initiatives:* Measures the percentage of annual dollars expended to five largest initiatives. These initiatives may be a specific NGO initiative or closely aligned projects, such as several specific ethic group schools within one geographic region or medical treatment projects in various countries but affiliated through a common initiative. The greater level of concentration is assumed to indicate a higher level of specific expertise and offer a greater probability of contributing value-added or risk minimization. Dead-Founder foundations (foundations in the aggregate) make grants in 10 unregulated areas according to a recent study. Soros foundations concentrated 100% of their distributions to their top 5 initiatives. Soros' 100% represents that he is a very focused individual and utilizes Open Society as the almost exclusive domain for his philanthropy. This focused mission is consistent with the messages of NPB. The NPB Live-Founder CPs averaged 79%.

• *Average Dollar Grant and Average Annual Grant for The Top 5 Initiatives:* Average annual dollar distributions is for all grant in excess of $10,000 and the average annual grant for the top five initiatives is based on the methodology indicated in the Concentration of 5 Largest Initiatives metric. The larger amounts are assumed to indicate a higher value-added and passionate commitment to social sector initiatives. This is somewhat analogous to the commercial sector investment strategies of limited number of concentrated investment versus an index approach of making a sufficiently large number of small investments so no one investment can have a material impact on the investing entity's aggregate performance. The Dead-Founder foundations (with assets between $51 million and $999 million) average $60,000 to $110,000 in individual grants, which effectively prohibits detailed performance analysis. The George Soros Foundations made grants averaging $108.9 million to its top five initiatives metric. Soros' average grant size represents the best of all the CPs, which achieved a $19.5 million metric.

• *Percentage of Assets Invested in Indexed Equities:* Compares the average percentage of foundation assets invested in indexed equity funds in contrast to more aggressive alternative investments. Dead-Founders are approximately 40% to 60% invested in indexed equity funds. Indexed equity investments are essentially nominal because such successful business people and investors are rarely interested in the average and more focused on the impact of their funds and distributing them as quickly as possible.

B. Foundations:

1. Soros Foundations
2. Open Society Institute
3. Open Society Fund
4. Soros Foundation of Hungary: "Achieved tremendous amount with very little money," endowment $3 million a year.
5. Soros Charitable Foundation: utilized to fund the Open Society Institute.

Actually a network of foundations, including "national foundations," a group of autonomous organizations operating in over 30 countries. National foundations share the common mission of supporting the development of open society. The Open Society Institute (OSI) and the Open Society Institute-Budapest (OSI-Budapest) assist the national foundations by providing administrative, financial, and technical support, as well as by establishing "network programs" to address certain issues on a regional or network-wide basis. In 1997, the network spent a total of $428.4 million on philanthropic activities. The largest portion of these expenditures was devoted to education

C. Foundations Goals:

An "open society" is a society based on the recognition that no one has a monopoly on the truth, that different people have different views and interests, and that there is a need for institutions to protect the rights of all people to allow them to live together in peace. Broadly speaking, an open society is characterized by a reliance on the rule of law, the existence of a democratically elected government, a diverse and vigorous civil society, and respect for minorities and minority opinions. The term "open society" was popularized by the philosopher Karl Popper in his 1945 book *Open Society and Its Enemies.* Popper's work deeply influenced George Soros, and it is upon the concept of an open society that Mr. Soros bases his philanthropic activity. (www.soros.org)

Creating an Open Society: can't be defined, only explained. "We all act on the basis of imperfect understanding," need institutions and interests to live in peace, democratic form of government, orderly transfer of power, market economy, rule of law, to foster critical mode of thinking, supports people who staked their life on fighting for freedom, for open society."

Challenge intrusion of marketplace into appropriate area, deal with inequalities in distribution of wealth and social benefits from "marketplace fundamentalism," address adverse unintended consequences of perhaps well-intended policies.

WILL NOT DO: "Categorically opposed to supporting political parties," some have become too influential for their own good, most powerful in Ukraine.

D. Soros Foundations Information:

Soros Charitable Foundation
400 West 59th Street
New York, New York 10019
Fiscal Year: 1998
Assets: $163,151,475
EIN: 13-7003532
Ruling Year: TBD

The Soros Foundation – Newly Independent Baltic States
400 West 59th Street
New York, New York 10019
Fiscal Year: 1998
Assets: $207,748
EIN: 13-3480946
Ruling Year: TBD

E. Successful Ventures:

International Science Foundation: social sector investment of $100 million in less then 2 years

International Science Education Program

Science Education program: 20 Million due to clearly defined rules and efficiency

Central European University: need for an institution that would preserve and develop the spirit of the revolution, program strong enough to allow masters degrees after first year, will receive $10 million a year (at least) for next 20 years, headquartered in Budapest, branches in Prague and Warsaw

F. Attempted Ventures:

Mitteleuropa: Monthly magazine *Transitions*. $1 million grant in 1998, declining $250K a year to make self-sustaining. Circulation less than 8,000; 300,000 web visits a month. Urban, not business minded or entrepreneurial; did too little to get money.

First Commitment: South Africa goal to educate blacks to decrease the separation of race, provided first 80 scholarships then dropped.

China: 1988 foundation became embroiled in country's internal political struggle.

Poland: assumed Okno knew how to form/run a foundation.

Cultural Initiative Foundation in Moscow.

Worst: Prague in Czech republic, Charta 77: 3 million, wanted to set up foundation, past not put to rest, wanted to discuss old quarrels.

G. Biography:

Born: 1930, Budapest, Hungary

Faith: Jewish

Early years: Escaped Nazis because father bought false identity papers for family and places to hide. Left Hungary in 1947 and enrolled in London School of Economics. Influenced by philosopher Karl Popper. Moved to United States in 1956. In 1969, started Quantum Fund, which became one of most successful hedge funds ever, returning 32% annually between 1969 and 1999. In 1992, was called "man who broke the pound" for placing $10 bil lion in bets against British pound, netting at least $1 billion in profit.

Recently: Major reorganization of investment empire to cut risk profile, due to loss in hedge fund of $2 billion during 1998 Russian eco nomic collapse and additional $3 billion in the Spring of 2000 with the Nasdaq correction. Still manages $11 billion and claims that his family and he own 60% of the funds managed, though fund rivals think that number may be inflated. Now relying on outside money managers for advice with the departure of his chief strategist and counseling investors to expect more modest gains. Flagship Quantum fund renamed Quantum Endowment Fund; says his proceeds will be utilized to pay for his philanthropic pur suits.

H. Personal Assets:

$5 Billion, America's 400 Richest People, *Forbes*, 2000 Edition, 10.9.00.

I. Why Give:

As Soros told Time in 1997, "There was a large element of guilt and shame in my personal makeup. Therapy helped, but philanthropy was the cure." Borg, Linda, "Billionaire philanthropist to speak at Brown," *Providence Journal*, 10.20.99.

"I can afford it."

"I decided open societies were what really mattered."

J. Religious Influence: TBD

K. Books Written:

The Alchemy of Finance
Opening the Soviet System
Underwriting Democracy
Soros on Soros: Staying Ahead of the Curve
The Crisis of Global Capitalism

L. Books Read with Substantial Impact: TBD

M. Quotations:

"Market fundamentalism poses a more potent threat than communism." Unfettered capitalism gives markets too much influence. Markets are imperfect and are just as likely to lead to excesses as to equilibrium. Advocates "open societies" that encourage free press, political pluralism and human rights. Borg, Linda. "Soros: Regulate global economy," *Providence Journal*, 10.21.99.

"Charity goes against human nature. One of the paradoxes is that it makes people dependent. You can't rely on philanthropy to change the world."

Borg, Linda. "Soros: Regulate global economy," *Providence Journal,* 10.21.99.

"My own needs are for a more reliable stream of income to fund my charitable operation." Soros, George. "Letter to shareholders of Quantum Group of Funds," 4.28.00.

N. Interesting Facts:

Funded construction of two campuses for new Central Europe University in Prague and Budapest. But, after studying behavior on Prague campus, terminated funding for Czechs. "This isn't charity, you know." Lewis, Michael, "Heartless Donors," *New York Times Magazine,* 12.14.97.

Paradox of Charity: "Charity tends to turn recipients into objects of charity, and that is not what it is intended to accomplish" – corrupting influence: recipient and giver, "People flatter him and never tell him the truth"

Use of Name: "a selfless benefactor was too good to be true," made to feel god-like, doing good fighting evil, felt "removed from humanity"

Recognition Change: in the beginning he avoided personal involvement, hence anonymity and shunned publicity, as revolution gained momentum he accepted the fact he was deeply involved.

O. Internet Resources:

Soros Foundation Network: www.soros.org

Open Society Institute www.soros.org/osi.html

Steven Spielberg

A. Overview:

Steven Spielberg's founding of the Shoah Visual History Foundation may well represent his most profiled social sector success. His foundations have leveraged his commercial sector talents into world-class multidimensional initiatives. Shoah has produced several documentaries including a 1999 Academy Award winner; produced an interactive CD that is being distributed globally; and developed web-based digital research archives of Holocaust testimonials with a goal of 50,000 testimonials.

Spielberg established the Righteous Persons Foundation, using mass media to engage broad audiences and encourage Jewish learning. In an exceptionally saga-cious statement, he dedicated his profits from Schindler's List (a highly success-ful commercial movie) to the Righteous Persons Foundation. In a progressive use of collaboration, he as teamed up with the American Association for School Administrators for a National Tolerance Initiative. Utilizing his networking and financial acumen, he founded the Partners in History and the Future campaign to assist in funding the Shoah Foundation. Furthermore, his foundations continue to work with outside resources in virtually every aspect of their work.

As for insightful perspectives, he approves of identifying his name with social sec-tor projects only if it further enhances the efforts, which occurs in approximately 20% of the situations in which he becomes involved.

This Working Book quantifies four metrics that benchmark the efficiency and effectiveness of foundations. Steven Spielberg's initiatives rank quite favorably in comparison to both CP foundations profiled (Live-Founder Foundations) and foundations in the aggregate (classified for simplicity as Dead-Founder Foundations).[269] Although the former is a subset of the latter, a recalculation of the aggregate metrics without the Live-Founder Foundation would only strengthen the comparative conclusions.

> • *Annual Percentage of Qualifying Distribution:* Calculates the percentage of distributions paid out of each foundation's net asset value. Foundations as a group distribute approximately 5.5%. Spielberg's foundations paid out 100% in 1998, well above the average. The weight-

ed average for the Live-Founders profiled as NPB CPs was an average of 65%. With the bulk of his interest in the Shoah foundation Spielberg has achieved a metric more representative of operating NGOs, which is its legally adopted structure. Spielberg's operating foundation, illustrates the attractiveness of a concentrated Intersectoral venture. Several other CPs utilize their foundations as effectively operating initiatives, which results in a significantly higher annual percentage distribution. In certain instances, CPs achieve an annual percentage in excess of 100%, and then replenish the foundation with new resources.

- *Concentration of 5 Largest Initiatives:* Measures the percentage of annual dollars expended to five largest initiatives. These initiatives may be a specific NGO initiative or closely aligned projects, such as several specific ethic group schools within one geographic region or medical treatment projects in various countries but affiliated through a common initiative. The greater level of concentration is assumed to indicate a higher level of specific expertise and offer a greater probability of contributing value-added or risk minimization. Dead-Founder foundations (foundations in the aggregate) make grants in 10 unregulated areas according to a recent study. Spielberg's foundation efforts register 100% of their distributions to their top 5 initiatives metric. Spielberg's 100% represents that he is a very focused individual and utilizes Shoah as the exclusive domain for his operating foundation. This focused mission is consistent with Intersectoral focus of NPB.

- *Average Dollar Grant and Average Annual Grant for The Top 5 Initiatives:* Average annual dollar distributions is for all grant in excess of $10,000 and the average annual grants for the top five initiatives is based on the methodology indicated in the Concentration of 5 Largest Initiatives endnote. Larger amounts are assumed to indicate a higher value-added and passionate commitment to social sector initiatives. This is somewhat analogous to the commercial sector investment strategies of limited number of concentrated investment versus an index approach of making a sufficiently large number of small investments so no one investment can have a material impact on the investing entity's aggregate performance. The Dead-Founder foundations (with assets between $51 million and $999 million) average $60,000 to $110,000 in individual grants, which effectively prohibits detailed performance analysis.

Steven Spielberg foundations registered grants averaging $21.4 million to each of top five initiatives metric as well as for the Average Dollar Grant, which – as mentioned – results from a single concentrated grant focus. Given the size of Spielberg's foundation this is an outstanding metric. His impressive operating entity allows him to distribute his revenues in a powerful example of Intersectoral enterprise. The Living-Founders studied averaged $29 million to their top five initiatives and $19 million for average dollar grants.

• *Percentage of Assets Invested in Indexed Equities:* Compares the average percentage of foundation assets invested in indexed equity funds in contrast to more aggressive alternative investments. Dead-Founders are approximately 40% to 60% invested in indexed equity funds. Indexed equity investments are essentially nominal because such successful business people and investor are rarely interested in the average and more focused on the impact of their funds and distributing them as quickly as possible.

B. Foundations:

Survivors of the Shoah Visual History Foundation

C. Foundations Goals:

Mission: The Shoah Foundation, a 501(c)(3) public charity, was established in 1994 to videotape and preserve the testimonies of Holocaust survivors and witnesses so that future generations can learn from the past. The Foundation has collected more than 50,000 eyewitness testimonies in 57 countries and 32 languages, and is committed to the broad and effective educational use of the archive worldwide. The Foundation's objectives include preserving the digital archive, cataloging for access, developing educational partnerships, producing educational products and promoting cultural understanding.

Programs: From 1994-98, the Foundation's main objective was videotaping 50,000 Holocaust testimonies worldwide. During this period, the Foundation produced three documentaries based on interviews about the Holocaust: "Survivors of the Holocaust (1995), "The Lost Children of

Berlin" (1997), and "The Last Days"(1998), which won an Academy Award for Best Documentary in 1999. The Foundation's first interactive educational CD-ROM, "Survivors: Testimonies of the Holocaust" is being distributed to schools in the United States and abroad and additional documentaries and educational materials are being developed. The current centerpiece of the Foundation's programs is the cataloguing of the testimonies in the digital archive so the public can access them. Each testimony is catalogued using sophisticated historical, library science, and information technology methods. Once catalogued, the testimonies will be available for access at sites around the world via state-of-the-art technology. In January 2000, the Foundation established a Department of Educational Resources through which it continues to produce and distribute educational materials to schools and the general public. In March 2000, Steven Spielberg announced the Shoah Foundation's creation of a National Tolerance Initiative in partnership with the American Association of School Administrators that will promote tolerance and embrace diversity in public schools.

Additional Comments: The Shoah Foundation's Partners in History and The Future Campaign has helped finance, and will continue to fund, the work of the Foundation. Achievements and ongoing goals include the videotaping of 50,000 testimonies, cataloguing the testimonies so they will be accessible to the public (ongoing), developing the technological infrastructure to disseminate the archive to educational institutions and museums throughout the world (ongoing), and creating documentaries and educational products (ongoing).

Accomplishments for Fiscal Year ending 12/31/1999

- Videotaped an additional 973 interviews, increasing the number of testimonies in the archive to 50,555.
- "The Last Days" won an Academy Award for Best Documentary Feature. Worldwide distribution of the film began in spring 1999.
- Released "Survivors: Testimonies of the Holocaust," the Foundation's first educational CD-ROM with an accompanying study guide for teachers.

Objectives for Fiscal Year Beginning 01/01/2000

• Cataloguing an additional 8,000 hours of testimony.
• Transmitting via fiber optic network a large part of the Foundation's archive to the Simon Wiesenthal Museum of Tolerance in Los Angeles, CA.
• Piloting a National Tolerance Initiative (in collaboration with the American Association of School Administrators) in five selected school districts around the country.

Self Assessment

The Foundation continues to work with outside consultants for every aspect of its work.
The cataloguing and archive is developed in consultation with archivists, historians, and information technology specialists. The Shoah Foundation's educational projects utilize educational specialists who evaluate materials. The National Tolerance Initiative is being conducted in partnership with the American Association of School Administrators.

D. Assets of Foundations:

Survivors of the Shoah Visual History Foundation
P.O. Box 3168
Los Angeles, CA 90078
Financial Info
Fiscal Year: 1997
Assets: $21 million
Income: $26 million
No. of Board Members: 4
No. of Employees: 500
No. of Volunteers: 4,000 more about leaders
EIN: 95- 4474965
Ruling Year: 1998
Year Founded: 1994

E. Successful Ventures:

Film Credits: (major credits as director)

The Sugarland Express, Jaws, Close Encounters of the Third Kind, Raiders of the Lost Ark, E.T., Indiana Jones and the Temple of Doom, The Color Purple, Empire of the Sun, Indiana Jones and the Last Crusade, Always, Hook, Jurassic Park, Schindler's List, The Lost World: Jurassic Park, Amistad, Saving Private Ryan, Men in Black, Twister, A.I., and Minority Report.

F. Attempted Ventures: TBD

G. Biography:

Born: 1947, Cincinnati, OH

Faith: Jewish

Early years: Grew up in "gentile suburbia" self-conscious about being Jewish. ("Something I was ashamed of." Dubner, Stephen J., "Steven the Good," *New York Times Magazine,* 2.14.99.) Second wife converted to Judaism and raising children Jewish. Began to see his religion as blessing, not a curse. Now doorways at his company Amblin Entertainment all have mezuzahs. Amateur filmmaker as a child. One of the youngest television directors at Universal Studios. As director, foregoes salary in exchange for share of gross. Most commercially successful director of all time despite partnership at Dreamworks with David Geffin and Jeffrey Katzenberg

Recently: Shoah Foundation.

H. Personal Assets:

$2 Billion, America's 400 Richest People, *Forbes*, 2000 Edition, 10.9.00.

I. Why Give:

In past was eager to have his name prominently associated with gifts, until a rabbi sat him down and said, "You know if you put your name on everything, it goes unrecognized by God." Now 80% is anonymous, 20% only where name attracts other moneys.

Could fund Shoah Foundation by writing check. But then would be *Spielberg* foundation. Spielberg associated with fantasy. Shoah Foundation trying to recreate social studies in America. Michael Berenbaum, Shoah Foundation president, Dubner, *Id.*

J. Religious Influence:

Experience of filming "Schindler's List," prompted establishment of Shoah VHF

K. Books Written:

The Last Days by Steven Spielberg, et al.
Amistad : 'Give Us Freedom' by Steven Spielberg (Editor), et al.
Saving Private Ryan by Steven Spielberg (Editor), et al.
(Numerous other film related writings)

L. Books Read with Substantial Impact: TBD

M. Quotations:

"Schindler's List" and the Shoah Foundation have reshaped his thinking. "They've given me more of a moral responsibility to make sure I'm not putting someone else's agenda in front of the most important agenda, which is creating tolerance." . . . The Shoah Foundation is a vital outlet for his altruism. Dubner, Stephen J., "Steven the Good" *New York Times Magazine*, 2.14.99

N. Interesting Facts:

Code of Morality: a Boy Scout is trustworthy, loyal, helpful, friendly, courteous, kind, obedient, cheerful, thrifty, brave, clean, and reverent.

Reverent to God, country, family and entertainment, goodness to trump evil.

"When people in Hollywood talk about him it is as if they are talking about God, with one difference people are not afraid to badmouth God I don't think its politically correct to stand up and say anything against him."

Affected by experiences of youth, feeling like an outsider, being Jewish in gentile suburbia. Issue of tolerance/intolerance reflected in films and in purpose of Shoah Foundation. When began to see Judaism as more of blessing than curse, was ready to make "Schindler's List."

O. Internet Resources:

Survivors of the Shoah Visual History Foundation: www.vhf.org
Righteous Persons Foundation: www.s2k.org/Spielberg.html

Michael Steinhardt

A. Overview:

Michael Steinhardt, one of the world's most respected investors and money managers, has passionately committed his talent to social sector missions. The *NYT* reports that Steinhardt now manages a portfolio of "enthusiasms," one of which is philanthropy. "'What Michael wants to do is be an agent of change, by being very provocative and challenging,' says Gershon Kekst, a friend who is also active in Jewish philanthropy."[270]

Steinhardt co-founded (with Charles Bronfman) Birthright Israel, an innovative and quantifiably measured initiative, which is also a prime example of collaboration with both private and public entities. He obtained co-ownership of the Forward newspaper, possibly the largest Jewish (English language) weekly in the United States. Through considerable effort he is widely considered an internationally acclaimed proponent and sponsor of universal protection, study, and exhibition of historically significant Judaica objects. With focused effort, he is an aggressive supporter of multiple New York area high schools and Jewish social and cultural centers. His leadership role supporting the Israel Museum includes global network building and financing. He is also the lead sponsor of a visionary project at the Brooklyn Botanical Gardens. One of his most notable achievements is his mentor role in developing future Jewish community leaders. More recently, he has become increasingly engaged with several higher education institutions: joining Brandeis University's board, becoming chairman of the board of Tel Aviv University, and pledging $10 million to the School of Education at New York University, where he is a trustee. In the spring of 2001, the school will be named in his honor.

This Working Book quantifies four metrics that benchmark the efficiency and effectiveness of foundations. Michael Steinhardt's initiatives rank quite favorably in comparison to both CP foundations profiled (Live-Founder Foundations) and foundations in the aggregate (classified for simplicity as Dead-Founder Foundations).[271] Although the former is a subset of the latter, a recalculation of the aggregate metrics without the Live-Founder Foundation would only strengthen the comparative conclusions.

• *Annual Percentage of Qualifying Distribution:* Calculates the percentage of distributions paid out of each foundation's net asset value. Foundations as a group distribute approximately 5.5%. Steinhardt's foundations paid out 37% in 1998, well above the average. This average percentage is above 6 times the dead-founder average. Several other CPs utilize their foundations as effective operating initiatives, which results in a significantly higher annual percentage distribution. In certain instances, CPs achieve an annual percentage in excess of 100%, and then replenish the foundation with new resources.

• *Concentration of 5 Largest Initiatives:* Measures the percentage of annual dollars expended to five largest initiatives. These initiatives may be a specific NGO initiative or closely aligned projects, such as several specific ethic group schools within one geographic region or medical treatment projects in various countries but affiliated through a common initiative. The greater level of concentration is assumed to indicate a higher level of specific expertise and offer a greater probability of contributing value-added or risk minimization. Dead-Founder foundations (foundations in the aggregate) make grants in 10 unregulated areas according to a recent study. Steinhardt foundations concentrated 63% of their distributions to their top 5 initiatives, which is in line with the 79% for the NPB CP group. Such high metrics illustrates specific and focused initiatives strategic management.

• *Average Dollar Grant and Average Annual Grant for the Top 5 Initiatives:* Average annual dollar distributions is for all grants in excess of $10,000 and the average annual grant for the top five initiatives is based on the methodology indicated in the Concentration of 5 Largest Initiatives endnote. Larger amounts are assumed to indicate a higher value-added and passionate commitment to social sector initiatives. This is somewhat analogous to the commercial sector investment strategies of limited number of concentrated investments versus an index approach of making a sufficiently large number of small investments so no one investment can have a material impact on the investing entity's aggregate performance. The Dead-Founder foundations (with assets between $51 million and $999 million) average $60,000 to $110,000 in individual grants, which effectively prohibits detailed performance analysis. Michael Steinhardt foundations made grants averaging

$974,000 to each of top five initiatives. This metric surpasses the dead-founders by a multiple of almost 12 times on average. Steinhardt's Average Dollar Grant, while relatively lower, remains approximately 2.6 times greater than the foundation average.

- *Percentage of Assets Invested in Indexed Equities:* Compares the average percentage of foundation assets invested in indexed equity funds in contrast to more aggressive alternative investments. Dead-Founders are approximately 40% to 60% invested in indexed equity funds. Indexed equity investments are essentially nominal because such successful business people and investor are rarely interested in the average and more focused on the impact of their funds and distributing them as quickly as possible.

B. Foundations:

1. Judy and Michael Steinhardt Foundation
2. Steinhardt Family Foundation

C. Foundations Goals: TBD

D. Assets of Foundations:

Judy and Michael Steinhardt Foundation
1185 6th Ave
New York, NY 10036-2601
Fiscal Year: 1997, Assets: $ 47 million
EIN: 13-3357500 Ruling Year: 1987

Steinhardt Family Foundation
1185 6th Ave
New York, NY 10036-2601
Fiscal Year: 1999 Assets: $ 35,035.
EIN:13-7067570 Ruling Year: 1995

E. Successful Ventures:

Chairman of the Investment Committee - NYU
Democratic Leadership Council - Major Contributor
Birthright Project - Provides free trip to Israel to any Jewish youth in the world.

F. Attempted Ventures:

Steinhardt-Baer Productions: Movie production company that has not had any success to date.

G. Biography:

Born: 1941, Brooklyn, NY.

Faith: Jewish

Early years: Father, a jeweler, gave him shares of stock for his bar mitzvah. Began studying broker's reports, following stock prices, and spending time at a Merrill Lynch office. Graduated high school at 16 and Wharton School of Finance at 19. Briefly wrote for *Financial World*. Became known as one of the top special-situations analysts. In 1967, started investment firm and became chief trader. 1978 took sabbatical; spent time pursuing numerous interests including starting a real estate and construction business in Israel, reading the Old Testament with a rabbi and visiting Israel several times. Thought he had quit, but after one year returned. In 1994, after a rare 3-week vacation in China, he returned to New York to find his investment funds had lost 4% of their value while he was gone. Although upset, he sat down and went right back to work. A year later investors were stunned when he announced he was winding down his four high-performing hedge funds after 28 years.

Recently: Since retirement Steinhardt has been notably active in a number of endeavors including:

- A major contributor to the Democratic Leadership Council, which seeks a third road for American politics outside the established political parties.
- Part of an investment group that took control of Israel's largest bank – Bank Hapoalim – in 1997. The group has now divested itself of half of its original stake.
- In September 2000, Steinhardt was asked to sell his 40% stake in Israel's Maritime Bank because of his controlling interest in Bank Hapoalim.
- In 1995, bought a 50% stake in the Forward Newspaper, a nationally distributed Jewish publication. His daughter also works at the paper.
- Merged/Donated Jewish cultural center at 67th Street in New York City with the 92nd Street Y, the 126 year-old Jewish institution known for its classical music concerts and literary readings. The five-story, 22,000-foot brownstone will become the eighth center in the Y's chain of cultural institutions.[272]

H. Personal Assets: Over $300 million in personal liquid assets. "Art, Wildlife and a Bit of Investing," *NYT* 11.12.00.

I. Why Give:

"I try to focus on innovation. I'm not interested in contributing to existing organizations, many of which I regard as vestigial. I think the Jewish world needs risk-taking. Unfortunately, the Jewish establishment is glacially slow in doing that."

J. Religious Influence:

Although a self-declared atheist, Steinhardt has made the traditional Friday night Shabbat dinner a centerpiece of his family's life. An avowed secularist, he has long engaged in religious discussions with Orthodox rabbis. His Jewish journey has taken him on a roundabout route. It is one that finds him in a place without any theological comforts, but where the possibility of making a substantial contribution is its own reward.

K. Books Written: TBD

L. Books Read with Substantial Impact:

> Fascinated by the Holocaust, has read most of books on subject. Train, Id.,
> at 38.

M. Quotations:

> Steinhardt has contributed $10 million to Makom (Hebrew for "Place") .
> Its objective is to create a gateway to Jewish life through cultural interests
> that appeal to the younger generation, from art and music to literature and
> filmmaking, in an open, pluralistic and accepting way. One of its projects
> is the renovation of a four-story building on Central Park West which will
> include space for a myriad of activities and areas such as poetry slams,
> text study, independent films, and locker rooms.

> "We hope the result will be a stronger sense of Jewishness," says
> Steinhardt, in terms of the members and participants marrying other Jews,
> attending synagogue, taking part in Shabbat dinners and increasing their
> interest in Judaism.

> "Is this just another singles scene approach or an attempt at religious out-
> reach?" Steinhardt offers. "I wouldn't deny either, or be ashamed. But nei-
> ther fits what this project is all about." Rather, he says, it is about creating
> a "beautiful facility and highly sophisticated environment" that will
> appeal to young Jews - not just singles - on a variety of levels.

> (Source: Rosenblatt, Gary, "The Wooing Of Gen-X: Philanthropist
> Michael Steinhardt plans to create cultural hangout here for under affili-
> ated Jews in their 20s and 30s," *The Jewish Week*, 1.2.98)

> "I find joy and meaning in the hope that I contribute something to a ren-
> aissance in the non-Orthodox Jewish world. The values of our communi-
> ty are the best that humankind has created, and to perpetuate it is, I think,
> worthwhile" (Source: Debra Nussbaum Cohen, "From Wall Street to phi-
> lanthropy, re-invigorating the Jewish community is Steinhardt's bottom
> line" *Jewish Telegraphic.*)

"I'm looking forward to the 21st century, because the economic problems that have plagued mankind will be largely ameliorated. We won't experience all the fears of the 20th century like, war, dangerous inflation or protracted down cycles. It's going to be a much more sanguine time for markets everywhere." (Source: Robert Lenzner, "The Hedger: An optimist on the sidelines" *Forbes* 11.16.98)

N. Interesting Facts:

Wife chairs the board of the American Friends of the Israeli Museum. Michael actively participates on the board.

Keen interest in history of Jewish people. Has visited Israel dozens of times and has business interests there. "He observes that his attachment to the place is for him a substitute for adherence to its religion." Train, *Id.*, at 38.

"I asked him how he proposed to save the next generation (his son was listening to our conversation) from the perils of excessive wealth. Steinhardt thought a moment, and then said that he hoped to accomplish this by transmitting the traditional values of his people — not his religion, but his people — to his children." *Id.*

O. Internet Resources:

Birthright Israel: www.israelexperience.org

INNOVATING FOUNDATIONS

With the increasing number of foundations it becomes important to locate foundations focused on "new" philanthropy. The following foundations are catalysts, addressing topic from venture philanthropy to educating social sector workers on the professional practices of "new" philanthropy.

Ave Maria Foundation: Ave Maria School of Law

www.avemarialaw.org

Ave Maria School of Law approaches legal education as a combination of faith and reason. With funding of $50 million, the Ave Maria seeks to combine Catholic faith, academic rigor, dedication to research and scholarship, and community dedication into a world institution for legal education and training.

Nathan Cummings Foundation

www.ncf.org

The Nathan Cummings Foundation is committed to finding innovative solutions to the challenges faced by the nonprofit sector. To this end, the Nathan Cummings Foundation has supported research on the commercialization of nonprofit spaces, accountability by

nonprofits, the professionalization of human services, and new paradigms for corporate giving.

Bill & Melinda Gates Foundation

www.gatesfoundations.org

The Bill & Melinda Gates Foundation's mission of increasing access to innovations in education, technology and world health leverages the expertise and infrastructure of existing organizations to maximize the philanthropic return on its investment. Chief among these initiatives is a $750 million lead grant to the Global Fund for Children's Vaccines. This donation will work towards reducing the historical 15 year period between the introduction of life-saving vaccines in the developed world and their introduction into the developing world by encouraging governments and NGOs to maximize their contribution to immunization efforts. The Gates foundation will then "fill in the gaps" as necessary.

echoing Green Foundation

www.echoinggreen.org

The Foundation provides catalyzing fellowships to social entrepreneurs, particularly those early in their philanthropic career. Currently, over 300 social entrepreneurs receive fellowships throughout the world. echoing Green Foundation has pioneered a unique venture philanthropy approach to its giving, providing financial, strategic, staff development, legal, and accounting assistance to their grantees. This integrated effort combines the identification, mentoring, and capacity building of emerging social entrepreneurs into a powerful engine for positive social change.

William and Flora Hewlett Foundation

www.hewlett.org

The William and Flora Hewlett Foundation understands that the challenges facing philanthropy in the future will require foundations to be much more active in determining goals and measuring effectiveness. Accordingly, they have devoted significant financial and intellectual resources to grappling with these issues.

James Irvine Foundation

www.irvine.org

Multiyear efforts of the James Irvine Foundation to improve nonprofit management and governance include the support of research in nonprofit, mergers, consolidation, joint ventures, acquisitions, and other strategic restructurings. Newly instituted efforts include the establishment of the Innovation

Fund (IF) which supports promising ideas and new strategies that add value to social enterprises.

Japonica Partners Affiliated Foundations

www.japonica.com/japonica/frames/community.html
www.unitedu.com
www.japonicaintersectoral.com

Japonica Partners and its Affiliated Foundations invest in and manage social sector initiatives focused on creating value through "best-in-class" strategies and tactics.

Japonica Intersectoral Investment Bank
Japonica Intersectoral's efforts are focused on the intersectoral segment of the social sector where quantifiable value metrics of the commercial sector converge with the socially powered motivations of the nonprofit sector.

Japonica Intersectoral's network of thought leaders, policy experts, and financial experts will apply the firm's global infrastructure to value creating initiatives which encompass capital market services, strategic financial advisory services, direct investment opportunities, and educational resources. By providing unparalleled financial technologies and a reservoir of industry knowledge to a select group of innovative foundations and NGOs, Japonica Intersectoral seeks to create "best-in-class" returns along a social enterprise investment spectrum.

United University

UnitedU.com believes that a significant need exists for innovative, accessible social sector education. The pronounced growth in NGOs over the past decade, combined with increasingly overlapping boundaries between the public and private sector, has created a demand for excellence at the core of social sector leadership board members and executive managers.

UnitedU.com will seek to provide world class course content for social sector executives via the Internet. Strategic business and entrepreneurial classes will create a paradigm shift for NGOs and include best practices in the areas of ROI Marketing, Executive Compensation, Creative Finance, Benchmarking, and Technology. Content and service will be paramount, with support from leading Internet software technologies.

Japonica-affiliated foundations have historically utilized the following to prioritize and manage their initiatives:

The Program Efficiency and Technology ("PET") Multiple. In order to ensure that Return on Investment and Optimal Resource Allocation Model objectives are met, potential projects must present an opportunity for value creation and meet the Foundation's PET Multiple criteria. The PET Multiple is the extent to which Foundation dollars can be leveraged to achieve an impact of several times the base contribution amount.

The PET Impact. Balancing the PET Multiple analysis is the impact on human lives. The prospective donation must have a meaningful impact of one or more lives, either physically or spiritually. Priority is given to those projects that will, in an immediate and measurable way: Save a life or lives, alleviate human suffering, and dramatically change a life or lives for the better.

The Robert Wood Johnson Foundation

On a quarterly basis, The Robert Woods Foundation publishes (via the Internet and other dissemination means) reports on the outcomes of its grants. These reports describe the problem addressed, the objectives and strategies, the results or findings, communications efforts, and any next steps. Reports also include dollars invested and, often, quantifiable outcome results.

Ewing Marion Kauffman Foundation

www.emkf.org

The Ewing Marion Kauffman Center is devoted to developing entrepreneurs in the for-profit and nonprofit sectors. By researching, identifying, teaching, and disseminating "state of the art" entrepreneurial skills, the center seeks to increase the success of emerging entrepreneurs. Education and encouragement are the prime drivers of this effort.

W. K. Kellogg Foundation
www.wkkf.org
W. K. Kellogg Foundation's Philanthropy and Volunteerism Efforts seek to "increase the ranks of new givers and to nurture emerging forms of philanthropy." Strong, multiyear, concerted investments of intellectual capital in the areas of social entrepreneurship, e-philanthropy, and venture philanthropy have fueled the W. K. Kellogg Foundation's innovative programs in the intersectoral arena. In particular, its Director of Venture Philanthropy, Thomas K. Reis, has advanced several powerful papers in innovative philanthropy. Regarding best practices, the foundation is developing a computerized knowledge management system to retrieve information on program goals and outcomes, and creating an internal task force to advance its standing as a learning organization. Also, the Foundation has made a strong commitment to education for nonprofit managers, creating distance learning opportunities through a collaboration involving Society for Nonprofit Organizations, University of Wisconsin Extension Service, and Murphy Communications, Inc.

John and Mary Markle Foundation
www.markle.org
Recognizing that the opportunities of the present may be pivotal in solving the challenges of tomorrow, the John and Mary Markle foundation plans to disburse its assets twice as fast as the 5% legal requirement. This innovative move is complemented by the foundation's bold move into intersectoral investing, funding both innovative nonprofit and for-profit entities.

Milken Institute
www.milken-inst.org
The Milken institute is devoted to the study of economic dynamics. Key areas of analysis include corporate finance, capital markets, and financial institutions; globalization, education, jobs, labor markets, and human capital. The institute aggressively initiates, supports and disseminates analytically engaging works to thought leaders, policy makers and other global decision makers.

Milwaukee Foundation Corporation
www.milwaukeefoundation.org
The Milwaukee Foundation takes an integrated approach to community development philanthropy, targeting small geographic areas and developing collaborative neighborhood projects for "housing, business and commercial development, and community infrastructure by building on the best practices of economic development in urban areas." The foundation cultivates com-

munity-based organizations designed to improve their capacity and success in creating community wealth.

Charles Stewart Mott Foundation
www.mott.org
The Mott Foundation has devoted several years of research and planning to the creation of the Fund for Innovation, Effectiveness, Learning and Dissemination (FIELD). FIELD will "identify, develop, support and disseminate best practices, and to educate policymakers, funders and others about micro-enterprise as an anti-poverty intervention." This creative approach to philanthropy will not only fund micro-enterprises but will also teach social entrepreneurs business, financial and marketing skills.

David and Lucile Packard Foundation:
www.packfound.org
The Foundation's Organizational Effectiveness and Philanthropy Program (OE/P) strives to "enhance the effectiveness of Foundation grantees, build the field of nonprofit management, promote philanthropy, and strengthen the nonprofit sector overall." Since 1983, the foundation has worked towards strengthening the management capacity of nonprofit organizations. Multi-year efforts have advanced the causes of organizational assessment, planning, board development, staff training, market research, evaluation design and evaluations, mergers and other restructuring efforts, executive transitions and executive search, and technology assessments and plans.

Ellis L. Phillips Foundation
www.agmconnect.org/epf.html
Seeing the need for innovative, creative approaches to fundraising, The Ellis L. Phillips Foundation initiated and funded the Catalogue for Philanthropy. This project has been crafted to "increase charitable giving in Massachusetts by creating a year-end catalogue showcasing philanthropy and presenting 100 examples of highly attractive and cost effective charitable institutions.

Roberts Foundation
www.redf.org
The Roberts Enterprise Development Fund (REDF). REDF builds on six years of effort to improve economic opportunities for the homeless and very low income individuals. A proactive leader in social enterprise, REDF operates 23 enterprises in the San Francisco Bay area. REDF takes a social return on investment (SROI) approach to its giving. REDF also "preaches what it practices" by sponsoring, publishing and disseminating a wide range of whitepapers on social enterprise, venture philanthropy, SROI and other innovative approaches to giving.

Rockefeller Brothers Fund
www.rbf.org
Cognizant of the increasing need by the social sector for financial, human, and structural resources, the Rockefeller Brothers Fund has devoted significant time, effort, and funds to the programs that focus on the development of resources, increased understanding, and accountability in the social sector.

The Survivors of the Shoah Visual History Foundation
www.vhf.org
The Survivors of the Shoah Visual History Foundation chronicles firsthand accounts of "survivors, liberators, rescuers, and other eyewitnesses of the Holocaust." The focus is on their experiences before, during, and after World War II.

The foundation's archive includes 200,000+ video tapes which consists of 100,000 hours+ of testimony, making the Shoah Foundation's archive the world's largest collection of digitized video testimonies. The Foundation is also developing new and innovative means to disseminate their archive, such as interactive CDs, to a wider audience of researchers, students and educators.

Soros Foundation: Open Society Institute
www.soros.org/osi.html
The Soros Foundation is devoted to

supporting, developing, and building open societies in more than 30 countries around the world. To these ends, it has expended hundreds of millions of dollars towards creative approaches to educational, social, and legal reform. A network of nationally based and global entities work synergistically to provide both regional expertise and macro wisdom. Soros Foundation programs include innovative approaches to economic/business development, Internet programs, privatization, and other areas requiring bold and proactive leadership.

Steinhardt Foundation
Birthright Israel
www.israelexperience.org
Concerned that younger generations of Jews were losing touch with their faith, two prominent Jewish philanthropist Michael Steinhardt and Charles Bronfman "jump started" Birthright Israel. Birthright Israel provides free 10-day tour of Israel to all North American Jews between the ages of 15 and 26. This $210 million program is designed to provide a tangible connection for Jewish youth to their heritage.

Surdna Foundation
www.surdna.org
The Surdna Foundation's Nonprofit Sector Support Initiative seeks to improve the effectiveness of nonprofit organizations by improving the nonprofit sector's ability to articulate its importance to public life, encouraging

collaboration among and within sectors, improve management, finance, leadership, and technology education in the nonprofit sector. Efforts have included grants to improve web based communication for nonprofits, develop a statistical measurement of nonprofit for-profit economic activity, and share social enterprise benchmarking efforts online.

Tides Foundation
www.tides.org
Cognizant of the increasingly important role technology plays in society, the Tides foundation developed eGrants . "eGrants.org is an online foundation that allows nonprofits to accept donations via the Internet and gives individuals an opportunity to make immediate and secure contributions to nonprofit groups working toward positive social change."

World Jewish Congress
www.virtual.co.il/orgs/orgs/wjc
The world Jewish Congress, an international federation of Jewish communities and organizations, founded the World Jewish Restitution Organization. The World Jewish Restitution Organization is devoted to recovering Jewish assets seized during World War II.

SOCIAL ENTERPRISE INVESTORS

Ashoka
www.ashoka.org

Ashoka is a global NGO devoted to social venture capital. Ashoka awards modest ($1,000s) stipends to "pattern changing visionaries." These Ashoka Fellows apply their creativity and determination to solving social problems on a macro scale. Since its inception, 1,000s of Ashoka Fellows in over 40 countries have made society improving changes in the areas of education, the environment, health, human rights, economic development and civic participation.

Calvert Social Venture Partners
www.greenmoney.com/calvertventures

One of the first social venture capital funds, Calvert invests in companies with a positive social impact that also meet the firm's venture capital risk and return requirements. Calvert provides financing, strategic advice, and assistance to its portfolio companies in the health and human services, education, environmental, and energy industries.

Community Foundation Silicon Valley
Silicon Valley Social Venture Fund
www.siliconvalleygives.org
www.siliconvalleygives.org/information1932/information.htm

Community Foundation Silicon Valley's Silicon Valley Social Venture Fund is a group of young professionals that "promotes intelligent, active and effective giving to non-profit organizations" in The Silicon Valley region. Emphasis is on using the venture philanthropy model to creating community wealth.

Community Partners
www.communitypartners.org

Community Partners is a nonprofit incubator focused on building civic capacity in Southern California. Community Partners approach includes assessment and creation of learning/technical assistance plans, direct, one-on-one technical assistance and support, group training based on mutually shared capacity-building priorities across projects and organizations, peer-to-peer learning built on formal and informal knowledge sharing, and connecting partners to important resources (e.g., written materials, publications, consultants).

235

Denali Initiative

www.denaliinitiative.org

A collaboration between the Manchester Craft Guild and several foundations, the Denali Initiative provides social entrepreneurs with the skills, tools and capital to better accomplish their missions. Denali Fellows are social entrepreneurs that participate in a three year training and development program in which they are educated by faculty from leading universities in the areas of marketing, financial planning, strategy and other managerial and entrepreneurial subjects.

echoing Green Foundation

www.echoinggreen.org

The Foundation provides catalyzing fellowships to social entrepreneurs, particularly those early in their philanthropic career. Currently, over 300 social entrepreneurs receive fellowships throughout the World. echoing Green Foundation has pioneered a unique venture philanthropy approach to its giving, providing financial, strategic, staff development, legal, and accounting assistance to their grantees. This integrated effort combines the identification, mentoring, and capacity building of emerging social entrepreneurs into a powerful engine for positive social change.

Entrepreneurs Foundation

the-ef.org

The Entrepreneurs Foundation seeks to encourage community involvement as a core element of company by providing capital and expertise to facilitate move to social entrepreneurs' to move to scale. With a focus on the Bay area and education and youth development, its 5 year goal is to invest $100 million in 15 community ventures.

Flatiron Partners
Flatiron Future Fund
Flatiron Foundation

www.flatironpartners.com

www.flatironpartners.com/index_future fund.html

www.flatironpartners.com/index_foundation.html

Flatiron Partners' Future Fund and Foundation invests in social enterprises. Their focus is on organizations that help prepare children for the new "digital society," educating and encouraging entrepreneurship "among minorities, women, and others with less traditional access to capital" and entrepreneurs to focus their efforts on solving social problems.

Japonica Intersectoral

www.japonica.com

Japonica Intersectoral's efforts are focused on the intersectoral segment of the social sector where quantifiable value metrics of the commercial sector converge with the socially powered motivations of the nonprofit sector. Its network of thought leaders, policy experts, and financial experts will apply the firm's global infrastructure to value creating initiatives which encompass capital market services, strategic financial advisory services, direct investment opportunities, and educational resources. By providing unparalleled financial technologies and a reservoir of industry knowledge to a select group of innovative foundations and NGOs, Japonica Intersectoral seeks to create "best in class" returns along a social enterprise investment spectrum.

Joint Venture Silicon Valley Network

www.jointventure.org

Joint Venture Silicon Valley Network is a nonprofit civic incubator focused on initiatives aimed at improving the economic vitality and quality of life in Silicon Valley. Specific initiatives include Challenge 2000, an effort to create "systemic, sustainable, and measurable gains" in student achievement.

Morino Institute

www.morino.org

The Morino Institute is catalyst, facilitator, and incubator for new, particularly technology driven, society improving initiatives. Areas of focus include community, youth services, and learning, specifically as they relate to venture philanthropy efforts.

New Profit Inc.

www.newprofit.com

New Profit Inc. provides financial and developmental support to the most promising social enterprises. Emphasis is on using benchmarks and performance measurements to make managers of NGOs accountable for creating social change.

New School Venture Fund

www.newschools.org

New Schools Venture Fund supports innovation in education. Specific efforts include a plan to invest in "10-20 of the most promising, scalable education ventures in the country."

Peninsula Community Foundation Center For Venture Philanthropy

www.pcf.org

www.pcf.org/pcfsite/stratphil/strat-phillinks/cvp.html

The Peninsula Community Foundation's Center for Venture Philanthropy is the "birthplace of venture philanthropy." For over 35 years, the CVP emphasizes giving that has a measurable impact on "civic investment" in the San Francisco Bay Area.

Roberts Foundation

www.redf.org

The Roberts Enterprise Development Fund (REDF). REDF builds on six years of effort to improve economic opportunities for the homeless and very low income individuals. A proactive leader in social enterprise, REDF operates 23 enterprises in the San Francisco Bay area. REDF takes a social return on investment (SROI) approach to its giving. REDF also "preaches what it practices" by sponsoring, publishing and disseminating a wide range of whitepapers on social enterprise, venture philanthropy, SROI and other innovative approaches to giving.

Robinhood Foundation

www.robinhood.org

Robinhood Foundation seeks to end poverty in NYC. Efforts focus on using venture philanthropy techniques to find, support and nurture strong social enterprise organizations and hold them accountable for their results.

Silicon Valley Community Ventures

www.svcv.org

Silicon Valley Community Ventures provides advice and financing to businesses that hire and/or are located in economically disadvantaged San Francisco Bay Area Communities. Specific resources include networking forums, business planning tools, software, equipment, training courses, legal services, public relations support, and employee recruiting and retention services.

Social Venture Partners

www.svpseattle.org

Social Venture Partners applies the venture capital to its giving. They commit time, money and expertise to create partnerships with not-for-profit organizations. Focus is community based. Original entity located in Seattle, with affiliated entities in Austin, and Arizona.

The Three Guineas Fund
Women's Technology Cluster

www.womenstechcluster.org

The Three Guineas Fund is a public grantmaking foundation. Its mission is "to advance social justice primarily by creating opportunity for girls and women in education and the workplace. One of the Fund's primary projects is the Women's Technology Cluster, the first high tech incubator focused on women entrepreneurs.

Youth Services America
Fund for Social Entrepreneurs

www.ysa.org/fse/index.php3

Youth Services America's Fund for Social Entrepreneurs funds a three-year leadership development program for the leaders of innovative youth services organizations in the Washington D. C. region.

INTERSECTORAL QUESTIONS

Intersectoral Interview Assessment Questions

Key Philosophies:

1. How will an increase in baby boomer affluence, from both a booming economy and intergenerational transfer of wealth, affect philanthropy in the coming decades?

2. Is it a misnomer to define a "social entrepreneur" as: "a nonprofit manager with a background in social work, community development and/or for-profit business who pursues a vision of economic empowerment through the creation of nonprofit enterprises intended to provide expanded opportunity for those on the margin of our nation's economic and social mainstreams"? Why exclude those entrepreneurs seeking social change through commercial ventures?

3. Identify several of the best-in-class Social Entrepreneurs and/or Venture Philanthropists and describe the key distinguishing characteristics. How familiar are you with the work of Jed Emerson or REDF?

4. Discuss major categories of NGO enterprise. What has been your experience with social enterprise? If possible, discuss the alternatives discussed by Jed Emerson, Gregory Dees, Ed Skloot, Bill Shore, or Burton Weisbrod.

5. How does the "Virtuous Capital" model of philanthropy attempt to resolve several key aspects of traditional VC practices that may run afoul with NGO & foundation cultures, such high risk investments, management changes, organizational control, and demand for high growth rates? How familiar are you with the work of Letts, Ryan, or Grossman?

6. Discuss your knowledge of the comparative view of three major sectors of philanthropic theory, *tzedakah*, stewardship, and secular thought leaders.

7. Which universities offer the best social sector education and why? Discuss the role of more classic business education plays in the "new philanthropy" model. What steps can the better graduate schools adopt to enhance their curriculum?

Minimizing Cost and Creating Value:

8. Discuss your views of the so-called tides of change that are effecting the social sector, e.g. scientific management, liberation management, war on waste, and the watchful eye. What is your familiarity with the work by Tom Reis or the W.K. Kellogg Foundation? How familiar are you with the work of Paul Light?

9. Discuss several tactics – in order of increasing impact – that a foundation can best create value. Which tactic do you believe can most often create the greatest value? How can foundations best develop their internal use of strategy? How familiar are you with the work of Michael Porter or Mark Kramer?

10. Discuss what is meant by a "Capacity Gap" existing in the social sector. What are several telling signs of a sizable Capacity Gap existing in an NGO or foundation? What strategies can be used to increase capacity at NGOs? Discuss your view of the state of MIS systems within the social sector, both for basic financial information and social metrics. What is your familiarity with the work by the Morino Institute?

11. Discuss your views as to whether private operating foundations

("POFs") create greater value than grantmakers by essentially eliminating the middleman and its associated costs and administrative processes. Should there be a call for more philanthropists to pursue POFs?

12. Is it possible for a private foundation to establish a commercial subsidiary? What are several of the most significant restrictions?

13. What is an appropriate ratio of costs/total funds raised for professional fundraising? Discuss both the direct and total cost of fund raising for internal efforts and external activities.

14. What are your views with regard to the amount of time and effort NGO executives dedicate to fund raising? What impact do you believe this has on NGO effectiveness?

15. What are some of the more effective uses of technology for social sector organizations in the new economy? Should organizations and their funders first focus on internal efficiencies or move quickly to the web to leverage currently favorable valuations?

16. Is the "new philanthropy" trend prevalent outside the US? Do greater opportunities exist in cultures where the nonprofit sector is still emerging and open to greater change? Discuss the statistics regarding annual trends in giving and foundation assets.

17. Of the various social sector industries (healthcare, education, human services), which present the greatest opportunities for socially-minded strategic philanthropist?

Measuring Efficiency:

18. What are your views on measuring the effectiveness and efficiency of social sector work? How familiar are you with the program outcome work by the United Way or the Inter-Agency Benchmarking and Best Practice Council or the National Partnership for Reinventing Government?

19. Discuss your views regarding the calculation and use of what several

social sector scholars and practitioners refer to as a blended social return or a social sector return on investment ("SROI")? How familiar are you with the work of Jed Emerson or REDF? How about Dennis Benson?

20. Does an absence of transparency in accounting negatively affect the ability of donors to evaluate the effectiveness of NGOs and foundations? Are Form 990 filings an adequate source of information? What on line sources exist for such information? What are your thoughts on Guidestar?

Use of Assets:

21. What is your view on how foundations should invest their assets? To what extent should they be utilized to advance the foundation's missions?

22. What is the average size of an annual grant for a billion dollar plus foundation? Are there economies of scale for foundations and NGOs? Should billion dollar plus foundations focus on relatively small ($40,000) grants?

23. What is the IRS minimum for foundation asset distribution annually? Should foundations allocate more of their assets than the government mandated 5%? Should the minimum be increased? How do you assess the trade-offs between current success and growth in asset levels?

24. What is a Program Related Investment ("PRI")? How can a PRI be effectively used by a foundation? At what point does a PRI count toward the 5% IRS calculation? What was the dollar volume of PRIs for the latest year for which information is available?

25. How do the anti-inurement and the 1996 Intermediary Sanction Act effect commercial activities of an NGO, the operations of a foundation, and the compensation in the social sector?

26. Can an NGO have stock ownership? To what extent are NGO security issuances regulated by the 33 or 34 Acts? What flexibility is there under

the regulation that no individual can profit from a 501(c)'s activities?

27. What alternatives are available to obtain financial information or tax files for NGOs or foundations? What are the regulatory requirements for disclosure?

28. What are your views on the current state of capital structure within the social sector and prospects for an evolution to those more characteristic within the commercial sector?

Social Sector vs. Commercial Sector:

29. How does increasing commercial and competitive pressures change the social sector landscape? Do they help or hinder the creation of community wealth? What are your views on strategic restructuring within the social sector? What is your familiarity with the work of David La Piana? What has been your experience with intersectoral situations such as: M&A, back office consolations, joint venture, public offerings, or fiscal sponsorships?

30. How would you compare social sector executives to commercial sector executives in the following categories: Finance? Marketing? Compensation structuring? Technology? Benchmarking? Budgeting? Virtuous capital?

31. Can social sector executive compensation be enhanced through commercial subsidiary equity and incentives? Discuss several of the alternatives social sector organizations can utilize to innovatively enhance compensation to attract the best and brightest.

32. How do the compensation packages of social sector executives compare to those of the commercial sector? How does the ratio of comparison change from graduation from college or grad school to a seasoned executive?

33. Who do you believe are the best-in-class capital-philanthropists and the lowest ranking CP's? Importantly, what are the factors that influence your views? How familiar are you with the writing by Andrew

Carnegie? Discuss your views with regard to the efforts of the following CPs: The Bronfman Brothers, Bill Gates, Michael Milken, Tom Monaghan, George Soros, Steven Spielberg, or Michael Steinhardt.

Resistance to New Philanthropy:

34. Why do the majority of NGOs adamantly oppose benchmarking efforts? To what extent is their justification valid? What sources of best practice or benchmarking information exist for the social sector and what are the sources? How familiar are you with the Internet resource sites such as Benchnet, The International Benchmarking Exchange, The Drucker Foundation, or the London Benchmarking Group?

35. Many say a turn in terminology away from business terms is required when encouraging social sector organization to engage in private sector practices such as marketing and benchmarking. Can this ultimately sanitize the process and undermine efforts to initiate change? How familiar are you with the work of Camp, Watson, or Bogan?

36. What has been your experience with misfortunate situations within the social sector? NGOs? Foundations? Law of Unintended Consequences? Or Wasted Fund?

37. What do you see as the consequences for an unlimited demand for funds by NGOs or within Endowments?

38. Discuss your views on the existence of small and fragmented NGOs and the practical considerations for going to scale.

39. What do you see as the consequences of an absence of critical advocates within the social sector? No SEC? No research analysts? No catalysts?

40. How do you see the sophistication of the media with regard to PR for the social sector?

Appendix E

Sectarian Support for NP Benchmarking

Jewish Guidelines on Giving – *Tzedakah:*

The Jewish concept of philanthropy is embodied in the word "*tzedakah*" which is derived from a word meaning "just" and "righteous." *Tzedakah* is given because a person has a responsibility to take care of fellow human beings who are in need. This giving is not a matter of choice, but rather of obligation. Specific guidelines are detailed regarding how much to give, how to calculate what should be given and the forms of *tzedakah*.

The Torah indicates an obligation to "tithe," that is, give ten percent. Impulse giving is specifically and strongly discouraged in order to prevent impulse giving and to fulfill the *mitzvah* of *tzedakah*, predetermine amount should be established, either in a fixed percentage or a specific amount of money. A *mitzvah* is a "commandment of God." There are 613 *mitzvot* in the Torah. *Tzedakah* is considered one of the greatest because it involves in joining with God in working towards the sustenance and preservation of the world, and the dignity of human beings.

The medieval philosopher and legalist Moses Maimonides identified the following eight stages of *tzedakah*. The highest stage is the stage eight.

Stage One: [Lowest] The person who gives reluctantly.

Stage Two: The person who gives less than what he or she should, but gives graciously.

Stage Three: The person who gives what he or she should, but only after being asked.

Stage Four: The person who gives before being asked.

Stage Five: The person who gives without knowing the recipient, but the recipient knows the giver.

Stage Six: The person who gives knowing the recipient, but without the recipient knowing the identity of the giver.

Stage Seven: The person who gives completely anonymously: neither giver nor recipient knows the other.

Stage Eight: [Highest] The person who gives a gift or a loan or gives a job, or goes into business partnership, so the recipient becomes self-supporting, and no longer needs *tzedakah*.

Importantly, there is specific guidance on how to calculate *tzedakah*. The *ma'aser kerofim* is the traditional term for the tithe on money income.

1. The base on which it is calculated is one's income including recurring income like wages and ordinary profits, plus non-recurring income such as inheritances and capital gains.
2. One gives *tzedakah* on capital, but it is calculated on each asset only once, not annually. The period for which the calculation is made should be from Rosh Hashanah to Rosh Hashanah or a shorter fiscal period between those holidays, although other authorities allow the period to be a year and starting on any date convenient for the donor.
3. Losses may be offset against profits, and the calculation is then done from the net profit. Losses may not be carried forward to future fiscal periods.
4. Expenses truly justified for business purposes may be deducted from income subject to *ma'aser kerofim*. Food and lodging while on business travel may be deducted, but only to the extent that they exceed costs that would have been incurred at home.
5. Cash or accrual accounting may be used, but once chosen, the accounting method should be used consistently.
6. Some authorities do not require ma'aser kerofim on profits resulting purely from inflation. For example, if the value of one's home appreciates 3% but the rate of inflation was 2%, only the difference is subject to *ma'aser kerofim*. Taxes may be deducted from income. There are differences of opinion whether only taxes based on income or all taxes may be deducted from income subject to *ma'aser kerofim*.
7. *Ma'aser kerofim* may be paid in cash, merchandise or with one's labor. Labor is valued at the rate usually charged by the worker. Only 90% of

the value may be deducted from an existing obligation; the remaining 10% is *ma'aser* on the value of the work done.

Useful resources on *tzedakah* include: the just-*tzedakah*.org web site and Rabbi Wayne Dossick's *Living Judaism* (HarperCollins, 1995), and Moses Maimonides (1135-1204 AD) magnum opus, *Mishnah Torah*.

Christian Concept of Stewardship:

In addition to the Parable of the Talents contained in *Matthew 25: 14-30,* there is a very similar story called the Parable of the Gold Coins contained in *Luke 19: 11-27.* Both speak to the principles of comparative assessment, quantitative measurement, maximizing return on investment of the four T's (time, talent, treasures, and tenacity), reallocation of resources to those who will provide the highest return, and desire to expand a positive initiative.

Christianity proactively espouses the responsibility of giving and the duty to do so responsibly. "From everyone who has been given much, much will be demanded; and from the one who has been entrusted with much, much more will be asked." Time, talent and money are regarded as gifts from God and that those who receive these gifts are "trustworthy stewards," that is, someone who manages property belonging to someone else. Furthermore, it remains a Christian's awesome responsibility to make a return on that which he or she has received. The Parable of the Rich Fool speaks to the importance of those to whom much has been given to wisely use their resources and continue to endeavor to greater good regardless of accumulated wealth or successes *(Luke 12: 13-21).* An ancient Christian Armenian moral story, "The Foolish Man", expands upon the Rich Fool parable by stressing the importance of seeking value, working smartly, the negative consequence of seeking and placing luck over the wisdom of work, and the importance of recognizing value that may not be obvious upon first glance. The consequences in these parables are not positive for those who fail to live by the teachings, which is a perspective not typically associated with New Testament teachings.

In selecting recipients, there are various factors one should consider. Just as in any other investment, Christians should get the best benefit of their investments in God's work. Organizations that manage their funds best should be given priority. Support for a particular type of initiatives should go to the most efficient and productive. One should expect that leaders of an initiative can provide a clear, concise plan for accomplishing God's work and a reasonable idea of costs and time. Cautionary signs include the lack of written goals and objectives, heavy debt burden, bad credit history, unfinished projects, significant staff turnover, and unfocused solicitation of support.

Christianity affirms 10% as the desired level of giving, although the method for calculating the tithe is not as formalized. However, those who practice tithing, especially common among Mormons, are often cited as simply deducting 10% of their weekly or monthly income even before taxes and setting it aside for their church or other charity.

The idea that giving should be done with humility and anonymity is as important as the giving itself. Furthermore, giving can be in the form of time, services, non-cash gifts or property.

Useful resources on Christian Stewardship obviously include the Bible, both the Old and New Testaments. Also, Larry Brukett's *Giving and Tithing* (Moody Press, 1998) contains useful practical observations, material from the 1999 National Conference of Catholic Bishops segment on "Stewardship Conference Offers Lessons for a Lifetime" offer operational insights, a book titled *Parables of Jesus* published by the Diocese of the Armenian Church of Canada: Montreal (1998) provides a basic summary of useful parables, and *Armenian Tales* by the National Center of Aesthetics: Yerevan (1999) provides unique material on Armenian Christian wisdom.

CONCEPT COMPARISON GLOSSARY

Best Practices: Best practices are the byproducts of the benchmarking process. They are successful innovations or techniques of top-performing organizations, which are often classified into processes, programs, or policies. Most effectively applied, Best Practices are represented as quantified metrics. Quantification of Best Practices is often referred to as a Best Practices metric. The same terminology exists in the commercial sector.

Blended Return on Investment ("Blended ROI"): The blended return is the combination of both a social return on investment ("SROI") and a financial return on investment ("FROI"). The methodology to determine the statistics may vary as well as the relative weighting of each. Furthermore, its application as a discount rate in the traditional corporate finance or portfolio management sense may merit customization.

Capacity Building:
Capacity allows an organization to see how effective it is at executing its mission, how market needs are changing, and where it could improve its process-es. Beyond measuring outcomes, capacity allows an organization to analyze its programs in terms of effectiveness, efficiency, cost, timeliness and client satisfaction, all against the backdrop of a dynamically changing environment.

Dead-Founder Foundation: A foundation where the founder or substantial funder is no longer active in management. Such founder need not be deceased. Furthermore, commitment of special talents by the founder or substantial funder beyond the traditional "write-a-check" is required to be excluded from this definition.

Deliverable Opportunity: Similar to the commercial sector concept of Nuggets of Value, Deliverable Opportunities are specific situation outputs or deliverables, be they processes, programs, or policies that offer opportunities for improved performance in a NGO.

Enablers: The process, practices, and methods that underlie the implementation of best practices and work to achieve specified goals. Enablers are also referred to as characteristics that

249

seek to isolate certain of the more quantifiable reasons for the achievement of benchmark performance. Enablers may be the factors that underlie nuggets of value in the commercial sector or deliverable opportunities in the Social Sector. On a cautionary note, be wary of "false enablers" that are misleading explanations.

Intersectoral: The blending of two or more sectors working collaboratively and using their resources, inherent perspectives, experience, and management tools to achieve common goals.

Market Multiples: In the commercial sector, one of the more frequently used tools of measurement is market multiples, especially for public companies and in situations of private market transactions. As CPs probably know, historically the most widely recognized multiple was the price/earnings multiple ("P/E Ratio"). More recently the multiples have expanded to include revenue and cash flow multiples. And even more recently with the explosion of the new economy, market multiples to an even wide-range of measurement have developed, including market value to vision.

Live-Founder Foundation: A foundation lead by a founding or substantially funding passionate capitalist/philanthropist. Proactive involvement is often considered a necessary prerequisite. Financial allocation involvement only is

an insufficient qualification.

Multiplier/Discount Effect: The Multiplier Effect or the Discount Effect is intended to serve as the social sector version of the Return on Investment in the commercial sector. A Multiplier Effect exists when performance either equals or exceeds that of the pervious (or latest) best practice or its cost is either equal to or less than the previous (or latest) best practice. The Discount Effect is the converse of the Multiplier Effect. A Discount Effect exists when the organization under review displays a lower level or performance or is expending a higher level of costs for comparable product or services.

New Philanthropy Benchmarking ("NPB"): New philanthropic benchmarking ("NPB") builds on a synergist collaboration of commercial sector benchmarking, progressive social sectors strategies, and contemporary financial markets analytical tools. NPB is evaluated within the context of macro issues such a stakeholder considerations and comparative conclusionary financial metrics. On a micro level, insights are offered on process sequence as well as organizational execution suggestions.

Nuggets of Value: Represent specific opportunities to create value by improving current operations or by financial engineering previously ignored by the market and management. Comparing current operations to the practices of selected benchmark companies often provides ideas for these Nuggets.

Operational Philanthropy:
Commercial relationships between social sector organizations and commercial organizations, whereby the decision of the commercial organization to enter into the relationship is in part motivated by social sector considerations. Such relationships include foundations, Intersectoral organizations, NGOs, publicly traded companies, and – possibly – governmental entities.

Performance Gap: The Performance Gap is either the aggregate dollar or unit difference between the situation output or deliverable being assessed and the best practice performance metric. This gap is obtained by multiplying the difference (the Performance Margin) times the number of units involved. Performance Gap can be for one specific deliverable or output, a group, or for an entire organization. A Performance Gap is powerfully utilized when applied to an entire organization. In the commercial sector, the Performance Gap for the entire organization can also be referred to as the Value Gap.

Performance Margin: Performance margin is the difference between the sit-uation output or deliverable being measured and the best practice. This can be expressed in dollars or unit terms and preferably in its most basic form. Illustrative examples include cost per meal, percentage of utilized assets, or fees paid per physician visit. Although not necessarily a percentage calculation, the Performance Margin in the social sector is compared to the Profit Margins in the commercial sector given the similar objective of measuring and comparing a comparable metric.

Profit Margin: Profit Margin is defined in using various percentage calculations including pre-tax margin, after tax margin, gross margin variable contribution margin, etc.

Program Related Investments: A Program-related investment ("PRI") is an investment by a foundation that meets the following three tests:

- Its primary purpose is to further the exempt objectives of the foundation.
- To no significant purpose is the production of income or the appreciation of property (i.e. a prudent investor seeking a market return would not enter into the investment).
- It is not used to lobby or support lobbying.

In addition, as with any grant, a PRI may not be used to generate significant private inurement for any individual or corporation. In the 1969 Tax Act, Congress created inducements for the use of PRIs to encourage foundations to use their assets in ways that would further their philanthropic ends. In particular, the entire amount of the PRI is counted as a qualifying distribution in the year in which it is made, and all PRIs are specifically exempted from classification as jeopardizing investments. (Brody and Weiser)

Shareholder/Stakeholder: Public companies that have varying degrees of obligations to multiple constituencies. Although current trends support greater concern for stockholders, other stakeholders such as customers, management, employees, suppliers, and communities receive significant consideration.

Social Capital: Social capital begins with human capital: the development of self-sufficient individuals who are mutually supportive and have the generosity and skills to create the structures, organizations, and resources needed for healthy and equitable communities. Ultimately, the ability of social structures and systems to help people achieve their goals for the common good is perceived as "social capital." (Reis)

Social Capital Markets: Also referred to as the U.S. Nonprofit Capital Market. The Social Capital Markets includes both traditional and innovative sources of funding for social sector organizations, especially NGOs. Historically, discussions of funding in the social sector have focused primarily on grants, annual fund raising, direct mail, and endowments. More recently the components of this market have become understood to include financial sources more customary to the commercial sector, including access to public markets, private institutional markets, and funds generated from commercial ventures. (J. Emerson)

Social Enterprise: Social Enterprise is the application of innovation management and program development strategies in an effort to address critical issues facing society. Individuals who engage in social enterprise, often referred to as Social Entrepreneurs, draw upon the best thinking in both the commercial and social sectors in order to advance their social agenda. (REDF)

Social Enterprise Spectrum: A starting point for thinking about strategy and structure in the social sector by considering the nature of key stakeholder relationships. The spectrum is anchored by two theoretical extremes that are relatively rare in practice. At one end, the purely philanthropic organization relies exclusively on donations for operating both expenses and capital, uses only volunteer labor, receives in-kind donations, and gives away its product or services. At the other end of the spectrum, the purely commercial enterprise mediates all its transactions through economic markets. (Dees)

Social Entrepreneur: Plays by the role of change agent in the social sector by:

- relentlessly pursuing opportunities to create and sustain social value,
- applying innovative approaches in their work and their funding
- acting boldly without being constrained by the resources currently in hand, and
- exhibiting a heightened sense of accountability to the various constituencies they serve (communities and investors) for the outcomes they create. (Dees)

Social Sector: The social sector is the sector of the economy that encompasses organizations seeking to advance social missions. Such organizations would most typically include NGOs (including 501(c) nonprofits), foundations, and possibly certain intersectoral ventures.

Social Venture Capital/Venture Philanthropy/Virtuous Capital: Social Venture Capital/Venture Philanthropy/Virtuous Capital is the philanthropic application of venture capital principles and practice. Venture Philanthropy assists social sector organizations in the plan, launch and management of new programs or social purpose enterprises. In addition to grants, Venture Philanthropists provide networking, management advice and an array of other supports to organizations within a given portfolio of charitable investments.

Stakeholder: Stakeholders include all the multiple constituencies of an NGO. These include, among others, funders, sponsors, donors, clients, patrons, management, employees, volunteers, suppliers, and community in general. This concept parallels the commercial sector term of stockholder/stakeholder without the often-dominant emphasis on stockholder value.

Value Gap: Value Gap is the difference between a company's current value and its potential value approximately two years subsequent to acquisition. Value Gap is based on utilizing existing business lines only.

APPENDIX G

CAMP'S REASONS & RESULTS CHART*

Key Reasons for Benchmarking and Contrasting Results

Without Benchmarking **With Benchmarking**

Defining customer requirements

Without Benchmarking	With Benchmarking
Based on history or gut feeling	Straight reality
Perception	Objective evaluation
Low fit	High conformance

Establishing effective goals and objectives

Without Benchmarking	With Benchmarking
Lacking external focus	Credible, unarguable
Reactive	Proactive
Lagging industry	Industry leading

Developing true measure of productivity

Without Benchmarking	With Benchmarking
Low commitment	High commitment

Industry best practices

Without Benchmarking	With Benchmarking
Not invented here	Proactive search for change
Few Solutions	Many options
Average of industry progress	Business practice breakthrough
Frantic catch-up activity	Superior performance

* Camp, Robert C., Benchmarking; The Search for Industry Best Practices that Lead to Superior Performance, Wisconsin, ASQC Quality Press, 1989.

CAMP'S BEST OF THE BEST CHART[a]

Best of Best in Commercial Sector

Subject	Company	Says Who ...
Benchmarking	AT&T, Digital Equipment Corporation, IBM, Motorola, Texas Instruments, Xerox	Port and Smith [b]
Benchmarking	Digital Equipment Corporation, Florida Power & Light , Ford, IBM/Rochester, Motorola, Xerox	Altany [c]
Billing/collection	American Express, Fidelity Investments, MCI	Port and Smith
Billing/collection	American Express, MCI	Altany
Customer focus	General Electric (plastics), Wallace Company, Westinghouse (furniture systems), Xerox	Altany
Customer satisfaction	Federal Express, General Electric (plastics), L.L. Bean, Xerox	Port and Smith
Customer service	Federal Express, L.L. Bean, The Limited, Marriott, Procter & Gamble	Foster [d]
Design for manufacturing assembly	Digital Equipment Corporation, NCR	Altany
Distribution and logistics	L.L.Bean, Wal-Mart	Port and Smith
Employee empowerment	Corning, Dow Chemical, Millikin, Toledo Scale	Port and Smith
Empowerment	Honda of America, Millikin	Altany
Employee suggestions	Dow Chemical, Millikin, Toyota	Altany
Equipment maintenance	Disney	Port and Smith
Flexible manufacturing	Allen-Bradley/Milwaukee, Baldor Electric, Motorola/ Boynton Beach	Altany, Port and Smith
Health care programs	Allied-Signal, Coors	Port and Smith
Inbound transportation	Digital Equipment Corporation, Dow Chemical, Motorola, 3M, Xerox	Foster
Industrial design	Black and Decker (household products), Braun, Herman Miller	Altany
Leadership	General Electric/Jack Welch, Hanover Insurance/ Bill O'Brien, Manco/Jack Kahl	Altany

(a) Camp, Robert C., *Business Process Benchmarking: Finding and Implementing Best Practices,* Wisconsin, ASQ Quality Press, 1995.

Subject	Company	Says Who ...
Benchmarking	AT&T, Digital Equipment Corporation, IBM, Motorola, Texas Instruments, Xerox	Port and Smith
Benchmarking	Digital Equipment Corporation, Florida Power & Light , Ford, IBM/Rochester, Motorola, Xerox	Altany
Billing/collection	American Express, Fidelity Investments, MCI	Port and Smith
Billing/collection	American Express, MCI	Altany
Customer focus	General Electric (plastics), Wallace Company, Westinghouse (furniture systems), Xerox	Altany
Customer satisfaction	Federal Express, General Electric (plastics), L.L. Bean, Xerox	Port and Smith
Customer service	Federal Express, L.L. Bean, The Limited, Marriott, Procter & Gamble	Foster
Design for manufacturing assembly	Digital Equipment Corporation, NCR	Altany
Distribution and logistics	L.L.Bean, Wal-Mart	Port and Smith
Employee empowerment	Corning, Dow Chemical, Millikin, Toledo Scale	Port and Smith
Empowerment	Honda of America, Millikin	Altany
Employee suggestions	Dow Chemical, Millikin, Toyota	Altany
Equipment maintenance	Disney	Port and Smith
Flexible manufacturing	Allen-Bradley/Milwaukee, Baldor Electric, Motorola/ Boynton Beach	Altany, Port and Smith
Health care programs	Allied-Signal, Coors	Port and Smith
Inbound transportation	Digital Equipment Corporation, Dow Chemical, Motorola, 3M, Xerox	Foster
Industrial design	Black and Decker (household products), Braun, Herman Miller	Altany
Leadership	General Electric/Jack Welch, Hanover Insurance/ Bill O'Brien, Manco/Jack Kahl	Altany

(b) Port, Otis, and Geoffrey Smith. 1992. "Beg, borrow, and benchmark." *Business Week,* 30 November, 74-75.

(c) Altany, David. 1991. "Share and share alike: Benchmarkers are providing the wisdom of mother's reproach." *Industry Week,* 15 July, 12-16.

(d) Foster, Thomas. 1992. "Logistics benchmarking: Searching for the best." Distribution 96 no. 3 (March):30-36.

APPENDIX I

20 BENCHMARKING ASSESSMENT QUESTIONS

Benchmarking Section:

1. Benchmarking is:
   a) only for entrepreneurial corporations
   b) only when there is a Profit Margin
   c) for any situations dealing with the investments of time, talents, treasures, and tenacity
   d) for any type of corporation excluding NGOs

2. Benchmarking is not:
   a) identifying areas where improvement would make the most significant difference to the bottom line
   b) finding out how the best companies meet the "Best Practices" standards
   c) adapting and applying lessons learned from others work
   d) a process which promotes the "let's do it" attitude

3. Which of the following is a common theme behind benchmarking?
   a) benchmarking is not used in the social sector because people think that social sector jobs should not be assessed
   b) benchmarking is not used in the social sector because it is a lot less risky then it sounds
   c) the process of benchmarking takes a lot of time and effort to be successful
   d) all of the above

4. Which statement proves that many social sector participants believe that NGOs do not have stakeholders?
   a) there are no stockholders
   b) corporations only have stakeholders
   c) stakeholders are not funders, management, or patrons
   d) all of the above

5. Which of the following is a justifiable complaint about benchmarking in a foundation?
   a) isn't benchmarking a profit maximizing, competitive weapon, and therefore inconsistent with a mission driven NGO?
   b) will the social sector service culture resist the analysis and learning that benchmarking requires?

c) when managers are overburdened, staffs don't like comparisons, funders don't value
overhead, and customers lack
market mechanisms, who will
drive benchmarking?

d) none of the above

6. Employees protest against NPB
because:
a) change causes them to leave
their comfort zone
b) they fear having to do more
work
c) their unproductive attitude
could be exposed and they
could lose their jobs
d) all of the above

7. Why do commercial sector organizations share benchmarking information?
a) companies expect and value
reciprocal information
b) they share generally available
and non-highly proprietary
information
c) they know the difficulty their
competitors will have implementing processes
d) all of the above

8. When assembling a benchmarking
team what are the characteristics you
look for?
a) a large group who are not
organizers or managers, but
intellectuals

b) a small team of motivated people who are comfortable with
data, well networked, and
management focused
c) a small group of individuals
each assessing different projects on their specific qualifica-
tions
d) one person who assesses all
the data and then makes the
decision

9. When looking to have a significant
impact with the assets your controlling, which of the following would
not be helpful to hear?
a) From evaluating our
"Performance Gap," we
noticed that we could easily
implement this newer procedure with a high probability of
success
b) By comparing different aspects
such as budget demands, management problems and per-
formance issues, we could
have a more significant impact
on our mission by taking the
following course
c) when we tried to benchmark
our missions to others we
found ours to be so unique
that our process was unable to
be compared
d) none of the above

10. Which of the following reasons
reaffirms that external benchmarking

works for NGOs as well as internal benchmarking?

   a) external benchmarking focuses on getting the most out of your assets

   b) external benchmarking is used effectively for corporations on a daily basis

   c) external benchmarking allows you to find faster, cheaper and better ways to assess goals

   d) all of the above

11. Internal benchmarking can be less effective than external because:

   a) it does not help an organization figure out how to meet their goals or improve

   b) external benchmarking lets you learn from others who have already made mistakes, and find a successful way to increase efficiency

   c) when you're internally focused you don't have a concrete understanding of where your competition is

   d) all of the above

12. When assessing the "Performance Gap," (in business terms, the "Value Gap") which of the following steps is not important?

   a) significance of impact

   b) the burdens it could place on the inefficient

   c) time to get it

   d) probability

Implementation Process Section:

13. Which of the following structures applies directly to benchmarking in NGOs?

   a) Motivations

   b) Missions

   c) Management

   d) all of the 3M's apply directly

14. What percentage of problems involves benchmarking solutions, and what percentage of problems have solutions that involve changing culture, philosophy and processes, respectively?

   a) 50% and 50%

   b) 90% and 10%

   c) 10% and 90%

   d) 100% and 0%

15. How often does benchmarking need to occur?

   a) once

   b) annually

   c) rarely

   d) continually

16. After the implementation, the follow-up steps monitor the progress. Which of the following are the reasons for monitoring the progress?

1. resistance to change

2. to maintain day to day contact, keeping everyone involved

3. old habits die hard

4. implementation often gets stuck

5. some management egos have dark

sides
   a) 1, 4, 5
   b) 1, 2
   c) all of the above
   d) none of the above

17. Implementation of benchmarking works best when:
   a) there is day to day check up on all levels to make sure implementation is going smoothly
   b) when the managers have direct and strong control over the employees
   c) when a company is in such dire need for change that only a turn around will save employee's jobs
   d) all of the above

Best Practices Section:

18. How do best practices and Benchmarking work together?
   a) benchmarking is more than "Best Practices," but also comparative measurements, active goal setting, and implementation
   b) benchmarking finds appropriate "Best Practices" and puts them into action
   c) benchmarking helps an organization learn exactly where their performance lags and helps them to focus on the application of Best Practices
   d) all of the above

19. Which of the following are not Best practices?
   a) byproducts of the benchmarking process
   b) successful innovations or techniques of other top-performing organizations
   c) ideas which cut against the grain of many social sector cultures
   d) none of the above

20. Which of the following are common implementation problems?
   a) staff insists they already have the lowest prices
   b) employee botch any attempts to implement what they learned
   c) difficult to persuade employees that a competitor with a mediocre reputation can do anything good
   d) all of the above

APPENDIX J

ANSWERS AND EXPLANATIONS TO 20 BENCHMARKING ASSESSMENT QUESTIONS

Question 1: Answer: c
Explanation: Benchmarking is a tool that compares situations, including investments. The four T's of time, talents, treasures, and tenacity are the four areas in which one can make a philanthropic investment. Reminding us, any investment can be benchmarked with other investments, even in the social sector.

Question 2: Answer: d
Explanation: The Benchmarking process requires time. Benchmarking deliverables or outputs need to be determined, assessments and calculations made, and then they need to be implemented. The "let's do it" attitude directly opposes the attitude required for successful Benchmarking.

Question 3: Answer: d
Explanation: Unfortunately, a common theme in NGOs is that because people are doing social work they feel there is no need for assessments. A *New York Times* article written by Claudia Deutsch states: "Old habits die hard, even ones that employees rail against.

When employees complained a few years ago of slow reimbursements, the Xerox Corporation studied 26 companies to find a way to speed up the payments. Problem was, the new system entailed new forms, did away with cash advances and required people to carry more than one corporate credit card. It took months longer than management expected for employees to embrace the new system. 'Everyone resisted the changes, even those that were unhappy with the old way,' recalled Warren D. Jeffries, manager of customer services benchmarking for Xerox." As previously stated in the answer to question number two, Benchmarking requires time.

Question 4: Answer: d
Explanation: All to often NGO managers myopically view their constituencies as restricted to only a limited number of groups, when in fact their constituencies are quite similar to commercial public company stakeholders. Without fully understanding the multiple stakeholders of commercial public companies, NGO executives risk reaching firm conclusions without the facts.

263

Furthermore, they frequently fail to understand that stakeholders are in fact funders (similar to a public company's stockholders), management (including employees), and patrons, which are really their customers.

Question 5: Answer: d
Explanation: Benchmarking can be used to maximize profit or performance. Maximizing performance is not against NGO missions. Service Cultures can resist analysis and learning, but effective managers can assuage their efforts.

Question 6: Answer: d
Explanation: Employees in NGOs are used in a different environment then employees in the commercial sector. Not all levels of people in the social sector are used to the changes that are occurring.

Question 7: Answer: d
Explanation: Commercial sector companies share information frequently. The information they share is never highly proprietary, but useful when comparing aspects of outputs to maintain a competitive status. Large companies like Wal-Mart don't hide their processes because they know that their competitors could not implement their processes as well as they do.

Question 8: Answer: b
Explanation: A small team is best because of the communication that takes place in teams. It is easier for a small team to make a decision than a large team. Motivation is key to expediting the Benchmarking process. Management focus is imperative as well as comfort with data and comfort with contacting.

Question 9: Answer: c
Explanation: The capability of implementing a new procedure with a high probability of success is an idea that sounds helpful. A way to have a more significant impact on your mission is also an idea that sounds helpful. However, the inability to draw comparisons because of your unique processes is the most common unrealistic excuse. Apples to apples comparisons are undoubtedly the easiest, but the benefit of Benchmarking is that it compares processes allowing apples to oranges comparisons.

Question 10: Answer: d
Explanation: External Benchmarking can be more beneficial than internal Benchmarking. External Benchmarking provides answers and solutions. When your processes are not as efficient as the ones you're comparing it to, you can use the more efficient process as a model solution. This statement does not mean that other process will work perfectly without changes. Adjustments will need to customize the model solutions.

Question 11: Answer: d
Explanation: See answer to question number 10.

Question 12: Answer: b
Explanation: When assessing Performance Gaps the significance of impact, time to get it, and probability are important in deciding which best practice to implement. The burdens placed on the inefficient are not important because if the inefficient were being efficient then they and you would not being in a situation to worry about their potential burdens.

Question 13: Answer: d
Explanation: Motivations, missions, and management apply to all social sector investments. The 3M's provide a reminder that during the Benchmarking process Benchmarking can get complicated. Sticking to the clearly set out motivations, missions, and management will increase the benefits of Benchmarking.

Question 14: Answer: c
Explanation: Claudia Deutsch, in her *New York Times* article "Competitors Can Teach You a Lot, but the Lessons Can Hurt," presents the fact that Benchmarking attacks only 10% of the problem and the other 90% involves changing your culture, philosophy and processes, respectively. These numbers confirm that cultural issues are most always present and can negate the Benchmarking process.

Question 15: Answer: d
Explanation: Benchmarking needs to occur continually. The Best Practice changes frequently. To maintain efficient practices and maximum performance, changes need to be occurring frequently to keep up with the times.

Question 16: Answer: c
Explanation: Monitoring the process need to occur for a variety of reasons. Already mentioned in the explanation to question 15 are culture issues. Culture issues involve resistance to change, because old habits die hard and some management egos have dark sides. Maintaining day to day contact is important because implementation often gets stuck. Of course there are other reasons for monitoring progress, but these are just a few of them.

Question 17: Answer: d
Explanation: Implementation is a very difficult part of the Benchmarking process. As discussed in the explanation to question 18, culture issues create problems. Two good ideas are to have day to day check ups and managers with direct and strong control over employees. An example of when there are not culture issues is when a company is in such dire need for change that only a turn around will save employee's jobs. This example illustrates that the resistance to change is normally unfounded and just created by unmotivated employees.

Question 18: Answer: d
Explanation: Benchmarking is a process of comparative measurements, active goal setting, and implementation. Best Practices are individual processes, which create the current best Multiplier Effect. Benchmarking helps an organization learn exactly where their performance lags and helps them to focus on the application of the Best Practice.

Question 19: Answer: d
Explanation: Best Practices are byproducts of the benchmarking process, successful innovations or techniques of other top-performing organizations, and ideas that cut against the grain of many social sector cultures. The definitions of Benchmarking and best Practices are compared in the answer to question 20.

Question 20: Answer: d
Explanation: All of these implementation problems fall under cultural issues. These three problems are more examples of possible cultural issues. The amount of cultural issues that arrive may seem over whelming and stressful. Benchmarking is not easy, but it can maximize performance.

DUAL STEPS BENCHMARKING PROCESS

Benchmarking Study Phases and Benchmarking Execution Steps

Benchmarking Study Phases:

1: *Familiarization*: familiarity with operating practices in the industry sector

2: *Development of Information-Gathering Instruments*: collection of information regarding operating practices, qualitative and quantitative measurements, financial statements, and expense records

3: *Development of Data Analysis Program*: development of a standard system of measurement

4: *Information Gathering*: process of accessing information through CFOs

5: *Data Analysis, Normalization and Input*: normalization of data so all numbers are calculated on a relative scale

6: *Development of Internal Performance Objectives*: standardization to a bell curve

7: *Firm-Level Performance Evaluation*: creating system to measure performance gap

8: *Preparation of Participant Study Report*: report containing evaluation of performance, overview of operating practices, and performance information data

Benchmarking Execution Steps:

1: *Identify What is to be Benchmarked*: what processes are to be benchmarked

2: *Identify Comparative Organizations*: identify best competitors for comparisons

3: *Determine Data Collection Method and Collect Data*: how data will be collected

4: *Determine Current Performance "Gap"*: determine where gap exists and what represents

5: *Project Future Performance Levels*: was gap understood in terms of actions required

6: *Communicate Benchmark Findings and Gain Acceptance*: were the findings communicated and commitment established from affected organizations

7: *Establish Functional Goals*: was best practice information understood so functional goals to incorporate benchmarking findings established

8: *Develop Action Plans*: action plans to lessen the "Gap" was action plan implemented

9: *Implement Specific Actions and Monitor Progress*: were benchmarks incorporated with the management and financial processes

10: *Recalibrate Benchmarks*: recalibrate and determine if benchmarking has become institutionalized

APPENDIX L

SELECTED BLENDED ROI & PRESENT VALUE MODEL ISSUES AND RESPONSES

Overview, Issues and Responses[a]

Abstract: There appears to be at least five issues requiring resolution prior to advancing the practical application of both the SROI[b] and Present Value to the social sector. The benefits are obvious; but, the consequences – while significantly positive – may be less so. The benefits include a more effective allocation of resources, an accelerated investment of funds into the social sector, and a higher level of market/financial-

---

(a) Materials obtained from www.UnitedU.com.

(b) REDF believes the social and economic value created by the nonprofit sector has not been appropriately tracked, calculated and attributed. As the nonprofit sector continues to compete for limited charitable dollars, it will be increasingly important to go beyond evaluating whether a program is a "good cause" to analyzing if it can be considered a "sound and smart investment." REDF's efforts to calculate the Social Return on Investment (SROI) of its portfolio of social purpose enterprises is one attempt to analyze and describe the impact of these enterprises on the lives of individuals and on the communities in which they live. REDF's approach to calculating SROI includes measuring the tax dollars saved by helping the people who work for REDF portfolio social purpose enterprises reduce their dependency on public assistance, homeless shelters, and other government-supported services. SROI enables nonprofit organizations to calculate the social cost savings generated by their social purpose enterprises. This cost savings data, in combination with the social impact findings from OASIS, can be a powerful tool for social sector managers in advocating for financial support of their work. REDF has produced SROI Reports on each enterprise in its portfolio, detailing the financial results of the enterprise, the social cost savings generated, and the impact of the social purpose enterprise on individual social outcomes.

based competition. The consequences are vast and would impact all members of the social sector, including foundations, NGO, CPs, and social sector executives.

First Issue: How can a framework be developed to rank projects by social desirability?

Response: A periodic market survey index. Such an index would provide the results of a periodic survey of social sector funder (social sector capital markets) indicating quantitative rankings of preferences for a comprehensive range of social sector or social subsector initiatives. The survey would be cross-categorized by three primary funder types, e.g., CPs, foundations, and individuals. The output would be sufficiently comprehensive to include both projects and capacity related programs. The ranking would be on a scale of 0.1 to 1.0, with the lower number indicating the more highly valued social investments. These statistics would then be used to adjust social returns (SROIs) and social financial returns ("FROI"[c]) (on a basis weighted for NGO project funding mix and NGO dollars

		CPs		Fnds		Inds		All
Urban:		0.20x		0.40x		0.60x		0.40x
Program		0.20x		0.20x		0.20x		
Capacity		0.20x		0.60x		1.00x		
Suburban:		0.80x		0.60x		0.40x		0.60x
Program		0.80x		0.40x		0.20x		
Capacity		0.80x		0.80x		0.60x		

(c) Financial Return of Investment ("FROI") can refer to both the financial return of financial assets or the financial return of an investment in social sector or intersectoral investment.

(d) The blended return is the combination of both SROI and FROI. The methodology to determine the statistics may vary as well as the relative weighting of each. Furthermore, its application as a discount rate in the traditional corporate finance or portfolio management sense may merit customization. Select factors considered in constructing BROI/DR Scale: ease of understanding, simplicity of calculation, non-negative connotations, comparability to commercial financial concepts, ease of application, DR moves in reverse direction to BROI, and applicability to calculating Social Purchasing Power and Present Social Value.

invested) by dividing the respective IRR's to obtain a market proxy Blended ROI.[d] An example table may prove illustrative. For supporting detail see "Multiple Programs with FROI & SROI and Multiple Funders — Pluralistic within Funder Categories."

Second Issue: How can a higher SROI provide a lower discount rate[e] so as to reward the more desirable projects with a greater present value?

Response: An effective and practical approach appears to be a simple conversation table. This conversion table essentially transforms (reverses) the higher SROIs to a lower discount rate. The table is intuitively appealing as it includes most frequently encounter FROIs and likely encountered SROIs, provides a non-negative stigma beginning SROI at 10%, is uniformly consistent, and is quite easy to understand and apply. For example, a 20% SROI translates to a 50% discount rate and a 40% SROI to a 30% discount rate. For an application, see "Comparisons of PSV under Varying BROI, FROI, and Years to Full Investment Scenarios."

BROI/DR Scale:

BROI	0%	5%	10%	15%	20%	25%	30%	35%	40%	45%	50%	55%	60%	65%	70%
DR	70%	65%	60%	55%	50%	45%	40%	35%	30%	25%	20%	15%	10%	5%	0%

(e) Discount Rate ("DR") is the rate at which social projects are discounted to determine the projects present social value. DR is structured such that the more socially desirable a social project, the lower the DR, and, consequently, the greater Present Social Value.

(f) The present value in dollars (discounted at an specified annual percentage rate) of projected social benefits obtained from a social or Intersectoral investment. Present Social Value is a function of: (a) payout, (b) Discount Rate, "DR", and (c) years since 1st investment. For instance, if payout equals $20mm DR equals 20% and years since 1st investment equals 4 years, then Present Social Value equals $20mm/(1.20^4)=$9.66mm.

However, both BROI and DR have practical uses in financial assessment of both foundations and NGOs. For example, in calculating Present Social Value[f], utilizing the discount rate satisfies the objective of providing a greater Present Social Value to those projects a with a higher social return. When calculating the projected Social Purchasing Power,[g] BROI provides the more appropriate metric by discounting future financial assets with an appropriately greater rate for those projects yielding a greater social return.

The actual calibration of the scale deserves careful assessment in part based on the BROIs achieved by NGOs, foundations, and Intersectoral entities and projects. For example, a BROI of 55% may be too high or relatively quite rare in order to achieve an unchanging projected social value with a 15% return on financial assets.

Third Issue: With regard to foundations, how does this approach integrate varying financial returns?

Response: The model provides for independent assumptions of projected returns on a foundation's investment assets. The model also provides for independent annual distribution scenarios.

Fourth Issue: With regard to foundations, how does this approach integrate the varying lives to full social investment, e.g. three years to essentially perpetuity?

Response: The model provides for independent assumptions regarding years to full social investment, including a proxy for the in-perpetuity foundation. The methodology utilized assumes a planned simple arithmetic division of initial

---

(g) The projected social dollar value of foundation assets based on the interaction between of the BROI and the FROI, assuming no payout. Social Purchasing Power is a function of a) initial assets, b)Discount Rate "DR" c) Financial Return on Investment FROI and d) years since first investment. For instance, if initial assets were $100mm, DR equals 5%, FROI 15%, and years since 1st investment equals 1 year, then Social Purchasing Power equals (1.15/1.05)*$100m=$109.5mm.

assets over the planned years to full investment. For a graphic visualization see: "Present Social Value of $100mm Assuming 20% DR 50% BROI, and Various Years to Full Investment/ Approximate Payout Distributions."

CPs may find comparing the charts particularly useful in assessing what could be called crossover points varying the years to full investment of an endowment's assets. For example, in comparing the three-year scenario with the perpetual proxy (the twenty-five-year scenario), note the ladder pattern of the crossover where the Present Social Value of the three-year equals or exceeds the twenty-five year for all BROIs/DRs should the FROI on financial assets be projected at zero. However, for each five percentage point increase in FROI on financial assets, the crossover BROI decreases by five percentage points. In more concrete terms, assuming a projected FROI on financial assets of 10%, a three-year plan to fully invest an endowment's fund in the social sector would provide a greater Present Social Value for all BROIs until 60% and above. Should the endowment management really believe that its FROI on financial assets would actually achieve a historically unprecedented 30%, then a BROI of 40% would be required to be indifferent between fully investing social assets in either three or twenty-five years.

Fifth Issue: Does the model offer the potential to calculate both Social Purchasing Power and Present Social Value?

Response: Yes. With regard to Social Purchasing Power, the model can project the changing values based on three variables: BROI/DR, Return on financial assets, and annual payout rates. For example, Social Purchasing Power will increase when SROI exceeds FROI, decline when reverse, and remain unchanged when equal, without annual distributions. As for Present Social Value, the model provides the ability to calculate this metric based on the same three variables previously cited. For examples, assuming SROI exceeds FROI, an earlier full investment will yield a greater Present Social Value than a later, lower annual payout scenario. For a graphic illustration see: "Social Purchasing Power and Varying, Discount Rates/ BROIs."

Multiple Programs with
FROI & SROI and Multiple Funders

(Pluralistic within Funder Categories)

A.

	CPs	Fnds	Inds	All
Urban:	0.20x	0.40x	0.60x	0.40x
Program	0.20x	0.20x	0.20x	
Capacity	0.20x	0.60x	1.00x	
Suburban:	0.80x	0.60x	0.40x	0.60x
Program	0.80x	0.40x	0.20x	
Capacity	0.80x	0.80x	0.60x	

B. NGO Funding Composition - Annual Latest Year

	Dollars Invested	Weight
CPs	$600	60%
Fnds	$300	30%
Inds	$100	10%
	$1,000	100%

C. Dollars invested and IRR Assumptions

	Dollars Invested	IRR	Weight
FROI	$300	8%	30%
SROI	$700	14%	70%
Total	$1,000		100%

D. Project classification assumptions within FROI and SROI
100% of FROI is Suburban
100% of SROI is Urban

E. Investor Allocation in Programs

	(FROI) Suburban		(SROI) Urban	
	Dollars Invested	Weight	Dollars Invested	Weight
Program	$250	83%	$400	57%
Capacity	$50	17%	$300	43%
	$300	100%	$700	100%

F. Calculation of Social Beta

Suburban	Weight	60% CPs	30% Fnds	10% Inds
Program	83%	0.80	0.40	0.20
Capacity	17%	0.80	0.80	0.60
WT	100%	0.80	0.47	0.27
				0.65

Urban	Weight	60% CPs	30% Fnds	10% Inds
Program	57%	0.20	0.20	0.20
Capacity	43%	0.20	0.60	1.00
WT	100%	0.20	0.37	0.54
				0.29

G. Calculation of FROI/SROI and Respective Discount Rates

	IRR	Social Beta	
FROI (suburban)	8% /	0.65	12.3% FROI 57.7% Discount Rate
SROI (urban)	14% /	0.29	48.3% SROI 21.7% Discount Rate

H. Calculation of Blended ROI and Discount Rate

	Weight	DR	F/S ROI's
FROI	30%	57.7%	12.3%
SROI	70%	21.7%	48.3%
BROI	100%	32.5%	37.5%

BROI	DR
37.5%	
	32.5%

Calculation Steps for
Multiple Programs with FROI & SROI and Multiple Funders

As this is a hypothetical case study, detailed notes of elaboration serve a more heuristic purpose in contrast with the detailed notes for a situation specific evaluation and analysis.

• **Step A:** The Multiple Programs with FROI and SROI and Multiple Funders (pluralistic within funder categories, which effectively means "greater dollars, greater influence") begins with the periodic market survey index as Step A. The periodic market survey index is discussed in the first issue's response. The betas in this index assist in Step F: Calculation of a Social Beta.[h]

• **Step B:** NGO Funding Composition – Annual Latest Year calculates the weight of dollars invested by each group of funders. Each group's dollars invested is divided by the total dollars invested by all funders to calculate their respective weight. These weights are then used in Step C: Dollars Invested and IRR Assumptions.

• **Step C:** Step C calculates the weight of dollars invested in FROI and SROI investments. Similar to Step B, the weight is calculated by dividing the dollars invested in either FROI or SROI investments by the total dollars invested in both groups together. The IRR numbers are calculated and established by the NGO.

• **Step D:** Project Classification Assumptions with FROI and SROI provides NGO information used in Step F to calculate the Social Beta. Step D assumes the classification that 100% of FROI is allocated to suburban investments while 100% of SROI is allocated to urban investments.

• **Step E:** Investor Allocation in Programs calculates the respective weights of program and capacity separately under both FROI and SROI investments. The weights are calculated by dividing the individual dollars invested in program or

---

(h) A quantitative evaluation of a project's social desirability. Social Beta is ranked on a scale of 0.1 to 1.0 with the lower number indicating the more highly valued social investment, Unlike a financial beta, social beta is not associated with historical volatility.

capacity by the total dollars invested in both. The dollars invested in programs and capacity under both FROI and SROI are provided by the NGO.

• **Step F:** Calculation of Social Beta is done for both the Suburban and Urban programs separately. The calculation utilizes the weights established in Step E and the Social Betas from the periodic market survey index in Step A. Each category of funder is listed with their weights from Step B (60%CPs, 30%Fnds, and 10%Inds). An average of the program and capacity betas from the index is calculated with their respective weights as the WT (working total). The WTs are then multiplied by their respective funder percentage weights and all added to calculate the Social Beta. The same process is undergone with the Urban as the Suburban.

• **Step G:** Calculation of FROI/SROI and Respective Discount Rates takes the IRR from Step C and divides it by the Social Beta.

• **Step H:** Calculation of the Bl table, calculating the FROI. The Discount Rate is then calculated using the BROI/DR Scale. Both the FROI and the SROI calculations utilize the separate IRRs and Social Betas. Ended ROI and Discount Rate uses the weights established in Step C and the DR and F/S ROIs from Step G. The weighted averages are both calculated to establish the final BROI and DR.

Comparisons on PSV under Varying
BROI, FROI, and Years to Full Investment Scenarios
(In millions of dollars. Assumes initial financial assets of $100mm)

3 year

		FROI on Financial Assets						
BROI	DR	0%	5%	10%	15%	20%	25%	30%
0%	70%	$ 37.9	$ 39.2	$ 40.5	$ 41.8	$ 43.2	$ 44.6	$ 46.1
5%	65%	39.9	41.2	42.6	44.1	45.6	47.1	48.7
10%	60%	42.0	43.5	45.0	46.6	48.2	49.8	51.5
15%	55%	44.3	45.9	47.6	49.3	51.0	52.8	54.7
20%	50%	46.9	48.7	50.5	52.3	54.2	56.2	58.2
25%	45%	49.8	51.7	53.7	55.7	57.8	59.9	62.1
30%	40%	53.0	55.1	57.2	59.4	61.7	64.0	66.4
35%	35%	56.5	58.8	61.2	63.6	66.1	68.7	71.4
40%	30%	60.5	63.1	65.7	68.4	71.2	74.0	76.9
45%	25%	65.1	67.9	70.8	73.8	76.8	80.0	83.2
50%	20%	70.2	73.4	76.6	79.9	83.3	86.9	90.5
55%	15%	76.1	79.6	83.2	87.0	90.8	94.7	98.8
60%	10%	82.9	86.8	90.9	95.1	99.4	103.9	108.4
65%	5%	90.8	95.2	99.8	104.6	109.5	114.5	119.7
70%	0%	100.0	105.1	110.3	115.8	121.3	127.1	133.0

5 Year

		FROI on Financial Assets						
BROI	DR	0%	5%	10%	15%	20%	25%	30%
0%	70%	$ 26.6	$ 28.0	$ 29.6	$ 31.2	$ 33.0	$ 34.9	$ 36.9
5%	65%	28.3	29.9	31.6	33.4	35.4	37.5	39.8
10%	60%	30.2	31.9	33.9	35.9	38.1	40.5	43.1
15%	55%	32.3	34.3	36.4	38.8	41.2	43.9	46.8
20%	50%	34.7	37.0	39.4	42.0	44.8	47.8	51.1
25%	45%	37.5	40.0	42.8	45.7	48.9	52.4	56.1
30%	40%	40.7	43.6	46.7	50.1	53.7	57.7	61.9
35%	35%	44.4	47.7	51.3	55.1	59.3	63.9	68.8
40%	30%	48.7	52.5	56.6	61.1	66.0	71.2	76.9
45%	25%	53.8	58.2	63.0	68.2	73.9	80.0	86.7
50%	20%	59.8	64.9	70.6	76.7	83.3	90.6	98.4
55%	15%	67.0	73.1	79.7	87.0	94.9	103.5	112.8
60%	10%	75.8	83.0	90.9	99.6	109.0	119.3	130.5
65%	5%	86.6	95.2	104.8	115.2	126.6	139.1	152.7
70%	0%	100.0	110.5	122.1	134.8	148.8	164.1	180.9

10 year

BROI	DR	FROI on Financial Assets						
		0%	5%	10%	15%	20%	25%	30%
0%	70%	$ 14.2	$ 15.3	$ 16.5	$ 17.8	$ 19.4	$ 21.2	$ 23.3
5%	65%	15.3	16.5	17.9	19.5	21.3	23.4	25.9
10%	60%	16.5	17.9	19.5	21.4	23.6	26.2	29.2
15%	55%	18.0	19.6	21.5	23.7	26.4	29.5	33.1
20%	50%	19.7	21.6	23.9	26.6	29.8	33.5	38.0
25%	45%	21.7	24.0	26.8	30.1	34.0	38.7	44.3
30%	40%	24.1	27.0	30.3	34.4	39.3	45.2	52.3
35%	35%	27.2	30.6	34.8	39.9	46.1	53.7	62.9
40%	30%	30.9	35.3	40.6	47.1	55.1	64.9	76.9
45%	25%	35.7	41.3	48.1	56.6	67.0	80.0	96.0
50%	20%	41.9	49.1	58.1	69.3	83.3	100.8	122.6
55%	15%	50.2	59.7	71.8	87.0	106.1	130.2	160.5
60%	10%	61.4	74.4	90.9	111.9	138.7	172.7	215.8
65%	5%	77.2	95.2	118.5	148.4	186.7	235.9	298.5
70%	0%	100.0	125.8	159.4	203.0	259.6	332.5	426.2

25 year

BROI	DR	FROI on Financial Assets						
		0%	5%	10%	15%	20%	25%	30%
0%	70%	$ 5.7	$ 6.2	$ 6.7	$ 7.3	$ 8.0	$ 8.9	$ 10.0
5%	65%	6.2	6.7	7.3	8.0	8.9	10.0	11.4
10%	60%	6.7	7.3	8.0	8.9	10.0	11.4	13.3
15%	55%	7.3	8.0	8.9	10.0	11.4	13.3	15.8
20%	50%	8.0	8.9	10.0	11.4	13.3	15.8	19.4
25%	45%	8.9	10.0	11.4	13.3	15.9	19.5	24.9
30%	40%	10.0	11.4	13.3	15.9	19.6	25.1	33.7
35%	35%	11.4	13.3	15.9	19.6	25.3	34.2	48.9
40%	30%	13.3	15.9	19.7	25.4	34.6	50.0	76.9
45%	25%	15.9	19.7	25.6	35.0	51.2	80.0	133.3
50%	20%	19.8	25.7	35.5	52.4	83.3	142.0	255.9
55%	15%	25.9	35.9	53.7	87.0	151.8	281.6	545.0
60%	10%	36.3	55.0	90.9	163.1	312.2	624.8	1282.6
65%	5%	56.4	95.2	176.0	348.8	724.6	1543.3	3318.0
70%	0%	100.0	190.9	393.4	851.2	1887.9	4219.2	9395.2

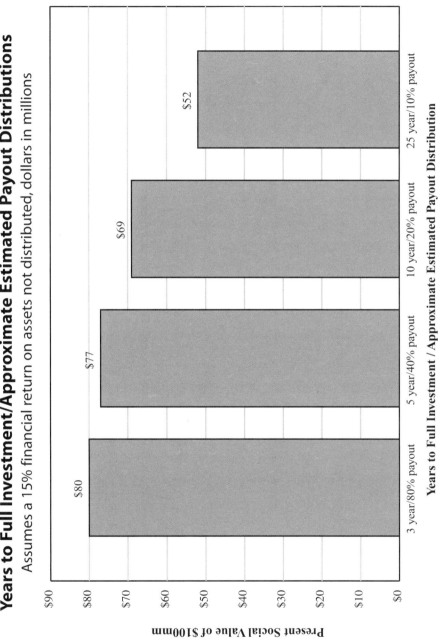

Present Social Value of $100 Million Assuming 20% DR/50% BROI, and Various Years to Full Investment/Approximate Estimated Payout Distributions

Assumes a 15% financial return on assets not distributed, dollars in millions

Present Social Value of $100mm

$90
$80
$70
$60
$50
$40
$30
$20
$10
$0

3 year/80% payout — $80
5 year/40% payout — $77
10 year/20% payout — $69
25 year/10% payout — $52

Years to Full Investment / Approximate Estimated Payout Distribution

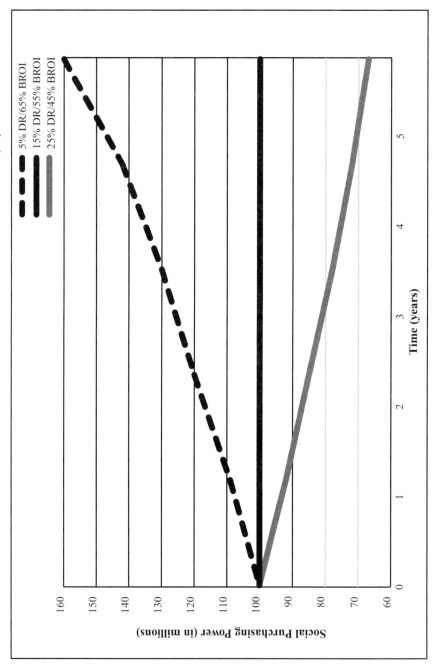

Projected Social Purchasing Power and Varying Discount Rates/BROIs

Assumes $100 million in initial financial assets, 15%, and no payout

APPENDIX M

BENCHMARKING INTERNET SITES

The Advisory Board Company (ABCO)

www.advisory.com

The Advisory Board provides best practices research and analysis to the health care industry, focusing on business strategy, operations, and general management issues. They provide these services through discrete annual programs to a membership of more than 2,000 hospitals, health systems, pharmaceutical and biotech companies, health care insures, and medical device companies. ABCO offers 13 distinct membership programs focused on identifying best-demonstrated management practices, critiquing widely-followed but ineffective practices, analyzing emerging trends within the health care industry, and supporting institutions' efforts to adopt best practices to improve performance. Each program charges a fixed annual fee and provides members with best practices research reports, executive education, and other supporting research services. The Advisory Board has an affiliation with The Corporate Executive Board.

APQC (International Benchmarking Clearinghouse)

www.apqc.org

APQC's approximately 500 members include over 100 social sector organizations in industries including higher education, government, health and human services, and faith based organizations. APQC's members receive access to proprietary best practices data in over 350 categories of value to NGOs including human resources, information management, learning organizations, recruiting, and women's issues as well as best practices derived from and oriented specifically towards NGOs. Database assets include online case studies, metric resources, benchmarking bibliographies, APQC proprietary research and presentations, an online membership directory, and a list of selected Internet resources. Additionally, members have access to member only events including conference discussions and work sessions as well as the support of a designated account manager and special pricing on APQC products and service.

Benchnet

www.benchnet.com

Benchnet is a large scale, daily updated, subscription based web service devoted to sharing experiences, superior business practices, and increasing the quality industry quality standards. The 2,500 companies in 50 countries that are members of benchnet engage in online forums and email surveys which collect, evaluate, and disseminate quality benchmarking data. Many of these surveys appear daily via email to members. Benchnet provides members the ability to request and construct their own (via the Internet) interactive surveys. Soon to be added functions include online placement services for employers seeking candidates for employment and candidates seeking employers to work for in the benchmarking industries and an online interactive self assessor & diagnostic function.

Best–in-Class

www.best-in-class.com

Best practices LLC is a research and consulting firm that specializes in best practices benchmarking. Emphasis is on qualitative as opposed to quantitative data and analysis. Best practices combines research, scholarship and "field" experience to provide a deep reservoir of benchmarking knowledge to apply to its clients' needs. Key features include a sizeable database on business operations, customer service, human resources, Internet, knowledge and database, and sales and marketing. The site also offers an online rapid quote service for benchmarking projects.

The Center for What Works

www.whatworks.org

This website is currently under construction, but the description of its search functions take a step towards creating a benchmarking society much like the established for-profit society. However, assessment is withheld until further developments.

The Corporate Executive Board Company (EXBD)

www.executiveboard.com

The Corporate Executive Board provides best practice research and analysis focusing on corporate strategy, operations, and general management issues. The best practice research identifies and analyzes specific management initiatives, processes, and strategies that have been determined to produce the best results in solving common business problems and challenges. They provide research and analysis on an annual basis to a membership of 1,745 worldwide. At December 2000, the average annual price per subscription was approximately $30,600. The Corporate Executive Board has an affiliation with The Advisory Board. Several of its Intersectoral members include Harvard University, Duke University, University of Virginia, US Department of Commerce, US Department of Treasury, and The US National Security Council.

The Peter F. Drucker Foundation for Nonprofit Management

www.pfdf.org

The Peter F. Drucker foundation's mission is to "lead social sector organizations toward excellence in performance." To this end, the foundation collects, evaluates, and disseminates "Innovations of the Week." Innovations of the Week are given to NGO programs and are selected based upon the difference organizations have made on the lives of the people they've served. To be considered, programs must further the mission of the organization, have specific and measurable outcomes, exemplify innovation by demonstrating a "new dimension" of performance, have made a difference in the lives of the people it serves, and serve as a model that can be replicated or adapted by other organizations.

The Inter-Agency Benchmarking and Best Practice Council and The National Partnership for Reinventing Government

www.va.gov/fedbest

www.npr.gov/initiati/benchmk

These sites grew out of Al Gore's national partnership for reinventing government. The sites have excellent benchmarking background material but they are no longer very active. The Inter-Agency Benchmarking and Best Practices Council web site has a Best Practices Knowledge Base but it is not an active repository of best practices.

The main site does have some best practices but nothing after 1997.

The London Benchmarking Group (The Corporate Citizenship Company)

www.corporate-citizenship.co.uk/benchmrk.htm

The London Benchmarking Group, a consulting firm, specializes in corporate community relation benchmarking. It seeks to "better define measures of efficiency and effectiveness of all types of community involvement activity by using benchmarking techniques." Chief goals include the establishment of a UK standard for recording, valuing and reporting corporate community involvements. Approximately 20% of their client base is NGO and government organizations.

APPENDIX N

INTERNET RESOURCES

Alliance for Community Technology
www.communitytechnology.org
Alliance for Community Technology contains an extensive online database of technology tools for NGOs. Detailed information on the strengths/weaknesses of specific technologies are provided for groupwork solutions ASPs, e-philanthropy sites, web conferencing, and other technologies, Emphasis is on comparison and benchmarking for better selection of technology solutions.

e-philanthropy Database
www.communitytechnology.org/databases/ephil
Organization effectiveness resources for NGOs. A currently best-in-class database. Categories of classification include:

- e-Commerce Shopping/Profit Sharing
- Fund-raising and Advertising
- Philanthropy and Donor Services
- Knowledge and Capacity Building
- Volunteering and Service
- Social Advocacy and Action

Events and Auctions
- Portals/Full Spectrum Services

Guide Star
www.guidestar.com
Guide Star provides access to an online searchable database of over 640,000 NGOs in the United States. The NGO operational and financial information (including 990 filings) located at Guidestar increase transparency in the social sector and are a valuable resource for benchmarking NGOs.

The Roberts Enterprise Foundation:
www.redf.org
The Roberts Enterprise Foundation's website is based on venture philanthropy. This site offers free publications from REDF on philosophy and practice of social entrepreneurship, venture philanthropy, and the ever-changing social sector. Additional papers are available by other individuals exploring the many challenges of social sector enterprise and investing in social change organizations.

The United Kingdom Charity Commission:

www.charitycommission.uk.org

The United Kingdom took an exemplary step establishing a commission that has the power of a court to review and regulate NGOs. The commission differs from the IRS in that if offers guidance and best practice examples for NGOs and that it has objectives aimed at restructuring NGOs to become more accountable.

Appendix O

Benchmarking Advisor Sampling Summary

Appendix O contains a limited sampling of prospective benchmarking advisors who profess capabilities to conduct subsector benchmarking studies. The material is based on interviews with the firms and likely team members. Each summary was provided to the respective firms for general comments; however, no right to modify was extended. No representation is made as to the accuracy of the information. CPs may find this information useful as part of a more extensive evaluation, but in no way should this material be considered accurate on its face. CPs may also wish to use this list a simply the beginning of an more extensive evaluation and selection process. Although possibly not available as of the publication date, NPB seeks to provide comment on a range of firms including: Charles E. Napier Company, Ltd.; Best-In-Class, Inc., and Arthur Anderson LLP.

Charles E. Napier Company, Ltd.

Introduction[a]

Charles E. Napier Company, Ltd. ("CEN") is a small boutique management consulting firm focused primarily on commercial sector performance benchmarking and improvement. Its managing executive, Harvey Goodwin, possesses an excellent understanding of the highest value-added levels of benchmarking for firm wide performance. CEN's expertise includes a limited number of NGOs. Prior assignments include a diverse group of global initiatives. The firm's work product appears ideally suited for New Philanthropy Benchmarking, as it offers organization and process level Performance Gap metrics, Deliverable Opportunity observations, and execution and assessment information that facilitate the determination and improvement of Multiplier/Discount Effects. Below are listed a selection of CEN's strengths and weaknesses.

Strengths:

- Process directly compatible with NP Benchmarking
- Principal has 18 years experience in benchmarking and appears very cost effective
- Principal commits to be primary staffing member on assignment
- CEN has worked in the public and private sector, domestically and internationally
- Firm and principal flexible on terms and process

Weaknesses:

- Firm has undefined access to diverse team members
- Social sector is not primary area of expertise
- Relatively non-brand name firm may provide some challenges in obtaining access and cooperation of targeted benchmarks
- Questionable experience with latest technological innovations
- Travel and miscellaneous expenses may be somewhat greater than more proximate organizations; however, this may be off-set by non-major city inherent expenses, as CEN is located in Ottawa, Canada

1. Prior Relevant Experience in

Benchmarking: Substantial experience having managed Interfirm Comparison Programs (IFC) covering numerous diverse industries such as upholstered furniture, printed circuit board manufacturers, trading houses, and Canadian book publishers. CEN has some experience with social sector and governmental entities.

Performance: The core of CEN's practice is performance measurement. Each study provided a competitive performance comparisons to develop sector-specific operating models. CEN, as part of its basic service, identifies areas of competitive strengths and weakness providing performance enhancement recommendations.

Social sector: Limited to serving several Canadian governmental agencies such as the Canadian International Development Agency, the Solicitor General of Canada, and the Ministry of Science and Technology.

International: Engagements have included benchmarking in Europe, Canada, and the U.S.

2. US Size of Firm

Although CEN is relatively small with a limited number of fully dedicated employees, firm has historically expanded teams to well over a dozen members for larger projects. Firm appears to posses a unique boutique status.

3. Project Compensation

CEN proposed to complete a project as specified for a fee estimated at approximately $20,000, staffing with a two-member team as appropriate. A second person is expected to be utilized for approximately 30% of the project. CEN's estimate is based on 36 person-days, at Cdn$850 or US$570, which consists of 8-hour days and includes an estimate of six travel days. CEN indicated willingness to consider incentive compensation elements that would include a discount to its standard fee for a significant incentive premium payment on success of investment in NGO benchmarked. Premium based upon success of investment in NGO benchmarked.

4. Time to Completion

CEN estimates the study could be completed in approximately 6 weeks baring any unforeseen delays associated with scheduling conflicts with the benchmarked organizations. CEN did not expect any significant differences, including compensation, if project were allowed for an extended completion over 18 week period. Guidance regarding person days allocated to project. Project phases are estimated by CEN as follows: Phase 1: 3 days, Phase 2: 4 days, Phase 3: 3 days, Phase 4: 5 days. Phase 5: 2 days, Phase 6: 5 days, Phase 7: 6 days, and Phase 8: 2 days. In addition, to 30 person hours, an additional 20% (6 days) were added for travel days. An additional two days may be necessary at the beginning of the project for industry specific discussions with operating and financial staff at one or more of the target organizations.

5. Quality of Previous Presentations

CEN's performance benchmarking case study of the Canadian Book Publishers (as published in Robert Camps' Global Benchmarking Case Studies book) is clearly an exemplary work product in assessing best practice Performance Gaps and providing quantitative concrete suggestion to minimize Discount Effects. The case study also provides post-study assessment of value-added and benefits realized.

6. Flexibility of Structure
CEN's prior projects support the firm's claim of positive flexibility in accommodating its clients. The firm's principal and designated team leader has provided consistent representations. Research supports this assertion. CEN displays considerable enthusiasm for a NPB project as described.

7. Previous Background
CEN's principal, Harvey Goodwin, has degrees in Mechanical Engineering from McGill U., International Business from Centre d' Etudes Industrial in Switzerland, and Technology Management from MIT. He has over 40 years of experience, having worked for 23 years at Alcan in Europe, Africa, and North America, 5 years with Bell Northern Research and since 1982, a management consultant in Canada. He is president of CEN and a CEO of two other management consulting firms.

(a) Parameters of assignment provided to each prospective benchmarking advisor included the following: evaluation of the five organizations of which two will be NGOs and three commercial firms; social sectors of interest will be in the areas of either health care, low income housing, education, or human services; assessment of approximately 30 to 50 different parameters; field research will include one day of research at each organization; the process will adhere to a customary 8 phase format and written output presentation will include determining benchmarking metrics and operating practices, quantification of Performance Gap evaluation, best practice identification, and performance improvement observations addressing quantification of costs and benefits of Deliverable Opportunities and Multiplier/Discount Effects.

Best Practices, LLC

Introduction[a]

Best Practices, LLC ("BP") is a small business research and consulting firm specializing in best practice benchmarking. BP maintains its own proprietary best management practice database, which is constantly updated through its own ongoing research. Its President and founder, Chris Bogan, is a recognized expert and author of highly acclaimed books concerning benchmarking and best practice performance improvement. BP's expertise includes a large number of Fortune 1000 companies but a limited number of NGOs. Prior assignments include a wide range of diverse companies studying areas such as customer service, knowledge management, sales and marketing, strategic partnerships, and leadership. Although BP, as of this writing, has limited experience with the investor perspectives of New Philanthropy Benchmarking, the firm does possess the sufficiently impressive talents to allow them to be considered as an alternative. However, BP may require a comparative greater investment of CP time to advance subsector studies, and the firm's traditional incentive compensation structure may sire unproductive counter-currents. Below are listed select BP strengths and weaknesses.

Strengths:

- World leader in benchmarking with proprietary best practice management databases maintained by a staff of 25 employees and utilized worldwide.
- Principal has written two highly acclaimed books relating to benchmarking and quality of world-class companies.
- BP has worked primarily in the public sector with multinational companies.
- Utilizes a more consultantcy-based/conceptual structural approach to performance and economic metrics.
- Firm and principal flexible on terms and process.

Weaknesses:

- Will require knowledge transfer from the Commercial to the Social Sector where BP has limited experience.
- NPB investor perspective a new process, which will likely mandate sig-

nificantly greater investment of client time at all stages of process.

- Standard economic terms offer potentially unproductive counter-currents, e.g. higher profit pre-project fixed-fee with less time and extra fee if encounter unfamiliar metrics.
- Limited ability to leverage existing database for use on a social sector project.
- Given BP's organizational structure, Bogan can only commit limited time to any project.
- Arguable lack of national brand-name at CEO and board level may effectively limit BP's ability to open doors; accordingly, BP estimates considerable additional time and cost should project entail this role.

1. Prior Relevant Experience

Benchmarking: BP is considered among the world leaders in benchmarking, evidenced by an impressive list of multinational clients. Industry experience includes financial services, pharmaceuticals, and telecom. BP has limited experience with municipalities and Social Sector organizations. Projects appear to offer limited NPB experience.

Performance: BP is a leader in the field of best practice performance improvement. It offers a selection of services and products designed to assist clients improve their performance by analyzing the winning practices of leading corporations.

Social Sector: Limited to working with city governments such as Portland, Oregon and Dallas, Texas.

International: Engagements have included working with many multinational firms and their databases are sold on all 5 continents. However, databases may have limited application to NPB sub sector projects.

2. US Size of Firm

BP is a relatively small firm with 25 employees. It appears that they are adequately staffed to handle any sized engagement that they normally encounter, as their list of clients shows.

3. Project Compensation

BP estimates that on a fixed fee basis a subsector project – as outlined – would cost between $75,000 and $150,000 excluding travel and expenses. Travel and expenses would add an additional 10% to 15% to the total cost. Staffing would consist of a senior level team leader who would attend each of 5 site visits with a second or third team member if deemed necessary. The number of metrics being analyzed would determine a final fixed cost. NPB investor perspective is a new process for BP, which will likely mandate significantly greater investment of client time at all stages of the process. Standard economic terms offer potentially unproductive counter-currents, e.g. higher profit pre-project fixed-fee with less time and extra fee if encounter unfamiliar metrics. This issue should be addressed to develop a win-win for all parties involved. BP estimates considerably greater costs if project entails "opening-doors" for prospective organizations.

4. Time to Completion

BP estimates that sub sector study would require approximately 10 weeks to complete, baring any unforeseen delays associated with scheduling conflicts with the projected 5 organizations to be benchmarked. It appears that BP is comfortable estimating that the Phase 1-8 work would take approximately 4 weeks to complete for each individual firm.

5. Quality of Previous Presentations

BP material assessed includes a *Xerox Corp. Site Visit Report* and executives summaries of *Managing SG&A Expenses* and *Merger & Acquisition Integration Excellence*. Each summary is high on concepts with little hard-core investor financial metrics. Tables of contents appear to indicate bulk material, which may be much more suited for BP target middle-level management audience.

6. Flexibility of Structure

BP has a documented client list that supports its assertions that it is flexible in fulfilling the requirements of its diverse customer base. Bogan will only play a small role in the overall project. Team managers will be responsibly to ensure the project is properly executed with uniform standards. Process seems rather established with heavy focus on utilizing existing database and consultantcy-based/conceptual structural approach to performance and economic metrics.

7. *Previous Background*

BP's principal, Christopher Bogan graduated from Amherst College and the Harvard Business School. He has co-authored the book *Benchmarking for Best Practices: Winning Through Innovative Adaptation*, and authored *The Baldridge: What it is, How it's Won, How To Use It to Improve Quality in Your Company*. He has 25 years of industry experience.

Keith Symmers is a Vice President and the #2 executive at BP. He graduated from the University of Virginia and received a Harvard MBA. Prior to joining BP he served in the US Navy and was an Officer specializing in financial management, operational excellence, and served as a Nuclear Plant Manager, a Strategic Consultant and a Training Officer. At BP he specializes in best business practices relating to business operations, technology, and manufacturing.

(a) Parameters of assignment provided to each prospective benchmarking advisor included the following: evaluation of the five organizations of which two will be NGOs and three commercial firms; social sectors of interest will be in the areas of either health care, low income housing, education, or human services; assessment of approximately 30 to 50 different parameters; field research will include one day of research at each organization; the process will adhere to a customary 8 phase format and written output presentation will include determining benchmarking metrics and operating practices, quantification of Performance Gap evaluation, best practice identification, and performance improvement observations addressing quantification of costs and benefits of Deliverable Opportunities and Multiplier/Discount Effects.

Arthur Andersen LLP

Introduction[a]

Arthur Andersen LLP is one of the largest consulting and accounting firms in the world with nearly 80,000 employees worldwide. The Metro New York Not-for-Profit Group consists of a group of professionals with expertise in accounting, auditing, tax and consulting matters. One of the most significant areas of growth in this practice has been in the area of operational reviews (agreed upon procedures format). Arthur Andersen has significant experience reviewing the current operations of NGO clients and analyzing their policies, procedures and internal controls from a best practices perspective. The Metro NY NFP group is able to draw upon the significant resources throughout the firm and frequently work with our practices within the firm such as the National Higher Education consulting practice. Its performance with NPB is currently under review, especially concerning macro-level NGO performance metrics. Team structure and terms of engagement will probably parallel characteristic of major multi-national organizations. Below are listed select Arthur Andersen strengths and weaknesses.

Arthur Andersen's commercial sector Global Best Practices group has yet to be reviewed. However, it's benchmarking, best practices, and continuous improvement appear to offer considerable potential. Their four service areas include: best practices reviews, custom benchmarking, benchmarking tool box, and benchmarking workshops. Within the custom benchmarking area, a sub-specialty performance analysis, which offers similarities to NPB – "Determine the performance gap, negative or positive, and assess which process improvements are a priority [for the client]". The Universal Process Classification Scheme provides a framework of 13 core business processes and more than 140 sub-processes.

Strengths:

- Dedicated NGO personnel resources
- Access to firm-wide resources
- Brand name value
- Firm-wide best practices data base
- Significant experience with institutions of higher education, foundations and voluntary health and welfare organizations.
- Significant best practices experience

Weaknesses:

- Undetermined NPB benchmarking skills
- Major firm issues, especially responsiveness and competitiveness
- Prior projects appear more focused on micro rather than macro considerations
- The Metro NY office maintains a separate Healthcare Consulting Practice that is not part of the Metro NY NFP Group
- Work product format to be determined
- No significant experience in the low-income housing sector.

1. Prior Relevant Experience
Benchmarking: Arthur Andersen has experience performing various benchmarking studies in the higher education field in particular. Arthur Andersen has also assisted specific clients in benchmarking various entities within a significant controlled group of entities. Certain personnel also have experience with benchmarking comparisons for United Way affiliated entities.

Performance: Various financial and operating measurements can be developed of various NFP groups from both a quantitative and qualitative perspective.

Social Sector: The firm has significant experience with institutions of higher education, foundations and voluntary health & welfare organizations. Our work has been primarily performed on a local, regional or U.S. national level.

2. US Size of Firm
Arthur Andersen LLP is one of the largest consulting and accounting firms in the world with nearly 80,000 employees worldwide. Typically, a 3 person team is used consisting of a partner, principal and manager with the senior official (partner) conducting most of the onsite meetings.

3. Project Compensation
Project fees to be determined once the agreed upon procedures and specific scope of the project are determined and finalized with a client. Not unlike other firms, Arthur Andersen performs a standard new client review and approval process before new clients are accepted and a formal arrangement letter is issued. Fees are typically quoted in a range plus out of pocket expenses. The average weighted

consulting fee per hour is generally in the range of $ 225 - $ 275. Cost for project prototype as describes remains unknown. Potential appears to exist for cost somewhat in excess of competitive alternatives based on rigid hours billing terms. However, this maybe offset by specific arrangement.

As for the four subsectors considered, the following were general guidelines provided by the Metro New York Non-for-Profit Group. Of course, these are fee estimates, which would require customization for the specific assignment subsequent to agreed upon procedures and parameters.

- Higher Education - Fee range of $ 150,000 to $ 200,000 plus out of pocket
- Expenses. This work would be performed by the Metro NY NFP Group and the
- National Higher Education Consulting Group.
- Human Services - Fee range of $ 200,000 to $ 250,000 plus out of pocket expenses
- Managed solely by Metro NY NFP Group.
- Healthcare - Would be managed by a separate Healthcare Consulting Group in Metro NY which is not part of our NFP Group; accordingly no estimate is provided.
- Low Income Housing - the firm does not have experience in this area, and therefore did not provide a quotation.

4. Time to Completion
Once the specific scope of the project is determined and the agreed upon procedures finalized, an exact timetable would be determined and included in the written arrangement letter. Most projects can be completed in less than two months.

5. Quality of Previous Presentations
Arthur Andersen has been rated as the top leader in client satisfaction among the Big 5 firms in a recent Emerson Study. More details regarding this Emerson study are available upon request. The Metro NY NFP group has received outstanding client satisfaction ratings over each of the past several years. These claims are based upon unreviewed representations by Arthur Andersen. Based on review of a sample output, CPs can expect a more traditional consultantcy fair.

6. Flexibility of Structure

Due to the agreed upon procedures format Arthur Andersen typically employ, there may be significant flexibility in determining the scope of the project and the output from the project. At times, written amendments to the original arrangement letter may also be made as the work progresses for scope changes. However, as in many commercial and social sector projects, mid-stream assignment changes can be relatively- as well as absolutely expensive.

7. Previous Background

Arthur Andersen project teams consist of a partner with significant NGO experience as well as fully dedicated NGO principals and managers with significant industry experience. The exact project team would be determined once the timetable for this project is decided. As with any large organization, junior-level staffing and heavy team loading may be an issue. Members of Group have yet to publish public materials.

(a) Parameters of assignment provided to each prospective benchmarking advisor included the following: evaluation of the five organizations of which two will be NGOs and three commercial firms; social sectors of interest will be in the areas of either health care, low income housing, education, or human services; assessment of approximately 30 to 50 different parameters; field research will include one day of research at each organization; the process will adhere to a customary 8 phase format and written output presentation will include determining benchmarking metrics and operating practices, quantification of Performance Gap evaluation, best practice identification, and performance improvement observations addressing quantification of costs and benefits of Deliverable Opportunities and Multiplier/Discount Effects.

APPENDIX P

FURTHER READING AND INFORMATION

Books and Articles:
Abelson, Reed. "Charities Investing: Left Hand, Meet Right," *New York Times*, 11 June 2000.

——. "Charity Led by General Powell Comes Under Heavy Fire, Accused of Inflating Results," *New York Times*, 8 October 1999.

——. "Foundation Giving Is at $23 Billion High," *New York Times*, 29 Mar. 2000.

——. "New Philanthropists Put Donations to Work," *New York Times*, 6 July 2000, sec. B1.

——. "Some Charities Cash In by Playing the Name Game," *New York Times*, 30 December 1999.

Anderson, Mary B. *Do No Harm: How Aid Can Support Peace - or War*. London: Lynne Rienner Publishers, Inc., 2001.

Andrews, Fred. "Thinking Great Thoughts Without Great Money," *New York Times*, 12 January 2000.

Arenson, Karen W. "Art, Wildlife and a Bit of Investing," *New York Times*, 12 November 2000.

——. "Princeton to Replace Loans with Student Scholarships," *New York Times*, 28 January 2001.

——. "Cornell Will Open a Medical School in the Persian Gulf," *New York Times*, 9 April 2001

——. "For Rensselaer Polytechnic, a Record-Setting Gift With No Strings Attached," *New York Times,* 13 March 2001.

Armstrong, David and Pesta, Jesse. "MIT, India Are Close to Asian Media Lab Pact," *Wall Street Journal*, 12 February 2001.

"At Goldman Sachs a Bonanza for Charities," *New York Times,* 12 December 1999.

Backer, Thomas E. "Innovation in Context: New Foundation Approaches to Evaluation, Collaboration, and Best Practices, study conducted for the John S. and James L. Knight Foundation." November 1999.

Banks, David. "Bill Gates Donates $6 Billion to His Charitable Foundation," *Wall Street Journal,* 23 August 1999.

——. "Gates Earmarks $750 Million to Spur Work on Vaccines," *Wall Street Journal,* 27 August 1999.

Barringer, Felicity. "Moving Beyond the Four Horsemen of the Philanthropy Beat." *New York Times*, 20 November 2000.

——. "Public Radio at Center of Ownership Debate," *New York Times,* 5 March 2001.

Barrett, Amy. "Affairs of Estate: Questions for William H. Gates Sr." *New York Times Magazine*. 18 March 2001.

Benson, Dennis K. "PY97 Return on Investment; Technical Report." Worthington, Ohio: Appropriate Solutions, Inc., March 1999.

Benson, Dennis K. "Return on Investment: Guidelines to Determine Workforce Development Impact." Worthington, Ohio: Appropriate Solutions, 1999.

——. "Return on Investment: An Essential Metric for One-Stops." Reno, Nevada: Annual Conference of the National Association of Workforce Development Professionals, 21-24 May 2000.

Billitteri, Thomas, J. "Roberts Fund Puts Its Venture-Philanthropy Approach to the Test," *The Chronicle of Philanthropy*, 1 June 2000.

——. "Technology and Accountability Will Shape the Future of Philanthropy," *The Chronicle of Philanthropy,* 13 January 2000.

Blazek, Jody. "Unrelated Business Income - A Primer," *Board Member,* July/August 1999.

Bogan, Christopher E. English, Michael J. *Benchmarking for Best Practices: Winning Through Innovative Adaptation*. New York: McGraw-Hill, Inc., 1994.

Borg, Linda. "Billionaire Philanthropist To Speak at Brown," *Providence Journal,* 20 October 1999, B1.

——. "Soros: Regulate Global Economy," *Providence Journal*, 21 October 1999, B1.

Bronfman, Edgar M. *The Making of A Jew*. New York: G. P. Putnam and Sons, 1996.

Camp, Robert C. *Benchmarking: The Search for Industry Best Practices that Lead to Superior Performance*. New York: ASQC Quality Press, 1989.

——. *Business Process Benchmarking: Finding and Implementing Best Practices*. Wisconsin: ASQ Quality Press, 1995.

——. *Global Cases in Benchmarking: Best Practices from Organizations Around the World*. Wisconsin: ASQ Quality Press, 1998.

Stanton, Gregory. "Going Mainstream: NPOs Accessing the Capital Markets," Capital Markets Access Program: 2001.

Carlton, Jim. "WSJE: Dot-Orgs Become A Role Model For Some Start-Ups." *Wall Street Journal*, 13 March 2001.

Carnegie, Andrew. *The Gospel of Wealth*. Massachusetts: Applewood Books, 1889.

Charles, Babington. "Clinton Urges a New Web of Giving," *Washington Post*, 23 October 1999.

Cherry, Elyse. "NO EXIT: The Challenge of Realizing Return on Community Development Venture Capital Investments." The Ford Foundation, October 5, 2000.

"Clintons Hold Forum on Philanthropy," *New York Times,* 23 October 1999.

Community Wealth Ventures, Inc. *Venture Philanthropy: Landscape and Expectations*. Morino Institute, 2000.

Dees, J. Gregory, et al., Enterprising Nonprofits: A Toolkit for Social Entrepreneurs. New York. John Wiley & Sons, Inc., 2001.

Demarche Associates, Inc. *Spending Policies and Investment Planning: A Structure for Determining a Foundation's Asset Mix*. Washington, DC: Council on Foundations, 1999.

Deutsch, Claudia H. "Competitors Can Teach You a Lot, but the Lessons Can Hurt: The Many Obstacles to Benchmarking." *New York Times,* 19 January 1999.

Dillin, John. "Newly Rich Escalate Estate-Tax Fight," *The Christian Science Monitor*, 7 September 2000.

Dubner, Stephen, J. "Steven The Good," *New York Times Magazine,* 14 February 1999.

Dundjershi, Marina. "To Live Forever, Foundations Should Give Away the Minimum, Report Says," *The Chronicle of Philanthropy,* 18 November 1999.

Dunn, Julie. "Maybe Charity is Contagious," *New York Times*, 9 September, 2000.

Ehrbar, Al. *Stern Stewart's EVA (Economic Value Added): The Real Key to Creating Wealth.* New York: John Wiley & Sons, Inc., 1998.

Elkind, Peter. "The man who sold Silicon Valley on giving," *Fortune*, 27 November 2000.

Emerson, Jed. "A Social Capital Markets Analysis: Inquires into the Nature of Investment, Elements of Return, and A Blended Value Proposition," *Working Paper in Draft*. Internal Working Group Version: July 2000.

Emerson, Jed, J. Gregory Dees, Christine W. Letts, and Edward Skloot. *The U.S. Nonprofit Capital Market: An Introductory Overview of Developmental Stages, Investors and Funding Instruments*. Roberts Enterprise Development Fund, 2000.

Emerson, Jed and Tuan, Melinda. *The Roberts Enterprise Development Fund: Implementing a Social Venture Capital Approach to Philanthropy — A Case Study*. Graduate School of Business Stanford University, 1998.

Emerson, Jed and Jay Wachowicz. "Riding on the Bleeding Edge: A Framework for Tracking Equity in the Social Sector and the Creation of a Nonprofit Stock Market."

Emerson, Jed, Jay Wachowicz, and Suzi Chun. *Social Return on Investment: Exploring Aspects of Value Creation in the Nonprofit Sector*. Roberts Enterprise Development Fund, 2000.

Finance Authority of Maine. *A Study of the Availability and Sources of Venture Capital in Maine*. 15 March 1995.

Fisher, Ian. "Can International Relief Do More Than Harm?" *New York Times*, 12 February 2001.

Forbes, Daniel P. "Measuring the Unmeasurable: Empirical Studies of Nonprofit Organization Effectiveness," *Nonprofit and Voluntary Sector Quarterly,* Vol. 27 No. 2 (1998), 183 – 202.

"Foundation Center Announces Estimates for 1999 Foundation Giving," *Foundation Center,* 29 March 2000.

"Foundation Growth and Giving Estimates: 1999 Preview." *Foundation Today Series: The Foundation Center,* 2000.

"Foundation Growth and Giving Estimates 2000 Preview." *Foundation Today Series: The Foundation Center,* 2001.

Freudenheim, Milt. "Blue Cross Offers to Aid Uninsured in Bid to Be For-Profit," *New York Times,* 3 April, 2001.

Frumkin, Peter. "Failure in Philanthropy," *Philanthropy*, July/August 1998.

Gallagher, Michael K. "More-Effective Foundations: Making the Dream a Reality." *The Chronicle of Philanthropy,* 13 January 2000.

Goldberg, Carey. "Auditing Classes at M.I.T., on the Web and Free," *New York Times,* 4 April 2001.

Goodman, Randolph M. and Arnsbarger, Linda A. "Trading Technology for Equity: A guide to participating in Start-Up Companies, Joint Ventures and Affiliates." New York: New York University 27th Conference on Tax Planning for 501(c)(3) Organizations 1999 (Chapter 2), Matthew Bender & Company, 1999.

Gootman, Elissa. " UJC Prepares to Squelch Public Airing of Disputes: Curb Overseas Allocation." *The Forward,* 12 May 2000, A1.

Golden, Daniel. "Rensselaer Polytechnic Gets Huge Cash Gift From Donor," *New York Times,* 13 March 2001.

Gore, Al. "Serving The American Public: Best Practices in Performance Measurement. – Benchmarking Study Report," *National Performance Review*, June 1997. 16 July 2000.

Gorov, Lynda. "Spreading the Wealth," *Boston Globe,* 28 November, 1999.

Greenberg, Joel. "Trips to Renew Jewish Ties Set Off Debate Over Costs," *New York Times,* 8 January 2000.

Greenfield, Karl Taro and David S. Jackson. "A New Way of Giving," *Time,* 24 July 2000, 49-57.

Grobman, Gary M. *Improving Quality and Performance in Your Non-Profit Organization*. Pennsylvania: White Hat Communications, 1999.

Hafner, Katie. "Technology Boom Too Tempting for Many Government Scientists," *New York Times*, 9 September 2000.

Hardy, Quentin. "The Radical Philanthropist," *Forbes,* 1 May 2000.

Hakim, Danny. "Huge Losses Move Soros to Revamp Empire," *New York Times,* 29 April 2000.

Hartocollis, Anemona. "As Election on Privatizing Schools Winds Down, Call Goes Out for Plan B," *New York Times,* 1 April 2001.

Harvard University Hauser Center for Nonprofit Organizations, the Urban Institute Center on Nonprofits and Philanthropy. "When Exempt Organizations Conduct Exempt Activities as Taxable Enterprises: A Seminar on Emerging Issues in Philanthropy" November 30, 2000.

Horvath, Peter. "Why We Give," *The American Benefactor*, Winter 1997.

Hruby, Linda and Schwinn, Elizabeth. "Big Funds See a Dip in Assets," *The Chronicle of Philanthropy*, 22 February 2001.

Hunt, Albert R. "Charitable Giving: Good but We Can Do Better," *Wall Street Journal*, 21 December 2000.

Inter-Agency Benchmarking & Best Practices Council. *A Taxonomy of Common Processes to Use for Collecting and Sharing 'Best Practices.'* Government Process Classification Scheme, GPC Scheme Version 1.01, 1 October 1996.

Janofsky, Michael. "Antidrug Program's End Stirs Up Salt Lake City," *New York Times*, 16 September 2000.

Jedrey, Christopher M. "Permissible Business Arrangements Between Taxable and Tax-Exempt Organizations." Boston: McDermott, Will & Emery.

Johnston, David Cay. "A Larger Legacy May Await Generations X, Y, and Z." *New York Times* 20 Oct. 1999.

——. "For Checking Out a Charity Remember the Number 990," *New York Times*, 20 November 2000

——. "Foundations Can Give More, and Protect Assets, Study Says," *New York Times,* 5 October 1999.

——. "Tax Returns of Charities to be Posted on the Web," *New York Times,* 18 October 1999.

Juran, J.M. *Juran on Quality By Design*. New York: The Free Press, 1992.

Kirkpatrick, David P. "Soros Concedes Goof in Book: Global Economy Didn't Collapse," *New York Times*, 12 August 2000.

——. "2 Harry Potter Spinoffs Done for Charity." *New York Times,* 12 March 2001.

Kogelman, Stanley and Thomas Dobler. *Sustainable Spending Policies for Endowments and Foundations*. New York: Goldman, Sachs & Co., November 1999.

Kohm, Amelia et al. "Strategic Restructuring: Findings from a Study of Intergrations and Alliances Among Nonprofit Social Service and Cultural Organizations in the United States." *Discussion Paper PS -24*. Chapin Hall Center for Children, June 2000.

Kramer, Mark R. "Venture Capital and Philanthropy: A Bad Fit," *The Chronicle of Philanthropy,* 22 April 1999.

Kronholz, June. "Gift of $128 Million to DePauw Proves to be a Mixed Blessing," *Wall Street Journal,* 8 March 2001.

La Piana, David. "Beyond Collaboration: Strategic Restructuring of Nonprofit Organizations." James Irvine Foundation, 1997.

Letts, Ryan, and Grossman. *High Performance Nonprofit Organizations Benchmarking: An Organizational Process That Links Learning and Results*. New York: John Wiley and Son, Inc., 1999.

Levy, Steven. "Behind the Gates Myth," *Newsweek,* 30 August 1999.

Lewin, Tamar. "In an Uncertain Climate, Philanthropy Is Slowing," *New York Times*, 19 February 2001.

——. "Foundation Grants Surged Last Year Despite Slowing Economy," *New York Times,* 27 March 2001.

Light, Paul C. *Making Nonprofits Work: A Report On the Tides of Nonprofit Management Reform*. Washington, DC: Brookings Institution Press, 2000.

——. *Sustaining Innovation: Creating Nonprofit and Government Organizations That Innovate Naturally*. San Francisco: Jossey-Bass Publishers, 1998.

Lowell, Stephanie. "Careers In The Nonprofit Sector." Boston: Harvard Business School Publishing, 2000.

Magnet, Myron. "What Makes Charity Work?" Chicago: Ivan R. Dee, 2000.

Marchetti, Domenica. "Delivering on His Word," *The Chronicle of Philanthropy,* 7 October 1999, p 1.

Maren, Michael. *The Road to Hell: The Ravaging Effects of Foreign Aid and International Charity.* New York: The Free Press, 1997.

Markoff, John. "Intel Joins Cancer Research Effort," *New York Times,* 4 April 2001.

Marks, Alexandra. "Drawing a Line in the School Yard," *The Christian Science Monitor*, 8 September 2000.

Massey, William. "e-philanthropy and the New Accountability Agenda," *Independent Sector,* www.independentsector.org, 14 August 2000.

McCully, George. "Is This A Paradigm Shift?" *Foundation News and Commentary,* March-April 2000.

McGarvey, Craig. " A Third Way," *Foundation News and Commentary,* May-June 2000.

McKinnon, James D. "Charity Groups are Torn on the Tax Repeal: Worried over Effects, Wary of Offending Donors," *Wall Street Journal*, 10 August 2000.

McNeil, Donald G. Jr. "Oxfam Joins Campaign to Cut Drug Prices to Poor Nations," *New York Times*, 13 February 2001.

Mehrling, Perry. *Spending Policies for Foundations: The Case for Increased Grants Payout*. National Network of Grantmakers, 1999.

Milken, Michael. " Manager's Journal: Advice for Bill Gates." *Wall Street Journal,* 4 October 1999: A42.

Miller, Lisa. "Thomas Monaghan's Scope, Style Stir Rancor in His Local Diocese," *Wall Street Journal*, 21 June 2000.

Miller, Lisa. "Titans of Industry Join Forces To Work For Jewish Philanthropy," *Wall Street Journal,* 4 May 1999.

Morino Institute. "2001 Venture Philanthropy: The Changing Landscape," 2001.

Morris, Kathleen. "The Reincarnation of Mike Milken," *Business Week*, 10 May 1999.

Moss, Michael and Jim Rutenberg. "Writer's Philanthropic Hopes Ending in Bitter Court Fight," *New York Times,* 11 July 2000.

Myers, Michele Toela. "A Student Is Not an Input." *New York Times,* 26 March 01.

Nelson, Stephen J. "What Can Managers Learn From Nonprofits?" *Harvard Management Update*, 1999.

"New Alliance to Develop Drugs to Fight Tuberculosis," *Philanthropy New Digest*, 10 October 2000, Volume 6, Issue 42.

Norris, Floyd. "Top Soros Fund Manager Victim of Technology's Fall," *New York Times,* 29 April 2000.

Nostrand, A.D. "Misuse, Abuse of Metrics in Corporations and Health Care," *Providence Business News/High Technology Monthly*, 31 July 1999: 5B.

O'Keefe, Mark. "Wealthiest in the World Wield Power Through Philanthropy," *San Francisco Chronicle*, 21 January 2001.

Okten, Cagla and Weisbrod, Burton A. "Differential Taxation of Nonprofits and the Commercialization of Nonprofit Revenues," *Journal of Public Economics*, Vol. 75, 2000.

Olect, Joan. "Swollen Charities: Should They Give More: A Debate is Raging Over Those Billions in Stock-Market Gains," *Business Week,* 29 May 2000.

Pear, Robert. "Nonprofit Groups Accused of Bilking Lunch Programs," *New York Times,* 2 October 1999.

"People: Today's Philanthropists Reflect Changing Attitudes." *Philanthropy News Network.* 2 February 1999.

Plantz, Margaret C. et al. "Outcome Measurement: Showing Results in the Nonprofit Sector." United Way of America Online Resource Library. July 1999. www.unitedway.org/outcomes/ndpaper.htm.

Porter, Michael E. and Mark Kramer. "Philanthropy's New Agenda: Creating Value," *Harvard Business Review*, November-December 1999.

Press, Eyal and Washburn, Jennifer. "The Kept University," *The Atlantic Monthly*, March 2000.

Purdum, Todd S. "The Benefactors; Moving heaven and Earth for the City of Angels," *New York Times*, 12 August 2000.

"Raiders of the Lost Jobs," *Public Employee Magazine*, January 1998.

Reis, Tom. "Unleashing New Resources and Entrepreneurship for the Common Good." Michigan: W. K. Kellogg Foundation, 1999.

Renz, Loren, Cynthia W. Massarsky, Rikard R. Treiber and Steven Lawrence. "Program Related Investments: A Guide to Funders and Trends." USA: The Foundations Center.

——. "Foundation Growth and Giving Estimates." USA: The Foundations Center, 2001.

"Report Says Charities Get Little Pledges," *New York Times,* 31 December 1999.

Revkin, Andrew C. "Nonprofits Facing Ethical Challenges Over Sales of Land," *New York Times*, 16 September 2000.

Ring-Cassidy, Elizabeth. "Conference Contrasts Church Social Teaching To Ideologies," *Wanderer,* 18 May 2000.

Roberts Foundation and Homeless Economic Development Fund. "New Social Entrepreneurs: The Success, Challenge and Lessons of Non-Profit Enterprise Creation." September, 1996.

Roberts Enterprise Development Fund. "SROI Overview/Reports." 2001.

Robertson, Pat. "Mr. Bush's Faith-Based Initiative Is Flawed." *The Wall Street Journal.* 12 March 2001.

Roth, Katherine. "Paul Newman Urges Companies to Open a Little Wider for Charity." *Providence Journal,* 19 November 1999.

Salamon, Lester M. "Holding the Center: America's Nonprofit Sector at a Crossroads." New York: The Nathan Cummings Foundation, 1997.

Saul, Jason. *Benchmarking Workbook for Nonprofit Organizations.* Wilder Publishing Center. TBP.

Scholl, Jaye. "The Pilgrim: Don McClanen Offers the Wealthy a Different Kind of Freedom." Barron's, 18 September 2000.

Sealey, Kelvin Shawn, et al., ed. *Social Enterprise*. Massachusetts: Pearson Custom Publishing, 2000.

"Selling Off Seagram," *The Forward,* 23 June 2000.

Shore, Bill. *Revolution of the Heart: A New Strategy for Creating Wealth and Meaningful Change*. New York: Riverhead Books, 1995.

Shore, Bill. *The Cathedral Within*. New York: Random House, 1999.

Sievers, Bruce. "If Pigs Had Wings," *Foundation News & Commentary,* November/December 1997.

Sievers, Bruce and Tom Layton. "Best of the Worst Practices," *Foundation News and Commentary,* March-April 2000.

Skloot, Edward. *The Nonprofit Entrepreneur: Creating Ventures to Earn Income*. The Foundation Center, 1988.

——. "The Second Gilded Age: Time for a New Bargain." *The Chronicle of Philanthropy,* 2 May 2000.

Smalhout, James H. "The World Bank's New Clients." Barron's, 25 September 2000.

Smart Money. "Give and Take." SmartMoney.com. <www.smartmoney.com>. 2 January 2001.

Social Investment Forum. *1999 Report on Socially Responsible Investing Trends in the United States*. SIF Industry Research Program, 4 November 1999.

"Socially Responsible Investing in U.S. Tops Two Trillion Dollar Mark." Social Investment Forum News, 4 November 1999.

Sorkin, Andrew. "March First to Eliminate 3,500 Jobs," *New York Times,* 27 March 2001.

Soros, George. "Letter to Quantum Group Shareholders from George Soros," *New York Times,* 28 April 2000.

Stamler, Bernard. "Charities Award Grants, Then Pay to Evaluate How the Money is Spent," *New York Times*, 20 November 2000.

"Standards for Excellence: An Ethics and Accountability Code for the Nonprofit Sector." Baltimore: Maryland Association of Nonprofit Organizations, 1998.

Stanley, Alessandra. "Modern Marketing Blooms In Medieval Vatican Library," *New York Times,* 8 January 2001.

Streeter, Ryan. "Where the Mission Meets the Market." Welfare Policy Center of the Hudson Institute, www.welfarereformer.org., January 2001.

Stehle, Vince. "Putting Charities in Business," *The Chronicle of Philanthropy*, October 1999.

Steinberg, Jacques. "Harvard's $2.1 Billion Tops Colleges' Big Fund-Raising," *New York Times*, 7 October 1999

Stewart, G. Bennett III. *The Quest For Value: A Guide for Senior Managers*. New York: Harper Business, 1999.

Stone, Melissa A. et al. "Research On Strategic Management in Nonprofit Organizations: Synthesis, Analysis, and Future Directions." *Administration Society* Vol. 31 No. 3 (1999): 378 - 423.

Strouse, Jean. "How to Give Away $21.8 Billion," *New York Times Magazine,* 16 April 2000.

Swinney, R. Andrew. "Collaborating with Virtuous Capital," *Foundation News and Commentary,* May-June 2000.

"The 2000 Study on Wealth and Responsibility." *Bankers Trust*, Boston College Social Welfare Research Institute and the University of Massachusetts Boston Center for Survey Research, Summer 2000.

Tokasz, Jay. "Putting a Cold, Hard Number on the Value of Good Works," *New York Times*, 20 November 2000.

Twersky, Fay. *Webtrack and Beyond: Documenting the Impact of Social Purpose Enterprises*. The Roberts Enterprise Development Fund, 2000.

Uchitelle, Louis. "Working Families Strain to Live Middle-Class Life," *New York Times*, 9 September 2000.

United Way of America. "Focusing on Program Outcomes: A Guide for United Way." 1996.

——. "Measuring Program Outcomes: A Practical Approach." 1996.

University of Minnesota. "John M. Olin Foundation," Research Review, June 1998.

Varchaver, Nicholas. "Can Anyone Fix the United Way?" *Fortune*, 27 November 2000, 171-180.

Verhovek, Sam Howe. "Bill Gates Turns Skeptical on Digital Solution's Scope," *New York Times*, 3 November 2000.

Vice President Gore's National Partnership for Reinventing Government. *Benchmarking Reports*, 16 July 2000.

Watson, Gregory H. *Strategic Benchmarking: How to Rate Your Company's Performance Against the World's Best*. New York: John Wiley and Son, Inc., 1993.

——. *The Benchmarking Workbook: Adapting Best Practices for Performance Improvement*. Oregon: Productivity Press, 1992.

Weisbrod, Burton A., Editor, "To Profit or Not To Profit: The Commercial Transformation of the Nonprofit Sector." United Kingdom, Cambridge University Press, 1998.

Williams, Caroline. "Financing Techniques for Non-profit Organizations: Borrowing From the For-Profit Sector." President's Committee on the Arts and Humanities, Washington, D.C., 1998.

Williams, Grant. "Government, Charities, and Business Will Join Forces, Bush Advisor Predicts," *The Chronicle of Philanthropy,* 13 Jan. 2000, page 24.

——. "The Bush Brand of Charity," *The Chronicle of Philanthropy*, 6 April 2000.

Williams, Roger M. "Inside The Gates." *Foundation News and Commentary,* May-June 2000: 32-37.

Wyatt, Edward. "Confusion, Then Fervent Opposition to a Plan to Privatize 5 Schools," *New York Times,* 31 March 2001.

——. "Higher Scores Aren't Cure-All, School Run for Profit Learns," *New York Times,* 13 March 2001.

Zernike, Kate. "Antidrug Program Says It Will Adopt a New Strategy," *New York Times*, 15 February 2001.

——. "Gap Widens Again on Tests Given to Blacks and Whites," New York Times, 25 August 2000.

Zich, Janet. *The New Face of Philanthropy.*

Zimmerman, Rachel. "Student Protesters Target Universities Profiting From Research on AIDS," *Wall Street Journal.* 15 April, 2001.

APPENDIX Q

EXECUTIVE EDUCATIONAL ALTERNATIVES

Harvard University and Affiliates:

Harvard Business School is consistently top-ranked in terms of providing non-profit focused MBAs, and has a respected executive education program with regards to general management. However, HBS only offers two programs within the executive education program directed toward non-profit executives.

These programs, Strategic Perspectives in Non-profit Management ("SPNM") and Governing for Non-profit Excellence ("GNE") are part of HBS's Initiative on Social Enterprise, an effort created to respond to the growing social and economic importance of the non-profit sector and its interrelationship with business. Courses are primarily taught using the case-study method. Case studies are augmented by lectures, guest speakers, multimedia presentations, computer simulations, Internet explorations and group discussions.

These programs generally tend to attract individuals serving on boards of large institutional not-for-profits, hospitals, universities, as opposed to venture philanthropists interested in starting grass-roots social enterprises.

Benefits of these programs:
- A significant number of the cases studied in these programs were actually written and researched by the program's instructors. Instructors are highly committed to involvement in the non-profit world, serving on boards of world-renowned institutions, consulting with managers of foundations and, often times, founding and growing organizations that serve the public good.
- High quality and diverse enrollment. Participation in the SPNM program is limited to CEOs, Executive Directors, and senior-level managers with substantial policy and program responsibility. Participation in GNE is determined by level of leadership and experience on non-

315

profit boards. Both programs boast extremely diverse cultural, educational and professional backgrounds.
- Networking opportunities. High level of peer-to-peer interaction presents the opportunity to meet a large number of like-minded executives with similar goals.
- Name recognition.

Drawbacks of these programs:
- HBS's Executive Education only offers a small selection of programs focused on non-profits and social enterprise relative to top executive education programs at other institutions.
- The two programs offered at HBS are of one week or less in duration, and provide a lot of exposure to broad concepts, but fail to provide depth on individual subject matter.
- Enrollment is high in each program, as is the student-teacher ratio. Harvard relies upon peer-to-peer learning, and participants do not receive as close attention from instructors/facilitators as in other programs.

Strategic Perspectives in Non-profit Management
The SPNM Program will next be offered in 2001. The following information is based on the program offered in June 2000.

Program length:	6 days
Hours of instruction:	9:00AM - 3:30PM, with case discussion before and after classroom instruction
Format:	Integrates interactive classroom sessions with structured and informal small-group sessions
Tuition Fees:	$3,950 (includes lodging and most meals)
Enrollment:	90 students

Key objectives of this program include:
- Understanding core management concepts
- Applying these concepts strategically
- Learning how to implement change within the organization

Following are a series of case studies relevant to this program:
Virtuous Capital: What Foundations Can Learn from Venture Capitalists,

Christine Letts, William Ryan and Allen Grossman
How can foundations and non-profits learn to be more effective with their limited resources? They should consider expanding their mission from investing only in program innovation to investing in the organizational needs of nonprofit organizations as well. Venture capital firms offer helpful benchmarks for developing hands-on partnering skills. In addition to putting up capital, they closely monitor the companies in which they have invested, provide management support, and stay involved long enough to see the company become strong.

New Profit, Inc., James Heskett and others
Having founded what they called a "venture philanthropy" operated like a hybrid between a venture capital fund and a philanthropy, New Profit's organizers are confronted with two issues: 1) the role that "investors" would be asked to play in the organization, and 2) the way in which management tools such as the Balanced Scorecard could be put to work in the service of the philanthropy.

The Roberts Enterprise Development Fund: Implementing a Social Venture Capital Approach to Philanthropy, Daniel Kessler and others
This case looks at the experience of the Roberts Enterprise Development Fund ("REDF") which transformed its philanthropic practice into a social venture capital practice in 1997 with a portfolio of nonprofit enterprises in the San Francisco Bay Area. It also analyzes the applicability of a private venture capital model to social enterprise, including evaluating the changing nonprofit and philanthropic marketplace and looking in depth at one attempt to implement a social venture capital practice.

Notable amongst the Faculty of 14 who teach this program:
James Austin, chairman of HBS's Initiative on Social Enterprise
- HBS faculty member since 1972
- Special White House advisor on food policy

Stephen A. Greyser, faculty co-chair of SPNM
- Board member and national vice chair of the Public Broadcasting Service
- Advisory Committee for the Getty Museum Management Institute
- Initial chair of the Trustees Marketing Committee for the Museum of Fine Arts (Boston)

Allen Grossman
- President and CEO of Outward Bound from 1991 through 1997
- Joined Harvard faculty to work exclusively on the challenges of creating high-performing non-profits
- Founded the Going to Scale Project in 1994 and has chaired the project since its inception

Regina Herzlinger
- Currently researching the transformation of the American health care industry and managerial challenges in the non-profit sector
- Board member of eight large publicly held organizations
- Elected one of the most outstanding instructors of the MBA Class

James L. Heskett, faculty co-chair of SPNM
- Faculty co-chair of the Denali Initiative in social entrepreneurship
- Sales and Marketing Executives International - Marketing Educator of the Year Award

Rosabeth Moss Kanter
- Conceived and led the Business Leadership in the Social Sector Project, which involved over a hundred national leaders, including U.S. Senators, Governors, corporate CEOs and the First Lady
- Consulting clients include Bell Atlantic, BankBoston, Monsanto, IBM, Gap Inc., Novartis, British Airways, Volvo, and several large Asian financial conglomerates

Governing for Non-profit Excellence: Critical Issues for Board Leadership
This Program will next be offered November 2001.

Program length:	3 days
Hours of instruction:	9:00AM - 3:30PM, with case discussion before and after classroom instruction
Format:	Integrates interactive classroom sessions with structured and informal small-group sessions
Tuition Fees:	$2,850 (includes lodging and most meals)
Enrollment:	Limited to 90 students

Key objectives of this program include:
- Strategic planning
- Managing mission transitions and organizational transformations
- Achieving financial sustainability
- Attaining effective relationships between the board and the CEO
- Structuring and managing alliances
- Creating a productive, flexible board structure

Case studies relevant to this program include:

Working on Non-profit Boards, Don't Assume the Shoe Fits, F. Warren McFarlan
Most business professionals will spend some time on a non-profit board. Their involvement usually backfires. Despite similarities between the for-profit and non-profit sectors, governance differs in several key areas. Understanding these differences will make it easier to move from one environment to the other.

Effective Oversight, A Guide for Non-profit Directors, Regina Herzlinger
A non-profit needs a powerful and proactive board of directors to provide oversight. The board must assume the roles played in a business by owners and the market, ensuring that the nonprofit accomplishes its mission efficiently and devising its own system of measurement and control. Four questions help board members create such a system: 1) Are the organization's goals consistent with its financial resources? 2) Is the organization practicing intergenerational equity? 3) Are the sources and uses of funds appropriately matched? 4) Is the organization sustainable?

United Way of America: Governance in the Non-profit Sector, Jay Lorsch
Discusses the management practices of William Aramony at the United Way of America (UWA). First, the case describes the United Way movement, focusing on both the local chapters and the national organization. Second, it sets forth the Washington Post reports that lead to the UWA scandal. Third, it shows how the Board of Governors, the local chapters, Aramony, and donors responded to the scandal.

Teaching Purpose: To analyze the role that the board of directors plays in governing a nonprofit institution.

Notable faculty:
James Austin, Stephen Greyser, Allen Grossman, Regina Herzlinger (see SPNM bios above)
V. Kasturi Rangan, chair of the HBS marketing faculty
  • Founded and chaired "Strategic Perspectives in Non-profit Management"
  • Founding co-chair of the HBS Social Enterprise Initiative
  • One of the principal creators of the Social Enterprise Research Forum
  • Studies the role of marketing in non-profit organizations, especially how it influences the adoption of social products and ideas

As previously mentioned, one of the drawbacks of Harvard's general management approach is that neither of these programs provide in-depth analysis of several issues highly relevant to non-profit management and governance. In HBS's defense, program representatives do state that classroom instruction facilitates the investigation of subject matter(s) deemed relevant but not covered in the syllabus (not made available to non-registrants). Several programs within Harvard's Executive Education program do focus on subject matter in the for-profit world. They are as follows:

Contemporary Finance: SPNM touches upon this subject, but it is fully explored in the for-profit world within *Finance for Senior Executives,* a two-week program that investigates the corporate financial system, business strategy and financial controls, financial strategy and execution, and mergers, strategic alliances and restructuring. This course, which costs $10,500, will next be offered in 2001. Finance as it relates to non-profits is not specifically addressed in this program.

Marketing: Several marketing programs are offered, but the subject matter covered in these programs is not specifically relevant to marketing as it relates to the social enterprise. General marketing strategies are covered in the SPNM course.

Technology: *Delivering Information Services* addresses the issue of managing the information infrastructure of an organization for maximum advantage. This course is focused on improving shareholder value of for-profit companies, but provides insight into the implementation of a sound IT plan for any organization.

Benchmarking: This subject is fully explored within the bounds of SPNM. Through case study, participants are instructed on successful techniques of benchmarking for both non-profit and for-profit enterprises.

Compensation Issues: None of the courses or modules within courses offered at the Executive Education program at HBS specifically focus on compensation issues.

Venture Capital Techniques: Allen Grossman, one of the SPNM instructors, co-wrote a case study specifically addressing this subject – specifically, the implementation of successful venture capital techniques in the non-profit world. Another course offered within the executive education program, *Venture Capital: Revolutionizing Corporate Investments,* also addresses this topic.

Budgeting: SPNM gives a general overview of budgeting strategies, but doesn't fully explore this issue. None of the general management courses offered within the Executive Education program at HBS specifically focus on budgeting issues.

HBS MBA Program
HBS offers one of the top MBA programs in the world focusing on social enterprise. HBS has made social enterprise a priority for all MBA students through implementation of the Initiative on Social Enterprise, which:
- makes social enterprise a required module within the General Management curriculum,
- facilitates cross-registration at other Harvard Graduate Schools,
- offers an established program of non-profit fellowships,
- establishes a field-based elective program in which students work directly with leading non-profit organizations on major strategic challenges, and
- makes available to students an established field-based elective program.

A new seminar called Effective Leadership of Social Enterprise exposes students to leaders who have been extremely effective at strengthening non-profit management.

More than 50% of HBS graduates go on to serve on non-profit boards at some point in their career. This has led HBS to put more emphasis on social enterprise, specifically governance issues as they relate to non-profits.

The Hauser Center for Non-profit Organizations, at Harvard's John F. Kennedy School of Government ("KSG"), offers one executive education program.

<u>Strategic Giving</u> is targeted toward individual philanthropists who want to move beyond traditional methods of giving and develop new practices with a greater social impact. Designed for range of participants from the well-established giver who wishes to reevaluate his/her giving philosophy to the new philanthropist seeking to make sense of the vast range of methods.

Assessment: This is a new course, first offered in March 2000. It is taught through a collaboration of esteemed faculty from both HBS and KSG. The most valuable aspects of this program are the participants' confidential discussions of their own major philanthropic activities, which promotes self-analysis: What are my personal values and how are they reflected in my giving practice?

Program length:	3 days, Wednesday afternoon through Saturday morning
Hours of instruction:	8:00AM – 4:30PM
Format:	Case study augmented by group discussion. Group sessions give the opportunity to present the challenges faced in giving, and to seek ideas from their colleagues.
Tuition Fees:	$3,500 (includes most meals, no lodging)
Enrollment:	Limited to 50 students; not for professional managers of foundations

Key objectives of this program include:
- Evaluation of personal values and interests and how they relate to serving public need
- Evaluation of personal resources and level of personal involvement
- Evaluation of organizational structures that yield the best results
- Proper assessment of the work of particular non-profit organizations

Notable faculty:
Jim Austin (HBS, bio above)

Christine Letts (KSG), Executive Director, Hauser Center. Ms. Letts has served as Commissioner of the Indiana Department of Transportation, was the first Secretary of the Indiana Family and Social Services Administration, and is a member of the several boards including the Boston Music Education Collaborative.

Diana Barrett (HBS) currently serves on the Finance Committee of Partners Healthcare System and is Chair-Elect of the Board of the Spaulding Hospital, a major affiliate of the Massachusetts General Hospital.

Peter Frumkin's (KSG) current work focuses on how nonprofit organizations go to scale. He consults and serves on the boards of several for-profit and nonprofit organizations. He is on leave from HBS this year and is currently co-founding and serving as president of the Bridge Group, a nonprofit consulting firm affiliated with Bain & Company.

Distance Education: In fall 1999, Professor Mark Moore, Director of The Hauser Center, designed curriculum and taught the first distance-learning course for executive education. The Hauser Center has not made a decision as to whether or not this course, or other web-based courses, will be offered.

Stanford University:

Like Harvard, the non-profit management program for MBA students at **Stanford Business School** is extremely well respected, but opportunities for non-profit executive education are limited. Stanford Business School offers two executive education programs of interest directed toward non-profit executives.

These programs, Non-Profit Management and Philanthropists are offered at the Center for Social Innovation. As at Harvard, courses are taught primarily using the case-study method, augmented by peer review sessions.

Benefits:
- Within the MBA Program, Stanford has a very strong Public Management Initiative.
- For those interested in the healthcare industry, Stanford boasts a strong group of professors with practical and research backgrounds in that field. Stanford Business School offers a wide variety of cutting-edge programs and courses relating to healthcare.
- Approximately 25% of Stanford's MBA students are active participants in the Public Management Program (described below). For decades Stanford has received solid commitment from its administration to non-profit education. This has led to the creation and support of a variety of workshops, conferences, work-service projects, seminars and a top-notch guest speaker series.
- Close proximity to Silicon Valley gives Stanford access to the world's top technology companies.
- Stanford Management Internship Fund and Loan Forgiveness Program at MBA school makes available a wide range of public sector jobs for graduates, and results in a strong network of Stanford graduates in the non-profit field.
- Annual Public Management Initiative: the Initiative for 2000-2001 is technology-focused – building a bridge across the digital divide.

Drawbacks:
- Lacks breadth at the executive education program – there are only two executive education courses for the non-profit professional.
- Lacks depth at the executive education program – the two programs are both of extremely short duration, less than three days in length.

• As at Harvard, students do not receive as close attention from instructors as in other programs. Stanford relies on the peer review sessions to provide detailed feedback.

Non-Profit Management
This course will be offered in the summer of 2001. Course content is not currently being made publicly available, but the syllabus will focus on strategic thinking. This course is directed toward those who would like to hone their ability to develop coherent big picture strategy, not for individuals interested in exploring specific issues such as marketing, technology, venture capital techniques, etc. The syllabus for this program is currently under development, and information will be released in December 2000.

Philanthropists

Program length:	Two and one-half days – Wednesday, November 1 through Friday, November 3, 2000.
Hours of instruction:	12:00PM – 4:30PM (Wednesday), 8:45AM – 4:30PM (Thursday and Friday)
Format:	Case study, augmented by peer review sessions. Dinner with faculty on Wednesday evening.
Tuition Fees:	$3,500 (includes meals, but no lodging)
Enrollment:	By invitation only, please contact Karen Jacobsen at (650) 723-2165 for information.

Key objectives of this program include:
- Exposure to innovative approaches to philanthropy
- Determining a framework for how much to give
- Developing a compelling philanthropy mission and strategy
- Action plan for pursuing the mission
- Learning to engage different cultures and communities

The following faculty members will be among those teaching this course:
J. Gregory (Greg) Dees, Faculty Director
- Primary research interest – the challenges of bringing entrepreneurial skills into the non-profit sector
- Selected publications – Enterprising Non-Profits; Challenges of

       Combining Social and Commercial Enterprise
- Teaches MBA course on Social Entrepreneurship
- Editorial Review Board: Business Ethics Quarterly

Daniel Kessler
- Primary research interest - Economics of health care
- Selected cases - Asian Neighborhood Design; Roberts Enterprise Fund: Implementing a Social Venture Capital Approach to Philanthropy
- Teaches MBA courses on Social Entrepreneurship; Political Economy of Health Care in the United States

William Meehan
- Selected publications – "A Hard and Soft Look at IT Investments," "Six Principles of High-Performance IT," "Applying the High-Performance Organization Framework"
- Teaches MBA course on Strategic Management of Non-Profits
- Member of Board of Directors – United Way, Philanthropic Research Inc.

A two and a half day program provides the participant with enough time to meet a number of people interested in similar subject matter, to touch upon several interesting and highly relevant topics, and to listen to a few faculty members speak who have done some very interesting work in the field of non-profit management and philanthropy. It does not provide enough time to go into any depth on any of the subjects, so one must allow for significant post-course independent study to explore any particular topics in depth. Several courses at Stanford's executive education program and MBA program do allow for further investigation into the following topics:

Contemporary Finance: Stanford offers a Financial Seminar for Non-Financial Managers. This is next available in November 2001.

Marketing: There is an MBA course offered on Public and Non-profit Marketing.

Technology: The Public Management Initiative at the MBA program this year is focused on developing projects to mobilize business leaders to create universal technology access and to promote education and economic opportunity for the underprivileged. The Institute for Educational Leadership Through Technology is to be offered in the Spring 2001. Multiple courses focusing on technology are available in the executive education program (for-profit focus, but still applicable). Stanford's location in Silicon Valley is a plus.

Compensation Issues: Human Resource Executive Program is to be offered September 9 - 14, 2001. One of the session topics in this program is evaluating and rewarding performance.

Venture Capital Techniques: Both the Non-profit Management and Philanthropist programs emphasize the value of utilizing the hands-on venture capital approach, and review transferable tactics to the non-profit world.

MBA Program
The Public Management Program at **Stanford Graduate School of Business** was founded in 1971 in order to bring together business and government leaders and to effectively prepare MBA students for work in the non-profit sector.

Approximately one quarter of students in Stanford's MBA program are members of the Public Management Program ("PMP"). The PMP is a voluntary association of students committed to public service; admission only requires completion of the PMP essay question on the MBA application.

PMP students are not required to take any specific courses. However, Stanford does offer a Certificate in Public Management with the following areas of specialization that require specific course study:

- General Public Management
- Non-Profit Management
- Social Entrepreneurship
- Public Policy: Education, Environment or Healthcare

Stanford requires that all MBA students take a course on Management in Non-Market Environments. This course focuses on the formation of business strategy for addressing issues and interacting with the non-market environment.

The ability to work on independent projects, the accessibility and openness of faculty, and quality of guest speakers are just a few of the strengths cited by Stanford MBA graduates. The quality of the student body is also unilaterally praised.

Distance education: Stanford makes available a series of audio and video clips over the Internet on a wide variety of subjects. Several of the files provide overviews of programs available at the University, others are self-contained discussions of particular issues, and some are interviews of high profile entrepreneurs and businessmen. There are currently no programs specifically tailored for the non-profit professional that are available over the web.

Yale University:

Yale University's School of Management

With regards to executive education, **Yale University's School of Management** "Yale SOM" offers no set program catering to social sector executives. It only offers customized programs directed towards for-profit and non-profit executives. Each program is specifically tailored for the needs of its participants, and can range from short seminars to more extensive educational programs. The executive education department routinely draws upon the resources of other Yale schools and departments. This Working Book only analyzes Yale SOM's non-profit MBA program. SOM is the top business school in the nation for non-profit business education. Founded in 1974, Yale's SOM was, from the very beginning, envisioned to be a combination of a business school and an institute of public policy. For years the school has churned out graduates who have brought business savvy to the non-profit and government sectors.

In recent years, Yale SOM has set about to remake itself as a more mainstream business school with closer ties to corporate America. In 1998 Dean Jeffrey Garten, chief architect of this transformation, took the big step of changing the degree awarded by the SOM from the MPPM to the traditional MBA.

Yale retains its dual public-private focus. Nearly every course at Yale uses cases from both public and non-profit institutions, giving students' perspective in both sectors. It is expected that SOM graduates will move back and forth between sectors more often than other MBAs.

Strengths:
- Public/private sector program unique amongst business school programs
- Extraordinary faculty has depth and breadth of practical experience in the non-profit sector
- Vast selection of course offerings on non-profit management and organization
- Strong diversity of background amongst students, many of whom have non-profit/government backgrounds
- Broad network of contacts outside of Yale in the non-profit sector
- Strong ties to other graduate schools within Yale University facilitates joint study and full-fledged joint degrees

Weaknesses:
- Weak Information Technology program. This area is seeing improvement, as eight courses focused on Information Technology have been created within the past three years
- Not as strong as the top schools in traditional MBA disciplines (i.e., finance, marketing, technology)
- Recruiting effort is weak

Instruction consists primarily of lectures (estimated at 50%). Students also study cases (often NGO-focused as highlighted above) and are asked to participate in real-world projects.

Ten courses are required in the first year of all students in each of the following areas:
- Accounting, Statistics, Economic and Decision Analysis, Strategy, Leadership and Team Building, Organizational Behavior, Marketing, Operations, and Finance

In the second year, students who wish to concentrate in either non-profit management or public management will meet the following requirements:

Non-profit Management Concentration
Required course:
- Strategic Management of Non-profit Organizations

Four units from the following courses:
- Entrepreneurship: Business Planning for New Cultural Institutions
- Understanding and Evaluating the Financial Statements of Not-for-Profit Organizations
- Institutional Funds Management
- Program Evaluation

This concentration also requires the student to take courses outside the Yale SOM within his or her interest area (i.e., health care, arts, environment).

Public Management Concentration
Required course:
- Policy Modeling

Eight units from the following courses:
- Managing New York, Managing in New York

- Transportation and the Environment
- Housing and Community Development
- Introduction to Planning and Development
- Intermediate Planning and Development
- Healthcare Finance and Healthcare Economics
- Microeconomic Applications: Interacting with the Public Sector
- Strategy and Policy in the Healthcare Sector

Notable faculty members at Yale SOM involved with Non-profit Work include:
William Goetzmann, Director of International Center of Finance
- Background in arts and media management.
- Former documentary filmmaker, "Nova," "American Masters" series
- Former Director Denver Museum of Western Art

Sharon Oster, Professor of Finance and Entrepreneurship
- Ms. Oster is a specialist in competitive strategy, industrial organization, the economics of regulation and antitrust, and non-profit strategy.
- Works include Strategic Management for Non-profit Organizations, which analyzes management strategy and applies concepts originally designed for the for-profit sector to the management of non-profit institutions.
- Named best instructor in a 1994 Business Week survey of business schools.

Katherine O'Regan, Associate Professor of Economics and Public Policy
- Ms. O'Regan researches issues affecting the urban poor. She also works on the role of community organizations in the field of community development.
- Consulted for U.S. Department of Housing and Urban Development, Connecticut Department of Human Resources, and New Haven Legal Assistance.
- Works include "Non-profit and For-Profit Partnerships: Rationale and Challenges of Cross-Sector Contracting"

Douglas Rae, Professor of Organization and Management
- Mr. Rae specializes in the political economy of cities, electoral politics, political ideology, and power relations.
- Former Chief Administrative Officer of New Haven
- Fellow of the American Academy of Arts and Sciences and former Guggenheim Fellow
- Former President of Leeway, Inc., non-profit organization serving AIDS patients
- Consulted by the Parliament of Spain, Government of Netherlands Antilles, and BBC

Some sample courses of interest on Non-profit Management/Organization other than those offered within the concentration include:

Contemporary Finance: *Corporate Finance II* focuses on financial management from the perspective of inside the operating entity. Cases cover the public and private sector as well as the interface of the two.

Marketing: *Services Marketing: Strategies for Non-profits and For-profits* examines how marketing strategies can be used to attract not just customers, but volunteers, gifts, and other resources. *Product Planning and Development* deals with the development and introduction of new products and the management of existing products. Cases studied represent a wide variety of products and services from the non-profit and public sectors.

Compensation Issues: *Strategic Human Resource Management* explores compensation issues as they relate to the non-profit organization, as well as many other human resource issues.

Columbia Business School:

Columbia Business School's executive education program is the top-ranked program in the world according to a study performed in 2000 by the Financial Times. It is designed to capture the "ability of users to put into practice newly-acquired skills on their return to work." Approximately two-thirds of each class is filled by referrals from alumni.

Columbia Executive Education offers a wide range of non-degree programs, among them a special course for non-profit managers - The Institute for Not-for-Profit Management ("INM"). INM was the first of its kind, established in 1975.

INM offers:
- Executive Level Program.
- Middle Management Program.
- Leadership Development Program.
- Customized Programs.

These intensive programs are not for the faint-of-heart. Participants have generally developed the specific expertise required to work within their field, but need to better develop their managerial skills. Instructors work closely with students to learn these skills and to efficiently employ them in the workplace.

Benefits:
- Low student-teacher ratio; 10 instructors are assigned to each program of 24-26 students.
- Culturally diverse group of participants with work experience in a variety of segments of the non-profit sector.
- Faculty contains a large number of practitioners, with extensive experience working with non-profit organizations.
- In-depth instruction in a wide variety of specific non-profit management verticals.
- State of the art instructional resources.

Drawbacks:
- No emphasis on the implementation of technology within non-profit organizations.
- No stated distance learning or web-based initiatives.

Executive Level Program
This program is designed for executive directors and strategic planners for large organizations.

Program length:	Nineteen days, consisting of three non-consecutive weeks in residence in Harriman, NY and four days on the Columbia University campus.
Hours of instruction:	8:30AM – 5:00PM
Format:	Course instruction consists of one-on-one coaching, team building, and lecture. Instruction is application-focused, supplemented with minimal case study.
Tuition Fees:	$7,500 (includes lodging and meals)
Enrollment:	averages 24 to 26 students per course

Key objectives of this program include:
- Development of personal and professional objectives for the individual manager.
- An understanding of the usefulness of financial information for decision making and reporting.
- Development of a comprehensive framework for choosing institutional purposes and directions, consistent with the organization's mission and values.
- The ability to negotiate and to manage conflict.
- Proficiency in managing an organization's relations with its various constituents, respond to threats and opportunities, and achieve strategic goals.
- Completion of the Strategic Management Project – the development of a comprehensive strategic plan for the organization the participant manages.

Topics of interest explored and overviewed by this course include:
Contemporary Finance and Budgeting: *Accounting, Budgeting, and Finance* explores the limits and effectiveness of financial information in financial planning for non-profit organizations.

Marketing: *Marketing, Public Relations and Fund Development* gives an overview of marketing for non-profits; provides analysis of segmentation, positioning and orientation; and allows for in-depth exploration of marketing tactics.

Technology: Limited discussion. The executive level program discusses the use of the Internet in deploying effective fund raising strategies. Outside of this, participants can take advantage of a number of for-profit executive education programs including: *E-Commerce: Creating New Strategic Advantage; E-B2B: Winning in the Digital Economy; E-Valuation: Maximizing the Value of Internet Ventures; and E-Law: Legal Issues Surrounding the Internet.*

Venture Capital Techniques: *The Strategic Management* module discusses the employ of entrepreneurial thinking within the management of a non-profit organization.

Middle Management Program
This program is designed for program directors or executive directors of small organizations.

Program length:	7 days
Hours of instruction:	8:30AM – 5:00PM
Format:	Course instruction consists of one-on-one coaching, team building, and lecture. Instruction is application-focused, supplemented with minimal case study.
Tuition Fees:	$3,400 (includes lodging and meals)
Enrollment:	averages 24 to 26 students per course

Three variations of this program exist with differing thrusts:
- All fields of non-profit service
- Community development organizations
- Youth service organizations

Each of these programs is essentially an abbreviated version of the executive management program tailored towards an audience of mid-level managers.

Leadership Development Program

Program length:	5 days
Hours of instruction:	8:30AM – 5:00PM with occasional evening sessions
Format:	Course instruction consists of one-on-one coaching, team building, and lecture. Instruction is application-focused,

	supplemented with minimal case study.
Tuition Fees:	$3,800 (includes lodging and meals)
Enrollment:	averages 24 to 26 students per course

Participants can expect to:
- gain the practical tools and methodologies to build and motivate teams,
- develop an ability to plan and manage change, and
- learn to create a climate that encourages diversity and promotes creativity and innovation.

Teaching methodologies include case analysis, lectures, 360-degree feedback, one-on-one coaching sessions and small group discussions and exercises. The coaching sessions are designed to develop a real-world action plan to achieve stated goals.

Columbia remains unique in its broad-based offerings of intensive management education to senior and mid-level executives of non-profit organizations – social services, community development, health, education, philanthropy, advocacy, religion, arts and culture. Customized programs are also available.

The following key faculty members will be teaching these courses:
Murray Low
- Executive Director, Center for Entrepreneurship
- Teacher of executive seminars on entrepreneurship
- Leading authority on entrepreneurship in independent, corporate and not-for-profit settings
- Founder, Columbia Entrepreneurship Program

Thomas Ference
- Adjunct Professor, Finance and Economics

Michael Feiner
- Adjunct Professor, Management Teacher of executive seminars on entrepreneurship
- Faculty Director, Leadership Development Program

Columbia MBA Program
Columbia allows students to concentrate in one of thirteen areas for its MBA program, including Public and Non-profit Management ("PNPM").

Courses of interest within PNPM include:
- *Financial Management in the Non-profit Sector:* This course focuses on financing the mission of non-profit organizations. The syllabus also covers endowment management and MIS applications to day-to-day operations.
- *Consulting in the Non-profit Sector:* Participants complete a twelve-week consulting project, examine case studies, and listen to guest lectures.
- *Cost-Benefit Analysis:* Provides an ability to broaden the scope of cost-benefit analysis from simply cash flow analysis to include concepts such as the valuation of intangibles like life, health and time, and public goods and externalities such as pollution.

Other positives of PNPM include strong community involvement by:
- supporting such endeavors as Net Impact, an organization that promotes a speaker series,
- organizing a set of panel discussions, and
- promoting fund raising for summer internships in the non-profit sector.

The Small Business Consulting Project is a student-led organization that provides services to small businesses and non-profits. Also, the PNPM Program boasts a strong alumni group that is very active within the University.

United University:

United University ("UnitedU") is an emerging alternative executive education initiative, uniquely structured for social sector executives and those engaged in the Intersectoral arena. Proprietarily unique, UnitedU's mission is to facilitate positive social sector transformation based on a belief that there are virtually boundless opportunities for maximum initiative value creation. UnitedU seeks to provide customized and flexible educational offerings via a collaboration of mediums, especially those leveraging technology. Its comparative distinguishing innovations include: superior Intersectoral course offerings and content, unique executive time/value sensitive formats, and both structured class interaction as well as 24/7 access.

UnitedU is a proactive response to the demand for quality instruction of business management skills for leaders of benchmark social sector and intersectoral organizations. Content and instruction are provided by accomplished professionals from leading universities, consulting firms, corporations, and social sector organizations.

The typical scholar at UnitedU is a senior social sector executive who is in a position to affect immediate and dramatic change within their organization. They have a strong desire to network, and are early adopters of new technologies. They are proactive scholars to whom lifelong learning and continuous improvement is an integral part of life. Time is at a premium for this executive.

Benefits:
- UnitedU courses are designed specifically for executives seeking the optimal blend of commercial and social sector education - intersectoral. Course subjects cover a comprehensive spectrum of the best of these intersectoral offerings including ROI Marketing, Contemporary Technology, Contemporary Financial Engineering, Executive Compensation, Benchmarking, Social Entrepreneurship, Virtuous Capital, and Budget Process & Discipline.
- UnitedU's propriety case studies teach social sector executives what they need to know quickly and efficiently. Cases are expressly created for the social sector or Intersectoral executive, unlike many schools where social sector cases are merely modified to address NGO issues; or are norm-focused NGO qualitative war stories. The content is passionate in message and seeks to provide material that can be directly and

immediately applied for rapid results. Value creation is a consistent mission of all classes and materials; and a rigorous focus on hard metrics provide unique compelling offerings. Only essential information is included in its executive summary format. Designed for individual review, only the most macro, value added, insights are taught.

- The UnitedU program is structured with the understanding that time is at a premium for the UnitedU student. Unlike traditional case studies that are written in a lengthy story format, UnitedU cases are executive summaries that focus on the crucial points and exclude non-essential information. The scholar's valuable time is further conserved by completion of a pre-course diagnostic test that allows instructors to tailor coursework specifically to meet individual needs and objectives to avoid repetition. Unlike traditional schools, syllabi for UnitedU programs are not static.
- UnitedU's pioneering method of Internet-based instruction provides global access to course material 24 hours a day, 7 days a week. This gives the scholar the flexibility to fit coursework into a crowded schedule. Parallel CD's are also available for remote learning when access to the Internet is not available or optimal.
- The global reach of Internet-based instruction creates unique networking capabilities/opportunities that are unavailable at traditional programs. The scholar's student profile is always present, allowing for scholars to systematically seek out peers rather than the haphazard network opportunities that occur at traditional programs.
- UnitedU provides one-on-one instruction of dynamic material from world-class faculty and team members.

Weaknesses:

- This program is not designed for individuals who will not take advantage of the power of the Internet and leverage the abilities of new technologies. The vast majority of programs available at top universities around the world have not developed a strategy for embracing the Internet. These programs are generally more interested in maintaining the status quo of instruction than in creating a new paradigm.
- Individuals who would rather "sit back" and absorb a set syllabus, and are satisfied with only a limited ability to determine which topics are discussed in courses would be better off in a traditional program.
- Those without considerable passion for positive social sector transformation need not apply.

Program length: 5 to 6 weeks per course
Hours of instruction: 1-1.5 hours each week (two classes ranging from 30 minutes to 45 minutes each)
Outside reading: 2-3 hours each week (two hours of outside reading for every one hour of class time)

UnitedU courses are offered on a number of highly relevant topics to the social sector executive, including:

ROI Marketing
  • Measurement and Accountability
  • Strategic Micromarketing
  • Leveraging the power of brand equity
  • Leveraging public relations and communications opportunities
  • The use of the Internet as a marketing tool

Instructor: Norman Shawchuck, Ph.D.
  • Author and consultant for NGO and spiritual organizations
  • More than 20 books on spirituality, conflict management and leadership
  • Ph.D. in Organizational Systems from Northwestern University

Case Topics:
Ad Council looks at social advertising ROI practices using various media.
AMA College Board examines how to effectively leverage one's brand to compete with commercial entities.
BirthRight Israel looks at the importance of micromarketing and segmentation.
Business School Initiatives compares various marketing strategies.
Focus on the Family examines effective marketing & distribution, effective segmentation, and brand management strategies.

Contemporary Technology
  • Management issues of the New Economy
  • Benchmarking and Business Strategy
  • Overview of technology as it relates to NGOs
  • Impact of the Internet on NGOs Operating efficiencies afforded by new technologies

Instructor: David Altshuler
- Executive Director of TCN, a consultancy that provides NGOs with telecommunications and IT advice and solutions
- Responsible for all aspects of TCN's telecommunications and technology products and services
- Former President and CTO of Mutual Analytics
- 1999-2000 Irey Grant Lecturer in Business Law at The Law School at the University of Pennsylvania
- Former instructor at The Wharton School and Aresty Institute

Case Topics:
Business School Initiatives examines the steps leading business schools are taking to embrace, or not embrace technological advances.
Virtual Jerusalem looks at the effective use of technologies to further the mission of an organization.
Social Venture Capital discusses the benefits of leveraging Internet technology by benchmark NGOs.

Contemporary Financial Engineering
- Introduction and analysis for better management
- Compensation issues
- Cutting edge financial techniques including M&A and restructuring
- Cultivating untapped assets
- Investment Banking ideas for NGOs.

Instructor: Paul Kazarian
- Founding and Managing Partner, Japonica Partners and Japonica Intersectoral
- Efforts include tender offer for Chicago Northwestern Corp, Acquisition of Allegheny International, IPO of Sunbeam-Oster, and restructuring proposal of Borden
- Former Investment Banker, Goldman Sachs & Co.
- Graduate Bates College, MA Brown University, MBA Columbia University

Case Topics:
Ad Council and *BirthRight Israel* examine the positive impact of Joint Ventures/Alliances with other organizations.

AMA/College Board and *Business School Initiatives* look at how to make use of untapped assets.
Social Venture Capital explores the increased competition between NGOs and commercial organizations.

Executive Compensation

Description: Initial design plans for the course include the following topics: comparative social sector to commercial sector packages, trends in social sector compensation, talent mobility both intra and inter sectors, value creation performance compensation packages, and ill-conceived programs.
Instructor: TBD
Cases: Under Development

New Philanthropy Benchmarking

Description: New Philanthropy Benchmarking builds on a synergist collaboration of commercial sector benchmarking, progressive social sectors strategies, and contemporary financial markets analytical tools. NPB is evaluated with the context of macro issues such a stakeholder considerations and comparative conclusionary financial metrics. On a micro level, insights are offered on process sequence as well as organizational execution suggestions.
Instructor: TBD
Cases: Under Development

Social Entrepreneurship/Social Venture Capital

Description: Under Development
Instructor: TBD
Cases: Under Development

Budgeting Process and Discipline

Description: Under Development
Instructor: TBD
Cases: Under Development

ILLUSTRATIVE PUBLICLY TRADED COMPANIES WITH INTERSECTORAL MISSIONS

Arts & Culture
A.C. Moore Arts & Crafts (ACMR)
Artgallerylive.com (ALVV)
Baldwin Piano + Organ Company (BPAO)
Gallery of History (HIST)
Steinway Instruments (LVB)

Biotechnology
Amgen (AMGN)
Biogen (BGEN)
Celera (CRA)
Charles River Labs (CRL)
Genentech (DNA)
Human Genome Sciences (HGSI)
Medimmune (MEDI)
Millennium (MLNM)

Community Development
America First Apartments (APROZ)
Eldertrust (ETT)
Fannie Mae (FNM)
Freddie Mac (FRE)
Mid-America Apartment (MAA)
Rural/Metro Corp. (RURL
Senior Housing Properties (SNH))

Education
Apollo Group (APOL)
Career Education Corp. (CECO)
Corinthian Colleges (COCO)
DeVry (DV)
Edison Schools (EDSN)
ITT Educational Services (ESI)
Nobel Learning Communities (NLCI)
Strayer Education (STRA)
Sylvan Learning (SLVN)

Educational Publishing
Educational Development (EDUC)
Harcourt General (H)
Houghton Mifflin (HTM)
McGraw Hill (MGH)
Millbrook Press (MILB)
Scholastic, Inc. (SCHL)
School Specialty (SCHS)

Edutainment
Centra Software (CTRA)
eCollege.com (ECLG)
Learn2.com (LTWO)
Learning Tree (LTRE)
Mentergy Ltd. (MNTE)
Scientific Learning Corp. (SCIL)
Learning Star Corporation (LRNS)

Environment
ACCIXX (SFTY)
Clean Diesel Technologies (CDTI)
Clean Harbors (CLHB)
Earthcare Company (ECCO)
Earthshell Corp. (ERTH)
Ecology & Environment (EEI)
Environmental Elements (EEC)

Financial
Heller Financial (HF)
National Rural Utilities Cooperative Finance (NRU)
Silicon Valley Bancshares (SIVB)
Student Loan Corp. (STU)
USA Education (SLM)
Thornburg Mortgage (TMA)

Hospitals
HCA (HCA)
Health South (HRC)
Tenet Health Care (THC)
Triad Hospitals (TRI)
United Surgical Partners (USPI)
Universal Health Services (UHS)

Health Care Services
American Healthways (AMHC)
AMN Health Care Services (AHS)
DiVita (DVA)
Renal Care (RCGI)
Quest (DGX)
UniLabs (ULAB)

Health Support Services
Apria (AHG)
Aetna (AET)
Corvel (CRVL)
PacifiCare (PHSY)
United Health Group (UNH)
Universal Hospitals Services (UHS)

Human Services
Armor Holdings (AH)
Avalon Correctional (CITY)
Children's Comp. Services (KIDS)
Correctional Properties (CPV)
Correctional Services (CSCQ)
Ramsay Youth Services (RYOU)
Res-Care (RSCR)
Wackenhut Correction (WHC)

Long-Term Care
ARV Assisted Living (SRS)
Balanced Care Corp. (BAL)
Beverly Enterprises (BEV)
Capital Senior Living (CSU)
Greenbriar (GBR)
HCR Manor Care (HCR)
Kindred (KIND)

Medical Devices
Arrow Intl (ARRO)
Baxter Intl (BAX)
Beckman Coulter (BEC
Boston Scientific (BSX)
Guidant Corp. (GDT)
Integra Life Sciences (IART)
Johnson & Johnson (JNJ)
Stryker (SYK)

Professional Services
Arrow Intl (ARRO)
DigitalThink (DTHK)
National Computer Sys. (NLCS)
NCS Pearson Inc (PSO)
Orthodontic Centers of America (OCA)
Skillsoft Corp. (SKIL)
Smartforce (SMTF)

Information Technology
Affiliated Computer Services (ACS)
Care Sciences (CARE)
Click2Learn.com (CLKS)
Saba Software (SABA)
Smartforce (SMTF)

APPENDIX S

SOCIAL SECTOR MISFORTUNATE SITUATIONS

NGOs:
1. United Way

William Aramony was President of United Way of America for more than two decades. In 1995, he began serving a seven-year prison sentence for defrauding the organization out of more than $1 million over a five-year period in order to support a lavish lifestyle. Despite the conviction, a federal judge ruled that Aramony was entitled to pension benefits worth more than $2 million (after deducting approximately $2 million for damages, interests and costs to United Way). The pension plan had failed to provide for forfeiture of benefits. Recently, a second United Way president, Betty Beene, resigned after her attempts to impose national standards on local United Ways ignited a power struggle within the organization and threatened the organization's cohesion. Somewhere between 12% and 25% of local donations were being held back pending her resignation. The United Way back-office process has been compared to those existing in corporate America years ago. Beene, seeking to automate this process, put the United Way's national headquarters up as collateral for a multi-million-dollar line of credit to fund the technology. But, when the system was finally tested in 1999, the system reportedly failed, and the United Way took a $12.1 million write-off to cover the cost of the now dormant project. One local chapter opponent to Beene commented that her organization was not "old-school" but "cutting-edge" and pointed to the fact that it allowed donor matching, a practice that hasn't been seen as innovative for 15 years, as Fortune observed. The number of United Way donors had fallen more than 20 percent since 1987, but has since recovered significantly. In 1998 the United Way's share of all charitable contributions in the U.S. was 3.16% and by 1999 had declined to 1.98%. Relative to U.S. personal and corporate income, United Way contributions have declined 29% in the past 12 years, even though overall giving as a percentage of income rose 8.2%. Overhead is reportedly three to four percentage points higher than it was 10 or 15 years ago. Sources: Wee, Eric L., "Judge Says United Way Must Pay $2 Million Pension to Aramony," *The Washington Post*, 10.24.98; David Cay Johnston, "United Way faces crisis as president plans to leave." *The New York Times*, 9.19.00. Varchaver, Nicholas. "Can Anyone Fix the United Way?" *Fortune*, November 27, 2000. Pages 171-180.

Issues: Fraud; compensation; impact on public image; no forfeiture provision.

2. New Covenant Charter School (Albany, NY)
In its first school year of operation and after praise from New York's governor, New Covenant Charter School in Albany, NY saw the for-profit company managing its academic program resign, two principals quit, one-fourth of the school's students leave, and only 9% of its students meet or exceed state testing standards. Education Department found "'serious violations of law and of the school's charter,' including inadequate academic programs, building code violations and students who were missing or unaccounted for." The hastily opened school (rushed approval process without comment from stakeholders entitled to be heard under state law) was housed in trailers, with overcrowded classes being taught in hallways and carpets mended with duct tape. Furthermore, the State University of New York made similar findings and determined that the school lacked financial controls. It is uncertain whether school can be opened for 2000-2001 school year. Source: Wyatt, Edward, "Charter School's Problems Yield Cautionary Tale," *The New York Times*, 8.18.00.

Issues: Politics and publicity controlling process; mismanagement.

3. Child and Adult Care Food Program Federally Funded Lunch Program Fraud
As of 10.2.99, criminal charges had been filed against 44 officers of NGOs accused of defrauding the federal government of millions of dollars from its Child and Adult Care Food Program, a $1.7 billion a year program that provides meals to 2.4 million children in day care. The fraud took place by NGO groups known as "sponsors" that acted as middlemen between the government and day care homes and centers. The sponsors were supposed to monitor day care homes and review and pay claims for meals served. Claims were made for meals served to "nonexistent children" in fictitious day care homes. In other cases, the sponsors demanded kickbacks from legitimate day care providers. Some of the defendants padded their payrolls to justify bigger checks from the government. One sponsor owner even worked full-time for the state, monitoring the work of child case sponsors, including her own company. The inspector general investigating the frauds

said that "'Federal officials could have prevented or detected much of the fraudulent activity' if they had been more vigilant." Source: Pear, Robert, "Nonprofit Groups Accused of Bilking Lunch Programs," *The New York Times*, 10.2.99.

Issues: Fraud; lack of vigilance; pouring money in "black hole."

4. Operation Smile

In 1982, Operation Smile began a program of sending plastic surgeons overseas to fix cleft palates and lips of children in poor countries. The program received enormous praise and recognition along with support from Bill Gates, Charles B. Wang of Computer Associates, Warner-Lambert, Johnson & Johnson, and others. The husband (a noted surgeon) and his wife who founded the program never took salaries. However, beginning in 1997 allegations of shoddy medical practices and questions about the charity's direction and conduct precipitated a bitter internal struggle. A number of deaths during and after surgery and exaggeration of Operation Smile's size on its tax returns by including the value of medical services that volunteer nurses and physicians donated triggered withdrawal of Warner-Lambert's support and a $10 million pledge by Wang. The program was criticized for being more concerned than other charities with trying to impress donors with the sheer number of operations. Questions raised about who should conduct an internal inquiry and what should be reviewed to demonstrate "fundamental problem facing many nonprofit organizations: When a charity gets in trouble, who ought to slam on the brakes?" Source: Abelson, Reed, "Charges of Shoddy Practices Taint Gifts of Plastic Surgery," *The New York Times*, 11.24.99.

Issues: Ego of founders; publicity and numbers games hampering quality/value of services.

5. Adelphi University

In 1995-96 a highly publicized scandal developed surrounding financial dealings involving the president and board of trustees of Adelphi University on Long Island. The board had allowed university funds to be used to pay for the "extraordinary personal spending" of the president, Peter Diamandopoulos. In addition to average annual expenses of more than $100,000 a year for six years, the board provided Mr. Diamandopoulos with a $1.2 million Manhattan condominium (which Mr. Diamandopoulos had the option to buy from the university for $905,000), hundreds of thousands of dollars in furnishings and decorations for the condominium, and an $82,000 Mercedes. In 1994, Mr. Diamandopoulos' salary and benefits had amounted to $523,000 a year – the second highest total among American university presidents – and free residence in the president's house on the university campus. Meanwhile, enrollment had fallen by a third during the previous decade and tuition had more than doubled. University contracts for services (such as insurance, advertising, and legal services) with companies that were run by current board members raised the question of a possible *quid pro quo*. Moreover, Mr. Diamandopoulos' personal lawyer had also served as a lawyer for the university and had written the president's compensation package. The scandal was both embarrassing and highly divisive within the university community. Sources: Bruce Lambert, "Group at Adelphi asks regents to remove the trustees." *The New York Times*, 4.26.96; John Rather, "State's Adelphi inquiry raises larger questions on trustees." *The New York Times*, 5.26.96; Bruce Lambert, "Examining Adelphi president's perks, from a Mercedes to a million-dollar condo." *The New York Times*, 8.12.96.

Issues: Conflicts of interest; dishonest practices.

6. Los Angles Community Development Bank

Los Angles Community Development Bank is a government-supported lending institution. Its plan was to create inner-city jobs by lending to local companies that were not being serviced by commercial banks. Five years ago, politicians, including Vice President Al Gore, praised the bank and its objectives. The $435 million bank was financed by the US Department of Housing and Urban Development. However, of the $118 million in loans, all to businesses in economically depressed neighborhoods, $36 million have defaulted, and along the way, the bank exceeded its own lending limits in making a $24.1 million loan to a dairy project that eventually failed. Borrowers are suing the bank and its management claiming that bank-related incompetence forced them out of business. One company has won a $9.2 million judgment. The bank's problems have been attributed to "too much red tape," an overly politicized board, unrealistic expectations, and a doomed lending mechanism. Source: Business Diary, "A Costly Lesson About Best-Laid Plans," *The New York Times*, 7.30.00.

Issues: Departure from business plan; too much publicity; government involvement & red tape.

7. Project Pathways

Started in 1993 by the New York City School Construction Authority to place qualified vocational students into apprenticeship programs in the construction trades, Project Pathways was initially successful, placing 98% of students in apprenticeships within two years of graduation. However, in 1998 only 38% were placed and by early 2000, only 3% of the 1999 graduates had entered programs. A recent audit determined that the program was poorly administered, lacked monitoring, and failed to ensure that all parties were meeting their obligations. The program was expected to be replaced by a new program run by a new NGO. Union groups believe that the program should be run by a NGO while the employers' association urges greater reliance on private industry. Source: Sullivan, John, "Vocational School Training Effort Falls Short, Audit Says," *The New York Times*, 8.20.00.

Issues: Government involvement, agency distracted by other priorities, failure to establish and adhere to effective process.

8. Name Confusion

Organizations use names similar to those of well-established charities causing confusion for donors or outright fraud. The Wishing Well Foundation, formed in 1995, would tell potential donors, "I'm sure you've heard of us; we send terminally ill children to places like Disney World." The Minnesota attorney general sued the organization alleging that Wishing Well deliberately misled donors by implying that it was a local charity (it is based in Metarie, LA) and by preying on possible confusion with better-known charities, such as Make-A-Wish Foundation, founded in 1980. Internet search engines can be used to identify charities, but some search engines, like GoTo.com, give priority to organizations that pay for placement. Charities have been reluctant to sue "sound alikes," preferring to spend money of their missions rather than public relations or lawsuits. However, the consequence can be more than just confusion, but a loss of donor trust. Some organizations have become more active in protecting their names. For example, the Arthritis Foundation, American Cancer Society and American Heart Association joined in a suit against Citizens Action Group, which was the subject of two ABC News program "20/20" investigations, for using "confusingly similar" names like the National Cancer Association or National Heart Foundation to collect money. Source: Abelson, Reed, "Some Charities Cash in by Playing the Name Game," *The New York Times*, 12.30.99.

Issues: Fraud; protecting goodwill associated with charity name.

9. American Parkinson Disease Association

It was discovered in the mid-1990s that Frank Williams, executive director of the American Parkinson Disease Association, had embezzled an average of $80,000 a year over the course of a decade, depositing donations into a "temporary" bank account originally created for a charity walkathon. Though Williams's annual salary was in excess of $100,000, he felt overworked and underpaid relative both to directors of other comparable organizations and to the fund-raising obligations of his position. He expressed resentment at feeling underappreciated by the members of his board of trustees. Though Williams had been highly successful as a fundraiser and in attracting celebrity support for his organization, the scandal was a public relations disaster. Some chapters cut their ties to the association and at least one prominent board member, former congressman Morris Udall, resigned. Source: David Stipp, "Newstrends; I stole to get even: yet another charity scam." *Fortune*, 10.30.95.

Issues: Fraud.

10. Harvard's Russia Project

From 1992 to 1997, the United States Agency for International Development (USAID) paid Harvard University's Institute for International Development more than $40 million as part of an effort to help Russia "develop capital markets and rewrite Soviet-era civil laws." In May, 1997, the project was terminated by USAID on the grounds that individuals associated with the project had exploited their positions for private financial advantage, making investments in Russian industries and financial markets even as they advised the Russian government on policies that would directly affect the profitability of such investments. In September, 2000, the U.S. Justice Department sued Harvard and the individuals concerned for $120 million, alleging that the university had failed to exercise appropriate oversight and, moreover, that the defendants had "undercut the fundamental purpose of the United States' program in Russia – the creation of trust and confidence in the emerging Russian financial markets." Source: Steve Liesman and Carla Anne Robbins, "U.S. sues Harvard, 4 individuals, alleging fraud in Russia program." *The Wall Street Journal*, 9.27.00.

Issues: Conflicts of interest; fraud; unintended consequences.

Foundations:

1. Kyle Foundation

Author Tom Clancy established the Kyle Foundation, inspired by a young fan who died of cancer. He intended that the foundation use Internet technology to help children suffering from cancer and other illnesses talk with one another and learn about their diseases. Clancy donated more than $4 million, pledged one-third of the proceeds from his next movie, and used his connections to persuade others to contribute. But, after seven years, the foundation had spent more than $5 million on travel, salaries, fund-raising and furniture, yet did not have even a Web site. The salary for executive director Clancy hired climbed from $43,000 to $120,000. Although several people, including a board member who ran a $29 billion computer company, expressed concerns that the foundation was floundering and that its management was weak, Clancy took no action. The board member resigned. The mother of the boy for whom the foundation was named suggested that friends honor her son by donating to other charities. Finally, when Clancy's new wife voiced concerns, he sent in an accountant. The accountant's report disclosed that the foundation had spent almost $1.5 million on travel, consultants, and a one-time payment to the executive director for accrued vacation and sick pay. Clancy finally fired the executive director and filed suit against her for mismanagement and improper expenditures. Clancy is using the remaining foundation money to fund a pediatric oncology research chair. Source: Moss, Michael and Rutenberg, Jim, "Writer's Philanthropic Hopes Ending in Bitter Court Fight," *The New York Times*, 7.11.00.

Issues: Mismanagement; lack of oversight.

2. America's Promise

America's Promise—the Alliance for Youth, chaired by Retired General Colin Powell, works with corporations, charities and communities to provide children with five essentials it has identified: a caring adult, a safe place after school, health care, marketable skills and the chance to give back to the community. It promotes community forums to discuss how best to help young people and often matches companies and charities to work together. America's Promise claimed that it has generated commitments from corporations and charities of $300 million and "reached more than 10 million children." However, those claims are being questioned. For example, its 1999 Report to the Nation cited Hewlett-Packard for promising $4 million to help city students learn math and science. But, the company says that the gift had been approved well before it was contacted by America's Promise. Further, one critic says that if the claim about the number of children reached is true, it would mean that America's Promise has reached one of every five children in the nation. Others have noted that its mission is unclear. Moreover, the organization has refused to disclose how much it pays its top officials. (Gen. Powell takes no money from America's Promise, except for expenses when speaking on its behalf). PricewaterhouseCoopers acknowledges that a performance study it conducted was based on information supplied by America's Promise and that the information was not scrutinized and that the information could include multiple companies taking credit for the same effort. It has also been disclosed that the charity was not registered with state regulators as required for groups soliciting money. Source: Abelson, Reed, "Charity Led by general Powell Comes Under Heavy Fire, Accused of Inflating Results," *The New York Times*, 10.8.99.

Issues: Defining mission; measuring results; disclosure of financial information; attention to regulatory requirement.

3. Saint Francis of Assisi Foundation

As part of his enormous insurance fraud scheme, Marvin R. Frankel convinced Vatican clergy to allow him to associate the Saint Francis of Assisi Foundation, a B.V.I. trust formed in 1998, with a Vatican-based foundation. Frankel expressed his intention to use the foundation to acquire insurance companies and contribute investment profits to Catholic charities. Its financial statements indicated that it had almost $2 billion in assets as of March, 2000, although it is unclear how much, if any, money ever went into the foundation. Frankel even persuaded one of the clergyman to provide an affidavit stating that the funds contributed to the foundation came from "funds of the Holy See." The affidavit was used to support Frankel's lawyers' claims that the charity and its business dealings had the approval of the Vatican. No indication that any funds were taken donated by others to the foundation or any of the Catholic charities as a result of the scheme or that funds were embezzled from charitable sources. Frankel's Sources: Pacelle, Mitchell P. and Lohse, Deborah, " 'Saint Francis Foundation Becomes Focus of Questions," *The Wall Street Journal* Interactive Ed., 6.22.99; Stanley, Allesandra, How 2 Priests Got Mixed Up in a Huge Insurance Scandal," *The New York Time*, 6.26.99.

Issues: Fraud.

4. The Bernice Pauahi Bishop Estate

The Bernice Pauahi Bishop Estate (better known simply as the "Bishop Estate") is the largest private land holder in Hawaii and has world-wide assets estimated at between $5 billion and $10 billion. The sole beneficiary is the Kamehameha School (now a single institution), which educates more than 3,000 children of native Hawaiian descent, established in 1884. Trustees were to be appointed by justices of Hawaii's Supreme Court, acting in their private capacities. But in the past couple of decades the position of trustee became a political plum, awarded by the justices mostly to people with strong ties to the state's Democratic Party. A trustee's annual compensation would reportedly exceed $1 million. In 1998, responding to widespread criticism, four of the five justices excused themselves from making future appointments. In 1999, at the urging of the Internal Revenue Service, four of the five trustees were removed and the fifth voluntarily resigned. The IRS claimed that the trustees had (i) received excessive compensation, (ii) used estate funds for their personal expenses, (iii) focused on expanding the estate's lucrative commercial activities at the expense of its charitable purpose of running an educational institution, and (iv) improperly lobbied against federal legislation enacted in 1996 that penalizes excessive compensation or perks among non-profit officials and board members. A settlement was reached in 1999 under which the estate avoided losing its tax-exempt status going back to 1990 and safeguard measures were implemented removing the trustees from managing the estate's day-to-day operations. Additionally, the estate was required to review existing contracts and job classifications to insure that it was getting good value for necessary services and that contracts are obtained through open and competitive bidding. The settlement also provided for revisions of the estate's investment practices requiring that the charity's investments be handled in a way that supports its educational mission. Further, the estate agreed to strict guidelines on its employment of elected or appointed public officials.

Source: Purdum, Todd S., "For $6 Billion Hawaii Legacy, a New Day," *The New York Times*, 5.15.99; Greene, Stephen G., "Trustees Ousted in Hawaii," *The Chronicle of Philanthropy*, 5.20.99; Greene, Stephen G., " Bishop Estate to Pay IRS $9-Million But Retain Its Tax-Exempt Status," *The Chronicle of Philanthropy*, 12.16.99.

Issues: Self-dealing; breach of fiduciary duty; breach of loyalty; intermediate sanctions.

5. Foundation for New Era Philanthropy

In 1989, John G. Bennett, Jr., founded the Foundation for New Era Philanthropy, promising investors that wealthy anonymous investors would match their money after six months. Bennett claimed that New Era financed its philanthropic efforts with the interest earned from the invested funds. In 1991, Bennett invited non-profits to participate. During the next four years New Era took in more than $350 million. Participants included the American Red Cross, United Way, the Salvation Army, Wall Street money managers, Laurence Rockefeller and former U.S. Treasury Secretary William E. Simon. On May 15, 1995, *The Wall Street Journal* published an article suggesting that New Era was nothing more than a Ponzi scheme. Within hours of the publication, New Era filed for bankruptcy. Bennett was charged with fraud, filing false tax returns and money laundering, and is now serving a 12-year prison sentence. The New Era collapse has been described as one of the biggest scandals in the history of philanthropy. In the bankruptcy proceedings, charities received approximately 65% of what they placed with New Era. Sources: Stecklow, Steve, "New Era's Head Charged with Fraud," *The Wall Street Journal,* 9.30.96; SEC, Litigation Release No. 15637, 2/5/98; Case study, "Doubling Your Money in Six Months: The Foundation for New Era Philanthropy," Wake Forest University Law School, www.law.wfu.edu/courses/nonpro/CasebookSupp99.html.

Issues: Fraud; misplaced trust; informal management; pressure to find new sources of private funds.

Law of Unintended Consequences:

1. Foreign Aid to Africa

For over two centuries, missionaries, governments and NGOs have undertaken the task of trying to help Africans. Food, materials, and people (e.g. Peace Corps volunteers) have been sent to Africa to relieve hunger, dig wells or provide for other apparent needs. However, often the aid is either misguided or appropriated for the benefit of a few. For example, the leaders of a village convinced the Ministry of Education (allegedly by paying a bribe) to arrange for a Peace Corps volunteer to come to their village as a teacher. The idea was that a white teacher would attract students, school fees and donations to the school. But, when materials to build more classrooms arrived at the village, the leaders appropriated them to build additions to their houses and to expand their shops. Plus, aid agencies have little incentive to manage or question the system. In a food-for-work program, the more recipients signed up, even though many were too starved to work, the more government grant money was made available to administer the handouts. Source: Maren, Michael. *The Road to Hell: The Ravaging Effects of Foreign Aid and International Charity.* New York: The Free Press, 1997, pp. 1-12.

2. WHO's DDT in Borneo

In an attempt to control malaria in Borneo, the World Health Organization ("WHO") sprayed houses with DDT. The campaign killed mosquitoes and reduced the incidence of malaria, but it had side effects. House lizards ate the dead bugs, then cats ate the lizards and died from the accumulated insecticide. Without cats, the local rat population exploded – rats that could carry plague and typhus. Neighboring states donated cats to the affected upland regions. For the remote interior, the WHO and Singapore's Royal Air Force packed cats into perforated containers and dropped them into upland villages by parachute. Source: Strouse, Jean, "How to Give Away $21.8 Billion," *The New York Times, Sunday Magazine,* 4.16.00.

3. Russian Food Shipments

In 1999, the United States began shipping $1 billion in U.S. food aid to Russia. Officials from both sides claimed that the program was a win-win arrangement – Russians would be assured of food during a hard time and U.S. farmers would drain surpluses that were depressing commodity prices. In reality, the result would not be so rosy. Many Russians outside the government say they did not want the aid, and critics say the aid will not reach those who need it most. They note that Russia's problem is not a lack of food, but rather a lack of effective distribution and paying customers. Apparently Russian farmers have been exporting more grain than ever because they can't sell it at home. However, to avoid driving down prices, those portions of the aid shipped to the government are to be sold at market prices and would therefore not be available to those who could not pay. Earlier aid packages had been used by Western concerns to test market various products. For example, shipments of chicken legs so inundated the Russian market and drove prices down that Russian farmers had to destroy their chicken flocks because they could not afford to buy grain to feed them. Moreover, the same Russian officials and companies involved in the earlier aid package would be handling this one. Source: Whitehouse, Mark, "Western Food Shipments May Not Be What Russia Needs to Revive Economy," *The Wall Street Journal,* 3.12.99.

4. Aid in Response to War: Western Aid to Bosnia-Herzegovina, Rwanda, Liberia, Afghanistan and Sierra Leone
Wars and genocide in these countries have forced relief agencies and others to examine whether the aid they provide does more harm than good. For example, in organizing camps and shelters to comfort refugees driven from their homes in "ethnic cleansing" actions, humanitarian agencies were playing into the hands of the "cleansers." United Nations Secretary General Kofi Annan has said that relief efforts hide a lack of "will to address the root causes of conflicts." Some agencies are advocating a more cautious approach to relieving suffering, calling it "Tough Love." For centuries, humanitarian assistance has been guided by principles of neutrality, impartiality and consent of belligerents. Today, humanitarian emergencies often require both military intervention and relief aid. However, many combatants no longer respect the traditional rules. Lewis, Paul, "Humanitarians Worry The a Helping Hand Can Hurt," *The New York Times, 2.27.99*. Rony Brauman, "Hard Choices: Moral Dilemmas in Humanitarian Intervention" (Rowman & Littlefield, 1998)

5. Foreign Exchange Programs
Many educational exchanges between the United States and other countries have been undertaken with the intention of providing foreign students with training that will allow them to improve economic or social conditions in their homelands. Frequently, however, many of these students choose to remain in the U.S. after completing their education, thus depriving countries of origin of any benefit from the exchange and creating a "brain drain" of talented students away from less advanced nations. In one representative case, the public affairs officer at the American embassy in a former Soviet republic was forced to respond to accusations that two programs "are actually pursuing the goal of attracting smart youth from CIS countries to the USA." Virtually half the country's students do not subsequently return, and the American embassy warned that the programs, which cost U.S. taxpayers millions of dollars each year, might be frozen if the number of students choosing to stay in the United States continues to rise. Source: "Brain Drain May Halt US Educational Exchange Grants." *Courier*, 9.21.00.

Issues: Unintended consequences.

6. High-Risk Challenge Philanthropy
One danger of philanthropy is that would-be philanthropists may make the mistake of expecting that the promise of their resources gives them the right to dictate

policy to public and social-service sector institutions. Such expectations almost invariably meet with resentment from practitioners, as in the case of a generous Boston millionaire whose attempt to persuade six Massachusetts school districts to turn their elementary schools over to private management has encountered a chilly reception. The districts were promised $1 million each if the schools test scores did not exceed the district average after five years, but officials were unimpressed. "Why would we turn over a building, kids and the educational responsibility to an unknown group in running schools," asked one superintendent, "with the expectation that we'd only get a return on an investment if they failed?" Only one district so far has even been willing to discuss the issue. Source: "Review and Outlook: The Schools Millionaire" *The Wall Street Journal*, 9.14.00.

Issues: Naïve philanthropy; problematic relations between philanthropists and practitioners.

7. An Academic Mixed Blessing

CP generosity can trigger elevated expectations and competing institutional interests. Rensselaer Polytechnic Institute in Troy, N.Y, recently received an anonymous donation of $360 million, perhaps the largest gift ever to a U.S. college. Rensselaer has indicated in interest in using the gift "to catapult RPI into the top tier of technological-research universities."[273] Before doing so, it may be well-advised to benefit from the experience of Indiana's DePauw University, the recipient of a $128 million gift in 1995, that has learned of the unintended consequences of such an undertaking.[274] For DePauw, a 2,200 student school in central Indiana, the gift was more than 20 times its previous largest gift and, when added to its capital campaign then underway, helped triple the school's endowment. DePauw began "thinking at a different level." The gift was restricted to scholarships, so other funds DePauw had been using for aid was free to be spent elsewhere. The cost of modernizing the school's science building rose to $38 million from $5 million. Salaries were increased. Faculty sought to cut their teaching load from six courses a year to five. Full-time teachers rose by 30%, and full-time teachers required more office space than part-time faculty who had shared space if they had offices at all. "We've got scope creep," said the chairman of one of its departments. Tuition is up 20% since DePauw received the first payment from the gift in 1997. And, the task of fund raising has become more difficult, according to the school's president, as the size of the 1995 gift has become known.[275]

Wasted funds:

1. Gates Foundation
"You know, it would be possible to blow $100 billion" and have no impact at all, says Patricia Stonesifer, who manages the $21 billion Bill and Melinda Gates Foundation. Hardy, Quentin, The Radical Philanthropist, *Forbes Magazine*, 5/1/00.

2. Soros Foundation
"Charity goes against human nature. One of the paradoxes is that it makes people dependent. You can't rely on philanthropy to change the world." Borg, Linda, "Soros: Regulate global economy," *Providence Journal,* 10.21.99. Paradox of Charity: "Charity tends to turn recipients into objects of charity, and that is not what it is intended to accomplish" – corrupting influence: recipient and giver, "People flatter him and never tell him the truth."

3. Ted Turner's UN gifts
Several years ago, Ted Turner promised to donate $1 billion to the United Nations to be focussed on UNICEF. But, UNICEF has been criticized as wasteful with nearly half its budget being spent on its New York and regional offices. Giving intelligently is hard work. It demands research, patience and healthy skepticism. Unless practiced carefully, philanthropists' gifts may benefit primarily highly paid bureaucrats. Source: Frum, David, "Take My Billions, Please," *EnRoute*, 2.98.

4. Cost and terms of fund raising, external/internal, project, endowment, etc.
It has been argued that in certain circumstances the cost of endowment fund raising are much higher than meets eye on first inspection. One example cited in this regard concerned the efforts by a major east coast college to raise a $3 million endowment for a specific (from-scratch) faith-based center. The project sponsors indicated that only the IRS minimum of 5% would be established as the distribution hurdle and that fund management expense were estimated at approximately 2%. Even though the fund was clearly projected to earn much more given a planned heavy equity and alternative investment mix, some have urged that the cost really be measured relative to the amount distributed or 40% (2%/5%). Furthermore, the same observers have urged that the project overseers and funders view the cost of this fund raising approach as even much higher. This observation is quite critical of the annual use of such a small portion of the fund, i.e., $90,000

($3 million time 3% net funds spent). They contend that the opportunity cost of not utilizing a much greater percentage of the fund in a 3 to 5 year time frame carries a huge social cost. And, given the social mission of the project, they ask that this social opportunity cost be added into the all-in-cost of funding.

5. DARE (Drug Abuse Resistance Education)

Since 1983, 10,000 school districts in the United States have adopted the antidrug program DARE, in which police officers visit classrooms in an effort to discourage students from abusing illegal drugs, tobacco and alcohol. Although the program continues to grow in popularity, with more districts incorporating it into their curriculum each year, studies have indicated that DARE has no measurable effect in preventing later drug use by children who participate. Ross Anderson, mayor of Salt Lake City, Utah, recently cancelled the DARE program in his city's schools after concluding that "DARE is a complete waste of money and, even worse, fritters away the opportunity to implement a good drug prevention...." Anderson urged his superintendent to replace DARE, which had been costing the city $289,000 annually, with an alternative program with a better chance of producing results. Update: "In a striking shift, leaders of the nation's most widely used program to discourage drug use among schoolchildren have acknowledged that their strategy has not had sufficient impact and say they are developing a new approach to spreading their message."[276] In part, DARE is apparently responding to a change in perspective among federal education officials who distribute approximately $500 million in drug prevention money annually. As of 2000, DOE would no longer let funds from its office of safe and drug-free schools be allocated to DARE.[277] Records show DARE has $1.7 million from the Department of Justice, $215 million in indirect support from police departments, and $15 million in corporate support; indeed, "an industry has developed around the program and the sale of T-shirts, bumper stickers, textbooks, and even DARE affinity credit cards.[278] Since its founding 18 years ago, DARE is now taught in 75% of school districts nationwide and in 54 other countries.[279] "One six-year study by the University of Illinois found that the program's effects wore off by the senior year of high school: in fact, it detected some increase in drug use by suburban high school students who had taken the program."[280] Sources: Michael Janofsky, "Antidrug program's end stirs up Salt Lake City." *The New York Times*, 9.16.00. Zernike, Kate. "Antidrug Program Says It Will Adopt a New Strategy.*" New York Times*. February 15, 2001.

6. Overinvestment in Facilities

Community service organizations may feel that ownership or expansion of facilities will assist them in performing their missions by allowing them to acquire equity, giving them freedom and security in administering their programs, permitting them to accommodate more participants and offering them the chance to earn revenue through rentals of their space to other organizations. Lured by these and other inducements and negligent or unaware of accompanying disadvantages (such as debt and maintenance costs), such organizations may make investments in physical plants beyond their actual needs. The Nonprofit Finance Fund's feasibility study for its "Building for the Future" program reviewed a sample of Boys and Girls Clubs in the northeastern U.S. and concluded that that there is no correlation between physical plant and program management quality and that "square footage attracts neither members nor money." In fact, clubs spending the least on their buildings per square foot actually generated the highest proportion of revenues from building-driven activities. The study found that "dedicated leaders (not square footage) attract young people." Source: TBD.

7. Inexperienced Social Entrepreneurs

A senior religious leader from a distinct geographic area of a fourth world solicited a CP ("Capitalist/ Philanthropist") aggressively seeking funds for his religious program, and regaling the CP with stories of abject hardship. As represented, his entire religious program was being funded with an estimated $100,000 from a variety of sources, although no reliable financials or controls existed. This program included 17 geographically dispersed religious sites serving its members in a highly underdeveloped region. Stories of hardship abounded, including full-time religious staff being paid only $50 per month, malnourished children, nominal schooling, and almost non-existent prospects for employment. The religious leader claimed to have a wide range of deserving projects seeking funding but little venue to communicate the information to those with resources to assist. The CP's suggestions to communicate their messages via the Internet and attract resources were initially dismissed by the leader as prohibitively expensive.

The CP then offered to facilitate weekly publishing of brief summaries of worthy projects and other motivating stories on an Internet portal news site targeting the appropriate audience and absorb the cost request by the Internet site.

Several weeks after enthusiastically accepting the offer, the religious leader respectfully asked if it were possible to also receive some donation from the CP to help fund his budget. The CP offered $500 a month assuming 3 to 5 very short news briefs (100 to 200 words each) were provided weekly, expecting each would require no more than one hour to compose and e-mail. The annual donation would be $6,000 or 6% of the entire organization budget for an estimated 24 days of effort, an annualized rate of $72,000 ($31.25 per hour). To put this in context, within this region, annual compensation for professional non-religious teachers is $3,000 to $5,000 per year and religious staff earns supposedly less than $1,000 per year.

Quite surprisingly, the religious leader rejected the offer and suggested $500 for each of four "one-hour to compose" news briefs a week or $96,000 a year, almost 100% of the current budget. At $500 per hour, the religious leader found no difficulty in asking for an annualized compensation level of approximately $1 million. And, this request emerged from an initial claim of paying religious staff only $50 per month, managing 17 dispersed geographic sites on $100,000, and not having the funds to communicate project information via the Internet.

The CP progressed forward by posting the job/project offering directly on bulletin boards in various schools and religious sites in the region, hired several teachers, received a multiple of the initially expected productivity and effort - at the first proposed donation level - and proceeded to fund and raise additional funds for a wide range of competitively deserving regional projects in the impoverished region.

8. Oprah Winfrey's Families for a Better Life

This failure is one of the more common today in that it is an "unconstructive" failure in philanthropy, as it produces no knowledge because the funder either chose not communicate openly the results of the evaluation or did not conduct a sufficient evaluation. "Perhaps the most spectacular and wholly unconstructive failure in philanthropy occurred recently (article July/August 1998) in Chicago."[281]

In September of 1994, Ms. Winfrey announced that she would provide $3 million in funding to move 4,000 families out of public housing, off welfare, and toward independence. By 1996, the program had spent $1.3 million and had managed to serve only seven families. Of the five families, two dropped out of the program. The cost was from $250,000 to $400,000 plus per family. "Of course, these modest outcomes do not justify the program cost."[282]

No public narrative report on the program was written and no systematic outside evaluation was made available to other funders or the social sector. A wholly unconstructive failure that produced no systematic knowledge about the transition from welfare to work, it is particularly disappointing that this recent project proved so unconstructive, given the sizable resources that were invested, and the fact that information on what works and what does not in the area of welfare-to-work is now more urgently needed than ever before."[283]

APPENDIX T

INTERSECTORAL ILLUSTRATIVE EXAMPLES

A. Social Enterprise:
1. Social Entrepreneurship:
   a. Charityway.com, and many others, managed donations online for NGOs. Raised approximately $43 million. Its founder is Pete Mountanos.
   b. TransMedics, Inc., an organ transplant facilitator, raised $8 million. Expects to increase the supply of donor organs by 35%. Its founder is Dr. Waleed Hassanein.
   c. Edison Schools is a recent start up and publicly traded company that has assumed management of some of the most challenging public schools in the nation. Its visionary founder is Chris Whittle.
2. Commercialization:
   a. AARP's $150 million in licensing income.
   b. Girl Scouts $240 million in cookie revenues.
   c. National Geographic's advertising and subscription revenues.
   d. Bancroft, a $67 million residential treatment program for severely disabled children and adults.
   e. Stanford University Medical School's for-profit medical search engine, www.e-skolar.com.
   f. American Medical Association/ MEMED, for-profit JV linking doctors and patients through the Internet.
3. Operational Philanthropy:
   a. Pioneer's contract business for Boeing Inc. outsourcing.
   b. Universities and Federal Research: from 1981 to 1993, congressional earmarking for universities and colleges increased by over $750 million.
4. Contract Services:
   a. Lockheed-Martin IMS and Maximus, Inc. obtaining government welfare-human services contracts.
   b. Ivy League universities conducting corporate sponsored research projects.

    c. Columbia University's $140 million in projected 2000 income from licensing patents.

    d. Goodwill Industries and possibly Salvation Army are two of the world's largest NGO providers of employment and training services for challenged individuals.

B. Strategic Philanthropy & Restructuring:

  1. Capacity Building:

    a. REDF's Ongoing Assessment of Social Impacts (OASIS) - a cutting edge, comprehensive, social impact measurement system.

    b. ProFile - develops and services client tracking software for child welfare agencies. A joint venture between Ulhich Children's Home, The Catholic Charities, Lifelink Corp., Chicago Commons, and Ada S. McKinley.

    c. Partners for Community - management service organization between (MSO) (helps build capacity by combining overheads of NGOs) and Corporation for Public Management, New England Farm Workers' Council, Brightwood Development Corporation, Career Point, and International Language Institute of MA.

  2. Collaboration:

    a. United Negro College Fund management of Gates Billion Dollar Millennium Scholarship Program.

    b. Fathom.com - combined efforts of Columbia University, Cambridge University Press, London School of Economics, British Library and others to create a for-profit knowledge portal.

    c. Maryland Association of Nonprofits Survey observed that 58% of its members shared resources in 1998/1999.

    d. National Geographic/iExplore.com - National Geographic will acquire a 30 percent equity stake in iExplore, Internet resource for adventure and experiential travel. In addition, the firms will collaborate closely on the development of adventure and experiential travel content for magazines, television, and the Internet. National Geographic will provide content (articles, photography and images) for use on the iExplore.com site. Also, iExplore's site will be co-branded with the National Geographic logo.

  3. Managerial Efficiency Programs:

    a. Gates/Microsoft Library Technology Program.

    b. Community Wealth consulting business.

    c. The Morino Institute Netpreneur Program: a nonprofit organization created to advance Greater Washington's netpreneurs and the business they create.

4. Restructurings:
   a. Bronfman coordinated combination of three major Jewish organizations.
   b. Restructuring of National Association of Securities Dealers (NASD) from member owned to public stockholder owned.

5. Foundation Value Creation:
   a. Selecting Best Grantee: Steinhardt NYC schools selection.
   b. Signally Other Funders: Bronfman and Steinhardt on Birthright Israel; Monaghan 1000 plus member Legatus organization.
   c. Improving Performance of Grant Recipient: Soros's programs at Open Society; Spielberg's work on developing Shoah creations.
   d. Advancing the State of Knowledge and Practice: Milken's Knowledge Inc., and Cap CURE; Gates Drug research projects.

C. Social Capital Markets:

1. Innovative Financings:
   a. Recoverable grants- Provide for the return of capital under certain circumstances, treated as grants unless and until they are recovered- not considered PRIs by IRS.
   b. PRIs-over $700 million in existence, PRIs, program related investments, qualify for IRS 5% rule for distribution of financial assets. Additionally, PRI's economic returns (if any) will increase the endowment which can be used to advance the foundation's mission.
   c. College Board Initial Public Offering of testing service.
   d. Royalty payments for Children's Television Workshop (now Sesame Workshop) and National Wildlife Foundation.
   e. A reported public offering by securities by the Catholic in Brazil with the intent of providing a social return. Specifics to be determined.
   f. Japonica Intersectoral prospective blended SROI and FROI securities offerings.

2. Social Venture Capital
   a. Rensselaer Polytechnic Institute's venture capital incubator.
   b. Social Venture Partners in Seattle and Austin.
   c. Ashoka - Ashoka awards modest ($1,000s) stipends to "pattern changing visionaries" who apply their creativity and determination to solve social problems on a macro scale. Since its inception 1,000s of Ashoka fellows in over 40 countries have improved the social well

being of their communities.

d. Also, see Appendix C, Social Enterprise Investors.

3. Blended ROIs:

a. Roberts Enterprise Development Fund has several umbrella organizations that employ 600 individuals with [$200 TDB] million in projected revenue for 2000.

b. Total Renal Care publicly traded and serving 40,000 kidney dialysis patient annually had $1.5 billion in sales and a market capitalization of over $800 million.

c. Res-Care, a publicly traded company, delivers service and support to those with disabilities and special needs.

d. ITT Educational Services, a publicly traded company with $330 million in sales and almost $50 million in EBITDA, operates 67 educational institutes and serves over 26,000 students.

e. Bright Horizons Family Solutions provides day care centers to over 37,000 children with revenues of $300 million.

f. American Services Group provide health care solutions to correctional facilities and the military and has sales of in excess of $300 million.

4. M&A Transactions:

a. HMO conversations, e.g. PacifiCare, Columbia/HCA, SallieMae, FannieMae, etc.

b. Minnesota Public Radio's sale for $120 of catalogue business.

c. America's 2nd Harvest and FoodChain merger-influence from funders enabled the merger of two of the country's largest philanthropic entities devoted to distributing food to hungry Americans.

d. A Roman Catholic order of priests produced a feature film, "The Spitfire Grill," and reportedly marketed it for a $4 million profit.

APPENDIX U

MAIN OUTLINE

367

[1] Barringer, Felicity. "Moving Beyond the Four Horsemen of the Philanthropy Beat," New York Times, 20 November 2000.

[2] Tokasz, Jay. "Putting a Cold, Hard Number on the Value of Good Works," *New York Times,* 20 November 2000.

[3] *Ibid*.

[4] Light C. Paul. "Making Nonprofits Work: A Report on The Tides of Nonprofit Management Reform." The Aspen Institute Brookings Institution Press, 2000

[5] Morino Institute. "2001 Venture Philanthropy: The Changing Landscape." 2001, p.11.

[6] Weisbrod, Burton A. "To Profit or Not To Profit: The Commercial Transformation of the Nonprofit Sector." Massachusetts: Cambridge University Press, 1998, pp.5-6.

[7] Tuckman, Howard P. "Competition, commercialization, and the evolution of nonprofit organizational structures" 35. Edited by Weisbrod, Burton A. *To Profit or Not To Profit: The Commercial Transformation of the Nonprofit Sector.* Massachusetts: Cambridge University Press, 1998.

[8] *Ibid.,* 26.

[9] *Ibid.,* 39.

[10] Dees, Gregory J. Enterprising Nonprofits. Massachusetts: Harvard Business School Press, 1999, p. 147. The Dees Social Enterprise Spectrum illustrates a range from purely philanthropic to purely commercial issues, and also offers the motives, methods, and goals of the various stakeholder.

[11] Community Wealth Ventures, Inc. "Venture Philanthropy: Landscape and Expectations." Morino Institute, 2000, p. 15. Morino's work spans a spectrum

from pure social return on investment to pure financial return on investment. Viewing form left to right, the chart moves from traditional foundations, to hybrid foundations and social venture funds, which seek a blend of SROI and FROI, to community development funds, socially responsible FROI fund, and then to venture capital funds and other for-profit venture.

[12] Skloot, Edward. *The Nonprofit Entrepreneur: Creating Ventures to Earn Income*. The Foundation Center, 1988, p. 3.

[13] According to Skloot (pp. 3 to 7 of *The Nonprofit Entrepreneur*) there are many examples of entrepreneurial activity spread across a wide range of sector. He prefers to categorize the potential into these five categories: (1) "Program-related Products" including products for sales to organization members, participants, and the public at large, e.g. Girl Scout cookies that achieved gross sales in excess of $200 million in 1986, publishing activity such at the National Geographic which grossed $22 million in taxable advertising revenue in addition to its $152 million in untaxable subscription and membership revenues, and health related NGO's selling product such as Minnesota Public Radio. (2) Program Related Services such as gifts shops, food sales, and tours. The Metropolitan Museum of Art generated $40 million in revenue in 1986 and the Smithsonian generated $11 million in food and related sales. The American Jewish Congress is especially known for its tour programs. (3) Staff and Client Resources, where NGOs provide the expertise of their staff and clients in a variety of commercial ventures. WNET-13, the New York PBS, provides its production and post-production services to corporate and social sector clients. Numerous social service organizations have consulted for the private sector in designing alcoholism and drug treatment programs. According to Skloot, possibly the most lucrative area to develop in recent years is the long-term research contract between private corporations and universities. Some social service NGOs also employ their own clients in commercial activities, e.g. sheltered workshops such as Goodwill Industries, Salvation Army, and the Volunteers of America. (4) The Hard Property category includes the sale, lease, development, and rental of land and building. One example is Rensselaer Polytechnic Institute's decision to set aside campus facilities in "incubate" high technology industry and encourage successful ventures to stay in the local area. (5) Soft Property efforts encompass a cluster of income-earning assets that include copyrights, patents, trademarks, art and artifacts, and even mailing and membership lists. Two organization cited as being particularly active in this area in licensing products for royalty payments are the Children's Television Workshop (now, Sesame Workshop) and the National Wildlife Federation with its famous Ranger Rick character.

[14] Chapter Three of Burton A. Weisbrod's book "To Profit or Not to Profit: The Commercial Transformation of the Nonprofit Sector", titled " Modeling the nonprofit organization as a multi-product firm: A framework of choice" discusses three categories of goods to be sold by an NGO: 1. A preferred collective good, which is difficult to sell in private markets (e.g. donations- basic research, medical care for the poor, preservation of endangered animal species, or cultural heritage); 2. A preferred private good, which can be sold in private markets but which the nonprofit may wish to make available to some consumers independent of their ability to pay (e.g. user fees - access to higher education); and 3. A non-preferred private good, which is produced solely for the purpose of generating revenue for the preferred good (e.g. non-mission related - paid advertising on public television). See p. 49.

[15] Bill Shore's Chapter Eight, "You're Worth More Than You Think You Are," in *The Cathedral Within* offers a number of interesting insights. He categorizes defining assets as Things You Have + Things You Do: the three to four capabilities that can be leveraged to create community wealth. Other assets might include: access to celebrities, large membership, high-quality mailing lists, access to a low-cost workforce, knowledge of and credibility in local communities and neighborhoods, and an easily identifiable logo.

[16] Billitteri, Thomas, J. "Roberts Fund Puts Its Venture-Philanthropy Approach to the Test," *The Chronicle of Philanthropy.* June 1, 2000. Other works of direct interest of this point include: Emerson, Jed and Melinda Tuan. *The Roberts Enterprise Development Fund: Implementing a Social Venture Capital Approach to Philanthropy — A Case Study.* Graduate School of Business Stanford University, 1998.
Roberts Foundation and Homeless Economic Development Fund. "New Social Entrepreneurs: The Success, Challenge and Lessons of Non-Profit Enterprise Creation." September, 1996.

[17] Armstrong, David and Pesta, Jesse. "MIT, India Are Close to Asian Media Lab Pact," *Wall Street Journal*, 12 February 2001. With projected annual budget of $50 to $100 million, the Indian lab would outspend its counterparts in Ireland and the U.S.. The Irish government contributed about $35 million to host the European site and also provided a building to house the lab. The Indian government is reported to be providing 20% of the financing. The remained of the funding would come from private sponsors recruited by the government and MIT, much in the way the U.S. media lab taps large corporations. Media Lab Europe has an annual budget of about $29 million, while the U.S. lab on the MIT campus has a budget of nearly $40 million a year. The Media lab is well-know outside the U.S. prima-

rily because of the celebrity in technology circles of lab founder Nicholas Negroponte.

[18] Press, Eyal and Washburn Jennifer. "The Kept University," *The Atlantic Monthly*, March 2000. 46.

[19] Shore, Bill. *The Cathedral Within*. New York: Random House, 1999, 207.

[20] Arenson, Karen. "Cornell Will Open a Medical School in the Persian Gulf," *New York Times,* 9 April 2001.

[21] Markoff, John. "Intel Joins Cancer Research Effort," *New York Times*, 4 April 2001.

[22] Kirkpatrick, David. "2 Harry Potter Spinoffs Done for Charity," *New York Times,* 12 March 2001.

[23] Weisbrod, Burton A. "Modeling the nonprofit organization as a multiproduct firm: A framework for choice" in *To Profit or Not to Profit*, 58.

[24] Stanley, Alessandra. "Modern Marketing Blooms In Medieval Vatican Library," *New York Times*, 8 January 2001. The web site selling Vatican offerings is www.1451.com. The less positive situations referenced in the article include a failed 1988 licensing deal that resulted in the Vatican paying an $8.8 million settlement and $1.3 million in legal fees. The sad facts were apparently detailed in a lengthy 1998 New Yorker article.

[25] At a November 1998 conference, "Building Creative Assets," arts and culture foundations conferred with Hollywood entertainment industry to brainstorm about how to develop collaboration between entertainment industry and NGO art organizations. Coordinated by Americans for the Arts, the conference identified a number of pathways to such collaboration, both for Los Angles, the world capital of the entertainment industry, and the nation as a whole. Source: Becker, Thomas E. "Innovation in Context: New Foundation Approaches to Evaluation, Collaboration, and Best Practices." November 1999, 23.

[26] *Ibid.*

[27] La Piana, David. "Beyond Collaboration: Strategic Restructuring of Nonprofit Organizations." James Irvine Foundation, 1997, 5.

[28] Toward that more flexible embrace, La Piana give the funding community a simple list of questions that the social sector must ask itself as it considers restructuring: "(1) how can the options for NGO strategic restructuring be best defined and described, (2) is the climate right for strategic restructuring and will it improve the functioning of the individual NGO, (3) what pressures lead nonprofits to consider mergers, consolidation, and joint ventures, and what difficulties prevent them from bringing these efforts to fruition, (4) how can funders encourage NGOs to undertake strategic restructuring without being perceived as applying pressure to do so, and (5) what educational activities can funders promote to encourage strategic restructuring activities." La Piana, "Beyond Collaboration: Strategic Restructuring of Nonprofit Organizations." 5.

[29] Tuckman, "Competition, commercialization, and the evolution of nonprofit organizational structures," 40- 42.

Holding Company Alternatives:

- Strategy I: Unrelated Passive Income Strategy. For-profit activity where the sole purpose of producing income for the nonprofit parent, and the parent has nothing to do with the operations of the subsidiary.
- Strategy II: Passive Investment Cost Reducing. Its goal is to create competitive advantage by finding ways to lower the cost of delivering a service.
- Strategy III: Active Investment Revenue Producing. One in which the nonprofit involves itself in both the development and operation of its acquired subsidiary.

Joint Venture Alternatives: (Examples provided relate to the health care field, but have wider application)

- Ancillary-Service Ventures are partnerships between hospitals and physicians designed to provide services that the partners share in common.
- Third-Party Contracting Ventures are established to facilitate contracting with health insurance companies, HMOs, and similar organizations.
- Leased-Space Ventures are used by hospitals to facilitate construction of medical office building facilities.
- Specialty Ventures partner hospitals with specialized for-profits firms that provide services to complement or substitute those the hospital would otherwise provide.

[30] *Ibid.*, 42.

[31] CPs seeking further guidance of value creation opportunities now have the benefit of an expanding base of literature. Several worth noting include: James Austin's "Collaborative Challenge: How Nonprofits and Businesses Succeed Through Strategic Alliances," Curt Weeden's "Corporate Social Investing: The Breakthrough Strategy for Giving and Getting Corporate Contributions," Sagawa and Segal's "Common Interest - Common Good: Creating Value through Business and Social Sector Partnerships," Svendsen's "The Stakeholder Strategy: Profiting from Collaborative Business Relationships," and Bill Shore's *Revolution of the Heart: A New Strategy for Creating Wealth and Meaningful Change or The Cathedral Within.* And, to a lesser extent, chapters five and six of Clotfelter and Ehrlich's compilation "Philanthropy and the Nonprofit Sector in a Changing America." From a more statistical and study perspective, David La Piana, et al. in June of 2000, published findings from a study of integrations and alliances among nonprofit social service and cultural organizations in the United States.

[32] Shore, *The Cathedral Within*, 131-132. Furthermore, Shore disciple Guy Mulhair discusses a concept he calls "operational philanthropy." He urges companies to give his social sector organizations work instead of money. They will convert that to jobs and hire the people they won't hire. The corporations will receive products and services at a competitive rate. One of the more useful features of the book is an extensive list of successful social sector enterprises including a feature film by an order of Roman catholic priests (The Spitfire Grill); Minnesota Public Radio's sale of its catalog business for $120 million;; Store for Knowledge, a Los Angles based retail chain with an estimated $100 million in sales in 1998; Patagonia's social activism programs; Pioneer Human Services (which has become the largest and most self-sustaining human service agency of its kind) and Community Wealth Ventures, a subsidiary of Share Our Strength that provides consulting services to the social sector.

[33] Estelle, James. "Commercialism among nonprofits: Objectives, opportunities, and constraints." Page 285 in To Weisbrod, *To Profit or Not to Profit.*

[34] Salamon, Lester M. "Holding the Center: America's Nonprofit Sector at a Crossroads." New York: The Nathan Cummings Foundation. 1997. XIV.

[35] Shore, *The Cathedral Within*, 208.

[36] Williams, Grant. "The Bush Brand of Charity," *The Chronicle of Philanthropy*, 6 April 2000.

[37] *Ibid.*

[38] *Ibid.*

[39] "George W. Bush: Charity Pledges," *Chronicle of Philanthropy*, 6 April 2000. Seven elements of his faith-based plan follow: 1) Would change federal law and regulations to explicitly allow religious and other non-profit organizations to compete for government money to provide social services. 2) Would appoint a White House official whose sole responsibility would be to make sure faith-based groups were able to participate - without being "secularized or slighted" - in providing social services. 3) Would encourage states to establish similar offices by providing federal matching funds. 4) Would run a test program to determine the effectiveness of providing federal money to faith-based charities that work with prison inmates. 5) Would offer federal grants to faith-based and community groups that help the children of prisoners from low-income families. 6) Would make federal grants for drug treatment available to states with the requirement that non-medical, faith-based providers are eligible for the money on the same basis as other groups. 7) Would open certain federal after-school programs to greater involvement by faith-based and community groups.

[40] Smalhout, James H. "The World Bank's New Clients." Barron's. 25 September 2000, 59.

[41] *Ibid.*

[42] *Ibid.*

[43] The Foundation Center. "Foundation Growth and Giving Estimates: 1999 Preview." New York: The Foundation Center, 2000, 3.

[44] *Ibid.*

[45] *Ibid.*

[46] Steinberg, Jacques. "Harvard's $2.1 Billion Tops Colleges' Big Fund-Raising," *New York Times*, 7 October 1999.

[47] Hruby, Laura and Schwinn, Elizabeth. "Big Funds See a Dip in Assets," *The Chronicle of Philanthropy*, 19 February 2001.

[48] *Ibid.*

[49] Lewin, Tamar. "In an Uncertain Climate, Philanthropy Is Slowing," *New York Times*, 19 February 2001.

[50] Hruby, Laura et al., "Big Funds See a Dip in Assets."

[51] Lewin, Tamar. "Foundation Grants Surged Last Year Despite Slowing Economy," *New York Times,* 27 March 2001.

[52] The Foundation Center. "Foundation Growth and Giving Estimates," 2001.

[53] Schervish, Paul G and Havens, John J. "The 2000 Study on Wealth with Responsibility." Bankers Trust Private Banking, Boston College Social Welfare Research Institute, and the University of Massachusetts Boston Center for Survey Research. 2000.

[54] Johnston, David Cay. "A Larger Legacy Await Generations X,Y, and Z," *New York Times*, 20 October 1999.

[55] Salamon, Lester M. "Holding the Center: America's Nonprofit Sector at a Crossroads." New York: The Nathan Cummings Foundation, 1997, 51.

[56] Johnston, "A Larger Legacy Await Generations X,Y, and Z."

[57] Johnston, "A Larger Legacy Await Generations X,Y, and Z."

[58] Hunt, Albert R. "Charitable Giving: Good but We Can Do Better," *Wall Street Journal*, 21 December 2000. The report can be found on the Council's web site: "Philanthropy in the American Economy: A Report by the Council of Economic Advisers." This report is a follow-up to the 1999 White House Conference on Philanthropy.

[59] Dillin, John. "Newly Rich Escalate Estate-Tax Fight," *The Christian Science Monitor*, 7 September 2000.

[60] *Ibid.*

[61] Dunn, Julie. "Maybe Charity is Contagious," *New York Times*, 9 September 2000.

[62] Norton, Leslie P. "The Wealth Revolution," *Barron's,* 18 September 2000. 33.

[63] *Ibid.*

[64] *Ibid.*

[65] *Ibid.*, 34.

[66] *Ibid.*, 34.

[67] *Ibid.*, 34.

[68] *Ibid.*, 34.

[69] Scholl, Jaye. "The Pilgrim: Don McClanen Offers the Wealthy a Different Kind of Freedom," *Barron's,* 18 September 2000, 40.

[70] Uchitelle, Louis. "Working Families Strain to Live Middle-Class Life," *New York Times*, 9 September 2000.

[71] *Ibid.*

[72] *Ibid.*

[73] Zernike, Kate. "Gap Widens Again on Tests Given to Blacks and Whites," *New York Times*, 25 August 2000.

[74] *Ibid.*

[75] *Ibid.*

[76] Community Wealth Ventures, Inc. "Venture Philanthropy: Landscape and Expectations." Morino Institute, 2000, 1.

[77] La Piana, "Beyond Collaboration: Strategic Restructuring of Nonprofit Organizations," 14.

[78] Carnegie, Andrew. *The Gospel of Wealth.* Massachusetts: Applewood Books, 1889, 19.

[79] Magnet, Myron. "What Makes Charity Work?" Chicago: Ivan R. Dee, 2000, 145

[80] Reis, Tom. *Unleashing New Resources and Entrepreneurship for the Common Good.* Michigan: W. K. Kellogg Foundation, 1999, 1.

[81] Kristina A. Kazarian, Interview with Edgar Bronfman, Sr. New York, New York. 12 October 1999.

[82] *Ibid.*

[83] *Ibid.*

[84] *Ibid.*

[85] *Ibid.*

[86] Kristina A. Kazarian, Interview with Richard Marker. New York, New York. September 25, 1999.

[87] *Ibid.*

[88] Cabrera, Luis. "Gates, Allen Philanthropy Differs." Associated Press, 18 November 2000.

[89] Verhovek, Sam Howe. "Bill Gates Turns Skeptical on Digital Solutions' Scope," *New York Times*, 3 November 2000.

[90] *Ibid.*

[91] *Ibid.*

[92] Barrett, Amy. "Questions for William H. Gates Sr.: Affairs of State," *New York Times Magazine*, 18 March 2001.

[93] Moore, Geoffery. Conversation with Kristina Kazarian regarding Michael Milken and his Foundations. December 2001.

[94] Arenson, Karen W. "Art, Wildlife and a Bit of Investing," *New York Times*, 12 November 2000.

[95] Porter, Michael E. and Mark Kramer. "Philanthropy's New Agenda: Creating Value," *Harvard Business Review*, November-December 1999.

[96] Backer, Thomas E. "Innovation in Context: New Foundation Approaches to Evaluation, Collaboration, and Best Practices. Study conducted for the John S. and James L. Knight Foundation." November 1999, 1.

[97] Mehrling, Perry. *Spending Policies for Foundations: The Case for Increased Grants Payout.* National Network of Grantmakers, 1999.

[98] Dundjershi, Marina. "To Live Forever, Foundations Should Give Away the Minimum, Report Says," *The Chronicle of Philanthropy*, 18 November 1999. Kogelman, Stanley and Thomas Dobler. Sustainable Spending Policies for Endowments and Foundations. New York: Goldman, Sachs & Co., November 1999.

[99] Smart Money. "Give and Take." SmartMoney.com. www.smartmoney.com. 2 January 2001.

[100] Abelson, Reed. "Charities Investing: Left Hand, Meet Right." *New York Times* 11 June 2000.

[101] Mehrling, Perry. *Spending Policies for Foundations: The Case for Increased Grants Payout.*
National Network of Grantmakers, 1999. 1.

[102] Revkin, Andrew C. "Nonprofits Facing Ethical Challenges Over Sales of Land," *New York Times*, 16 September 2000.

[103] *Ibid.*

[104] *Ibid.*

[105] Arenson, Karen. "Princeton to Replace Loans with Student Scholarship," *New York Times*, 28 January 2001.

[106] Porter, Michael E. and Mark Kramer. "Philanthropy's New Agenda: Creating Value," *Harvard Business Review*, November-December 1999.

[107] In certain situations, CP analysis merited relative asset weighting, comparative

CPs	Annual Percentage Qualifying Distribution	Concentration of 5 largest Initiatives(a)	Average Dollar Grant (Approximates)	Average Dollar Grant for Top 5 Initiatives	Percentage of Assets Invested in Indexed Equities
Bronfman	43%	53%	$129,000	$934,000	40% to 60%
Gates	11%	60%	$3,524,000	$66,358,000	Nominal
Milken	18%	83%	$672,000	$1,360,000	Nominal
Monaghan	200%	93%	$1,360,000	$3,290,000	Nominal
Soros	49%	100%	$108,850,000	$108,850,000	Nominal
Spielberg	100%	100%	$21,411,000	$21,411,000	Nominal
Steinhardt	37%	63%	$222,000	$974,000	Nominal
Average	65%	79%	$19,453,000	$29,025,000	Nominal
Medium	43%	83%	$1,360,000	$1,360,000q	Nominal
High	100%(a)	100%	$108,850,00	$108,850,000	40% to 60%
Low	11%	53%	$129,000	$934,000	Nominal

annualization, adjustments for more recent information, and normalization of isolate aberrant data points. For example, the high-end of the range for annual distributions is 200% for the Live-Founders, but indicating the high end as the second ranking CP at 100% illustrates the point without creating the issues of associated with a percent exceeding 100%. The Gates asset base at the beginning of the year is utilized rather than monthly average as the $10.4 billion year to year increase places obvious on distribution execution. The detailed CP data is as follows:

(a) Grants to same and affiliated organizations, including intra-year grants and multi-location organizations, are combined; as are grants to comparable mission organizations.
(b) Excludes Monaghan at 200%.

[108] *Ibid.*

[109] Porter, Michael E. and Mark Kramer. "Philanthropy's New Agenda: Creating Value," *Harvard Business Review*, November-December 1999, 127.

[110] *Ibid.*

[111] *Ibid.*, 129.

[112] *Ibid.*, 129.

[113] *Ibid.*, 128.

[114] *Ibid.*, 128-129.

[115] *Ibid.*, 128.

[116] *Ibid.*, 128.

[117] Magnet, "What Makes Charity Work?" 145.

[118] Porter discusses four strategies to advance value creation: (1) The goal is superior performance in a chosen arena. (2) Strategy depends on choosing a unique position. (3) Strategy rest on unique activities. (4) Every positioning requires trade-offs.

[119] Porter, "Philanthropy's New Agenda: Creating Value," 126.

[120] Press, Eyal and Washburn, Jennifer. "The Kept University," *The Atlantic Monthly*, March 2000, 46.

[121] Horvath, Peter. "Why We Give." *The American Benefactor*, Winter 1997, 90-99.

[122] See, Appendix E: Sectarian Support for NP Benchmarking.

[123] Magnet, "What Makes Charity Work?" 148.

[124] One such organization that offers consulting services to those interested in philanthropy is The Philanthropic Initiative, Inc. out of Boston. One of their publications, "Philanthropy for the Wise Investor: A Primer for Families On Strategic Giving," contains a useful organization introductory framework. Seven areas worth mentioning: (1) The wise investor perspective, (2) Thinking strategically from four perspectives: identify and examine motivating reasons, align values with the philanthropic interests, find ways to truly make a difference, and organize the work of giving, (3) Simplicity and organization, (4) Building on due diligence, (5) Looking for gaps and leadership opportunities, (6) Leveraging your giving, and (7) Considering non-traditional approaches.

[125] Skloot, Edward. "The Nonprofit Entrepreneur: Creating Ventures to Earn Income." The Foundation Center, 1988, 7.

[126] Saul, Jason. "Benchmarking Workbook for Nonprofit Organizations," Wilder Publishing Center, TBP: 48.

[127] Morino Institute. "2001 Venture Philanthropy: The Changing Landscape." 2001, 5.

[128] *Ibid.*, 10.

[129] Gallagher, Michael K. "More-Effective Foundations: Making the Dream a Reality," "Chronicle of Philanthropy," 13 January 2000, 60.

[130] Dees, Gregory J. *Enterprising Nonprofits.* Massachusetts: Harvard Business School Press, 1999, 139.

[131] Powell, Walter W. and Owen-Smith, Jason. "Universities as creators and retailers of intellectual property: Life-sciences research and commercial development." 187. Weisbrod, Burton A. *To Profit or Not To Profit: The Commercial Transformation of the Nonprofit Sector.*

[132] *Ibid.*

[133] Porter, "Philanthropy's New Agenda: Creating Value," 130.

[134] Weisbrod, *To Profit or Not To Profit: The Commercial Transformation of the Nonprofit Sector,* 290.

[135] Emerson, Jed and Melinda Tuan. *The Roberts Enterprise Development Fund: Implementing a Social Venture Capital Approach to Philanthropy – A Case Study.* Graduate School of Business Stanford University, 1998: 17.

[136] Smart Money. "Give and Take." SmartMoney.com. www.smartmoney.com. 02 January 2001

[137] Emerson, Jed. "A Social Capital Markets Analysis: Inquires into the Nature of Investment, Elements of Return, and A Blended Value Proposition." *Working Paper in Draft.* Internal Working Group Version. July 2000. 27.

[138] Camp, Robert C. *Global Cases in Benchmarking: Best Practices from Organizations Around the World.* Wisconsin: ASQ Quality Press, 1998. 184.

[139] Certain of the more interesting case studies contained in the book include the following. NGO section: a benchmarking study on Improving the Outcomes of Cardiac Surgery by the Northern New England Cardiovascular Disease Study Group, and a benchmarking "On-The-Job Training - Singapore Productivity and Standards Board." NGO educational section: a benchmarking study on Enrollment Management at Babson College by Babson College, a benchmarking study on Collaborative Benchmarking in Higher Education by Oregon State University, and a Queensland University benchmarking study on Law Research Supervision at Queensland University, "Government Sector: Water Supply and Sewerage Benchmarking Study" by Australia's Department of Land and Water Conservation, a benchmarking study on First-Class Post Office Supply Chain by the UK Post Office, a study titled "Serving the American Public: Best Practices in Resolving Customer Complaints" by Vice President Al Gore's National Performance Review- Federal Benchmarking Consortium. Camp, Robert C. *Global Cases in Benchmarking: Best Practices from Organizations Around the World.*

[140] *Ibid.*, 397.

[141] *Ibid.*, 613.

[142] Weisbrod, Burton A., Modeling the nonprofit organization as a multiproduct firm: A framework for choice, "To Profit or Not To Profit," Weisbrod, ed., United Kingdom, Cambridge University Press, 1998, p. 50.

[143] Andrews, Fred. "Thinking Great Thoughts Without Great Money," *New York Times,* 12 Jan. 2000.

[144] "New Alliance to Develop Drugs to Fight Tuberculosis," *Philanthropy New Digest*, 10 October 2000. Volume 6, Issue 42. TB causes more than two million deaths each year, or about 5,500 deaths a day, most of them in the world's poorest countries. There hasn't been a new class of TB drugs developed in more than 30 years, and existing medicines are losing their efficacy as the disease continues to build up resistance to them. The Global Alliance is committed to improving TB control by discovering, developing, and making anti-TB drugs available — particularly in the countries worst hit by the disease — at affordable prices. The alliance expects the first new drug to be registered by 2010. "Development of Anti-TB Treatments Affordable in Worst-Hit Countries is Aim of New, Global Public-Private Partnership." *AScribe*

News 10/10/2000. Furthermore, an October 10, 2000 article in the *New York Times*, "Study Finds Poverty Deepening in Former Communist Countries", reported that at least 50 million children in Eastern Europe and the former Soviet Union live in poverty and are exposed to tuberculosis levels usually associated with the third world. Tuberculosis rates have risen in Eastern Europe, with an average 67.6 cases per 1,000 people in 1997. That compared with 49.6 percent in Arab states, 47.6 percent in Latin America and 35.1 percent in eastern Asia. Tuberculosis rates ranged from 20 per 1,000 in the Czech Republic to 80 per 1,000 in Lithuania, Turkmenistan, Latvia and Russia, and 150 per 1,000 in Georgia.

[145] Streeter, Ryan. "Where the Mission Meets the Market." Welfare Policy Center of the Hudson Institute. www.welfarereformer.org. (January 2001). Description of three models follow: Jobs/Community Partnerships - Local churches lead former welfare recipients and other job-needy individuals through faith-based employment curriculum, refer them to jobs provided by local business partners, and then maintain extended mentor relationships. Business Partnerships - ServiceMaster Corporation assists homeless shelters begin landscaping, housekeeping, and other service-related businesses by training their contracts with customers. It acts as subcontractor to the shelters. Investor Relationships/Partnerships - REDF, a foundation in the San Francisco Bay area, acts a philanthropic "venture capitalist" by providing nonprofit-run enterprises that serve homeless and other needy people with assistance in business strategy, capital, and other business-capacity enhancing services, including business analysts, MBA interns, and expanded area business networks.

[146] Emerson, Jed. "A Social Capital Markets Analysis," 33

[147] The Roberts Enterprise Development Fund. "SROI Overview: SROI Reports - REDF." 2001.

[148] Hardy, Quentin. "The Radical Philanthropist." Forbes. May 1, 2000.

[149] Powell, Walter W. and Owen-Smith, Jason. "Universities as creators and retailers of intellectual property: Life-sciences research and commercial development." Weisbrod, "To Profit or Not to Profit". 188.

[150] Benson, Dennis K. "PY97 Return on Investment: Technical Report." Appropriate Solutions, Inc. Ohio. March 1999. Benson material highlights three ROI calculations: ROI-T, ROI-D, and ROI-E. The time period of his studies under modeling ranges from 12 to 20 years. ROI-T is the Return on Investment to the Taxpayer, which seek estimate the amount of money which is theoretically avail-

able to be returned to the state and federal treasury. In one study for the Silicon Valley Private Industry Council (PY97 Return on Investment - Technical Report), ROI-T estimates potential savings in the Temporary Assistance to Needy Families program, potential savings in Food Stamp expenditures, projected increased personal income taxes to California and to the Federal government, and individual and company contributions to FICA. ROI-D is the Return on Investment Disposable Income. The theory behind ROI-D is that the goal of increasing an individual's economic independence is met not just by replacing public assistance dollars with wage dollars but by increasing the net amount of dollars the individual has to spend. ROI-D assesses whether or not this disposable income has increased. Increased earnings are reduced by lower welfare payments and by contributions to the tax base. According to Benson, if the result is a positive number, then new money has been made available to be spent in the local economy. ROI-E, the Return on Investment Economic Impact, appears to be similar to an economic multiple concept that seek to measure and estimate to the 'ripple' effect that each dollar has on an economy. ROI-E apparently uses an methodology similar to the US Department of Commerce developed Regional Input-effect Modeling Systems (RIMS-II model). ROI-E uses two RIMS-II multipliers in its calculations. The estimated increase in disposable income (ROI-D) and the total cost of the workforce programs are each subjected to different multipliers. Benson believes that the existence of the workforce programs in the community is a valid economic stimulus and is included as an economic benefit. Also included are the increased tax contributions and the increased FICA payments. The result is an estimate of what the workforce program and its results mean to the economy financially.

[151] Carnegie, *The Gospel of Wealth,* 15.

[152] Goddeeris and Weisbrod, "Conversion from nonprofit to for-profit legal status: Why does it happen and should anyone care?" in *To Profit or Not to Profit*, edited by Weisbrod, 143.

[153] University of Minnesota. Research Review: "John M. Olin Foundation," June 1998.

[154] Camp , Robert C. *Benchmarking: The Search for Industry Best Practices that Lead to Superior Performance*. New York: ASQ Quality Press, 1989.

[155] McNeil, Donald G. Jr. "Oxfam Joins Campaign to Cut Drug Prices to Poor Nations," *New York Times*, 13 February 2001. Oxfam indicated that it will pressure companies by attacking them before audiences on Wall Street and in the City

of London. Oxfam will also call for a $5 billion fund to subsidize research on curing diseases like malaria, elephantiasis, tuberculosis and sleeping sickness, which are endemic to poor countries. Campaigners like Oxfam have demanded that poor countries be allowed to change their patent laws so that they can import, without fear of trade retaliation, generic versions of anti-AIDS drugs, powerful antibiotics and other lifesaving medicines made in Brazil, Canada, India, or Thailand. Glaxo, the major drug company, claims that generic companies that manufacture patented drugs are "pirates of the high seas," and that Glaxo is giving these people drugs at costs, which are better than the generic houses can do, or simple giving them away. They view attacking the patent process would destroy the drug industry and hurt export earning.

[156] Bogan, *Benchmarking for Best Practices.* 234.

[157] Morino Institute. "2001 Venture Philanthropy: The Changing Landscape". 2001. The Flatiron Foundation of New York City. 73.

[158] Andrews, Fred. "Thinking Great Thoughts Without Great Money," *New York Times,* 12 January 2000.

[159] Johnston, David Cay. "For Checking Out a Charity Remember the Number 990," *New York Times*, 20 November 2000.

[160] *Ibid.*

[161] "George W. Bush: Charity Pledges." *The Chronicle of Philanthropy.* 6 April 2000.

[162] Robertson, Patrick. "Mr. Bush's Faith-Based Initiative Is Flawed," *Wall Street Journal,* 12 March 2001.

[163] Deutsch, Claudia H. "Competitors Can Teach You a Lot, but the Lessons Can Hurt: The Many Obstacles to Benchmarking," *New York Times,* 19 January 1999.

[164] Emerson, Jed and Melinda Tuan. "The Roberts Enterprise Development Fund: Implementing a Social Venture Capital Approach to Philanthropy – A Case Study." Graduate School of Business Stanford University, 1998: 11.

[165] Watson, Gregory H. *Strategic Benchmarking: How to Rate Your Company's Performance Against the World's Best.* New York: John Wiley and Son, Inc., 1993. 49.

[166] Lowell, Stephanie. "Careers In The Nonprofit Sector." Harvard Business School Publishing, 2000: 6.

[167] Light, Paul. *Sustaining Innovation: Creating Nonprofit and Government Organizations That Innovate Naturally.* San Francisco: Jossey-Bass Publishers, 1998: 121.

[168] Schochet, Bob. *Chronicle of Philanthropy.* c. 2000.

[169] Camp, *Benchmarking*, 285-326.

[170] La Piana, "Beyond Collaboration: Strategic Restructuring of Nonprofit Organizations," 9.

[171] Frank, Robert H. "What Price the Moral High Ground?" *Southern Economic Journal*, 63, July 1996, 1-17.

[172] Shore, "The Cathedral Within," 232.

[173] Dunham, Kemba J. "Getting Ahead: John W. Rowe," *Wall Street Journal*, 12 September 2000.

[174] Hafner, Katie. "Technology Boom Too Tempting for Many Government Scientists," *New York Times*. 9 September 2000.

[175] *Ibid.*

[176] *Ibid.*

[177] Ehrbar, Al. "EVA: The Real Key to Creating Wealth." John Wiley & Sons, Inc.: New York, 1998, 147-160.

[178] Lowell, Stephanie. "The Harvard Business School Guide to Careers in the Nonprofit Sector," Massachusetts: Harvard Business School Publishing, 2000. Two especially useful features are the subsector listing and the resources information on these subsectors. The subsector job categories include: [1] arts and culture (fine arts, performing arts, and public television and radio stations), [2] community economic development (housing development and workforce development), [3] community development financial institutions (community development loan funds, community development venture capital funds, community

development credit unions, microenterprise development institutions, and community development banks), [4] education (early childhood, K-12, higher education, and other education-related fields), [5] environment (advocacy groups, policy research organizations, preservation and land trusts, educational institutions, and environmental responsibility and 'green' marketing), [6] foundations (private/independent foundations, family foundations, community foundations, corporate foundations, and operating foundations), [7] government (federal government and state and local government), [8] health care (direct care providers, services supporting provision of care, insurance providers, public health, and medical supply, device, and pharmaceutical manufactures), [9] international aid and economic development (multilateral development organizations, relief organizations, international microfinace organizations, think tanks, private sector consultants, foundations, advocacy organizations), [10] Social services (umbrella organizations; aging; AIDS treatment, prevention, and advocacy; alcohol, and substance abuse treatment; children and youth; family support; domestic violence support; food security/hunger; homelessness; multiservice organizations) [11] Social purpose businesses (stand-alone social purpose businesses and subsidiary social purpose businesses), and [12] Socially responsible business/corporate community relations.

There is also an excellent Resource Road Map section that contains general social sector information as well as an impressive listing, for the subsectors mentioned above, of associations, publications, Harvard Business School case studies, and organizations. Extensive Internet source information is provided.

[179] Marks, Alexandra. "Drawing a Line in the School Yard," *The Christian Science Monitor*, 8 September 2000.

[180] *Ibid.*

[181] Goldberg, Carey. "Auditing Classes at M.I.T., on the Web and Free," *New York Times,* 4 April 2001.

[182] Nelson, Stephen J. "What Can Managers Learn From Nonprofits?" *Harvard Management Update*, 1999.

[183] Sievers, Bruce. "If Pigs Had Wings," *Foundation News & Commentary,* November/December 1997.

[184] Tokasz, Jay. "Putting a Cold, Hard Number on the Value of Good Works," *New York Times*, 20 November 2000.

[185] Sievers, Bruce and Tom Layton.. "Best of the Worst Practices." *Foundation News and Commentary,* March-April 2000: 1

[186] Janofsky, Michael. "Antidrug Program's End Stirs Up Salt Lake City," *New York Times,* 16 September 2000.

[187] *Ibid.*

[188] *Ibid.*

[189] Nelson, Stephen J. "What Can Managers Learn From Nonprofits?" *Harvard Management Update,* 1999: 4.

[190] Porter, Michael E and Mark Kramer. "Philanthropy's New Agenda: Creating Value." Harvard Business Review: November-December 1999: 130.

[191] Dunham, Kemba J. "Getting Ahead: John W. Rowe," *Wall Street Journal,* 12 September 2000.

[192] Barringer, Felicity. "Public Radio at Center of Ownership Debate," *New York Times,* 5 March 2001.

[193] Wyatt, Edward and Goodnough, Abby. "Confusion, Then Fervent Opposition to a Plan to Privatize 5 Schools," *New York Times,* 31 March 2001.

[194] Wyatt, Edward. "Higher Scores Aren't Cure-All, School Run for Profit Learns." *New York Times,* 13 March 2001.

[195] Hartocollis, Anemona. "As Election on Privatizing Schools Winds Down, Call Goes Out for Plan B," *New York Times,* 1 April 2001.

[196] Myers, Michele Tolela. "A Student Is Not an Input," *New York Times,* 26 March 2001.

[197] Williams, Grant. "Government, Charities, and Business Will Join Forces, Bush Advisor Predicts.*" Chronicle of Philanthropy,* 13 January 2000: 24.

[198] Watson, Gregory H. "Strategic Benchmarking: How to Rate Your Company's performance Against the World's Best." New York: John Wiley and Son, Inc., 1993: 194.

[199] Letts, Ryan, and Grossman. "High Performance Nonprofit Organizations Benchmarking: An Organizational Process That Links Learning and Results." New York: John Wiley and Son, Inc., 1999: 101-102.

[200] Johnston, David Cay. "United Way Faces Crisis As President Plans to Leave," *New York Times*. 19 September 2000.

[201] Emerson, Jed. "A Commitment to Accountability: The Coming Challenge to Venture Philanthropy." 2001 Venture Philanthropy: The Changing Landscape. Morino Institute. 2001. 22.

[202] Camus, Albert. *The Plague.*

[203] Anderson, Mary B., "Do No harm: How Aid Can Support Peace — or War." Lynne Reinner Publishers, Inc. Colorado and London, IK. 2001. 2

[204] Frumkin, Peter. "Failure in Philanthropy," *Philanthropy*, July/August 1998.

[205] *Ibid.*

[206] *Ibid.*

[207] Maren, Michael. The Road to Hell: The Ravaging Effects of Foreign Aid and International Charity. New York: The Free Press, 1997.

[208] Backer, Thomas E. "Innovation in Context: New Foundation Approaches to Evaluation, Collaboration, and Best Practices: Study conducted for the John S. and James L. Knight Foundation." November 1999. 3.

[209] O'Keefe, Mark. "Wealthiest in the World Wield Power Through Philanthropy," *San Francisco Chronicle* January 21, 2001. Also, see Philanthropy News Digest January 23, 2001.

[210] Magnet, Myron. "What Makes Charity Work?" Chicago: Ivan R. Dee, 2000. xii.

[211] Fisher, Ian. "Can International Relief Do More Harm Than Good?" *New York Times*, 11 February 2001.

[212] *Ibid.*

[213] Anderson, Mary B., "Do No Harm: How Aid Can Support Peace — or War." Colorado: Lynne Reinner Publishers, Inc., 2001. 2.

[214] Editorial, Review & Outlook..: "The Schools Millionaire, Lovett Peters," *Wall Street Journal*, 14 September 2000.

[215] Golden, Daniel, "Rensselaer Polytechnic Gets Huge Cash Gift from Donor," *The Wall Street Journal*, 13 March 2001.

[216] Kronholz, June, "Gift of $128 Million to DePauw Proves to Be a Mixed Blessing," *The Wall Street Journal*, 8 March 2001.

[217] Hardy, Quentin, "The Radical Philanthropist," *Forbes*, 1 May 2000.

[218] Soros, George. Brown University Speech. October 29, 1999.

[219] Carnegie, *The Gospel of Wealth*, 21.

[220] Stamler, Bernard. "Charities Award Grants, Then Pay to Evaluate How the Money is Spent," *New York Times*, 20 November 2000.

[221] Emerson, Jed, J. Gregory Dees, Christine W. Letts, and Edward Skloot. *The U.S. Nonprofit Capital Market: An Introductory Overview of Developmental Stages, Investors and Funding Instruments*. Roberts Enterprise Development Fund, 2000. 189.

[222] Williams, Caroline. "Financing Techniques for Non-profit Organizations: Borrowing From the For-Profit Sector." Washington, D.C.: President's Committee on the Arts and Humanities. 1998. Finance Authority of Maine. "A Study of the Availability and Sources of Venture Capital in Maine." 15 March 1995.

[223] Stanton, Gregory; Emerson, Jed; Weiss, Marcus. "Going Mainstream: NPOs Accessing the Capital Markets." Capital Markets Access Information: New York, 2001.

[224] Morris, Kathleen. "The Reincarnation of Mike Milken." *Business Week*. 10 May 1999. 95.

[225] Cherry, Elyse. "NO EXIT: The Challenge of Realizing Return on Community Development Venture Capital Investments." The Ford Foundation. 5 October 2000.

[226] Morino Institute. "2001 Venture Philanthropy: The Changing Landscape." 2001, 61.

[227] Okten, Cagla and Weisbrod, Burton A. "Differential Taxation of Nonprofits and the Commercialization of Nonprofit Revenues." *Journal of Public Economics*, Vol. 75, 2000. 255.

[228] "Watchdog Organization Recommends 15 Standards for Local Charities," *The Chronicle of Philanthropy*, 25 February 1999

[229] Shore, *The Cathedral Within*. 23.

[230] Two legal/regulatory areas appear to be the most frequently misinterpreted. The first being the structural flexibility of NGOs and the second the flexibility for innovative, incentive based executive compensation programs. Within the structural rubric, there appears to be a general perception that NGOs cannot have stock ownership and that this is somehow prohibited by the Federal government's – the IRS's – designation of the NGO as a 501(c). In fact, there appears to be little IRS prohibition to 501(c) stock ownership. The corporate ownership is an area of state governance. There are six possible strategies to address this issue: 1) there are a number of associations that have voting structures that are quite similar to stock ownership, 2) alternatives for a simulated stock ownership clearly is a productive area offering many alternatives, 3) some states specifically allow stock ownership of NGOs, 4) conversations are always an option with such organizations as HMOs, mutual insurance companies, or the NASDQ, 5) a number of states would welcome the opportunity to modified state rules and regulations to accommodate stock ownership NGO as has been done with Delaware with corporate governance, Alaska with estates and trusts, and Massachusetts with REIT's, and 6) for-profit commercial subsidiaries can be a viable alternative to address this issue. Interestingly, current research appears to indicate that 501(c)'s may be specifically exempt form the 33rd and 34th Acts; however, such a preliminary observation requires additional analysis (the purpose of this Working Book is not intended to provide legal advice, and there are specialized legal firms that can provide further information on this topic). This is no small observation, as it may allow room for innovative and progressive flexibility without arcane and inapplicable constraints. Furthermore, an avenue of future research addresses the constraints associated with 501(c) prohibitions specifying that no individual may profit from a 501(c). [Hopkins notes in Skloot book on page 12 a " the term (non-profit) means that a non-profit organization's profit may not be distributed to persons in their private capacities" and "that is why the federal law states that, in the case of some non-profit organizations, the organization's net earnings may not inure to the benefit of

persons in their private capacity."] A potentially worthwhile avenue of investigation is to determine the potential for a 501(c) to profit from its ownership of another 501(c). Some literature refers to this topic as the "non-distribution constraint." Such examples that might merit investigation include a foundations ownership's wish to create an HMO as commercial entity and take it public with the foundation maintaining control of ownership even to the point of having a special class of stock. This flexibility for 501(c) profiting from stock ownership in another 501(c) could allow for innovative forms of securities issuance and progressively sophisticated NGO capital structures. Furthermore, CPs should be particularly wary of those legal professionals who seek to unproductively and unwisely complicate the legal and regulatory issues in this area. This is not to say that the area is not complicated or requires highly specialized legal and regulatory professional advice.

A second are area often misinterpreted is that concerning social sector executive or other employees, including NGOs as well as foundations. Regarding any investigation in this area, CPs will mostly likely hear that either the anti-inurement rules and regulations or the 1996 Intermediate Sanctions Act specifically and uncategorically prohibit both NGO and foundation executives and other employees from above-the-norm financial compensation, especially incentive compensation. As mentioned above, some literature refers to this topic as the "non-distribution constraint." In fact, the governing promulgations do not appear to govern by an absolute prohibition of bonuses or incentive compensation, especially if such performance awards are tied to social sector performance of the mission of the NGO or foundation. Another alternative is to structure a for-profit subsidiary and accommodate the appropriate compensation via this venue. Of course, this should be completely transparent to the public. There has also been an active discussion of setting up separately funded pools for executive performance that would be outside the 501(c) structure. This may not be a necessary alternative if appropriate consideration is dedicated to the currently flexibilities that are available. CPs should also be prepared to hear that any such above-the-norm compensation could spark considerable bad press and cause a run on "hot money" donor base. Indeed, there is a growing body of consultants, especially among the major accounting firms, that offer incentive compensation programs for NGO executives that are in various ways tied to the market. In most cases they very unwisely suggest that this compensation not be directly and openly disclosed to the public. To this point, we strongly urge all CPs to insure that all compensation be disclosed and explained fueling, especially the logic supporting such a program. This would include allowing the executive to designate performance compensation to social sector programs of choice.

There are several sources of introductory reading on these topics, although they are limited to mostly contemporary perspectives. Chapter one of Edward Skloot's The Nonprofit Entrepreneur titled "The Legal Context of Nonprofit Enterprise" by Bruce R. Hopkins provides both a useful macro perspective as well as a limited collection of more detailed information. One interesting observation on page 11 reads: "Thus, the words nonprofit and enterprise do not harbor a conflict; they are quite compatible under the existing federal law structure. Those who assert them to be incompatible lack an understanding of the legal meaning of the term non-profit organization." He also notes on page 13 that "The organizational test principally requires, in the case of charitable organizations, that upon dissolution or liquidation the net income and assets of the organization be distributed to one or more other qualified charitable organizations." The issue of distribution of profits appears to focus significantly on dividends or other cash distributions, which may leave flexibility as to stock in otherwise money losing operations.

Burton A. Weisbrod's "To Profit or Not to Profit" contains several interesting chapters; Chapter 7: "Conversion from nonprofit to for-profit legal status: Why does it happen and should any one care?" offers several practical and value-added insights. Also, in "A Reader in Social Enterprise" edited by Kelvin Shawn Sealey, et al. Chapter 8: "Unrelated Business Income" by Jody Blazek is quite a practica and useful guide.

Two rather dense works worth the time to review for those CPs or associates interested or responsible in the tactical aspects of this area: Randolph M. Goodman and Linda A. Arnsbarger (both of Morrison & Foerster LLP) authored a 1999 of a Matthew Bender & Company publication (Chapter 2) entitled "Trading Technology for Equity: A Guide to Participating in Start-Up Companies, Joint Ventures, and Affiliates." Christopher M. Jedrey (McDermott, Will & Emery) authored a small piece entitled "Permissible Business Arrangements Between Taxable and Tax-Exempt Organizations."

Among the highlights in Goodman and Arnsbarger are these observations, presented here in summary form: "As a practical matter, the IRS has imposed this (loss of exemption) ultimate sanction infrequently and, when private inurement has been asserted, typically there has been inappropriate diversion of income or assets by those who control the organization" (2-6). "The courts and tax authorities recognize that an organization's legitimate activities will benefit private individuals and an absolute prohibition against any amount of private benefit is unwarranted - insubstantial private benefits, such as reasonable compensation or certain revenue-sharing or incentive arrangements with employees, will not jeopardize an organization' tax exempt exemption" (2-6). "Intermediate Sanctions: No taxes are imposed on the organization. Section 4958 of the Code imposes two-tier penalty tax on disqualified persons – those in a position to exercise substantial influence over organizational affairs, including their family members, and 35% controlled entities – who receive excessive compensation or other financial benefits for inadequate considerations. Under the first tier, the disqualified person must pay a tax equal to 25% of the excess benefit, i.e. the amount of the benefit exceeding fair compensation, Under the second tier, the disqualified person must pay an additional tax equal to 200% of the excess benefit if the transaction is not corrected by the time the IRS formally assesses the tax, up to a maximum of $10,000, on any organization manager who knowingly participates in the transaction" (2-8). "Exempt organizations are entitled to a rebuttable presumption of reasonableness where compensation or a property transaction is approved by its board (or an independent committee) that relies on data showing that the organization is receiving fair value and that it adequately documents its funding" (2-10). "Key issues in structuring capitalization include profit stream allocation, control considerations, and desired liquidation preferences. The final documents must spell out a number of equity-related issues, such as dividend rights or preferences. Voting rights issues to be addressed include whether the stock is voting or nonvoting, antidilution protection, preemptive rights, board representation, voting agreements, approval of certain major corporate events, or buy-out or first refusal provisions. Liquidation rights also must be addressed, such as any preferred interest." (2-21). "An additional advantage of the taxable corporate form involves disclosure. A taxable corporation, even a subsidiary, is not yet subject to the same public disclosure requirements as the exempt parent; corporate tax returns are confidential" (2-31). "On the other hand, an exempt organization could permit other exempt organizations to participate in the new equity without jeopardizing its exempt status, provided that the entity continues its exempt activities" (2-33).

Christopher Jedrey's article covers arms length arrangements (procedures, conflict of interests, and documentation), joint ventures, royalty arrangements, corporate sponsorship arrangements both permissible and prohibited, and Internet issues including corporate sponsorships. With regard to arms length arrangements, if the tax-exempt organization follows outlined, it is entitled to a "rebuttable presumption" that the transaction was on a fair-market-value basis and did not produce an "excess benefit" for the Disqualified Person. See above.

Useful readings on compensation are much more limited and generally address the gaps between the social sector and commercial sector.

[231] Dees, Gregory J. Enterprising Nonprofits. Massachusetts: Harvard Business School Press, 1999. Community Wealth Ventures, Inc., Venture Philanthropy: Landscape and Expectations. Morino Institute, 2000.

[232] Renz, Loren and Massarsky, Cynthia W. "Program Related Investment." New York: The Foundation Center, 1995., "Supply and Demand in the PRI Field - Do The Terms Apply? A Discussion Among Advisors to the PRI Study," 6-7.

[233] Baxter, Christie I. "Program-Related Investments: A technical Manual for Foundations." John Wiley & Sons, Inc. New York. 1997. 4.

[234] Weiser, John and Brody, Frances. "Introduction to Program-Related Investment." www.brodyweiser.com. April 2000. On the executive summary and on pages 55 and 58 of this study, the diverse categories noted include Community development, housing, health/metal health, education, arts/media, religion, environment, and human services-multipurpose. Half of all PRI dollars were invested in community development and housing, while another 18% was spent in the health field. In dollar amounts, nonsectarian NGOs accounted for approximately 74% and religious NGOs 20%. Nearly three-fourths of PRIs in the historical set amounted to at least $100,000, while more than one-in-six totaled $1 million or more. Close to two-fifths of PRI dollars and nearly an equal-share of PRIs' financed projects served the economically disadvantaged. Renz, Loren and Massarsky, Cynthia W. "Program Related Investment." New York: The Foundation Center, 1995.

[235] Renz, "Program Related Investment," ix.

[236] Baxter, Christie I. "Program-Related Investments: A Technical Manual for Foundations." John Wiley & Sons, Inc., New York. 1997, 1.

[237] Weiser, John and Brody, Frances. "Introduction to Program-Related Investment." www.brodyweiser.com: April 2000.

[238] *Ibid*. xii. Although funders represent all asset sizes, three out of the five held assets of $50 million or over which accounted for 87% of all PRI activity, based on a 1993 study. As noted on pages 48 and 50 of the study, approximately 66% of the PRI funding was by the top 10 funders. The big foundation names include : The Ford Foundation, The John D. and Catherine T. MacArthur Foundation, Pew Charitable Trusts, Richard King Mellon Foundation, Metropolitan Life Foundation, Meadows Foundation, Robert Wood Johnson Foundation, and the Rockefeller Foundation.

[239] Lingenfelter, Paul D. "Investing in Intermediaries: A Low-Cost, High-Impact Approach for Tackling Big Problems." Ed. Baxter, Christie I. "Program-Related Investments: A technical Manual for Foundations." Chapter 4, New York: John Wiley & Sons, Inc., 1997, 61.

[240] *Ibid.*

[241] La Piana, "The Nonprofit Merger Workbook."

[242] Carlton, Jim. "WSJE: Dot-Orgs Become A Role Model For Some Start-Ups," *Wall Street Journal*, 13 March 2001.

[243] "70% of Largest Social Investment Funds Earn Highest Performance Ratings In 1999." *Social Investment Forum News*. 25 January 2000.

[244] *Ibid.*

[245] Information obtained from www.japonicaintersectorial.com, September 2000). Full mission statement: Japonica Intersectoral is an investment bank dedicated to creating value in the intersectoral markets. The firm proactively cultivates opportunities in the segment of the social sector where quantifiable value metrics of the commercial sector converge with the socially powered motivations of the nonprofit sector. Here, "doing good and doing well" is synergistic. Japonica Intersectoral continuously seeks to strategically optimize its financial and intellectual capital for the benefit of its multiple constituencies, including: emerging growth NGOs, established NGOs, foundations, institutional investors, social sector professionals, and social sector executives/board members. The firm's value creating initiatives encompass capital market services, strategic financial advisory services, direct investment opportunities, and educational resources. Japonica Intersectoral's global constituents share a common mission of seeking best-in-class performance along a social enterprise spectrum of bringing transformative value to society and capturing economic benefits. Our franchise is devoted to building a transparent marketplace of creatively diverse investment instruments for traditional foundations and new institutional investors as well as established social sector operating organization seeking to strategically restructure and social entrepreneurs embarking upon start ups. Japonica Intersectoral's infrastructure is dedicated to an unparalleled standard of excellence. The firm's strong commitment to global diversity provides a comprehensive reservoir of intellectual talents and financial resources. Its organization structure of progressive concentric circles integrates the best resources across the social enterprise spectrum. Our global network of team members possess both demonstrated industry-specific performance and highly regarded

professional accomplishments. Complementing the commitment to innovation and the respect for tradition, every member of Japonica Intersectoral's network shares an uncompromising dedication to bring positive social change to our world community.

[246] Preliminary Criteria for Selecting Intersectoral Investments: Established Situations: 1. Strong internal and external team, with a sound program of substantial opportunities for value-added. 2. High relative market share and good relative perceived quality of offerings. 3. Strong core competencies. 4. Substantial, identifiable opportunities to improve services and offerings. 5. Attractive opportunities for blended ROI investments, especially via technology. 6. Potential opportunities for value harvesting and for-profit success stories. 7. Receptive avenues for mega-transformative organizational changes.

Preliminary Criteria for Selecting Intersectoral Investments: Emerging Growth 1. Strong internal management team, with skills and passion for accelerating growth. 2. Opportunities for high relative market share and excellent relative perceived quality of offerings. 3. Outstanding core competencies. 4. Ability to "go to scale" in a major market sector, preferably with rapid growth characteristics. 5. Significant opportunities for blended ROI investments, especially via technology. 6. Potential opportunities for value harvesting and for-profit success stories. 7. Receptive avenues for transformative organizational changes.

[247] Weisbrod, *To Profit or Not to Profit,* 58.

[248] Okten, Cagla and Weisbrod, Burton A. "Differential Taxation of Nonprofits and the Commercialization of Nonprofit Revenues." *Journal of Public Economics,* Vol. 75, 2000. 255.

[249] Freudenheim, Milt. "Blue Cross Offers Aid to Uninsured in Bid to be For-Profit." *New York Times,* 2 April 2001.

[250] Estelle, James. "Commercialism among nonprofits: Objectives, opportunities, and constraints." 285. Ed. Weisbrod, *To Profit or Not to Profit,* 1998.

[251] Goddeeris, John H. and Weisbrod, Burton A. "Conversion from nonprofit to for-profit legal status: Why does it happen and should anyone care?" 139. Ed. Weisbrod, *To Profit or Not to Profit.*

[252] Weisbrod, *To Profit or Not to Profit,* 48.

253 Estelle, James. "Commercialism among nonprofits," 285.

254 Steinberg, Richard. and Weisbrod, Burton A. "Pricing and rationing by non-profit organizations with distributional objectives." P. 76, Ed. Weisbrod, *To Profit or Not to Profit.*

255 Tedeschi, Bob. "E-Commerce Report." *New York Times*. 8 January 2001.

256 Emerson, *The U.S. Nonprofit Capital Market*, 189.

257 Metrics for Dead-Founder Foundations (foundations in the aggregate) are from Michael E. Porter and Mark Kramer, "Philanthropy's New Agenda: Creating Value." *Harvard Business Review*. November-December 1999.

258 Cabrera, Luis. "Gates, Allen Philanthropy Differs." *Associated Press.* home-news.excite.com. November 2000.

259 Verhovek, Sam Howe. "Bill Gates Turns Skeptical on Digital Solution's Scope," *New York Times*, 3 November 2000.

260 *Ibid.*

261 *Ibid.*

262 Porter and Kramer, *Harvard Business Review.*

263 Barrett, "Questions for William H. Gates Sr."

264 *Ibid.*

265 Moore, Geoffery. An interview with Kristina Kazarian regarding Michael Milken and his foundations. December 2001.

266 Porter and Kramer, *Harvard Business Review.*

267 Porter and Kramer, *Harvard Business Review.*

268 Porter and Kramer, *Harvard Business Review.*

269 Porter and Kramer, *Harvard Business Review.*

[270] Arenson, Karen W. "Art, Wildlife and a Bit of Investing," *New York Times*. 12 November 2000.

[271] Porter and Kramer, *Harvard Business Review*.

[272] "Center To Join 92nd Street Y," *New York Times*, 7 February 2001.

[273] Golden, Daniel, "Rensselaer Polytechnic Gets Huge Cash Gift from Donor," *The Wall Street Journal*, 13 March 2001.

[274] Kronholz, June, "Gift of $128 Million to DePauw Proves to Be a Mixed Blessing," *The Wall Street Journal*, 8 March 2001.

[275] *Id.*

[276] Zernike, Kate. "Antidrug Program Says It Will Adopt a New Strategy," *New York Times*, 15 February 2001.

[277] *Ibid.*

[278] *Ibid.*

[279] *Ibid.*

[280] *Ibid.*

[281] Frumkin, Peter. "Failure in Philanthropy." *Philanthropy*. July/August 1998.

[282] *Ibid.*

[283] *Ibid.*

INDEX

401

NOTES